A BRIEF HISTORY OF INDIA

SECOND EDITION

JUDITH E. WALSH

State University of New York
Old Westbury

Checkmark Books®
An Infobase Learning Company

A Brief History of India, Second Edition

Copyright © 2011, 2006 by Judith E. Walsh

Checkmark Books
An imprint of Infobase Learning
132 West 31st Street
New York NY 10001

Library of Congress Cataloging-in-Publication Data

Walsh, Judith E.
    A brief history of India / Judith E. Walsh. — 2nd ed.
        p. cm.
    Includes bibliographical references and index.
    ISBN 978-0-8160-8143-1(hardcover: alk. paper)
    ISBN 978-0-8160-8362-6 (pbk: alk. paper)
    1. India—History. I. Title.
    DS436.W34 2010
    954—dc22   2010026316

Checkmark Books are available at special discounts when purchased in bulk quantities for businesses, associations, institutions, or sales promotions. Please call our Special Sales Department in New York at (212) 967-8800 or (800) 322-8755.

You can find Facts On File on the World Wide Web at
http://www.infobaselearning.com

Excerpts included herewith have been reprinted by permission of the copyright holders; the author has made every effort to contact copyright holders. The publishers will be glad to rectify, in future editions, any errors or omissions brought to their notice.

Text design by Joan M. McEvoy
Composition by Mary Susan Ryan-Flynn
Map design by Dale Williams
Cover printed by Yurchak Printing, Landisville, Pa.
Book printed and bound by Yurchak Printing, Landisville, Pa.
Printed in the United States of America

This book is printed on acid-free paper.

For Ainslie Embree

CONTENTS

LIST OF ILLUSTRATIONS

LIST OF MAPS

LIST OF TABLES

ACKNOWLEDGMENTS

Book projects, like compulsive borrowers, accumulate many debts, and this brief history has been no exception to that rule. It is not possible to thank here by name the many people in my work and home lives who have been inconvenienced in one way or another by the demands of both the first and second editions of this project. But I am grateful to all for their sympathy, support, and generally high level of restraint. I would, however, especially like to thank my husband, Ned, and our daughter, Sita. They have been as inconvenienced as anyone by this project over the years it has gone on and yet have remained remarkably good humored about it.

A number of people have helped me with specific parts of this project, and I would especially like to thank them here. Lucy Bulliet read an early draft of the first chapters and several subsequent versions since then. I am grateful for her insightful comments and observations and for the general fun of those discussions. Lucy also provided the fine translation of the Rig-Vedic verse that opens the first chapter, for which I am also very grateful. I also want to thank Phillip Oldenburg for his generous loan of election slides for the book and Ron Ellis in Derby, United Kingdom, for his help in obtaining an old image of the Writers' Building in Calcutta. At Facts On File, Claudia Schaab, executive editor, and Melissa Cullen-DuPont, associate editor, have contributed many insights, suggestions, and great editorial feedback over the past years. I am grateful for all their help—and for their patience (or at least restraint) when I missed my deadlines.

At my college, SUNY at Old Westbury, I owe a special debt of gratitude to Patrick O'Sullivan, provost and vice president of academic affairs. Without Patrick's early support and encouragement, I could never have thought of undertaking this project. I also very much appreciate the good humor and support of my colleague, Anthony Barbera in Academic Affairs, and the chair of my department, Ed Bever, as I repeatedly missed meetings to finish the second edition.

As in the first edition, my special thanks here go to Ainslie Embree. Over the many years of thanking Ainslie in print and in person for his help, thoughts, comments, criticisms, and friendship, I have (almost) run out of things to say. Ainslie was the first person with whom I studied Indian history and is the best Indian historian I have ever known. The second edition of this book (as the first) is dedicated to him with continuing affection and gratitude.

NOTE ON PHOTOS

Many of the photographs used in this book are old, historical images whose quality is not always up to modern standards. In these cases, however, their content was deemed to make their inclusion important, despite problems in reproduction.

INTRODUCTION

Up to five years ago, American images of India pictured it as a land of religion, luxury, and desperate poverty—holy men sitting cross-legged by the roadside, fat maharajas on bejeweled elephants, or poverty-stricken beggars picking through garbage for scraps to eat. Now that image has begun to change. If Americans think of India today, they are more likely to imagine Indian workers in call centers taking jobs needed in the United States or slum kids winning fortunes on quiz shows as in *Slumdog Millionaire*—or, if they read the business news, they might imagine a population of consumer-crazed Indians drinking Coca-Cola or Pepsi and eating Kentucky Fried Chicken. The "Bird of Gold," the golden Indian economy, is on the rise, and by 2025, according to at least one group of American analysts, India's new globalized and liberalized economy could produce prosperity for more Indians and create an Indian middle class of more than 593 million (almost twice the size of the American population) eager to consume whatever global markets can provide.

These current images are, in their own way, no less exotic or distorting than images of the past. They do as little justice to the reality of Indian life and history as past stereotypes of poverty, religious conflict, and "holy" cows. India's 5,000-year history tells the story of a land in which both indigenous peoples and migrants from many ethnic and religious communities came to live together, sometimes in harmony and sometimes in conflict. The communal lives of the earliest Stone Age peoples; the mysterious bead-making ancient civilization of the Indus River Valley; the Sanskrit cultures of ancient India; the Islamic lifeways of Turks, Afghans, and Mughals; and the Western modernities of European colonizers—over past millennia, the contributions and lifeways of all these peoples, communities, and civilizations have been woven together into the rich tapestry that is India's past. But that history, it is important to note, is not owned by any *one* of these contributors or communities. It is the common heritage of them all. It is a heritage equally visible, and equally authentic, in the practices of a remote rural village or in the festivities of the yearly Republic Day Parade with which Indians celebrate India's independence and the birth of India's modern democracy in 1947.

It is this collective story of the Indian past that this brief history tells. As in the first edition of this book, themes important to this history include the great size and diversity of the Indian subcontinent, the origins and development of the Indian caste system, India's religious traditions and their use and misuse in past and present, and the complexities of democratic majoritarian politics within a country with many castes, minorities, and religious groups.

Unity and Diversity on the Indian Subcontinent

India is big according to any number of indexes—in landmass, in population, and in the diversity of its many peoples. In landmass, India is approximately one-third the size of the United States. In population, it is second in the world (after China) with a current population (estimated July 2009) of 1.157 billion people. The peoples of India speak 16 officially recognized languages (including English), belong to at least six major religions (having founded four of them), and live according to so wide a range of cultural and ethnic traditions that scholars have sometimes been tempted to define them village by village.

Instead of comparing India with other modern nation-states, a better approach might be to compare India with another large cultural region, such as the modern European Union. India today is three-quarters as large in landmass as the modern European Union with more than twice the European Union's population. Where the European Union is made up of 27 separate countries, India is a single country, governed centrally but divided internally into 28 regional states (and seven union territories). The peoples of the European Union follow at least four major religions; Indians today practice six different religions. Where the European Union population has 23 official languages, India has 16. Finally, the separate Indian regions, like the separate states of the European Union, are united (culturally) by shared religious and cultural assumptions, beliefs, values, and practices. Also as in the European Union, India is made up of multiple regional and local cultures and ethnicities.

As this brief history will show, the political unification of this vast and diverse South Asian subcontinent has been the goal of Indian rulers from the third century B.C.E. to the present. Rulers as otherwise different as the Buddhist Ashoka, the Mughal Aurangzeb, the British Wellesley, and the first prime minister of modern India, Nehru, have all sought to unite the Indian subcontinent under their various regimes. At the same time, regional rulers and politicians as varied as the ancient kings of Kalinga (Orissa), the Rajputs, the Marathas, the Sikhs, and the political leaders of contemporary Kashmir, the Punjab, and Assam have all struggled equally hard to assert their independence and/or autonomy from central control. The old cliché of the interplay of "unity and diversity" on the subcontinent still has use as a metaphor for understanding the dynamics of power relations throughout Indian history. And if this old metaphor encourages us to read Indian history with a constant awareness of the subcontinent's great size, large population (even in ancient times), and regional, linguistic, and cultural complexity, so much the better.

Caste

In this second edition, as in the first, the Indian caste system will be a major focus of discussion. From the third century B.C.E. to the present, the Indian institution of caste has intrigued and perplexed travelers to the region. Originally a Brahman-inspired social and religious system, caste divisions were intended to define people by birth on the basis of the religious merits and demerits believed to have been accumulated in their past lives. Most modern ideas about caste, however, begin with the observations of 19th- and 20th-century British officials and scholars. These men saw caste as a fixed hereditary system based on arbitrary customs and superstitions that forced Indians to live within a predetermined hierarchy of professions and occupations and created the "unchanging" villages of rural India. To such observers caste was a complete anachronism, a system that was anathema to egalitarian and competitive modern (that is to say, European) ways of life.

Many Western-educated Indians also believed that caste was an outdated system. In the early decades after Indian independence in 1947, such men believed that caste would simply wither away, an unneeded and outmoded appendage in a modern India organized on the principles of electoral democracy. But caste has not disappeared from modern India. Instead it has shown the flexibility and resilience that has characterized this institution from its origins. Caste has reemerged in modern India as an organizing category for Indian electoral politics and as an important component within new ethnicized 20th- and 21st-century Indian identities.

No short book can do justice to the complex historical variations or local and regional expressions of the Indian caste system. But this book will describe the ancient origins of the caste system, what scholars think it was and how scholars think it functioned, and it will suggest the many ways in which communities and individuals have adapted caste and caste categories and practices to their own needs and for their own purposes: to increase their own community's status (or decrease that of another); to incorporate their own community (or those of others) into broader local, regional, and/or imperial Indian political systems; and, in the modern world, to turn caste categories into broader ethnic identities and adapt them to the new demands of modern electoral politics. Caste has existed in some form in India from at least 600 B.C.E., but over the many centuries of this unique institution's existence, the single truth about it is that it has never been static.

Religion and Violence

From as early as we have Indian texts (that is, today from ca. 1500 B.C.E.), we have sources that tell us about Indian religions and religious diversity. Over the millennia different religions have lived together on the subcontinent, governed often by rulers of different religious persuasions—whether Buddhist, Jain, Hindu, Muslim, or Christian. Sometimes these communities have lived in peace with each other, sometimes in conflict.

Recent events—from the 1947 partition of the subcontinent into a Hindu-majority India and a Muslim-majority Pakistan to the rise to political dominance of Hindu nationalism in the late 1990s—have led to dramatic episodes of religious violence, in, for instance, the partition riots of 1947–48 and the Gujarat violence of 2002. Media reports of communal conflicts often present them as the result of a too-intense religiosity. "The problem's name is God," wrote the Indian novelist Salman Rushdie in the aftermath of brutal Hindu-Muslim riots in Gujarat in 2002.

Over the centuries, however, God has had considerable help with religious violence on the Indian subcontinent. One story India's history tells well is the story of how communities live together when their peoples take religion and religious belief seriously. This is not always an inspiring story. At times India's multiple religious communities have lived peacefully together, adapting aspects of one another's religious customs and practices and sharing in religious festivities. At other times communities have savaged one another, defining themselves in mutual opposition and attacking one another brutally. Thus—to use an ancient example—(Vedic) Hindu, Buddhist, and Jain communities competed peacefully for followers within the Indo-Gangetic Plain from the sixth to second centuries B.C.E. and throughout southern and western India during the first to third centuries C.E. But several hundred years later (from the seventh to 12th centuries C.E.), Hindu persecutions of Jain and Buddhist communities drove these sects into virtual extinction in southern India.

Religion and religious identities, when taken seriously, become available for use—and misuse—by local, regional, and political powers and communities. The exploitation of religion or religious feeling has never been the unique property of any single religious community (or any country, for that matter). Many, if not all, of India's kings and rulers turned extant religious sensibilities to their own uses. Sometimes the purpose was benign: The Buddhist emperor Ashoka urged his subjects to practice toleration; the Mughal Akbar explored the similarities underlying diverse religious experiences; in modern times, the nationalist leader Mohandas K. Gandhi used Hindu images and language to create a nonviolent nationalism. At other times rulers used religion to more violent effect: Southern Indian Hindu kings persecuted Jain and Buddhist monks to solidify their own political empires; Mughal emperors attacked Sikh gurus and Sikhism to remove political and religious competition. And sometimes the results of religious exploitation were far worse than intended, as when British efforts to encourage separate Hindu and Muslim political identities— "divide and rule"—helped move the subcontinent toward the violence of the 1947 partition. Or, to give another example, in the 1990s, when Hindu nationalists' efforts to build a Hindu temple on the site of a Muslim mosque resulted in widespread violence, riots, and deaths.

Who Is an "Indian"? Hindutva and the Challenge to Indian Secularism

At the heart of the religious violence and caste conflict in India from the late 19th century to the present, however, are questions about both ethnic identity and national belonging. These questions had not arisen in earlier centuries (or millennia) in part because earlier authoritarian rulers had had little need to pose questions of overall Indian identity. In part these questions did not arise because of the functioning of caste itself.

From very early the Indian caste system allowed diverse and differently defined communities to coexist in India, functioning together economically even while maintaining, at least in theory, separate and immutable identities. However, over the centuries of such coexistence, communities did, in fact, alter in response to groups around them, adapting others' practices, customs, and even religious ideas. Thus many Muslim communities in India as well as the 19th- and 20th-century Anglo-Indian British communities functioned as caste communities in India, even though caste had no basis or logic within their own religious ideologies. They related internally to their own members and externally to outsiders in ways often typical of Hindu castes. And movements such as the devotional (bhakti) sects of the 12th to 18th centuries appear within many different Indian religions even while sharing, across religious boundaries, similarities in expression and form. Still, however much ethnic and/ or religious groups might borrow or adapt from one another, the caste system allowed all these communities—to the extent that they thought of such things at all—to maintain a belief in the cultural and religious integrity of their own ideas and practices.

In the 19th century the needs of organizing to oppose British rule in India forced nationalist leaders for the first time to define an all-Indian identity. Initially, in the effort toward unifying all in opposition to the British, that identity was simply defined as "not British." Indians, then, were not white, not English speaking, not Western in their cultural practices. Later, however, the definitions began to be differently defined. Nationalists found themselves appealing to audiences on the basis of linguistic, cultural, or religious identities: as Bengali or Urdu or Tamil speakers; as Aryans or Dravidians; or as Hindus or Muslims. In the years after independence in 1947, these multiple identities often returned to haunt the governors of modern India, as ethnic and linguistic groups, their consciousness raised by earlier nationalist appeals, sought regional states within which their identities could find full expression.

After 1947, however, India also became a modern democracy—the world's largest democracy, in fact—and a country within which all adult citizens, male or female, were entitled to vote. For leaders such as Jawaharlal Nehru, India's first prime minister, Indian citizenship was a modern, completely secular status, conferred on adult men or women by virtue of birth (or naturalization) within the modern nation-state of India, a status that carried no requirements of particular linguistic, religious, or ethnic identities.

But the politics of majority electoral rule, and of nationhood itself, had its own logic. By the last decades of the 20th century the question of the nature of Indian citizenship had become one of the most compelling and contentious in Indian public life. Modern Hindu nationalists sought to create a politicized Hindu nation out of the 80 percent of the population who were Hindus. They proposed a new definition of Indian identity (if not quite of Indian citizenship): Hindutva. India would be identified not as a secular state but as a Hindu nation, a nation in which only those able to accept a Hindu identity might fully participate. By the turn of the century the question of whether India would be secular or Hindu had politicized not just Indian public life but all discussions of Indian history from the ancient river valley civilization of Harappa to the present. Which groups of Indians would be allowed to claim India's historical heritage as their own was very much in debate. As the Hindu nationalists won control of the central government in the elections of 1998 and 1999, it seemed as if the Indian majoritarian political system might become the vehicle for a new religiously defined Indian state.

The Bird of Gold

To the amazement of most political analysts, however, the Hindu nationalist party was defeated twice in the first decade of the 21st century, and the secular government of the previously governing Congress Party was returned to power. Congress's economic policies, in place since 1991, were seen as responsible for the booming growth of the Indian economy—policies that seemed to have wooed India's new middle class away from the Hindu nationalists. At the same time, Congress's calls for economic fairness and programs for rural employment captured a sizable portion of India's powerful rural vote and newly enfranchised lower caste and untouchable voters. Observers were left to wonder if the "bird of gold"—that is, a booming Indian economy—coupled with low-caste, untouchable, and rural voting majorities could trump the saffronized identity of Hindu nationalism.

These are the main themes and issues of *A Brief History of India, Second Edition* presented within a chronological framework throughout this book. The book opens with a survey of India's geography and ecology and with a discussion of prehistoric communities, the Indus River settlements, and early Aryan migrations into the Indian subcontinent. Chapter 2 discusses ancient India, the origins of Hinduism, Buddhism, and Jainism, the spread of early Sanskrit-based culture throughout the subcontinent, and the development of the caste system. Chapter 3 describes the entry of Islam into India and the growth and spread of Muslim communities and political kingdoms and empires. Chapters 4 and 5, taken together, describe the establishment of the British Raj in India and the impact of that rule on Indians both rural and urban: Chapter 4 specifically outlines, from the British point of view, the conquests and establishment of the British Empire; chapter 5 then discusses the multiple levels of Indian responses to the structures and ideologies introduced by British rule and to the economic changes the British Empire brought to the Indian countryside. Chapters 6 and 7 describe the origins of the Indian nationalist movement and its campaigns, under the leadership of Mohandas K. Gandhi, against British rule. Finally chapters 8 through 10 turn to postindependence India. Chapter 8 describes the creation of the modern republic of India and its governance through 1996, ending with the first abortive attempt of the Hindu nationalist party to form a government in that year. Chapter 9 discusses the social and demographic changes that have reshaped Indian society and the forms of popular culture that that new society developed from 1947 through 2009. Finally, chapter 10 carries the political story of the rise to power of the Hindu nationalist party in the elections of 1998 and 1999 up through their defeat by the Congress in both the elections of 2004 and 2009.

1

LAND, CLIMATE, AND PREHISTORY

Men, racing on fast horses, pray to me,
They call on me when surrounded in battle.
I cause the battle—I, generous Indra.
I, powerfully strong, raise the dust of the racing horses.

∎

Rig-Veda IV. 42.5 (Rgveda Samhita 1936, II:671; translated by Lucy Bulliet)

More than 50 million years ago a geological collision occurred that determined India's physical environment. The geographical features and unique ecology that developed from that ancient event profoundly affected India's later human history. The subcontinent's early human societies, the Harappan civilization and the Indo-Aryans, continue to fascinate contemporary scholars, even as modern Hindu nationalists and Indian secularists debate their significance for contemporary Indian life.

Borders and Boundaries

India is a "subcontinent"—a triangular landmass lying below the main Asian continent—bordered on three sides by water: in the east by the Bay of Bengal, in the west by the Arabian Sea, and to the south by the Indian Ocean. Across the north of this triangle stand extraordinarily high mountains: to the north and east, the Himalayas, containing the world's highest peak, Mount Everest; to the northwest, two smaller ranges, the Karakoram and the Hindu Kush.

Geologists say that these mountain ranges are relatively young in geological terms. They were formed only 50 million years ago, long before humans lived in India. Beginning several hundred million years ago,

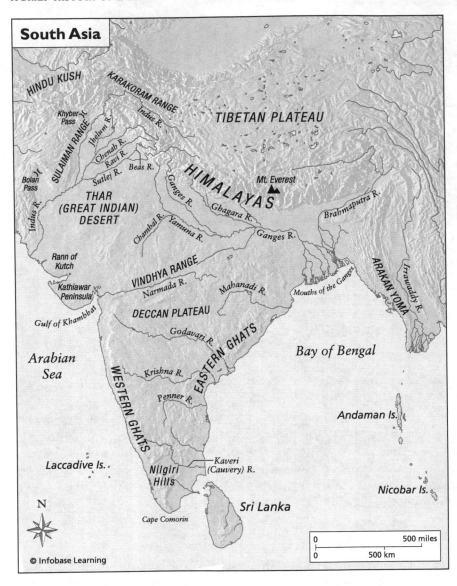

South Asia

HINDU KUSH

KARAKORAM RANGE

TIBETAN PLATEAU

Khyber Pass

SULAIMAN RANGE

Indus R.

Jhelum R.

Chenab R.

Ravi R.

Bolan Pass

Sutlej R.

Beas R.

Indus R.

HIMALAYAS

Mt. Everest

Ganges R.

Ghagara R.

Brahmaputra R.

THAR (GREAT INDIAN) DESERT

Chambal R.

Yamuna R.

Ganges R.

Rann of Kutch

VINDHYA RANGE

Narmada R.

Mahanadi R.

Mouths of the Ganges

ARAKAN YOMA

Irrawaddy R.

Kathiawar Peninsula

DECCAN PLATEAU

Godavari R.

Gulf of Khambhat

EASTERN GHATS

Bay of Bengal

Arabian Sea

WESTERN GHATS

Krishna R.

Penner R.

Andaman Is.

Laccadive Is.

Nilgiri Hills

Kaveri (Cauvery) R.

Nicobar Is.

N

Cape Comorin

Sri Lanka

| 0 | 500 miles |
| 0 | 500 km |

© Infobase Learning

the tectonic plates that underlie the Earth's crust slowly but inexorably moved the island landmass known today as India away from its location near what today is Australia and toward the Eurasian continent. When the island and the Eurasian landmass finally collided, some 50 million years ago, the impact thrust them upward, creating the mountains and high plateaus that lie across India's northwest—the Himalayas and the high Tibetan Plateau. Over the next 50 million years, the Himalayas

2

and the Tibetan Plateau rose to the heights they have today, with peaks, such as Mount Everest, reaching almost nine kilometers (or slightly more than five and a half miles) in height.

The steep drop from these newly created mountains to the (once island) plains caused rivers to flow swiftly down to the seas, cutting deep channels through the plains and depositing the rich silt and debris that created the alluvial soil of the Indo-Gangetic Plain, the coastal plains of the Gujarat region, and the river deltas along the eastern coastline. These same swift-flowing rivers were unstable, however, changing course dramatically over the millennia, disappearing in one region and appearing in another. And the places where the two landmasses collided became geologically unstable also. Today, the Himalayas continue to rise at the rate of approximately one centimeter a year (approximately 10 kilometers every million years), and the region remains particularly prone to earthquakes.

The subcontinent's natural borders—mountains and oceans—protected it. Before modern times, land access to the region for traders, immigrants, or invaders was possible only through passes in the northwest ranges: the Bolan Pass leading from the Baluchistan region in modern Pakistan into Afghanistan and eastern Iran or the more northern Khyber Pass or Swat Valley, leading into Afghanistan and Central Asia. These were the great trading highways of the past, connecting India to both the Near East and Central Asia. In the third millennium B.C.E. these routes linked the subcontinent's earliest civilization with Mesopotamia; later they were traveled by Alexander the Great (fourth century B.C.E.); still later by Buddhist monks, travelers and traders moving north to the famous Silk Road to China, and in India's medieval centuries by a range of Muslim kings and armies. Throughout Indian history a wide range of traders, migrants, and invaders moved through the harsh mountains and plateau regions of the north down into the northern plains.

The seas to India's east, west, and south also protected the subcontinent from casual migration or invasion. Here also there were early and extensive trading contacts: The earliest evidence of trade was between the Indus River delta on the west coast and the Mesopotamian trading world (ca. 2600–1900 B.C.E.). Later, during the Roman Empire, an extensive trade linked the Roman Mediterranean world and both coasts of India—and even extended further east, to Java, Sumatra, and Bali. Arab traders took over many of these lucrative trading routes in the seventh through ninth centuries, and beginning in the 15th century European traders established themselves along the Indian coast. But while the northwest land routes into India were frequently taken

3

by armies of invasion or conquest, ocean trade only rarely led to invasion—most notably with the Europeans in the late 18th century. And
although the British came by sea to conquer and rule India for almost
200 years, they never attempted a large-scale settlement of English
people on the subcontinent.

Land and Water

Internally the subcontinent is mostly flat, particularly in the north. It
is cut in the north by two main river systems, both of which originate
in the Himalayas and flow in opposite directions to the sea. The Indus
River cuts through the northwestern regions of the Indian subcontinent
(modern-day Pakistan) and empties into the Arabian Sea; the many tributaries of the Ganges River flow southeast coming together to empty into
the Bay of Bengal. Taken together, the region through which these rivers
flow is called the Indo-Gangetic (or North Indian) Plain. A third river,
the Narmada, flows from east to west into the Arabian Sea about halfway
down the subcontinent between the two low ranges of the Vindhya and
the Satpura Mountains. The Vindhya Range and the Narmada River are
geographical markers separating North and South India.

South of the Narmada is another ancient geological formation: the
high Deccan Plateau. The Deccan stretches a thousand miles to the
southern tip of India, spanning the width of southern India and much
of the peninsular part of the subcontinent. It begins in the Western
Ghats, steep hills that rise sharply from the narrow flat coastline and
run, spinelike, down the subcontinent's western edge. The plateau also
falls slightly in height from west to east, where it ends in a second set
of sharp (but less high) clifflike hills, the Eastern Ghats, running north
to south inward from the eastern coastline. As a result of the decreasing
west-to-east elevation of the Deccan Plateau and the peninsula region,
the major rivers of South India flow eastward, emptying into the Bay
of Bengal.

Historically the giant mountain ranges across India's north acted
both as a barrier and a funnel, either keeping people out or channeling
them onto the North Indian plains. In some ways one might think of
the subcontinent as composed of layers: some of its earliest inhabitants
now living in the southernmost regions of the country, its more recent
migrants or invaders occupying the north. Particularly when compared
to the high northern mountain ranges, internal barriers to migration,
movement, or conquest were less severe in the interior of the subcontinent—allowing both the diffusion of cultural traditions throughout the

4

entire subcontinent and the development of distinctive regional cultures. The historian Bernard Cohn once suggested that migration routes through India to the south created distinct areas of cultural diversity, as those living along these routes were exposed to the multiple cultures of successive invading or migrating peoples while more peripheral areas showed a greater cultural simplicity. In any event, from as early as the third century B.C.E. powerful and energetic kings and their descendants could sometimes unite all or most of the subcontinent under their rule. Such empires were difficult to maintain, however, and their territories often fell back quickly into regional or local hands.

Although the Indus, the Ganges, and the Brahmaputra (farther to the east) all provide year-round water for the regions through which they flow, most of the Indian subcontinent must depend for water on the seasonal combination of wind and rain known as the southwest monsoon. Beginning in June/July and continuing through September (depending on the region), winds filled with rain blow from the southwest up across the western and eastern coastlines of the subcontinent. In the west, the ghats close to the coastline break the monsoon winds, causing much of their water to fall along the narrow seacoast. On the other side of India, the region of Bengal and the eastern coast receive much of the water. As the winds move north and west through central India, they lose much of their rain until, by the time they reach the northwest, they are almost dry. Technically, then, much of the Indus River in the northwest flows through a desert; rainfall is meager and only modern irrigation projects, producing year-round water for crops, disguise the ancient dryness of this region. For the rest of India, farmers and residents depend on the monsoon for much of the water they will use throughout the year. Periodically the monsoons fail, causing hardship, crop failures, and, in the past, severe famines. Some observers have even related the "fatalism" of Hinduism and other South Asian traditions to the ecology of the monsoon, seeing a connection between Indian ideas such as karma (action, deeds, fate) and the necessity of depending for survival on rains that are subject to periodic and unpredictable failure.

Stone Age Communities

From before 30,000 B.C.E. and up to (and in some cases beyond) 10,000 B.C.E. Stone Age communities of hunters and gatherers lived on the subcontinent. The earliest of these human communities are known primarily from surface finds of stone tools. Paleolithic (Old Stone Age) peoples lived by hunting and gathering in the Soan River Valley, the

5

Potwar plateau regions, and the Sanghao caves of northern Pakistan and in the open or in caves and rock shelters in Madhya Pradesh and Andhra Pradesh. The artifacts are limited: stone pebble tools, hand axes, a skull in the Narmada River Valley, several older rock paintings (along with others) at Bhimbetka in Madhya Pradesh, and, at a different site in the same state, a natural weathered stone identified by workers as a "mother goddess." Later Mesolithic (Middle Stone Age) communities were more extensive with sites identified in the modern Indian states of Gujarat, Madhya Pradesh, Rajasthan, Uttar Pradesh, and Bihar. Small parallel-sided blades and stone microliths (less than two inches in length) were the tools of many of these Mesolithic communities who lived by hunting and gathering and fishing, with signs (later in this period) of the beginnings of herding and small-scale agriculture.

The beginnings of pastoral and agricultural communities (that is, of the domestication of animals and settled farming) are found in Neolithic (New Stone Age) sites at various periods and in many different parts of the subcontinent: in the Swat Valley and in Baluchistan in Pakistan, in the Kashmir Valley, in regions of the modern Indian states of Bihar, Uttar Pradesh, and in peninsular India (in the early third millennium B.C.E.) in northern Karnataka. The most famous and best known of Neolithic sites, however, is the village of Mehrgarh, in northeastern Baluchistan at the foot of the Bolan Pass. Excavations at Mehrgarh demonstrate that both agriculture (the cultivation of wheat and barley) and the domestication of animals (goats, sheep, and zebu cattle) developed during the seventh millennium B.C.E. (ca. 6500 B.C.E.). Although earlier scholars believed that settled agriculture and the domestication of animals developed on the subcontinent as a result of trading and importation from a limited number of sites in the Near East, contemporary archaeologists have suggested these developments were indigenous, at least in the regions of the Baluchistan mountains and the Indo-Iranian borderlands (Possehl 2002; Kenoyer 1998). Regardless of origins, by the third millennium B.C.E., the era in which the subcontinent's earliest urban civilization appeared along the length of the Indus River, that region was home to many different communities—hunting and gathering, pastoral, and farming—and this diverse pattern would continue throughout the Indus developments and beyond.

An Ancient River Civilization

The subcontinent's oldest (and most mysterious) civilization was an urban culture that developed its large city centers between 2600 and

FINDING HARAPPA

Traces of the Harappan civilization were discovered only in the 1820s when a deserter from the East India Company Army happened upon some of its ruins in a place called Haripah. This was the site of the ancient city of Harappa, but in the 19th and early 20th centuries its ruins were thought to date only to the time of Alexander the Great (ca. fourth century B.C.E.). In the early 1920s, the British Archaeological Survey of India, under the directorship of John Marshall, began excavating the sites of Harappa and of Mohenjo-Daro. The excavations produced a number of stamped seals, which puzzled and interested the archaeologists, but the site's great antiquity was not recognized until 1924 when Marshall published a description of the Harappan seals in the *Illustrated London News*. A specialist on Sumer read the article and suggested that the Indian site might be very ancient, contemporaneous with Mesopotamian civilization. The true date of Harappan civilization was subsequently realized to be not the fourth–third centuries B.C.E. but the third millennium B.C.E.

1900 B.C.E. along more than 1,000 miles of the Indus River Valley in what is today both modern Pakistan and the Punjab region of north-western India. At its height, the Harappan civilization—the name comes from one of its cities—was larger than either Egypt and Mesopotamia, its contemporary river civilizations in the Near East. But by 1900 B.C.E. most of Harappa's major urban centers had been abandoned and its cultural legacy was rapidly disappearing, not just from the region where it had existed, but also from the collective memories of the peoples of the subcontinent. Neither its civilization nor any aspect of its way of life appear in the texts or legends of India's past; Harappan civilization was completely unknown—as far as scholars can tell today—to the people who created and later wrote down the Sanskrit texts and local inscriptions that are the oldest sources for knowing about India's ancient past. In fact, until it was rediscovered by European and Indian archaeologists in the 19th and early 20th centuries, Harappan civilization had completely vanished from sight.

Who were the Harappan peoples? Where did they come from and where did they go? For the past 150 years archaeologists and linguists have tried to answer these questions. At the same time, others from inside and outside Indian society—from European Sanskritists and

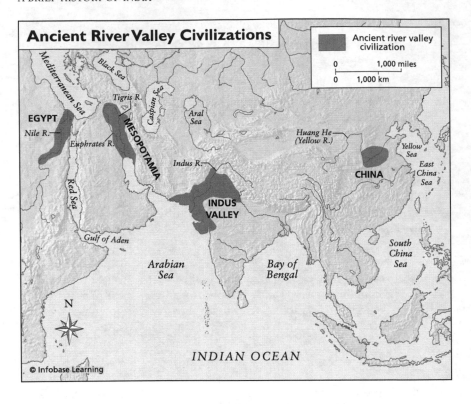

British imperialists to, more recently, Hindu nationalists and their secularist Indian opponents—have all sought to define and use the Harappan legacy.

Harappan civilization developed indigenously in the Indus River Valley. Its irrigation agriculture and urban society evolved gradually out of the smaller farming communities in the region, made possible by the Indus region's dry climate and rich alluvial soil. By the middle of the fourth millennium B.C.E. these agricultural communities had begun to spread more widely through the Indus Valley region. What caused an extensive urban, unified culture to develop out of the agricultural settlements of the region may never be known. But between 2600 and 1900 B.C.E. Harappan civilization appeared in what scholars call its "mature phase," that is, as an extensive civilization with large urban centers supported by surrounding agricultural communities and with a unified, distinctive culture. Mature Harappan settlements are marked, as their archaeological artifacts show, by increased uniformity in styles of pottery, by their widespread use of copper and bronze metallurgy and tools, by a uniform system of weights and measures, by baked brick

8

architecture, by planned layouts of cities with extensive drainage systems, by specialized bead-making techniques, and by distinctive carved steatite (soapstone) seals figured with animals and symbols that may represent a script.

Harappan civilization was at the southeastern edge of an interconnected ancient world of river civilizations that included Mesopotamia in Iraq and its trading partners farther west. Indus contacts with this ancient world were both overland through Afghanistan and by water from the Indus delta region into the Arabian Gulf. A wide variety of Harappan-style artifacts, including seals, beads, and ceramics, have been found in sites at Oman (on the Persian Gulf) and in Mesopotamia itself. Mesopotamian objects (although much fewer in number) have also been found at Harappan sites. Mesopotamian sources speak of a land called "Meluhha" with which they traded, from as early as 2600 B.C.E. to just after 1800 B.C.E. Scholars think Meluhha was the coastal region of the Indus Valley.

Urban Harappan civilization in its mature phase was at least twice the size of the two river valley civilizations farther to the east, either ancient Egypt or Mesopotamia. Harappan settlements spread across an area of almost 500,000 square miles and stretched from the Arabian seacoast north up the Indus River system to the foothills of the Himalayas, west into Baluchistan, and south into what is modern-day Gujarat. The total number of settlements identified with the mature phase of Harappan civilization is currently estimated at between 1,000 to 1,500. Out of these, approximately 100 have been excavated. It is worth noting, however, that the size of these mature Harappan settlements can vary widely, with most sites classified as small villages (less than 10 hectares, or 25 acres, in size) and a few as towns or small cities (less than 50 hectares, or 124 acres, in size). Only five large cities have been identified thus far in the urban phase of the Indus River civilization: Of these two, Mohenjo-Daro in Sind and Harappa in the Punjab are the best known and the largest, each perhaps originally one square mile in overall size.

Scholars now agree that not one but two great rivers ran through the northwest of the subcontinent at this time: the Indus itself (flowing along a course somewhat different from its current one) and a second river, a much larger version of the tiny Ghaggar-Hakra River whose remnants still flow through part of the region today. This second river system paralleled the course of the ancient Indus, flowing out of the Himalaya Mountains in the north and into the Arabian Sea. By the end

A zebu bull seal from Mohenjo-Daro. The Brahman, or zebu, bull on this Mohenjo-Daro seal is an animal indigenous to the subcontinent. Although zebu bull motifs are common in Indus art, the bull itself is only rarely found on seals and usually on seals with short inscriptions. (© J. M. Kenoyer, courtesy Department of Archaeology and Museums, Government of Pakistan)

of the Harappan period, perhaps as a result of tectonic shifts in the northern Himalayas, much of this river had dried up, and its tributary headwaters had been captured both by the Indus itself and by rivers flowing eastward toward the Bay of Bengal. Some suggest this was part of an overall climate change that left the region drier and less able to sustain agriculture than before. Animals that usually inhabited wetter regions—elephants, tigers, rhinoceroses—are commonly pictured on seals from Harappan sites, but the lion, an animal that prefers a drier habitat, is conspicuously absent.

Controversy surrounds contemporary efforts to identify and name this second river—and indeed the Indus Valley civilization itself. "Indigenist" Hindu nationalist groups argue that Indian civilization originated in the Indus Valley and later developed into the culture that produced the ancient texts of Hinduism, with some of its peoples migrating "out of India" to spread the indigenous Indian language farther to the east. In this context, journalists, scholars, and some archaeologists of the indigenous persuasion argue that the second river in the Indus Valley must be the ancient Sarasvati, a river mentioned in the oldest text of Hinduism, the Rig-Veda, but never identified in modern times. Indus civilization, according to this argument, should be called the "Sarasvati Civilization" or the "Indus Sarasvati Civilization" to indicate that it was the originating point for the later development of Hinduism and Indian civilization (Bryant 2001).

Harappan Culture

Mature Harappan cities were trading and craft production centers, set within the mixed economies—farming, herding, hunting and gathering—of the wider Indus region and dependent on these surrounding economies for food and raw materials. Mesopotamian records indicate that the Meluhha region produced ivory, wood, semiprecious stones (lapis and carnelian), and gold—all known in Harappan settlements. Workshops in larger Harappan towns and sometimes even whole settlements existed for the craft production of traded items. Bead-making workshops have been found at Chanhu-Daro in Sind and Lothal near the Gulf of Cambay in Gujarat. These workshops produced sophisticated beads in a wide range of materials, from carnelian and other semiprecious stones to ivory and shell. Excavations have turned up a wide range of distinctive Harappan products: Along with beads and bead-making equipment, these include the square soapstone seals characteristic of mature Harappan culture, many different kinds of small clay animal figurines—cattle, water buffalo, dogs, monkeys, birds, elephants, rhinoceroses—and a curious triangular shaped terra-cotta cake that may have been used to retain heat in cooking.

Harappan settlements were spread out over a vast region. Nevertheless "their monuments and antiquities," as the British archaeologist John Marshall observed, "are to all intents and purposes identical" (Possehl 2002, 61). It is this identity that allows discussion about Harappan cities, towns, and villages of the mature period (2600–1900 B.C.E.) as a single civilization. While scholars can only speculate about the nature of Harappan society, religion, or politics, they can see its underlying unity in the physical remains of its settlements.

Beads of many types and carved soapstone seals characterized Harappan culture. In addition Harappans produced a distinctive

11

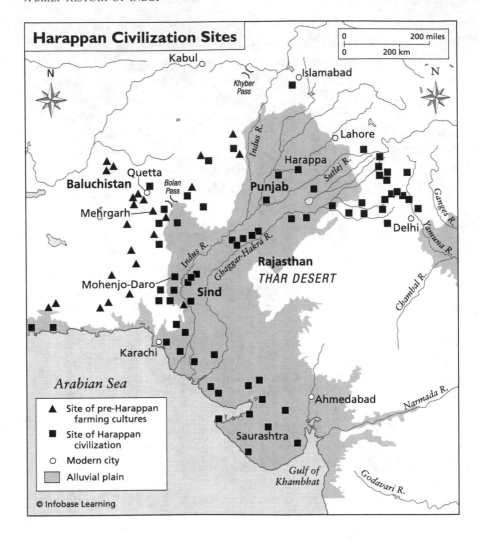

Harappan Civilization Sites

| 0 | 200 miles |
| 0 | 200 km |

N

Kabul

Khyber Pass

Islamabad

N

Lahore

Indus R.

Harappa

Sutlej R.

Ganges R.

Quetta

Baluchistan

Bolan Pass

Punjab

Mehrgarh

Delhi

Yamuna R.

Indus R.

Ghaggar-Hakra R.

Rajasthan
THAR DESERT

Chambal R.

Mohenjo-Daro

Sind

Karachi

Arabian Sea

Ahmedabad

Narmada R.

▲ Site of pre-Harappan
   farming cultures
■ Site of Harappan
   civilization
○ Modern city
▨ Alluvial plain

Saurashtra

Gulf of
Khambhat

Godavari R.

© Infobase Learning

pottery used throughout their civilization: a pottery colored with red slip and often decorated in black with plant and animal designs. They used copper (from nearby Rajasthan and Baluchistan) and bronze to make figurines, pots, tools, and weapons. Their builders used baked bricks produced in a standard size and with uniform proportions. Mature Harappan settlements are characterized by brick-lined wells and drainage systems (often hidden underground). These complex systems, as seen in Mohenjo-Daro, moved water off streets and lanes and removed wastewater from inside houses through vertical drainpipes through walls, chutes leading to the streets, and drains in bathing floors that fed into street drains.

READING THE INDUS SCRIPT

The Indus Valley civilization developed the symbols of what looks like a script, but scholars cannot yet read it. Harappans carved a line of symbols along the top of the square soapstone seals that characterized their society; usually they also carved an animal picture below the writing. Archaeologists find these seals in abundance in Harappan settlements. Like cylindrical seals used in Mesopotamia and in Central Asia, Harappan seals were probably used to mark ownership of goods and property or perhaps also as a kind of identity badge. The picture and symbols were carved in reverse, then the seal was fired to harden it. When stamped in clay, the writing was meant to be read from right to left. On the back of a seal was a small boss used either for holding the seal or for attaching a cord that let it hang around the neck. Indus symbols have also been found scribbled on the edges of pottery and on a three-meter-wide (9.8 feet) "signboard." The longest inscription is 26 symbols found on three sides of a triangular prism.

Approximately 400 different written symbols have been identified on Harappan seals, of which about 200 appear frequently. There are, thus, too many symbols for a phonetic alphabet but too few for a pictographic writing system. Instead, many scholars suggest, the system is logosyllabic, that is, its symbols represent both sounds and concepts (words, phrases, ideas) as is the case in Mesopotamian cuneiform or

(continues)

The front and back of a unicorn seal from Mohenjo-Daro with a relatively long, eight-symbol inscription. The back shows the boss common to Indus seals through which a cord could be run. The unicorn is the most common animal on Indus seals. (© J. M. Kenoyer, courtesy Department of Archaeology and Museums, Government of Pakistan)

READING THE INDUS SCRIPT *(continued)*

Egyptian hieroglyphics. Since the seals were first discovered in the 1870s, at least 100 different attempts have been made to decipher them. Indigenist proponents have claimed the Indus script to be an early form of Sanskrit (the ancient language of Hindu scriptures), but their claims have been widely rejected by both Western and Indian specialists on the subject. Two separate groups (one Soviet/Russian and one Finnish), using computer-based studies in an effort to "read" the symbols, have hypothesized that the writing was proto-Dravidian, that is, it represented an early script of the Dravidian languages of peninsular India. Most recently, several scholars shocked the Indological world with the theory that the symbols were not a language-based script at all. Instead, they argued, the signs represented nonlinguistic (religious or ideological) symbols (Farmer et al.). While both the Dravidian theory and the nonlanguage theory have received serious attention, neither is universally accepted. Indeed, many scholars suggest that the script will never be decoded. They argue that examples of this writing system are too short (too few symbols in a row) to allow them to decipher what was written on these mysterious seals.

Source: Farmer, Steve, Richard Sproat, and Michael Witzel. "The Collapse of the Indus-Script Thesis: The Myth of a Literate Harappan Civilization." *Electronic Journal of Vedic Studies* 11, no. 2 (2004). Available online. URL: http://www.safarmer.com/fsw2.pdf. Accessed August 25, 2009.

In their overall architecture, as well as in their drainage systems, Indus cities and even some smaller mature Harappan settlements show evidence of being planned societies. Although Harappa in the north and Mohenjo-Daro on the Indus to the south were about 350 miles apart, the cities have many similarities in planning and execution. These are the two largest sites yet found for the Indus Valley civilization and the most extensively excavated. Kenoyer (1998) estimates the size of Mohenjo-Daro at more than 200 hectares (more than 494 acres) and Harappa at 150 hectares (370 acres).

Both cities were oriented on a north-south axis. Both were built on two levels, and each level was surrounded by large mud-brick walls with gateways at intervals. The upper level, built on a brick platform, has been variously called a "citadel" or an "acropolis"; it held large buildings and structures whose function is still unclear. At Mohenjo-Daro

"Priest-King" from Mohenjo-Daro. Note that this figure is quite small, only approximately seven inches in height. (© J. M. Kenoyer, courtesy Department of Archaeology and Museums, Government of Pakistan)

the upper level also includes a large brick-lined bathing structure ("the Great Bath"), the sunken bathing section waterproofed by bitumen (tar). Both Harappa and Mohenjo-Daro contain large buildings either within the upper level or close to it whose function—granaries? warehouses?—scholars still debate.

The lower levels of both cities held residential areas and were built in rectangular sections with streets, running north-south and east-west, intersecting at right angles. Mohenjo-Daro's "lower town" may once have held 35,000–41,000 people. Harappa's population has been estimated at between 23,500 and 35,000. Urban homes in these cities were built around central courtyards—as are many Indian homes today—with inner rooms not visible from the street. Harappans also made careful plans for water. At Mohenjo-Daro one out of three homes had a well in an inside room. Latrines were built into the floors of houses, and wastewater (as noted earlier) was carried out of urban homes through complex brick drainage systems and outside the settlement areas through covered drains along the streets.

While archaeological excavations have provided a great deal of information about the material culture of Harappan civilization, the absence of oral or written texts still leaves many questions. Without additional sources scholars cannot know how Harappan cities were governed, how they related to the surrounding countryside, or even how they related to one another. Extensive water drainage systems and brick platforms that raised sections of settlements above the surrounding floodplain demonstrate Harappans' concerns with water and, perhaps, with protecting themselves against the periodic inundations of Indus Valley rivers. Walls and gates around areas of these cities may demonstrate a concern with protection from marauders, although many other settlements seem to lack defenses. Unlike Mesopotamia in the Near East, Harappan civilization had neither monuments nor large statues. One of the relatively few surviving human sculptures from the Harappan world is a seven-inch-high remnant that shows the upper torso of a bearded man. Is he a merchant, a king, or a priest? Although some have nicknamed this figure the "Priest-King," it is not known who or what the image was meant to represent.

The End of Harappan Civilization

By 1800 B.C.E. many of the main urban centers of mature Harappan civilization were abandoned or in decline, occupied on a much smaller scale and by communities whose cultures were very different from that of the earlier civilization. The upper levels of the city of Mohenjo-Daro show evidence of civic disorder and disarray—some 30 unburied skeletons lie in houses or lanes—and by 1900 B.C.E. the site was abandoned. The city of Harappa shrank in size, occupied in only one section and by a people whose pottery and burial customs (known as Cemetery H Culture) differed from those of earlier inhabitants. Other Harappan settlements—Ganweriwala, Rakhigarhi—disappeared entirely. One archaeologist estimates that the inhabited area of the Harappan region shrank to one-half its earlier size (Ratnagar 2001). The material culture of the mature Harappan period—as seen in Harappan-style seals and symbols, crafts using ivory or carnelian, metallurgy, standardized brick constructions—substantially disappears in settlements of the post–Harappan period.

Trade with Mesopotamia and the Oman region came to an end by 1800 B.C.E., and internal trade weakened. Mountain passes and trade routes through to Afghanistan and Baluchistan, which may have closed in the earlier period, seem to have reopened after 2000 B.C.E. (Ratnagar 2001). Archaeologists find evidence of Central Asian influences—whether through trade or the movement of peoples is debated—in artifacts from sites near the Bolan Pass (Sibri, Pirak, Quetta) and in the distinctive Gandharan Grave Culture found in the northern Swat Valley.

At many Indus region sites in the post–Harappan period, regionally defined cultures reemerge, their artifacts, buildings, and living styles replacing much, if not all, of the culture and products of mature Harappan civilization. The drying up of the Ghaggar-Hakra (Sarasvati) River forced many to abandon settlements along it. Archaeologists find evidence of Cemetery H Culture (fine fired red pottery urn reburials) in many sites throughout the Ghaggar-Hakra/Sarasvati River Valley and the southern Punjab. In Sind, a Jhukar pottery is found, associated with a culture using stone, bone, and some metal tools at Chanhu-Daro and Amri. Toward the south on the Kathiawar peninsula (Saurashtra) in Gujarat, new settlements appear, linked in style to earlier Harappan culture, but with a distinctive, regionally defined, culture.

Interestingly, aspects of Harappan civilization lived on in the material culture of the northwestern region. Full-size wooden bullock carts with solid wheels found in the area today are almost the exact duplicates of the small clay models from Harappan sites. Sewage drains continue to be common features of homes in this part of the north. Small Harappan figurines of large-breasted females remind many of "mother goddess" figures of more recent derivation. The posture of one broken Harappan statue, the torso of a man, is associated by some with the stance of the later dancing god Shiva. And a figure on an Indus seal sits cross-legged in a yogic pose common in later Hinduism.

INTO OR OUT OF INDIA

Over the past 150 years many groups have used the Harappan and Aryan legacies for their own purposes. The "Aryan invasion" theory originated in the 19th century, before the existence of Harappan civilization was even known, as part of Western linguists' efforts to account for similarities between Sanskrit and Western languages. This theory was used by 19th-century European scholars such as the Oxford don Friederich Max Müller to underline the "family" connection between "the Celts, the Germans, the Slaves [sic], the Greeks and Italians, the Persian and Hindus." All of these people at one time "were living together beneath the same roof. . . ." (Trautmann). Later British imperialists used the same theory to explain the inferiority of the Indian "race"—through mixing with indigenous peoples, Indians had degenerated from an earlier Aryan state—and, hence, the need for British rule. German Nazis in the 20th century claimed the Aryans were a superior "master race" whose descendants should rule the world. In the German formulation, however, the Indians, as Aryans, were part of the master race, not inferior to it.

The racial stereotypes and cultural supremacist assumptions inherent in the old Aryan invasion theory have been rejected in modern times, but the theory of a linkage between a wide number of "Indo-European" languages continues to be generally accepted. And many Western and Indian scholars (perhaps the majority, at least in the West) also accept the "Into India" theory as the most plausible explanation of the origins of Indian/Hindu religion and culture. That is, they argue that the peoples who composed the Rig-Veda (Hinduism's oldest text) were an Indo-European–speaking people who entered Afghanistan and the Punjab region of the subcontinent from the outside.

The linguistic connections of the into India theorists are widely accepted and unquestioned even by opponents of the theory themselves. Virtually all linguists and scholars accept that there is an Indo-European language family; the languages of western and eastern Europe, the Baltic and Slavic regions (from Poland to Russia), Iran, the South Asian subcontinent, and even the (ancient) Tocharian language of the Tarim Basin in China and the (ancient) language of the Hittites were all once part of a single language family, the Indo-European language family.

The origin of all these languages (according to the "into India" hypothesis) dates to the 4500–2500 B.C.E. period when a collection of tribes and/or tribal confederations lived together, in the steppe regions north and east of the Black Sea. These tribal communities and confederations were nomadic, warlike, used horses, and followed herds of cattle; they shared a common language (named proto-Indo-European as it existed before any of the later Indo-European languages developed). Beginning even before 2500 B.C.E. these tribes broke apart; some migrated into European lands or Slavic lands; others (known today as Indo-Iranians) moved south toward Iran and the Indian subcontinent. The term *Aryan* was used only by this later Indo-Iranian group; it is found in both the Iranian Avesta and the Indian Rig-Veda. (European scholars of the 19th century, however, mistakenly used Aryan to refer to the entire community from which the languages of Europe, Iran, and India derived [Bulliet].)

The into India scholars argue that the Indo-Aryans, the composers of Hinduism's most ancient text, the Rig-Veda, entered the subcontinent from the border regions to the northwest at some period before ca. 1500 B.C.E. Before reaching Iran, the Indo-Iranian communities had split: The Iranian-Aryans migrated south into Iran; the Indo-Aryans (as the India group is called) moved into the greater Punjab region of the subcontinent, sometime before ca.1500 B.C.E., the date by which it is thought the Rig-Veda was already composed (Witzel). In the same period, however, that is the centuries after the collapse of Harappan civilization (ca. 2000–1500 B.C.E.), other Indo-Iranian tribal groups may also have migrated into the subcontinent and/or settled along the Indo-Iranian borderlands. Thus from ca. 2000 B.C.E. to 1500 B.C.E. the subcontinent may have had multiple Indo-Iranian tribal communities either settled in, migrating through, or trading with its indigenous population.

Indigenist archaeologists and scholars and (more broadly) Hindu nationalist writers of the 20th and 21st centuries have challenged the into India theory, arguing that Indo-Aryan culture as seen in the Rig-Veda was indigenous to India; Aryans were the creators of the ancient Harappan civilization. Indigenist archaeologists (such as Jim Shaffer or B. B. Lal) argue that the reason archaeologists have failed to find the physical remains of the culture of the Indo-Aryans who composed the Rig-Veda is because these populations were indigenous both to the Indus region and to the subcontinent itself. Indigenist writers do not challenge the linguistic relationship between Indo-European languages; most often they ignore the linguistic issues in their writings. Some argue, however, that the linguistic connection

(continues)

INTO OR OUT OF INDIA *(continued)*

was created by Indian migrants who traveled "out of India," spreading the Indo-European language (and Aryan race) into Iran and Europe. According to this theory, the Hindus in India all descend from this original Harappan/Aryan race. As descendants of the original Indian people, Hindus are thus the only group who can legitimately claim the right to live in and govern the modern country of India.

The out of India theory is not widely accepted among Western scholars, and even in India itself it is far from universally accepted. Most scholars think that the into India theory, if problematic in many respects (the failure to "find" the archaeological remains of the Indo-Aryans who created the Rig-Veda being perhaps the major failing), is still the more acceptable theory for two reasons. One reason rests on linguistic evidence. The Sanskrit language has some linguistic features found only in it and not in other Indo-European languages. Those same features are also found in the Dravidian languages of southern India. It is difficult to believe that Sanskrit could have been the original proto-Indo-European language and not have carried these linguistic characteristics on to even *one* other Indo-European language.

The second major problem with the out of India theory lies in the absence of horses in the ancient Harappan region and sites. Indo-Aryan tribes were nomadic, pastoral people who fought their frequent battles in chariots driven by horses. But Harappan civilization has no evidence of horses: There are no horses on its seals; no remains of horses—although there are domesticated cattle and donkeys—found at its sites even in the greater Indus region before 1700 B.C.E. In the early 21st century, one enthusiastic proponent of the out of India theory attempted to improve the historical record by altering an image of a Harappan seal to make its bull (or unicorn) look like a horse (Witzel and Farmer). Such efforts show that current controversies over Harappa and the Aryan invasion are as much struggles for identity and political legitimacy in present-day India as they are arguments about the historical past.

Sources: Bulliet, Lucy. "The Indigenous Aryan Debate for Beginners." (New York: 2002); Trautmann, Thomas R. *Aryans and British India.* (New Delhi: Vistaar, 1997), p. 177; Witzel, Michael. "Autochthonous Aryans? The Evidence from Old Indian and Iranian Texts." *Electronic Journal of Vedic Studies* 7, no. 3 (2001): 1–115; Witzel, Michael, and Steve Farmer. "Horseplay in Harappa: The Indus Valley Decipherment Hoax." *Frontline.* 13 October, 2000. Available online. URL: http://www.flonnet.com/fl1720/17200040.htm. Accessed April 26, 2004.

What happened to Harappan civilization? British archaeologists in the mid-20th century, such as Sir Mortimer Wheeler (1890–1976), blamed its end on the "Aryan invasion," a mass movement of Indo-European–speaking warrior tribes from Iranian regions into the sub-continent. Few modern scholars agree that either an "invasion" or even tribal migrations into the subcontinent ended Harappan civilization. (Although many Western and Indian scholars do think that the period from ca. 2000 B.C.E. to 1500 B.C.E. saw numerous Indo-European–speaking tribal communities or confederations either migrating into or settling on the margins of the subcontinent region.) Scholars now look at a combination of factors to account for the end of the urban Harappan civilization: the end of trade links with Mesopotamia ca. 1800 that may have destroyed the Harappan trading economy; the increasing desiccation of the Ghaggar-Hakra/Sarasvati River region; the possibility that tectonic changes may have flooded the lower Indus in the Mohenjo-Daro region; and/or the possibility of endemic disease. Scholars even speculate on how Harappan ideology (about which nothing is known) might have contributed to the civilization's demise. Hindu nationalists of the 20th and 21st centuries claim Harappan civilization as the birthplace of Sanskrit and Hindu culture—an "out of India" idea that many "nonindigenists" strenuously dispute. In the end there are many questions and speculations but few firm answers.

Origins of the Aryans

By 1500 B.C.E. a tribal community living in the greater Punjab region of the subcontinent had composed a collection of hymns in praise of their gods. This community called themselves Aryans (a term that later meant "civilized" or "noble"). The hymns they composed eventually became the Rig-Veda, a sacred text in the modern Hindu religion, the oldest source for ancient Indian history and the only source of information about the origins and culture of the community that composed it.

The Indo-Aryans who composed the Rig-Veda migrated into the sub-continent from the mountains to the north and west. Linguistics theorize that these peoples were originally part of a larger Indo-European speaking subgroup, the Indo-Iranians, once living on the steppe lands north and east of the Caspian Sea. The Indo-Iranians migrated into south Central Asia where they then separated: one group, the Iranian Aryans, moved south onto the Iranian plateau; a second group, the Indo-Aryans, moved through the Afghan mountains into the Punjab region of the Indus plain.

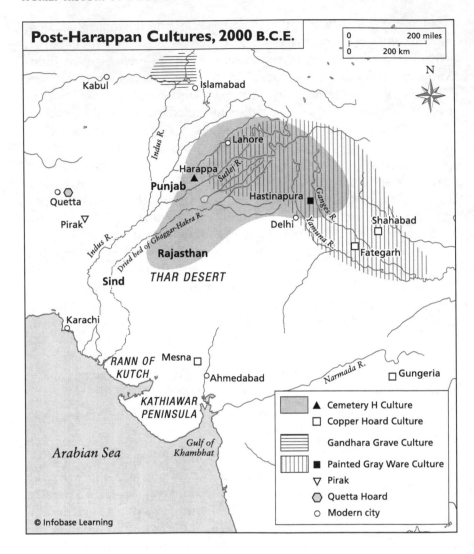

Post-Harappan Cultures, 2000 B.C.E.

Linguists base these migration theories on similarities between the ancient language, religion, and culture of the Iranian Aryans (as seen in the Avesta, the ancient scriptures of the Zoroastrian religion) and of the Indo-Aryans (as seen in the Rig-Veda). The languages of both peoples—as seen in these ancient texts—are so similar linguists say they are like dialects of the same language. Both peoples referred to themselves as Aryans. Their religions also had many similarities: similar gods with similar names, similar legends about these gods, and similar modes of worshiping these gods.

A century ago it was common to speak of the movement of these Indo-Aryan–speaking peoples as an invasion, a term that conjured images of platoons of mounted horsemen riding down onto the Indo-Gangetic Plain. Now historians are more likely to emphasize the gradualness of the process. Trade, regular and seasonal movements of seminomadic herding peoples, the migrations of tribal communities—these are all the means by which the Indo-Aryan peoples might have found their way into the subcontinent. By 1500 B.C.E. long-term trade and pastoral and migration routes had already linked India to Iran in the west and Central Asia to the north for more than a thousand years.

Archaeological evidence shows that many different tribes and cultures lived in the Indo-Iranian borderlands and in the northwestern mountains in the post-Harappan period (1900–1300 B.C.E.). But while artifacts found at numerous sites in this period show evidence of Central Asian influences and may suggest the presence of Indo-Iranian–speaking populations in the subcontinent, archaeologists have not linked any one of these cultures to the Indo-Aryan communities that composed the Rig-Veda. Excavators found evidence of camel and horse domestication at Pirak in Baluchistan from ca. 1700 B.C.E.—the first confirmed evidence of domesticated horses on the subcontinent. At a small nearby site, Sibri, and also at Pirak there were seals, not in the Harappan style, but in a style reminiscent of seals from early Indo-European sites in Central Asia. At the city of Quetta, an undated hoard of vessels and ornaments shows a style said to combine influences from Baluchistan, northern Iran, and Turkmenistan. In the Swat Valley region to the north, Gandhara Grave Culture (ca. 1700–1600 B.C.E.) has pottery similar to pottery found in northern Iran. Artifacts from Cemetery H Culture, excavated at the city of Harappa, show evidence of a population who now occupied only a small section of that ancient city. These people decorated their pottery with antelopes and peacocks and burned bones of their dead in clay urns.

Archaeologists argue over whether settlements in the post- Harappan period demonstrate the reemergence of regional cultures or the intrusion of "foreign" (that is, Central Asian, Indo-European–speaking) cultures into the area. Many believe the record now shows evidence of several different Indo-Iranian–speaking communities at different places in the region, although (as already indicated) no evidence links any of these communities to the particular Indo-European–speaking population, that is the Indo-Aryans, whose religion and culture are seen in the Rig-Veda. Interestingly, human physical remains from excavations throughout this region all fall within the same range of physical types. No "new" human subgroup entered the region in this period, perhaps because people within the larger geographical region had already interacted biologically (as they had economically) for more than a millennium.

Aryan Society

Whatever the means by which they made their way into the subcontinent, by 1500 B.C.E. Indo-Aryan tribes had established themselves in

THE VEDAS

The Vedas are the oldest and most sacred texts in Hinduism. These texts include the Rig-Veda, the Atharva-Veda, the Yajur-Veda, and the Sama-Veda. Each of these four Vedas was itself a collection of liturgical materials—hymns, for instance, and ritual sayings—used in the performance of Vedic rites. Attached to each of the Vedas, in turn, were three types of later explanatory, interpretive, and sometimes speculative texts: (1) the Brahmanas were texts that explained the Vedic hymns and rituals; (2) the Aranyakas were texts that gave even more esoteric and secret interpretations of Vedic rituals; and (3) the Upanishads were texts that gave later and yet more speculative interpretations of the rituals and the cosmic order in which they were set. The oldest of all the Vedas, the Rig-Veda, was probably composed by ca. 1500 B.C.E. on the basis of stories, legends, rituals, and religious practices perhaps already in existence for centuries. The rest of the Vedas, including the most important early Upanishads, were composed by ca. 500 B.C.E.

The four Vedas and (most of) their attached Brahmanas, Aranyakas, and Upanishads are classified in the Hindu tradition as *sruti* ("that which has been revealed" or, more literally, "heard"). These texts were sacred because they had been revealed to ("heard" by) the ancient rishis (seers). Their language was fixed and could not be altered or misremembered. These were all oral texts, not written down until well into the Christian era. To ensure their accuracy, the Brahman priests who were in charge of them developed an elaborate and precise method of memorization. The rest of Hindu religious scriptures were also considered important and sacred, but not in the same way as the Vedas.

Texts such as the epic poems (the *Mahabharata,* the *Ramayana*) and the law codes (the Laws of Manu among others) were all classified as *smrti* ("that which is remembered"). These *smrti* texts could be (and were) told and retold, embellished and added onto in any number of religious and secular contexts.

the Punjab region and had composed most of the hymns in Hinduism's oldest text, the Rig-Veda. That text is a collection of more than 1,000 hymns addressed to various Vedic gods. It has survived in an ancient and difficult version of the Sanskrit language (called Vedic Sanskrit), and even today many of its passages remain obscure and unintelligible. It is, nonetheless, the only source of information about the ancient peoples whose worldviews, beliefs, and practices would develop into the religion of a majority of Indian people.

The society described in the hymns of the Rig-Veda was nomadic and pastoral. Indo-Aryan society was divided into three classes: kings, priests, and commoners. Aryan life centered on cattle, horses, and warfare. This can be seen in the hymns' many metaphors involving cows, in their use of cattle as a sign of wealth, and in the special energy with which they condemn those who steal or threaten to steal Aryan herds. Indo-Aryans protected their herds (and stole cows from others) through warfare. This was a warrior culture whose major warrior god, Indra, was shown fighting against the "enemies of the Aryans," the peoples, that is, whose practices differed from those of the Aryans themselves.

The hymns also reveal Indo-Aryan society as pragmatic and utilitarian. Hymns ask the gods for wealth, cattle, progeny, prosperity, and health. The strong naturalistic elements in the Rig-Veda are represented by gods such as Agni (fire) and Surya (the Sun), each of whom is portrayed as the natural element itself. These natural elements and humankind are bound together in mutual dependence within the world's cosmic order (*rita*). The ritual of sacrifice, the focus of the hymns, is not only a means of flattering the gods and gaining gifts from them; it is also an act necessary to continue the world order.

But although the Rig-Veda would later be among the most sacred texts of the Hindu religion, many of Hinduism's basic ideas are missing from it. The hymns are not mystical or devotional in the fashion of later Hinduism. Nor do they mention key Hindu terms—such as karma (fate), dharma (duty), or reincarnation. The four classes (varnas) so important in later Indian society appear only in one late Rig-Vedic hymn. These concepts and categories, central to the Hindu religion and the social system in which it was embedded, only developed later, as the Indo-Aryans abandoned their nomadic, pastoral ways and settled down as farmers on the rich Gangetic plains.

2

CASTE, KINGS, AND THE HINDU WORLD ORDER (1000 B.C.E.–700 C.E.)

If the king fails to administer Punishment tirelessly on those who ought to be punished, the stronger would grill the weak like fish on a spit. . . .

■

The Law Code of Manu (Olivelle 2004, 107)

Indo-Aryans spread into the upper Ganges River Valley between 1200 and 400 B.C.E. Their superior Iron Age technology enabled them to dominate the many different tribes and communities living in Pakistan and northern India in 1200 B.C.E. and develop a farming civilization in the Gangetic region with urban centers of trade and power. By the early centuries C.E. a Sanskrit-based Aryan culture in which competing Hindu, Buddhist, and Jain religions vied for dominance had spread its cultural hegemony through all settled regions of the subcontinent.

India's Second Urbanization

Iron Age technology gave Indo-Aryan tribes the ability to move into the heavily forested regions of the Ganges River Valley and enabled them to dominate the region. Many scholars now agree that the sites in the Indo-Gangetic region characterized by Painted Gray Ware (PGW) pottery (ca. 1200–400 B.C.E.) are those of the Indo-Aryans. This pottery—a fine, wheel-made pottery decorated with black or red geometric patterns—was first found at sites from ca. 1200 B.C.E. along the northern Indus and then increasingly in the Ganges River Valley. Population pressures and the increasing desiccation of the Indus region may have

26

HOLY COW

There are no cow gods in Hinduism—not in the Rig-Veda or later Hinduism. The closest to a cow divinity are the divine wish-fulfilling cow, Kamadhenu (desire-fulfilling-cow), who appears in stories in the *Mahabharata,* the *Ramayana,* and the *puranas,* and the bull, Nandi, who is the "vehicle" of the great god Shiva.

Nevertheless cows have long had both practical and religious significance in India. The Indo-Aryans were a nomadic herding people when they migrated into the subcontinent. Their pastoral world valued cows, using them as a measure of wealth. One Vedic text reflected this in verses praising the cow:

The Cow is Heaven, the Cow is Earth, the Cow is Vishnu, Lord of Life....
Both Gods and mortal men depend for life and being on the Cow.
She hath become this universe: all that the Sun surveys is she.
(Embree et al.)

In the ecological conditions of the North Indian plains, however, the Aryans became farmers. As they moved from a pastoral to an agrarian way of life cows came to be seen as work animals, too valuable to be killed for food. Their milk products became the most precious of

(continues)

Mahabalipuram rock carving, ca. seventh century C.E., Pallava dynasty. This carving appears in the Krishna Mandapam, the largest of eight mandapams (shallow rock-cut halls decorated with rock carvings) carved during the Pallava dynasty at Mahabalipuram in south India. (courtesy of Judith E. Walsh)

HOLY COW *(continued)*

Indian foods. The five products of the cow—milk, curd, butter, urine, and dung—were traditionally seen to have great purifying powers.

The animal sacrifices that once were fundamental to Vedic Hinduism were abandoned over the centuries beginning with the Upanishads and later in response to Buddhist and Jain criticisms. As vegetarianism became more prevalent, prohibitions against cow slaughter became a fundamental feature of Hinduism. By the 12th century C.E. one legend circulated that a Chola king had executed his son because the boy had accidentally caused the death of a calf. This story (like another about a Gujarati Jain king who fined people for killing fleas) was apocryphal but shows how prestigious cow protection had become by this period. Even today, many religious Hindus will not eat beef, and wealthy Hindus may donate money to support *goshalas,* homes for the protection of cattle.

Source: Embree, Ainslie Thomas, et al., eds. *Sources of Indian Tradition. Vol. I: From the Beginning to 1800. 2d ed.* (New York: Columbia University Press, 1988), p. 41.

---

forced the Indo-Aryans to move farther east, clearing forests in the Gangetic region and settling in now mixed agricultural and pastoral communities, farming the land with teams of six and eight oxen. "Let the plough, lance-pointed, well lying with well smoothed handle turn up cow, sheep and on-going chariot frame and a plump wench. Let Indra hold down the furrow . . . let it, rich in milk, yield to us each further summer," says a ritual hymn from the Atharva Veda (quoted in Thapar 2002, 116). New iron tools and technology, widespread at PGW sites by 800 B.C.E., allowed the Indo-Aryan tribes to move into what are today the regions of Haryana and Uttar Pradesh. A finer, "luxury" pottery (Northern Black Polished Ware or NBPW, ca. 700–200 B.C.E.) marks the later spread of Aryan culture throughout the Gangetic region; it is this pottery that had also spread (perhaps through trade) as far south as the Deccan Plateau by 500 B.C.E.

All the later Vedic texts, as well as the core stories of the two great epics the *Mahabharata* and the *Ramayana,* were in existence by the fifth century B.C.E. (The epics, scholars believe, would continue to evolve and change well into the fourth century C.E.) Together, texts and excavations of the mid-first millennium B.C.E. show a western Gangetic plain dominated by Indo-Aryan tribal communities that had horses, iron tools, and weapons. These tribes had domesticated cattle, but they had now also become farmers, growing wheat, barley, and perhaps even rice. It is this PGW/Indo-Aryan society and its new way of life that spread throughout the Gangetic region.

Although the later Vedic texts rarely speak of towns, by ca. 500 B.C.E. India's second urbanization was well under way. The fertile alluvial soil of the Ganges River Valley combined with Indo-Aryan Iron Age technology to produce crop surpluses that allowed both population growth and the emergence of new cities. Silver bent bar coins and both silver and copper punch-marked coins also came into use in this period (ca. fifth century B.C.E.). "The number [of cities] is so great," reported a Greek envoy to the region in the late fourth century B.C.E., "that it cannot be stated with precision" (McCrindle 2000, 67). These new Gangetic towns and cities were built on the banks of rivers, enclosed by either a moat or rampart, and sometimes fortified. The city of Pataliputra (modern-day Patna), capital of the fourth–second century B.C.E. Mauryan Empire, enclosed an estimated 340 hectares (840 acres) within its moat and had, by one estimate, a population of 270,000 people (Allchin 1995, 69).

Urban settlements were not limited to the central Gangetic plains. Cities dotted trade routes through the northwest, Taxila below the Hindu Kush Mountains being the most famous. City sites have also been found to the east in the Gangetic delta, to the west on the Maharashtrian and Gujarat coasts, and along trade routes leading from the Gangetic valley into both central and peninsular India.

Vedic Hinduism

As the once-nomadic Indo-Aryans settled into agrarian life in the Gangetic region, the religion they had originally practiced changed and adapted. Key concepts of Hinduism, such as reincarnation, karma (actions, fate), dharma (obligations, duty), and the four *varnas* (classes) developed during this time. These new ideas were well adapted to agrarian (or even urban) settled life; they explained and justified the social and economic divisions of Gangetic society in terms of an individual's good or bad conduct in former lives. Taken together, these concepts created the basic worldview assumed by all indigenous religions in India.

The Vedic Hinduism (or Brahmanism) that developed out of the religion of the Rig-Veda in this period (ca. 1200–400 B.C.E.) was as different from modern Hinduism as the ancient Old Testament Hebrew religion was from today's Christianity. Vedic Hinduism centered on rituals addressed to Vedic gods, performed by Brahman priests around a sacred fire. Some gods represented the natural elements—Agni, the fire; Surya, the Sun; or Soma, the deified hallucinogenic plant used in rituals. Others had human characteristics or were associated with a moral or ethical principle: the god Indra was a mighty warrior, while Varuna stood for cosmic order (*rita*). In later Hinduism some of these Vedic gods (Indra, Agni, Surya) would become minor figures in the Hindu pantheon, while others, like Varuna, would disappear entirely. Gods barely mentioned in the Vedic texts—such as Vishnu—would later assume much greater importance.

Vedic fire rituals, from the simplest to the most elaborate, involved offerings of vegetable or meat foods or drink to the gods. In return the sponsor of the sacrifice might receive a powerful reign (if a king) or (if a householder) a good crop, a fruitful marriage, or a lifetime lasting a hundred years. Vedic rituals had no fixed place of worship—no temple, hall, or building was used—nor did they involve icons or images of the gods. Daily domestic rituals used a single fire and one priest, while public rituals—the accession of a king, the Horse Sacrifice—required at least three fires and many priests.

The Horse Sacrifice

The Asvamedha, or Horse Sacrifice, was a major ritual of Vedic times that continued in use well into the sixth and seventh centuries C.E. In this ritual a royal stallion wandered free for a year. The king's armies followed behind, either demanding tribute from all whose territories the horse entered or fighting them. At the end of the year, the horse was sacrificed in a ritual that associated the power of the king with the animal. Part of the ritual involved a pantomiming of the sexual coupling of the (dead) horse and the chief queen. Here is a depiction of that part of the ritual, as described in the Shatapatha Brahmana attached to the Yajur Veda:

> *A cloth, an upper cloth, and gold is what they spread out for the horse, and on that they "quiet" [kill] him. . . . When the water for washing the feet is ready, they make the chief queen (Mahishi) lie down next to the horse and they cover the two of them up with the upper cloth as they say the verse, "Let the two of us cover ourselves in the world of heaven," for the world of heaven is where they "quiet" the sacrificial animal. Then they draw out the penis of the horse and place it in the vagina of the chief queen, while she says, "May the vigorous male, the layer of seed, lay the seed"; this she says for sexual intercourse. (O'Flaherty 1988, 16)*

30

The Horse Sacrifice, 1780s. This 18th-century painting (attributed to the artist Sital Das) shows the Asvamedha (Horse Sacrifice). The chief queen sits on the platform with Brahmans and the sacrificial horse. The sacrificial fire burns in the center next to the plinth to which the horse is tied. In the upper left panel, the killing of the horse is shown. The Sanskrit text at the top identifies this as the Horse Sacrifice. (By permission of the British Library. India Office Prints & Drawings, Shelfmark J.5,21)

Unity and Diversity in the Upanishads

It was in the major Upanishadic texts (composed by ca. 500 B.C.E.) that the literal ideas of the Vedic rituals took on abstract, metaphysical significance. The Upanishadic texts described secret sessions in which holy men gathered in the forest to speculate on human life and the cosmos. In the Upanishads, for instance, the ritual of the Horse Sacrifice became an extended metaphor linking the horse with the cosmos itself: "Verily the dawn is the head of the horse which is fit for sacrifice, the sun its eye, the wind its breath. . . . When the horse shakes itself, then it lightens; when it kicks, it thunders; when it makes water, it rains" (Macnicol 1963, 43).

Upanishadic sages sought to draw out the hidden connections between the essence of life in each living thing and the creative force that brings all life into existence. Atman (the self) was the name the Upanishadic texts gave to the spark of life in each creature; Brahman (a neuter noun in this use) was the name for the ultimate force behind creation—not the Vedic gods (they were part of the universe) but

31

whatever enabled the universe and all its life-forms to come into existence. In the key insight of the Upanishads, atman and Brahman are understood to be one and the same: The essence of life in each being in the world (atman) is the same as the creative force (Brahman) that brings about all life. "As a spider sends forth its thread, and as tiny sparks spring forth from a fire," said one Upanishad, "so indeed do all the vital functions, all the worlds, all the gods, and all beings spring from this self [atman]. Its hidden name [upanishad] is: 'The real behind the real,' . . ." (Olivelle 1996, 26). Underlying the wild diversity of the universe is a simple unity. Each living being has a different form but the same "subtle essence." The differences—the forms, the changes—would be seen by later Hinduism as illusory and that illusion would be called *maya*. In the Upanishads the underlying unity is the point, the essential reality. "This whole world has that essence for its Self," says one wise Upanishadic sage to his son Shvetaketu. "That is the Real. That is the Self. That art thou, Shvetaketu" (De Bary 1958, 35–36).

Karma and Reincarnation

All Vedic sacrifices, from daily domestic offerings to the great Horse Sacrifice, were predicated on the assumption that their rituals produced consequences. But it was in the Upanishads (ca. 500 B.C.E.) that the belief took shape that humans also could experience the consequences of past acts through *samsara* (reincarnation, literally "the running around" "wandering"). At death, one Upanishadic passage explains, the most virtuous would go to "the worlds of brahman." Others—after the effects of their good deeds on Earth were used up—would return to Earth and "take birth in the fire of woman . . . [and] circle around in the same way." The least virtuous would "become worms, insects, or snakes" (Olivelle 1996, 83–84).

These new ideas of reincarnation and of karma (the effect of past actions on future lives) were also linked to the four classes, or *varnas*, of human society. These classes had first been mentioned in a late Rig-Vedic hymn. There they were created (as was the entire universe) out of the sacrifice of a primeval being, the "thousand-headed" "thousand-eyed" man (*purusha*): "His mouth became the brahman his two arms were made into the rajanyas [Kshatriyas], his two thighs the vaishyas; from his two feet the shudra was born" (Embree et al. 1988, 18–19).

In later Vedic texts (as in the Rig-Vedic verse) the four classes were both hierarchically ranked and occupationally defined. Brahmans performed the ritual sacrifices. They were the teachers, readers, and preservers of the sacred texts. Kshatriyas were the warriors and the kings, whose duty was to protect society. Vaishyas were the farmers and merchants. And Shudras were the servants. Rebirth into a higher class showed that one had been virtuous in past lives; rebirth at a lower level showed the opposite. *Moksha,* or escape from the cycle of reincarnation entirely, would become the ultimate goal of the Hindu religious tradition (as also of Buddhism, in which it is called "nirvana," and of Jainism). But moksha was too difficult for most to achieve. For most Hindus the goal of life was the fulfillment of the religious and social duties (dharma) of one's *varna* so as to acquire good karma and rebirth into a higher class: "Those whose conduct has been good," says the Chandogya Upanishad, "will quickly attain some good birth, the birth of a Brahman, or a Kshatriya, or a Vaisya. But those whose conduct has

THE VALUE OF A SON

66 **W**hat does one get by means of a son?" asks a sonless man to the sage Narada. The importance of a son in Hinduism is linked to his ability both to enable his father's spiritual progress in future lives by lighting his funeral pyre and to bring into the paternal home his wife (and dowry) when he marries. Here, from one of the Brahmanas, is the Vedic answer to the question:

If a father sees the face of his son born alive, he repays a debt through him and achieves immortality. As many joys as there are in the earth for creatures who have vital breath, as many as there are in fire, and as many as there are in water, greater than this is the joy that a father has in a son. Fathers have always crossed over the deep darkness by means of a son, for a son gives a father comfort and carries him across; the self is born from the self. What use is dirt or the black antelope skin (of the ascetic)? What use are beards and asceticism? "Seek a son, O Brahmins"; that is what people keep saying. Food is breath and clothing is protection, gold is beauty and cattle are marriage; a wife is a friend and a daughter is misery. But a son is a light in the highest heaven.

Source: O'Flaherty, Wendy Doniger, ed. *Textual Sources for the Study of Hinduism* (Chicago: University of Chicago Press, 1988), p. 20.

been evil, will quickly attain an evil birth, the birth of a dog, or a hog, or a Chandala [an Untouchable]" (Macnicol 1963, 161).

In the *Mahabharata* and the *Ramayana*—the great epic poems whose core stories were in existence by the fifth century B.C.E.—these ideas form the moral backdrop against which human lives and events play out. The fulfillment of the duties (dharma) of one's class determined what happened in future lives. "A Shudra," says the old grandfather in the *Mahabharata*, "should never amass wealth. . . . By this he would incur sin" (Embree and De Bary 1972, 82). This outline of a social system—and the concepts associated with it—remained fundamental to both Vedic and later Hinduism, as well as to all the heterodox religions indigenous to India.

Heterodoxy in North India
Cyclical Time, Reincarnation, and Karma

The Brahman priests who composed the early Hindu texts often spoke as if their world was exclusively dominated by Vedic Hinduism. But religious life on the Gangetic plains was heterodox and competitive. Wandering holy men, monks, and religious teachers were the norm in the urban towns and cities along the Ganges, particularly in the eastern regions of modern-day Uttar Pradesh and Bihar. Public rivalries and debates among contesting religious communities were common. Among the many heterodoxies of the period (ca. sixth–fifth century B.C.E.) Buddhist sources describe "six unorthodox teachers," not counting themselves. Each of the six led a different religious community with distinctive answers to the religious questions of the day.

However bitterly these religions competed, they shared fundamental assumptions about the process of time itself and the nature of life in the world. These assumptions originated in Vedic and Upanishadic Hinduism but by 500 B.C.E. had been so naturalized within Indian society that they were unquestioningly assumed to be the functioning nature of the world. The Hindu, Buddhist, and Jain view of time was and is cyclical, setting human life into an infinite expanse. In one of many Hindu myths that explore the origins of the world, the god Brahma creates the universe when he awakes each morning. He does this, the myth explains, for "play" or "sport." The universe he creates lasts for 4 billion 320 million years and then is destroyed. All of this occupies only one day in Brahma's life, and at the end of the day (and at the destruction of the universe) he sleeps. Next morning he begins all over again, creating the universe once again. In this way the god lives to the comfortable age of 108. On his death, a new Brahma is born who continues the cycle.

Each time Brahma creates the universe, it cycles through four ages (called *yugas*). The first of these, the Krita Yuga, is the longest and most perfect, but over time, a process of degeneration and decay sets in. By the last age, the Kali Yuga (the Black Age), the world has reached a condition of dangerous corruption, chaos, and degeneracy. It is in this age that we find ourselves at present. The Kali Yuga is the shortest of the four periods but a time marked by increasing disharmony, disorder among beings, and the continued disintegration of the universe itself. The end of this age brings with it the destruction of the universe and all creatures in it.

Vedic orthodoxy and the heterodox religions not only assumed a world in which time was cyclical, they took as a given that the process of life within those cycles was one in which reincarnation occurred based on the inexorable law of karma. Where reincarnation had been a new and secret idea when first introduced in the Upanishads, by the fifth century B.C.E. it had become the axiomatic base on which all indigenous religions rested. Reincarnation was a uniquely painful process, one which subjected the self to the pain and suffering of not one but an infinite number of lives. "In every kind of existence," sang the Jain poet, "I have suffered pains which have scarcely known reprieve for a moment" (De Bary 1958, 60). All teachers and religious schools of the period addressed the problems posed by karma and unending rebirth. One heterodox sect, the Ajivikas, argued that as karma was predestined, humans could do nothing to change it. Another—that of Ajita Keshakambalin ("Ajita of the Hair-blanket")—took an atheistic position. The monks of this school did not believe in rebirth and considered the concept of karma irrelevant, since nothing at all remained after death: "When the body dies, both fool and wise alike are cut off and perish. They do not survive after death" (Basham 1954: 296).

Three religions survived from the intense competition of the North Indian plains into modern times: Vedic Hinduism, Jainism, and Buddhism. The three were embedded in society in somewhat different ways. The Brahman priests of Vedic Hinduism were connected to both urban and rural society through their performance of rituals and their knowledge of (and monopoly over) the oral Hindu scriptures. Brahman holy men often lived outside urban centers in forest dwellings, alone or in small communities. Some even left society entirely, seeking spiritual salvation by adopting the life of a wandering *sannyasi* (ascetic).

LANGUAGES

Indians in the Gangetic region in the heterodox centuries, whatever their preferred religion, shared a common language base and by the early centuries C.E., if they were in the elite they would probably also know Sanskrit. By the fifth century B.C.E. there were two forms of the Sanskrit language in existence: Vedic Sanskrit, the form of the language used in rituals and preserved orally in the Vedas, and an early version of what would later become classical Sanskrit, described in a text by the Indian grammarian Panini dated to this period. This early version of classical Sanskrit was probably the form of the language in use in Panini's time, and it became the form of Sanskrit used in all later texts. Between the Mauryan and Gupta periods (300 B.C.E.–320 C.E.), Sanskrit spread throughout the subcontinent, and by the Gupta period (ca. 320–550 C.E.) it had become the medium for elite communication in most sections of India.

Ordinary speech of the time, however, was not in Sanskrit. The most ancient North Indian vernaculars were collectively called the Prakrits—a word that meant "unrefined" or "common" as opposed to Sanskrit, which meant "refined" or "elegant." The oldest Buddhist texts used a Prakrit (called Pali), as did most inscriptions before the Gupta period. Prakrit is also found in Sanskrit drama, in which women and low-caste characters speak it rather than Sanskrit. By the medieval period (ca. seventh century C.E.), Prakrits had been replaced in the north by the regional vernaculars known today: Hindi, Marathi, Gujarati, and Bengali, to name only a few. In South India the vernaculars were Dravidian languages, such as Tamil, Kanarese, Telugu, or Malayalam. Tamil *cankam* poetry (an anthology of Tamil poetry) of the first to third centuries C.E. shows that south Indian elites used both regional vernaculars and Sanskrit.

Followers of the heterodox schools of Buddhism or Jainism, in contrast, were more likely to live together in monastic communities called *sanghas* (assemblies). Monks and nuns were supported by lay communities, especially by trading and merchant families. By tradition the founders of both religions came from the Kshatriya *varna*. Thus, both Buddhism and Jainism implicitly challenged the idea that Brahmans had a monopoly over religious life. Buddhism and Jainism were also explicitly critical of Vedic animal sacrifices; both religions encouraged their members to practice ahimsa (nonviolence) and to give up the eating of meat.

Lay members of the Buddhist community were not allowed to work as either hunters or butchers, and religious Jains were even forbidden to farm (as that involved the killing of plants and living things in the soil). These heterodox criticisms and practices had a great influence on Indian society. Over the next centuries the practice of Vedic animal sacrifices slowly died out. By the Gupta period (ca. fifth century C.E.) a Buddhist traveler to India reported that vegetarianism was widely practiced among the higher Indian classes and that only the lower castes still ate meat.

Jainism

The name of this major heterodox religion of North India was derived from the Sanskrit word *jina,* meaning "to conquer." The Jain religion focused on the need to conquer or overcome the karmic influences that bound humans to the cycle of reincarnation. To escape this cycle, Jainism emphasized the unity of all life-forms and the religious, spiritual, and karmic dangers of violence against any of them.

The historical founder of Jainism was Mahavira (Great Hero) Vardhamana who lived during the sixth to fifth centuries B.C.E. Mahavira was said to be the 24th and last in a long line of "ford-makers" that stretched back, in the Jain worldview, through all history. (These ford-makers, or *tirthankaras,* were the Jain saints who created the means whereby humans could "ford the river" and achieve enlightenment.) According to Jain traditions, Mahavira was born into a warrior clan in the modern-day state of Bihar. He left home at age 30 to live the life of a homeless wanderer, begging for his food, at first wearing only a single garment that he never changed but later discarding this for complete nudity. In the 13th year of this ascetic life, Mahavira attained enlightenment. After that, it was said, he taught for 30 more years before dying at age 72 of ritual starvation in a village near the modern city of Patna. Traditionally, Jain sects have placed Mahavira's death at either 527 B.C.E. or 510 B.C.E., but, as Mahavira was a contemporary of the Buddha, ongoing recalculations of the Buddha's death (see below) will necessarily cause Mahavira's death to be placed much later, at or around ca. 425 B.C.E. (Dundas 2002).

Jainism taught that a living soul (*jiva*) was imprisoned in each and every material object. The actions of life led to the accretion of more and more matter (*ajiva,* or karma) onto these souls, an accumulation that led to the soul's continued rebirth within material forms. Only abstention from action—through a vow of nonviolence (ahimsa)—could decrease the matter adhering to the *jiva* and bring its release from reincarnation and (thus) the attainment of *moksha.* Once delivered from the physical body and all karma, the *jiva* rises to a realm of liberated *jivas* at the top of the universe where it will exist forever. All living forms—plants and animals as well as people—were believed to be inhabited by *jivas* and should not be harmed: "All breathing, existing, living, sentient creatures should not be slain nor treated with violence, nor abused, nor tormented, nor driven away," said an early Jain text. "This is the pure, unchangeable, eternal law which the clever ones, who understand the world, have proclaimed" (quoted in Dundas 2002, 41–42). Even in the modern era members of the Jain sect may cover their mouths with a fine mesh cloth as they walk in order to avoid breathing in insects or sweep the ground before them with a broom to avoid trampling any small creatures. Such actions may spring from a profound compassion for all living beings, but their religious justification lies in the fact that they enable the soul to escape the karma that might otherwise accrue from the death of these small beings. The ultimate logic of Jainism was the cessation of all life-sustaining activities, and in the past attempts to abstain completely from action led religious Jains (such as the founder Mahavira or, according to legend, the Mauryan emperor Chandragupta) to fast to death.

Monastic orders were necessary for such a strict life, and these orders were supported by a particularly devoted lay community whose members were encouraged to participate in the monastic experience as they could. Sectarian divisions within Jain communities arose gradually over the centuries following Mahavira's death, largely in disputes over whether monks should be naked or clothed. Those who wished to follow their founder (Mahavira) and remain naked (the "Sky-clad" or Digambara sect) argued against the wearing of clothes; those who thought this practice extreme and unnecessary (the "White Clad" or Shvetambara sect) argued for it. A mid-fifth century C.E. council (attended only by clothed monks) codified the Jain tradition along Shvetambara lines and confirmed the sectarian division. Scholars debate whether much real theological difference lay behind this division, but on one point at least the sects were deeply divided: Both agreed that women could not achieve salvation unless they were nuns and that women could not be nuns if that required them to be naked. Therefore, the Digambara (or naked) Jains insisted that women were not able to achieve salvation, while the Shvetambara (clad) sect argued that they could.

Buddhism

Like the Jains, early Buddhists believed that the goal of life was escape from the cycle of reincarnation (*moksha,* or nirvana). The Buddhist story that best illustrated this was the traditional story told about the life of the Buddha himself, Siddhartha Gautama. Siddhartha was the son of a king of the Shakya clan from the foothills of the Himalayas. Fearing prophecies that his son would become a wandering ascetic, the king raised him in great luxury, taking care to protect him from all pain and sorrow. He married the boy to a beautiful wife, and she soon gave Siddhartha a son. But on rare trips outside his father's palace Siddhartha was disturbed by a series of sights—an old man, a sick person, and a corpse—and by the realization that old age, illness, and death were the fate of everyone. When, on a fourth trip, he saw a holy man in the yellow robes of a wandering monk, Siddhartha realized that he too must leave home to seek a solution to the painfulness of life. During years of wandering he joined many different religious groups, but none helped solve his problem. Finally, sitting under the branches of a Bodhi tree (the tree of awakening), he resolved not to get up until he had found a solution. After 49 days, he arose. He had become the Buddha (the

The deer park at Sarnath north of the city of Varanasi was said to be the first place the Buddha preached after his enlightenment. It became a pilgrimage spot for Buddhists in later centuries and had numerous stupas. The emperor Ashoka erected a pillar at Sarnath in the third century B.C.E.; the Chinese pilgrim Faxian visited Sarnath in the fifth century C.E., as did another Chinese pilgrim, Xuanzang, in the seventh century. The Dharmekh Stupa, in the background here, was built between the fifth and seventh centuries C.E. (courtesy of Judith E. Walsh)

Enlightened one). In a deer park at Sarnath north of Varanasi he told an audience of five monks his solution. Life is sorrow, he said: "Birth is sorrow, age is sorrow, disease is sorrow, death is sorrow, contact with the unpleasant is sorrow, separation from the pleasant is sorrow, every wish unfulfilled is sorrow" (De Bary 1958, 102). The source of this sorrow is desire, the "craving which leads to rebirth." Only by ending all desire can people find peace in this world and achieve enlightenment. By following the "Middle Way"—the practices and mental disciplines of Buddhism—a Buddhist achieves nirvana (a state of final bliss in life and after death) and escapes the cycle of reincarnation forever.

By tradition the Buddha lived to the age of 80, preaching his "Middle Way" to a collection of disciples until he died at Kushinagara, a small town (now Kashia) in eastern Uttar Pradesh. Earlier historians placed the date of the Buddha's death at 483 B.C.E., but recent scholarship has concluded that a later date, between ca. 411–400 B.C.E., is more likely (Bechert et al 1996; Cousins 1996).

To become a Buddhist was to step outside the social classes of Hindu society and into a religious society whose obligations were defined by the Buddhist dharma (here used in the sense of "law" or "religion"). But the demands of this Buddhist dharma were not easy. A serious Buddhist had to remain celibate; refrain from harming living beings (that is, not eat meat); drink no wine; give up dancing, singing, and music (except for religious purposes); and abstain from sleeping in beds or receiving money. Such a severe discipline required monastic orders; committed Buddhists lived in monasteries or nunneries, endowed by wealthy lay Buddhists, or kings and rulers.

From Clan to King

Between ca. 1200 and 300 B.C.E. Indo-Aryan tribes cleared the forest regions of the northern Ganges River and settled down in farming communities prosperous enough to support cities throughout the region. From the Rig-Veda it is known that Aryan society was originally organized into tribal communities, clans dominated by elite warrior lineages. By the fifth century B.C.E., 16 large clans or tribes had consolidated claims over lands in the Gangetic region and begun to define themselves not by kinship but by the territories they claimed. Sources for the period called the lands of each of these clans a *mahajanapada* (great-clan's territory). Among the 16, some governed themselves through kings and some through oligarchic assemblies of a ruling clan or clans. Their capitals were fortified cities, often located along strategic trade routes, surrounded by the agricultural villages and towns they controlled. Five out of the six largest cities in the Gangetic region in this period were the political capitals of such "great-clan territories."

Political life in the Gangetic region, however, was just as volatile and competitive as religious life. Over the next century, these great-clan territories fought one another until only four remained. Magadha, located midway along the Ganges River, was the wealthiest of the four. In the mid-fourth century B.C.E., a soldier Mahapadma Nanda—said by some to be the son of a Shudra—seized power from the Magadha lineage and established his own kingdom. He made the Magadha capital city, Pataliputra (modern-day Patna), his capital and quickly brought most of the Gangetic region and the remaining great-clan territories under his control.

The core stories of both the *Mahabharata* and the *Ramayana* were initially composed in this period (ca. fifth century B.C.E.), and each may have something to say about the period's violence and changes. The *Mahabharata*'s core story tells of the struggle for control of a kingdom between two branches of a Kshatriya lineage, the Kurus and the Pandavas. In the war that ensues, all of the evil Kurus are killed, as are many children and supporters of the virtuous Pandavas. The *Ramayana*

GAMBLING IN ANCIENT INDIA

Dice and gambling were important in ancient India as far back as the Indus civilization. Oblong "stick dice," cubical six-sided bar dice (of the kind used even today in India to play pachisi), and cubical six-sided dice (like contemporary gambling dice) have been found at Indus excavations. The Rig-Veda itself contains a hymn—the "Gambler's Lament"—that shows the popularity of gambling in early Indo-Aryan society. The basic dice used in Indian gambling at the time of the epic *Mahabharata* were four-sided, and the names of the dice throws—*krita* (four), *treta* (three), *dvapara* (two), and *kali* (ace)—are the same as the names of the four *yugas* (ages) of the world. The losing streaks of compulsive gamblers figure prominently in the *Mahabharata*: In one major episode a dice tournament causes the virtuous Pandava brother Yudhisthira to lose both his kingdom and his wife, Draupadi, to his evil Kuru cousin. In a second story (also from the *Mahabharata*), King Nala's gambling compulsion almost costs him his wife, Damayanti.

tells of the banishment and long exile of Prince Rama, rightful heir to the kingdom of Ayodhya, his long search for his kidnapped wife, Sita; and the war he fights with the Sri Lankan demon-king Ravana to regain her. Today both epics are read as Hindu scriptures, texts that offer religious, moral, and exemplary stories. The violence of the epics, however, particularly the *Mahabharata,* may have had its origins in the violent clan warfare and struggles of the *mahajanapada* period. At the same time, the epics' preoccupation with questions of kingly inheritance and legitimacy may reflect both the growth of new ideas about monarchy and the weakening hold clans had on political power at this time.

Yet even as didactic texts such as the *Mahabharata* and the *Ramayana* insisted that kings came only from the Kshatriya *varna,* political events showed the opposite. Increasingly kingship was an ad hoc institution; that is, one defined as much by power and opportunity as by lineage or institutional sanctions. Kshatriya status (as historian Burton Stein suggested) was becoming an "achieved" status. The fact of seizing and holding power conferred royalty on whoever could successfully do it.

Alexander the Great

As the Nanda dynasty solidified its hold over the clan-dominated territories of the Ganges, to the north and west the ruler of a faraway empire prepared to invade India. In 331 B.C.E. Alexander of Macedon conquered the Persian Empire whose easternmost satrapy (province) included Gandhara and the northern Indus. Determined to assert control over all his Persian territories, Alexander and his army fought their way eastward. By 327 B.C.E. the Macedonians had subdued Bactria, come over the Hindu Kush Mountains, and crossed the Indus River. Alexander's army—as described by later Greek and Roman historians—numbered 125,000 men. They defeated tribal kings throughout the Punjab, but at the Beas River (an eastern tributary of the Indus) the soldiers mutinied and refused to go farther. Turning south the emperor fought his way down the Indus. He sent some of his army back to Mesopotamia by sea, while he and the remainder made the difficult land journey along the Iranian coast. Alexander's sudden death in Mesopotamia in 323 B.C.E. brought his campaigns to a sudden end.

Alexander's invasion of India had little lasting political impact. After his death, the eastern end of his empire, beyond the Hindu Kush, came under the rule of the Seleucids, a dynasty founded by one of his generals. Along the Indus, within a century the settlements left behind to govern Alexander's conquered lands disappeared, and the lands reverted to local control. Alexander's invasion did, however, bring India to the attention of countries to the west. The literate Greek scribes who accompanied him wrote about the eastern land through which they traveled. Their writings—the earliest Western sources on India—provoked an interest in this eastern region that continued down through the Roman Empire.

The Mauryans

In 321 B.C.E. the Nanda dynasty was overthrown in its turn by an officer in its army, Chandragupta Maurya. Chandragupta seized the Nanda capital at Pataliputra and the rich Magadha region. A treaty with the northwestern Seleucids ceded all of India south of the Hindu Kush to Chandragupta. By the end of the century he had conquered most of northern India, from west to east, and as far south as the Narmada River.

A Greek ambassador, Megasthenes, sent to Chandragupta's court by the Seleucid rulers in the north, left an account of his travels preserved by later Greek and Roman writers. Megasthenes was particularly impressed by Chandragupta's capital at Pataliputra. "The greatest city in India," he declared, it had 570 towers and 64 gates and was surrounded by a ditch "six hundred feet in breadth and thirty cubits in depth" (McCrindle 2000, 67). The emperor himself also impressed Megasthenes. "He . . . remains in court for the whole day," the ambassador wrote, "without allowing the business to be interrupted" (McCrindle 2000, 71). He even continued to hear court cases while attendants massaged him with wooden cylinders. According to Megasthenes, Chandragupta was personally cared for by a large number of women slaves. When he hunted, the Greek noted, "crowds of women surround him . . . some are in chariots, some on horses, and some even on elephants, and they are equipped with weapons of every kind, as if they were going on a campaign" (McCrindle 2000, 70–71). Yet, however wealthy and powerful the king, his life was not easy. Fearing assassination, Megasthenes reported, Chandragupta never slept during the day and at night he changed where he slept periodically to defeat any plots against his life.

Many legends surrounded the origins of the Mauryan dynasty and Chandragupta's life. Buddhist texts claimed that the Mauryans were descended from the Kshatriya Moriya clan, a clan related to the Shakyas (the Buddha's hereditary lineage), while Brahmanical sources suggested that Mauryans were Shudras. Two classical writers claimed

Chandragupta had met Alexander the Great during the latter's invasion of the Punjab. Chandragupta, who, according to one source, wanted Alexander to attack the Nandas to the east, so offended Alexander that he briefly imprisoned the Mauryan. An even later Indian legend claimed that Chandragupta Maurya was just a weak and ordinary man and attributed his rise to power to the advice of a wily Brahman adviser Kautilya. Even Chandragupta's death became the subject of legends. After ruling for 24 years, the Jain tradition says, the emperor abdicated, became a Jain monk, and traveled to the south where he fasted to death in the Karnataka region.

The Arthasastra

The clever minister Kautilya, who may have orchestrated Chandragupta Maurya's rise to power, was also said to have written a book on state-craft: the Arthasastra (Treatise on material gain). The text describes the art of running a kingdom: how to appoint ministers, officials, and judges; how to collect and keep revenues; how to wage war; how to manipulate and/or make treaties with neighboring kings. Its pragmatic "the-ends-justify-the-means" suggestions have often been compared to the 16th-century writings of the Italian political philosopher Niccolò Machiavelli.

The complex bureaucratic system that the Arthasastra described was probably more typical of the third-century C.E. Gupta period, during which the text was substantially revised and expanded, than of the fourth century B.C.E. But its practical and often brutal advice suited Indian political relations of many periods. "Make peace with the equal and the stronger . . . make war with the weaker" was its advice on political relations (Kangle 1972, 327). Create a network of spies, it advised, and include among them "secret agents in the disguise of holy men" (267). Eliminate treacherous ministers by poisoning the food they prepare for you, then have them put to death as traitors (194). The book explained in detail how a king in financial need might "replenish" his treasury: by taking more grain from farmers and more gold from traders or (this with several variations) by proclaiming a tree, a shrub, a house the site of a spectacular miracle and then living on the donations given by believers (296–301). In addition to all this, the book also included lists of magical potions and spells to be used against enemies or in case of a revolt. Among these were potions that could turn someone's hair white or cause leprosy and spells that made people or animals invisible (499–511).

Ashoka

The greatest Mauryan emperor—some say the greatest emperor India ever had—was Chandragupta's grandson, the emperor Ashoka (r. ca. 268–233 B.C.E.). Ashoka became emperor four years after his father Bindusara died and spent the early years of his reign solidifying and extending his empire. Scholars judge its size today by the edicts Ashoka had inscribed on rocks and pillars throughout India. Among these the Rock Edicts, inscribed on rock surfaces during the early part of Ashoka's reign, stretch at least 1,500 miles from the northern Himalayas into peninsular India and 1,200 miles across the widest breadth of the subcontinent. The Pillar Edicts, carved sandstone pillars topped with animal capitals, come from later in Ashoka's reign and most have been found in the Gangetic plain. The first Ashokan inscription was deciphered only in 1837, and even today additional inscriptions continue to be found.

These Ashokan edicts are not the first examples of writing from post-Harappan India but are very close to it. The earliest inscriptions found in India (after Harappa) are in *kharoshti*, a Persian script derived from Aramaic, and are from the Persian-ruled northwest of the late sixth century B.C.E. For the rest of India the earliest writing is in the Brahmi script, the script used in the Ashokan edicts and an ancient form of Indian writing from which all subsequent Indian scripts are believed to have developed.

Except for the edicts of the northwestern borderlands (which were written in Greek and Aramaic), the language of most Ashokan edicts was Prakrit, the general name for the spoken languages of northern India. The Brahmi script was commonly used to write North Indian Prakrits and even (in one example) to write the South Indian Tamil language. By medieval times, of course, both the Dravidian languages and the North Indian vernaculars were all developing separate, distinctive scripts. According to Buddhist traditions, Buddhist scriptures were written down as early as the first century B.C.E., but most Indian texts, secular and religious, were put into written form only in the early centuries C.E.

Ashoka's edicts are the main sources of information about the emperor and the tumultuous events of his career. Ashoka converted to Buddhism after a violent campaign against the eastern region of Kalinga (modern-day Orissa). His rock edicts tell us this battle took more than 100,000 lives and left the ruler questioning the purpose of such violence. Like his grandfather, Chandragupta, Ashoka had a preference for the heterodox religions. Buddhist sources say he had a son, Mahinda,

Remnant of Ashokan pillar, Sarnath. The base of this Ashokan pillar at Sarnath remains in its original site, and portions of its inscription can still be seen. Its capital (top), broken off during excavation and now on display in the Sarnath museum, was carved with four lions back to back, facing in four directions. The pillar edicts, carved sandstone pillars toped with animal capitals, come from later in Ashoka's reign and most have been found in the Gangetic plain. The first Ashokan inscription was deciphered only in 1837 and even today additional inscriptions continue to be found. (courtesy of Judith E. Walsh)

with a beautiful and devoutly Buddhist merchant's daughter. When, according to Buddhist traditions, the Third Buddhist Council met at Pataliputra at Ashoka's invitation, it adopted a plan to send Buddhist missionaries throughout India and the world; it was Ashoka's son Mahinda, according to Buddhist traditions, who took Buddhism south to the island of Sri Lanka.

Nonviolence and tolerance were the heart of the Buddhist dharma, Ashoka proclaimed in his edicts. Disturbed by the violence of the military campaign in Kalinga, the emperor expressed his great regret at the loss of life and suffering through his edicts there. Ashoka banned animal sacrifices at his capital and encouraged vegetarianism, in part by regulating the slaughter of animals for food. Where his grandfather, Chandragupta, had gone on hunting expeditions, Ashoka made pilgrimages to Buddhist holy places. His edicts urged the different religions and peoples in his empire to be tolerant: "Honour the sect of another," one inscription said, "for by doing so one increases the influence of one's own sect and benefits that of the other" (Thapar 2002, 202).

Ashoka called himself a *cakravartin*—a "universal ruler," the Sanskrit term for a ruler so powerful he established his righteous rule over all. In subsequent centuries this became a favorite title for kings large and small, regardless of religious affinity. Even as late as the eighth century C.E., Indian kings sometimes still combined their use of Vedic rituals with endowments to Buddhist or Jain monasteries or with donations for the building of Buddhist stupas—all to justify claims to the title of *cakravartin*.

How could a second-century B.C.E. ruler control an empire the size of Ashoka's? Although Ashoka traveled frequently throughout his realm and consulted with local officials, he probably had direct control over only the center of his empire: the wealthy Magadha and Gangetic region. This area had grown even more prosperous under Mauryan rule; its population now built more brick homes, dug more wells, and used more iron implements than they had in earlier periods. On one Ashokan pillar the emperor described his many public works in the area:

> On the roads I have had banyan trees planted, which will give shade to beasts and men. I have had mango groves planted and I have had wells dug and rest houses built every nine miles. . . . And I have had many watering places made everywhere for the use of beasts and men. (Thapar 2002, 203)

Outside this region and throughout their empire the Mauryans had certain core territories, important to them for trade or for crucial

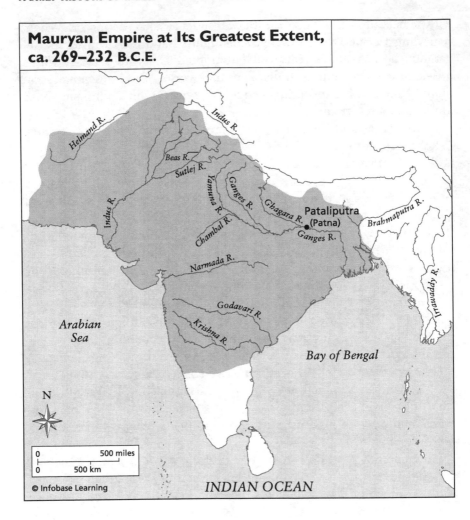

Mauryan Empire at Its Greatest Extent, ca. 269–232 B.C.E.

raw materials: cities such as Taxila in the north and Ujjain on the Indo-Gangetic Plain, regions such as Kalinga in the east and southern Karnataka in the west. The Mauryans ruled these areas through local governors, and trade routes linked them to the capital. Taxila in the northwest was the access point for trade beyond India's borders, while the Karnatak region was a rich source of gold. Beyond these core regions lay the empire's vast periphery: heavily forested regions or those that were less inhabited. Here the emperor or his ministers might travel safely—if accompanied by a large army—and they might leave behind an occasional inscription, but in most respects they had little control over these areas.

Ashoka died in 232 B.C.E. He was followed by a succession of weaker Mauryan rulers and the gradual shrinking of Mauryan territories. In 185 B.C.E. Pushyamitra Shunga, a Brahman general, overthrew the last Mauryan king and established the Shunga dynasty in a small segment of the earlier empire. Shunga rulers practiced an aggressive Vedic Hinduism. They restored Vedic animal sacrifices, including the Horse Sacrifice, and, according to Buddhist sources, they persecuted Buddhist monks.

Aryanization

By the end of the Mauryan period the Ganges River Valley was the hub for trade routes that ran north, south, east, and west through the Indian subcontinent. Some routes were initially created by migrating communities of Vedic Hindus, Buddhists, and Jains who traveled out of the Gangetic region to settle elsewhere. The Mauryan Empire had patronized these existing routes—and the communities that created

The Ajanta caves. The 30 Ajanta caves were carved into the hillside in a half-circle and occupied by Buddhist monks from the second century B.C.E. through the sixth century C.E. Sculptures and frescoes decorate the cave interiors and illustrate the life of the Buddha and stories from the Buddhist Jatakas (Birth Stories) about other incarnations of the Buddha. The caves were found in 1819 by British soldiers on a tiger hunt. They are in a horseshoe ravine above a riverbed, approximately 200 miles northeast of Mumbai (Bombay). (courtesy of Judith E. Walsh)

them—and had also established additional routes of its own, particularly to core regions of the empire. The rock inscriptions of Ashoka (third–second centuries B.C.E.) indicate the extent of these Mauryan trading connections.

But more than trade traveled along these routes. Brahman communities (and Vedic Hinduism) had spread throughout much of the subcontinent by the early centuries C.E. Buddhist and Jain monks, missionaries, and trading communities had also spread Sanskrit and Gangetic culture to other regions over these same centuries. Some scholars have called this movement "Aryanization," but while the culture spread by all these groups was certainly Sanskrit-based and may well have been derived from that of much earlier Indo-Aryans, it was not yet dominated by the Hindu religion.

To the north and west, the Gandharan region was known for its learned practitioners of Vedic Hinduism in the post-Mauryan centuries. But Gandhara also had large Buddhist communities that have left behind substantial archaeological remains. A famous second-century B.C.E. Buddhist text, *The Questions of King Milinda,* records the questioning of Buddhist monks by King Menander, an Indo-Greek (Bactrian) ruler and a convert to Buddhism in this region. Gandhara became a major Buddhist center again during the Kushan dynasty (first–third centuries C.E.). It was from this region that Buddhist monks traveled north out of the subcontinent and then east to take their religion across the Silk Road into eastern Asia.

Buddhist and Jain migrants and missionaries also traveled south and west. A Jain king named Kharavela ruled Kalinga (Orissa) in the mid-first century B.C.E. Trade routes that reached as far down the Narmada River as the Arabian Sea carried Jain communities into western regions, where they remained dominant through to the 10th and 11th centuries C.E. Buddhism also spread west into the Deccan hills; the caves at Ajanta, Ellora, and Elephanta had Buddhist orders settled in them through the early Christian centuries.

Buddhist missionaries from the Ganges region carried early Buddhism (Theravada Buddhism) into South India and on to Sri Lanka and Southeast Asia where it has remained the dominant form of Buddhism to this day. Within India a newer form of Buddhism—Mahayana (the Great Vehicle) Buddhism—became dominant in the centuries after the Mauryans. It was this religion that northern monks took into China and from there to Korea and Japan.

Little is known about South India before the beginnings of this period of "Aryanization." The region was peopled by pastoral or mixed agricultural pastoral communities beginning from the third to second millennia B.C.E., and its coastal regions developed urban civilizations in the late first millennium B.C.E. Its Dravidian languages—Tamil, Telegu, and Malayalam, among others—may have been indigenous to the south or may have been brought there, as some suggest, by migrants from the Harappan north. But from at least the Mauryan period, these south Indian languages coexisted with Sanskrit in the south. Early Jain cave inscriptions, dated to the second century B.C.E. are in the Tamil language but written in the Brahmi script, the same script used by the Mauryans. Tamil texts from the early centuries C.E. also show evidence of Sanskrit influences, although elite south Indians, whether migrant or indigenous, were probably literate in both Sanskrit and the Dravidian vernaculars.

Trade with Rome

By the first century C.E. trade routes throughout the subcontinent connected regional centers into both an interregional and an external trade: Iron came from mines in Rajasthan and other Indian regions; copper, from Rajasthan, the Deccan, and the Himalayas; precious and semiprecious stones, from peninsular India; salt, from the "salt range" of the Punjab; and spices, sandalwood, ebony, gold, and precious stones, from South India. These goods were traded within India and outside through trade with both the eastern Mediterranean and Southeast Asian regions.

Archaeological finds have documented the existence of trade between both the western and eastern coasts of India and the Roman Empire beginning as early as the first century B.C.E. and continuing through the seventh century C.E. Merchants who came to India were called *yavanas*. While this name may have originally been used for Indo-Greeks in the northwest (perhaps for Ionia in Greece), it quickly came to be used for all foreigners. *Yavanas* came from different parts of the Roman Empire and the Near East and from a wide range of ethnic populations: Greeks, Arabs, Egyptian Jews, and Armenians from western Asia, among others.

Black pepper was a major item of trade with the West along both the western and eastern coasts. This rich trade continued on the Malabar coast through the medieval period. Other items traded were spices, semiprecious stones, ivory, and textiles. Western products coming into India included wine, olive oil, and Roman coins—and in later centuries horses. The most popular Western commodity for Indians, however, were Roman coins. Hoards of such coins have been found throughout the Deccan and further south, most from the period of the Roman emperors Augustus (r. 27 B.C.E.–14 C.E.) and Tiberius (r. 14–37 C.E.). Indians had had a money economy and minted coins from as early as the fifth century B.C.E., but the Roman coins may have been hoarded for use as a high-value currency, since gold coins were largely missing from these areas.

Indian traders were active at both the Indian and the foreign ends of this maritime trade. Archaeological sites on the Red Sea have turned up potsherds with the names of Indians written in Tamil (in Brahmi script) and in Prakrit. In India archaeologists have identified the port of Arikamedu (near Pondicherry in Tamil Nadu) as the site of an ancient southeast Indian port mentioned in a mid-first-century C.E. Greek seafaring geography—*The Periplus of the Erythraean Sea*. Excavations there revealed Roman pottery, beads, and evidence of wines imported from southern Italy and Greece. Arikamedu seems to have traded with the eastern Mediterranean region from as early as the first century B.C.E.

Both coasts of South India were also linked by trade with Southeast Asia. An impetus for this trade may have been the rich Roman trade—the profitability of goods sold to the West sent Indian traders farther east looking for additional sources for spices. Both trading settlements in Southeast Asia and trading connections that ran as far east as Java and Bali are known.

Post-Mauryan Dynasties

In the centuries after the Mauryan Empire the porous border of north-western India became even more so. Traders, migrants, and invaders from Central Asia and Iran fought their way through the northwest mountains to settle in the subcontinent. The most prominent among these were the Indo-Bactrian-Greeks (or simply Indo-Greeks), the Scythians (Shakas), and the Kushans. While some of these tribal communities maintained their languages and ethnic identity through several centuries, others adapted their Indian kingdoms to local culture.

Indo-Greek kings ruled small kingdoms in northern India from ca. second to first centuries B.C.E. These Greeks had originally been settled as Persian tributaries in Bactria in Central Asia, but in the second century B.C.E. some kings moved south over the Hindu Kush to conquer lands in the subcontinent. Most of what is known of them comes from their multilingual coins—Greek on one side, Prakrit on the other. Their most famous ruler was the Buddhist convert King Menander (known in India as Milinda), who ruled ca. 155–130 B.C.E.

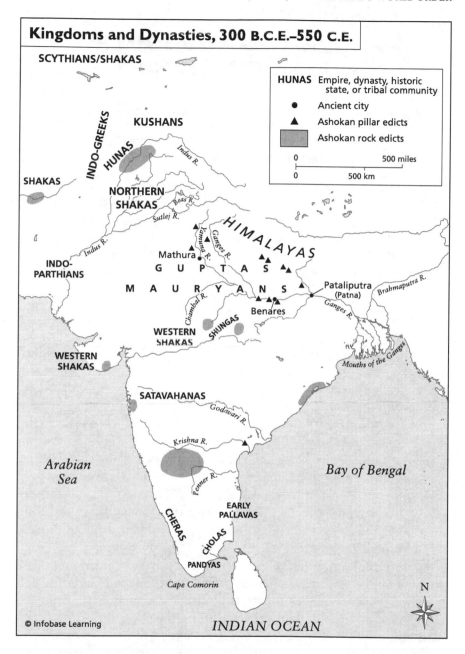

Kingdoms and Dynasties, 300 B.C.E.–550 C.E.

SCYTHIANS/SHAKAS

HUNAS — Empire, dynasty, historic state, or tribal community

● Ancient city

▲ Ashokan pillar edicts

▨ Ashokan rock edicts

0 — 500 miles
0 — 500 km

INDO-GREEKS

KUSHANS

HUNAS

SHAKAS

NORTHERN SHAKAS

Indus R.

Beas R.

Sutlej R.

HIMALAYAS

Mathura

Yamuna R.

Ganges R.

GUPTAS

INDO-PARTHIANS

Indus R.

MAURYANS

Chambal R.

Pataliputra (Patna)

Brahmaputra R.

Benares

Ganges R.

WESTERN SHAKAS

SHUNGAS

WESTERN SHAKAS

Mouths of the Ganges

SATAVAHANAS

Godavari R.

Krishna R.

Arabian Sea

Bay of Bengal

Penner R.

CHERAS

EARLY PALLAVAS

CHOLAS

PANDYAS

Cape Comorin

N

© Infobase Learning

INDIAN OCEAN

The Scythians (Shakas) were Central Asian horsemen, a nomadic peoples forced to migrate south and west into Iran and India by stronger tribes to their east. In successive attacks in the late second–first

ST. THOMAS AND SOUTH INDIAN CHRISTIANS

According to legend, the Christian apostle St. Thomas was brought to the northwestern region of India soon after the Crucifixion by the Parthian (Pahlava/Iranian) king Gondophares. After making his first converts at the Parthian king's court, St. Thomas was said to have preached in other regions of India and was martyred by an unidentified Indian king; some legends place this martyrdom in the modern city of Chennai (Madras). Other legends say St. Thomas arrived on the Malabar coast ca. 52 C.E. A group of Persian Christians are said to have migrated to Kerala ca. 500 C.E., and Christian churches on the Malabar coast and in Sri Lanka are noted by ca. sixth-century travelers. These South Indian Christian communities developed into the modern-day Syrian Christians.

centuries B.C.E. the Shakas defeated the northern Indo-Greek rulers and moved into Gandhara and then farther south. A later branch of the Shakas (called the Western Shakas) ruled over parts of Rajasthan and Sind through the fourth century C.E.

The Kushan, tribes of the people known to the Chinese as the Yueh-zhih, migrated south from Central Asia in the first century C.E., defeating most of the Shaka kings and creating a unified empire that lasted into the third century C.E. Their most powerful king, Kanishka (whose reign began in C.E. 78 or 144), ruled an empire that may have equaled Ashoka's in size: It stretched from Bactria through northern India to Varanasi on the Ganges. Kanishka was also a great patron of Buddhism, which flourished under his rule in the Gandharan region.

In south India the Satavahana (or Andhra) dynasty ruled a Deccan kingdom below the Narmada River between the first to third centuries C.E. The Satavahanas allied themselves with Vedic Hinduism; their first major ruler even celebrated the Horse Sacrifice. Farther south were three lineages that Ashoka's edicts once claimed to have defeated: the Cholas, the Cheras, and the Pandyas. Tamil *cankam* poetry (ca. first–third centuries C.E.) shows these lineages in constant combat with one another. The Chola lineage was associated with the Coromandel coast; the Cheras, with Kerala and the Malabar coast; and the Pandyas, with the southernmost tip of the subcontinent.

The Guptas

Historians often label the Gupta period as "classical" because it brings to fruition a Sanskrit-based culture begun in earlier centuries. By ca. 400 C.E., early in the Gupta period, Vedic Hinduism, Buddhism, and Jainism had spread throughout India. Brahman priests had composed most of the great Sanskrit texts and scriptures of Hinduism, most recently the Hindu law codes and the Puranas (Ancient tales), a collection of legends focused on key gods and goddesses. The *Mahabharata* and the *Ramayana* had reached their final forms. During the Gupta dynasty (ca. 320 C.E.–ca. mid-sixth century), this Sanskrit-based culture, now spread across India, reached a peak of creativity that included the production of secular literature, poetry, and art, of which the Sanskrit plays and poems of the court writer Kalidasa are the best-known example.

But the Gupta period also saw the reformulation of much of the earlier tradition. As much as it is "classical," Gupta India should also be seen as the starting point for new forms of Hinduism, Hindu political relations, and Hindu social institutions.

The Gupta dynasty was founded in the Ganges River valley ca. 320 C.E. by a man who took the name of the founder of the Mauryan dynasty, Chandragupta. This proved prophetic, for the Guptas' empire would reconquer much of the territory once held by earlier Mauryan kings. The base for the Guptas was (as it had been for the Mauryans) the Gangetic plains. The founder's son, Samudragupta (reigned ca. 330–380), also made Pataliputra his capital. Samudragupta's conquests created an empire that reached from Assam in the east through the Punjab and as far to the west as the territories of the Scythians (western Shakas) allowed. The third Gupta king, Chandragupta II (reigned ca. 380–415), became legendary in later centuries as King Vikramaditya, a wise and benevolent ruler about whom many tales and stories circulated. Chandragupta II extended Gupta territory to its greatest size. After his successful campaign against the Shakas, his dynasty controlled all of North India from the Indus in the west to Assam in the east and was acknowledged even by regional rulers south of the Narmada River. A Chinese Buddhist monk, Faxian, who lived in India for six years during Chandragupta II's reign, commented on the peacefulness of Indian society in this period.

But where the Mauryans had favored heterodox religions, Gupta kings identified themselves and their dynasty more with elite Sanskrit culture and with the new devotional, temple-based Hinduism—even though the Guptas continued to endow Buddhist monasteries and stupas. The Guptas built and endowed Hindu temples, and they wrote

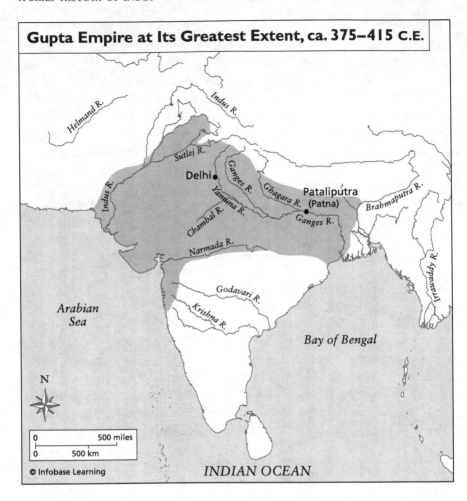

Gupta Empire at Its Greatest Extent, ca. 375–415 C.E.

inscriptions on these temples in Sanskrit (not Prakrit), now the elite written language of India. Samudragupta boasted of having performed the horse sacrifice and claimed the title of universal ruler (*cakravartin*). The Guptas also used Hindu rituals to formalize the incorporation of defeated tribes and kings into their empire. In a consecration ritual attended personally by the emperors, they reconsecrated defeated kings as tributary subordinates; the defeated ruler became a regional king of his land, paying tribute to and attending occasional audiences with the Gupta *cakravartin* but otherwise ruling independently in his land. Where the Mauryans had maintained control over only the center and a few core regions of their empire, the Guptas, through tributary relationships, attempted to control most of it.

STUPAS AND TEMPLES

Buddhist stupas and cave temples were built in India as early as the second century B.C.E. Stupas were round structures that held relics of the Buddha and were perambulated by devotees. They were built through donations from kings and laypeople from at least the time of Ashoka. The earliest freestanding Hindu temples in the subcontinent, however, date only to the Gupta period (fourth–mid-sixth centuries C.E.). These structures were small in comparison to the temples of later centuries; most had flat roofs and were built of thick masonry without mortar. The temple design of sixth century C.E. has remained the standard even to the modern period. At the center of the temple is a small, dark shrine room containing the image of the chief deity, and outside this is a larger hall and a porch through which worshippers enter. A large tower rises over the core shrine room, and the whole building complex is set within a rectangular courtyard, sometimes (in later buildings) enclosing a temple tank. The great Hindu temples were built under the patronage of the South Indian dynasties of the fifth to 12th centuries: the Pallavas, Chalukyas, and Cholas. In the north many older temples were destroyed by Muslim invaders, and most large temples, even in Varanasi, are recent. Two large famous temple complexes dating to the 12th and 13th centuries can be found in Orissa: the Jagannatha temple in the city of Puri and the temple to Surya (the sun god) at nearby Konarak.

Jagannatha temple at Puri, Orissa. Built in the 12th century on the east coast of India, this is one of the most famous Hindu temples in India. The temple's main deity is Jagannatha (Vishnu), worshipped in addition to his brother, Balabhadra, and his sister, Subhadra. (courtesy of Judith E. Walsh)

The successors of Chandragupta II, however, were unable to maintain his vast empire. In the north, beginning in the mid-fifth century, the Hunas—a Central Asian tribe related to the White Huns—repeatedly attacked the empire and even occupied its western regions in the early decades of the sixth century. These attacks, combined with the dynasty's failure to produce a strong ruler, weakened the Guptas. By the mid-sixth century, the Gupta successors were ruling only small fragments of the once great empire, the remainder having fallen back into the hands of regional and local rulers.

Puranic Hinduism

In the early centuries C.E. Hinduism developed into a temple-based, devotional religion. This new form of Hinduism maintained the sanctity of earlier Vedic texts and the preeminent position of the Brahman priest, even as the dominant forms of Hindu worship (puja) became devotional and focused more exclusively on the gods Shiva or Vishnu (and Vishnu's incarnations) or on the worship of Devi (the Goddess).

Whereas Vedic Hinduism had placed rituals performed by Brahman priests at the center of human efforts to control the cosmos, both the Upanishads and the later heterodox religions saw the goal of life as attaining *moksha*—in Buddhism, nirvana—and escaping the cycle of reincarnation. Bhakti (the devotional worship of a god) developed out of these ideas. Its first mention is in the Bhagavad Gita (Song of the blessed one), a long addition to the *Mahabharata* dated to ca. the first century C.E. (Thompson 2008). In the Gita, the prince Arjuna stands in his chariot on the battlefield, beset by doubts about the morality of going to war against his own grandfather and cousins. Arjuna's charioteer, the god Krishna in disguise, explains that even though such conduct may seem immoral, it is simply Arjuna's Kshatriya dharma. But dharma is just one of many paths by which men can find liberation from rebirth. The best of all these paths, Krishna says, is that of bhakti. Then Krishna reveals himself to Arjuna in his true form—he is the universe itself, all the cosmos is incorporated within him. Krishna says, "Whatever you do—whatever you eat, whatever offering you make, whatever you give, whatever austerity you perform—Arjuna, do it all as an offering to me!" (Thompson 2008, 47). Through bhakti, Krishna explains, karma ends, and liberation from rebirth is achieved.

The idea of devotion to a god as the center of religious life was accompanied in the early centuries C.E. by the rise in importance and centrality of the Hindu temple and of worship in that temple to its god.

Krishna instructs Arjuna on the efficacy of bhakti (devotion) in this modern rendition of a famous scene from the Mahabharata. The scene is carved on a wall of the 1938 Lakshmi Narayan Temple (Birla Mandir) in New Delhi, built by the industrialist B. D. Birla and inaugurated by the nationalist leader Mohandas K. Gandhi. (courtesy of Judith E. Walsh)

Where ancient Vedic rituals had taken place in the open and without images, now an image (*murti*) believed to embody the god being worshipped was installed at the heart of large temple complexes. Where Vedic religious life had centered on the performance of rituals, now religious life—for both priests and individual worshippers—was based on tending and worshipping the temple deity. The new gods worshipped in this way were celebrated in a new collection of Hindu texts: the Puranas. Written down no earlier than the fourth century C.E., these texts retold myths and legends associated with gods such as Vishnu, Shiva, or Devi and described the correct ways to worship them. While older Vedic gods such as Agni, Surya, and Indra continued to have a place within the Hindu pantheon, it was Vishnu (and his nine avatars, or incarnations), Shiva, or the Goddess who were the focus of the stories and tales of the Puranas and of devotional, temple-based worship.

Kings and Emperors

For centuries Indian kings had fought one another, the loser forced to accept subordination (or often death) at the hands of the winner. "The big fish eats the small fish," as the Indian proverb puts it. The Gupta dynasty, however, attempted to replace these older ad hoc relations with a more formal relationship, a tributary system. Under the Guptas such

59

relations could stretch in a descending spiral from the great emperor himself down to the headman of a local village, with tribute passed up to each successive overlord. From the Gupta period onward rulers' titles increasingly inflated their place in these graded rankings: Even the smallest vassal king might title himself "great king" (*maharaja*), while kings of any importance at all would insist on being called "Great King of Kings and Supreme Lord" (*maharaja-adhiraja-paramabhattaraka*).

In this system dharma was "king." "This dharma is the sovereign power ruling over kshatra [royal power] itself," explains an early Upanishad (De Bary 1958, 241). In the Laws of Manu, one of a number of Hindu law codes composed between ca. 200 B.C.E. and 200 C.E., society is to be governed by the *varna* system, its duties and obligations overseen by Brahman priests. The king's role was only the maintenance of these structures as they already existed: "The king was created as the protector of the classes [*varnas*] and the stages of life, that are appointed each to its own particular duty, in proper order" (Doniger and Smith 1991, 131). Whether he was as great as a *rajadhiraja* (king of kings) or *cakravartin* or as "little" as the head of a small village, the ruler functioned to preserve dharmic order.

The set of regional tributary relations begun by the Guptas remained the model for Indian political relations through the medieval period. Within this system kings spent most of their time trying to survive. A 12th-century text chronicling the lives of the kings of Kashmir (the *Rajatarangini*) shows us the likely fate of a ruler. If ministers did not plot against him, relatives did not overthrow him, or his wives did not have him murdered, his own sons might cause his death. Sons, like crabs, the traditional warning goes, survive by destroying their fathers.

Another way to think of this political system, as anthropologist Bernard Cohn once suggested, is as a means for channeling the agricultural surplus of peasants up through the various levels of power to the ruler with the greatest force. Describing the 18th-century king of Varanasi, Cohn wrote,

> Politically the Raja of Benares had to face in two directions. He fought a continuous and devious battle to be completely independent of the Nawab [a more powerful ruler and theoretically his overlord]. He also had to keep in check lineages and local chiefs and rajas who had power within his province. (1960, 422)

The central issue was tribute, and the measure of a superior's success was the amount he could collect from his subordinates. Success for subordinates, on the other hand, lay in the degree to which they could elude payment. By tradition, the king owned the land and had the right to a portion of the crop. But these rights existed within a system in which collection signified superiority and willingness to pay signaled weakness.

Rulers could not dispense with the regional and local powers beneath them, however, because they lacked the ability to collect the tribute themselves. Therefore collection was delegated from superior to subordinate, from the "emperor" down through the various levels of political power to the level of the dominant caste in each village. Within this pyramid, village communities were the most stable units, the units most easily dominated and controlled by local clan or caste lineages over long periods of time. In some parts of the subcontinent, long-term regional control was also possible. Certain regional divisions—Bengal in the east, for instance, and the Deccan in the southwest—slip in and out of India's history, held by one group, then by another. Unification of larger areas was hard to achieve—and even harder to maintain. As the territory of a king expanded, he became increasingly vulnerable to challenges from more stable regional and/or local kings below him.

If the origins of a regional tributary political system can be placed in the Gupta period, however, it should also be recognized that the Guptas, to some degree, simply put an institutional and ritual face on a system of political relations that had existed long before them. Even with their reconsecration of defeated rulers the Gupta dynasty still existed within a largely ad hoc system of kingship and empire. The skill of a ruler and/ or the luck or circumstances in which he found himself had as much to do with his success as anything else. Whether an emperor or a "little king," rulers spent their days protecting or extending their power over and against that of other rulers around them. Only with the Mughals in the medieval period and even later with the British are there political systems that attempt to challenge the tributary system.

Caste, *Varna*, and *Jati*

The term caste comes from the Portuguese word *casta*, first used during the 16th century to describe the Indian social system. Indigenous terms for social groups in both the ancient and modern periods were *varna* (class) and *jati* (birth group). The four *varnas*—Brahman, Kshatriya, Vaishya, and Shudra—appear as early as the Rig-Veda and in both Hindu and non-Hindu sources. Each *varna* was identified very early with a hereditary occupation—priest, warrior, farmer/merchant, and servant, respectively—and by the time of the early Upanishads the different and unequal duties of these groups were justified by karma and the individual's acts in former lives. *Jatis* were lineages, clans, and/ or families whose membership was determined by birth. Different *jatis* might interact economically, but their social contact was restricted; for instance, people married, shared meals, or participated in funerals only with members of their own birth group.

In contrast to the four *varnas* whose hierarchical order was universally known and acknowledged throughout the subcontinent, *jatis* were local or regional groups. Members of a village *jati* would know their status relative to other *jatis* in their immediate region, but there was no all-India hierarchy for these groups. *Jati* status changed from region to region—and over time. Village studies from North India in the 20th century have shown that *jatis* whose economic circumstances change can raise their *varna* status through a process sociologists call "Sanskritization"—the adoption of customs defined in Sanskrit texts as appropriate for a higher *varna*. If a *jati* can maintain such practices over several generations, their new *varna* status will be accepted. Conversely, groups that fall on hard times and are forced to adopt social customs associated with lower *varnas*—the eating of meat, for instance—can "lose caste" as a result. Untouchable communities in northern India, Bernard Cohn found, explained their low status in just such historical terms, as a loss of caste caused by poverty and the necessity of adopting practices associated with untouchability sometime in the ancient past.

If one thinks of the caste system in terms of *jatis, varnas,* and the connections between them, one can appreciate the complexity and flexibility of this social institution. Villages never remained "unchanged" over time. Instead, the caste system allowed frequent changes of social position, and *jatis* "lost caste" or raised it as their historical and economic circumstances changed. One example of a *jati* group whose status changed dramatically over time are the Kayasthas, a group from the Gangetic region that was classified as Shudra in the Gupta period. By the 11th century Kayastha status had improved dramatically as its members came increasingly to work as scribes and administrators for political rulers. Individual kings in ancient India, frequently came from non-Kshatriya origins; in the fourth century some Puranic texts try to fix these *varna* aberrations by providing non-Kshatriya kings with appropriate royal genealogies. Similarly the Hindu law codes (ca. 200 B.C.E.–200 C.E.) try to fix the shifting *varna* statuses of all these groups by offering elaborate classifications for groups that did not fit ordinary *varna* categories: a Brahman who marries a Shudra, for instance.

Birth groups were a way to give *varna* status to a wide range of peoples (and religions) who might otherwise not fit into *varna* classifications. From the mid-fifth century B.C.E. through the Gupta period, Indian society had to adjust to the presence of many new and/or non-Aryan groups: the heterodox followers of Buddhism and Jainism and also Indo-Greeks, any number of Central Asian tribes, and South Indian Dravidian-speaking communities, to name just a few. Local and regional societies could integrate these peoples by considering each of them as a separate *jati* and assigning a *varna* status appropriate to the group's economic wealth or political power. In this sense jatis functioned as a way to bring a wide range of non-Hindu peoples under the rubric of a Hindu (Aryan) *varna* system that in origin had been a Brahman view of society, not historical reality.

Women in Ancient India

Day and night men should keep their women from acting independently;
for, attached as they are to sensual pleasures, men should keep them
under their control. Her father guards her in her childhood,
her husband guards her in her youth, and her sons guard her in her old age;
a woman is not qualified to act independently.

■

The Law Code of Manu (Olivelle 2004, 155)

Although this much quoted passage from the Laws of Manu illustrates women's subordination to men in ancient India, other texts and sources give a more varied picture of how women lived and were expected to behave. Passages from the Rig-Veda suggest an early society in which unmarried girls and young men freely associated and in which women took part in public ceremonies such as the Horse Sacrifice. The Upanishads show two learned women (Maitreyi and Gargi) participating in philosophical speculations. By the early centuries C.E., however, knowledge of the Vedas had become forbidden to Hindu women (as also to Shudras), and women were described as an inferior class who could obtain *moksha* only after rebirth as men. Only in the heterodox sects of Buddhism and Jainism did women still have access to religious scriptures. In this same period the Arthasastra notes that the *antahpur* (women's quarters) of a king's harem was secluded and closely guarded and that wives who drank, gambled, or left home without permission were fined. A different impression, however, from the same period appears in stories describing young girls who visit temples without chaperones and in sculptures showing unveiled women watching processions from open balconies. Although it had long been customary for women's literacy to be forbidden, a 10th–11th-century Khajuraho sculpture shows a woman holding her writing tablet.

Hindu religious scriptures reveal a deep ambivalence toward women. On the one hand, in the Laws of Manu a wife is the "lamp" of her husband's home, and if she brings him children (preferably sons), she is called a Lakshmi, the goddess of good fortune (Doniger and Smith 1991, 200). According to the *Mahabharata*,

> The wife is half the man,
> the best of friends,
> the root of the three ends of life,
> and of all that will help him in the other worlds. (Basham 1958, 181)

On the other hand, women and women's sexuality are frequently portrayed as dangerous and uncontrollable. "Good looks do not matter to them, nor do they care about youth," says Manu. "'A man!' they say, and enjoy sex with him, whether he is good-looking or ugly" (Doniger

SATI

Sati (also spelled suttee) was the Hindu practice in which a newly widowed wife chose to be burned or buried alive with her husband's corpse. The custom was not mandatory for Hindu women and was never widely practiced, occurring mostly in the Ganges River Valley, the Punjab, and Rajasthan. The woman who chose to become a sati, it was commonly believed, was reunited with her dead husband in the afterlife. In the brief period before her death, the sati was thought to have magical powers to curse or bless those around her.

Mention of satis appears sporadically in Hindu scriptures (some claim as early as the Rig-Veda), while travelers reported witnessing satis from the fourth century B.C.E. The custom was common among Central Asian tribes, however, leading some scholars to suggest it became more common with the movement of these tribes into India after 200 B.C.E. Among Rajputs (a military caste of northern India), widows' suicides (*jauhar*) often followed the death of a Rajput king in battle. Sati was made illegal by the British in 1829. A recent case was the sati of a young Rajasthani college student in 1987.

and Smith 1991, 198). Religious scriptures are unequivocal, however, about the need for a woman's absolute duty to serve her husband "like a god." As stated in the Laws of Manu, "A virtuous wife should constantly serve her husband like a god, even if he behaves badly, freely indulges his lust, and is devoid of any good qualities . . . it is because a wife obeys her husband that she is exalted in heaven" (Doniger and Smith 1991, 115).

By custom high-caste widows were not allowed to remarry, and a wife demonstrated her extreme devotion to her dead husband by becoming a sati (the one who is true), a woman who was burned or buried alive with her husband's corpse. As late as Mauryan and Gupta times, widow remarriage was still possible, but by the medieval period the ban on widow remarriage extended even to child brides widowed before the marriage was consummated. Widows were expected to live lives of austerity, their atonement for having had the bad karma to survive their husbands. By custom widows were to shave their heads, wear only simple white saris and no jewelry, and eat only once a day a simple vegetarian meal with no condiments.

Harsha

After the Gupta period and before the Muslim incursions of the 13th century, only one ruler was able to create a substantial North Indian empire. This was Harshavardhana (r. 606–647 C.E.). Harsha inherited his elder brother's small Punjab kingdom at the age of 16 and soon after added to it the nearby lands of his widowed sister. Making his capital in the city of Kanauj, he expanded eastward, eventually controlling lands as far east as the Ganges delta and as far south as the Narmada River. Harsha claimed the title of *cakravartin* and, like the Guptas, controlled his empire by gifting lands and subordinate status to the kings he defeated. Later Buddhist texts claimed Harsha as a convert. The Chinese Buddhist monk Xuanzang, who visited India during Harsha's reign, claimed that kings only took the throne after receiving permission to do so from a Buddhist semigod (a bodhisattva). When Harsha died without an heir in 647, his empire quickly fell back into the hands of local and regional powers.

By the seventh century elites who identified with a Sanskrit-based, Indo-Aryan culture dominated all regions of the Indian subcontinent. A revitalized, temple-based Hinduism was coming to dominance, particularly in the south. Invading tribes of the past centuries had been successfully incorporated into local and regional life, and relations among

India's political elites had attained a stasis of ever-present warfare and intrigue. Harsha, as it turned out, would be the last Hindu king to rule a great North Indian empire. All future imperial powers in India would govern with an eye on events and contexts far beyond India's borders: on the court of the Baghdad caliph, for instance, or (eventually) on the Parliament of a British queen.

3

TURKS, AFGHANS, AND MUGHALS (600-1800)

We placed our feet in the stirrup of resolve, grabbed the reins of trust in God, and directed ourselves against Sultan Ibrahim, son of Sultan Sikandar, son of Bahlul Lodi the Afghan, who controlled the capital Delhi and the realm of Hindustan at that time.

■

The Baburnama: Memoirs of Babur, Prince and Emperor (Thackston 2002, 320)

In the eighth century C.E. the armies of a newly energized Arab Empire brought the religion of Islam to India. The Central Asian Turks and Afghans who conquered India in the centuries that followed were fierce warriors. As rulers, however, they struggled with their commitment to Islam and their minority status among a greater Hindu population. The Mughal emperor Akbar found the most successful resolution to this conflict. The Mughal war machine he created maintained Mughal dominance over most of India until the 18th century.

Islam Enters India

In 622 the Mecca-born Arab Muhammad (570–632) and a small number of followers established themselves and their new religion, Islam (meaning "submission"), in the Arabian city of Medina. This date marks the start of a rapid military expansion that within a century had created the Islamic Empire, the most powerful empire the Western world had ever known. At its height this empire controlled the Mediterranean Sea and lands from Spain in the west through the Middle East and as far east as India.

Islam spread quickly through the lands conquered by the Arabs. As the third "religion of the book," Islam claimed a heritage that included both Judaism and Christianity. At the heart of Islam was submission to

67

the will of Allah, the one, only, and omnipotent God. Muhammad was "the seal of the prophets," the last in the line of human transmitters of Allah's message that began in the Old Testament. For Muslims, as for Jews and Christians, human history began with Allah's creation of the world and would end in a Last Judgment, when human souls would be punished for their sins or rewarded for their virtues.

By the time armies from the new Islamic Empire entered India in the eighth century, Muhammad was long dead, and political power over the expanding empire had been placed in the hands of a caliph. The caliph's office (caliphate) was located, at the empire's height, ca. 750–1258, in the city of Baghdad. The Qur'an, Allah's revelations to Muhammad, had been written down in Arabic. Islam had already divided into two competing sects: the Sunnis, a majority sect that based its teachings on Islamic law (the sharia) as interpreted by special theologians-scholars (the *ulama*); and the Shiites, a minority sect that followed the charismatic teachings of the 12 imams, the true spiritual descendants of Muhammad, the last of whom would disappear in the 12th century. Islam's mystic tradition, Sufism, would begin only later, in the eighth century, and between the 13th and 15th centuries the great Sufi orders would spread throughout north India.

Dar al-Islam

In many ways Muslim rulers in India behaved just as Hindu, Buddhist, or Jain kings before them. They increased their lands through battle. They bound defeated rulers to them through alliances and gifts. They endowed buildings and supported the religious activities of religions other than Islam, and they adapted themselves and their courts to local Indian institutions, culture, and customs. Islam and Hinduism mutually influenced each other's social structures, art, architecture, and religious practices for more than 1,200 years.

But Islam also had a well-defined location outside the Indian subcontinent. When Muslims prayed, they faced in the direction of the holy city of Mecca. When they recited the Qur'an, they were encouraged to recite it in Arabic, for no translation was authentic. As often as they could, good Muslims should join the annual religious pilgrimage to Mecca (the hajj). In all their dealings—religious, social, or political— they should see themselves as part of a brotherhood of Muslims and seek to spread Islam and its teachings. All these practices tied Indian Muslims, kings, courts, and elites to the Arabian Peninsula and its centers of Islamic scholarship and law.

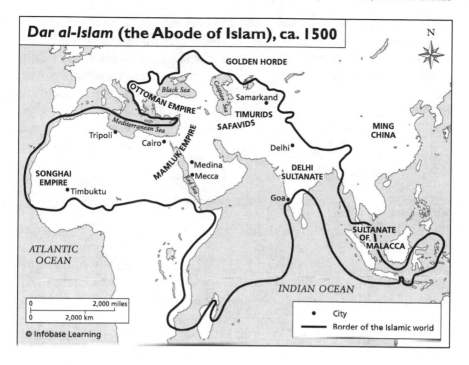

Muslim rulers, courts, and communities also saw themselves within a worldwide Muslim context. They were part of a global network of places—*dar al-Islam* (the Abode of Islam)—where Muslim peoples observed the religion of Allah, or where Muslim kings and/or powerful men maintained Islamic practices even while ruling non-Muslim populations. The strictest interpretation of Islamic injunctions would have required a jihad (holy war) against all non-Muslims, the destruction of all infidel temples and churches, and the death or conversion of all nonbelievers. The realities of ruling a large non-Muslim population, however, caused Muslim rulers in India, as elsewhere, to give the Hindu population the protected status of *dhimmis* (protected peoples), a status previously applied to "peoples of the book," that is to Jews and Christians. This allowed the continuation of Hindu religious rites and customs on payment of a yearly tax. To satisfy their own orthodox *ulama*, however, Muslim rulers would sometimes declare their local conflicts a jihad (holy war) or deface prominent local temples.

In the wider Muslim world (*dar al-Islam*), elite Muslims found others like themselves with whom they could share their knowledge of and perspectives on Islamic laws, customs, and practices. When the Moroccan-born Ibn Battuta traveled the world in the 14th century, he met many non-Arab peoples and encountered non-Muslim cultures. But although he traveled from Spain and North Africa to sub-Saharan Africa, India, and China, for most of his travels he remained within an elite Islamic world and with "individuals who shared his tastes and sensibilities and among whom he could always find hospitality, security, and friendship" (Dunn 1986, 7). In India, as elsewhere in the medieval world, Muslim kings and their related elites lived with a deep awareness of their location within an Islamic network of places and peoples linked throughout the world.

Arabs and Turks

By 711, Arab military commanders attacked and eventually conquered the western region of Sind. In the northwest, by the 10th century, independent Persian Muslims controlled the lands between Persia and the Oxus River (later called Amu Darya). Buddhism, which had flourished earlier in these regions, was abandoned as Turkic tribes converted to Islam.

Arab traders, new converts to Islam, had been settled peacefully in permanent communities along India's west coast from as early as the mid-seventh century. Arab merchants replaced moribund Roman trade routes with global routes that linked India to both the Mediterranean world and to Southeast Asia. Like the Christian communities that had settled in Kerala, Muslim traders were given land, allowed to maintain their own religion, and incorporated, as *jatis,* into the west coast's political and social structures. The Mappila (Moplah) community on the Malabar Coast and the Navayat Muslim community in the Konkan are the modern descendants of these early Arab settlements.

Mahmud of Ghazni

In the late 10th century, a Turkish military slave, Sabuktigin, established an Afghan kingdom centered on the city of Ghazni and, in 986, attacked and defeated a neighboring Hindu ruler who controlled lands between Kabul and the northwest Punjab. Sabuktigin's son, Mahmud of Ghazni (r. 998–1030) continued his father's raids into India, carrying out between 16 and 20 raids in the years between 1000 and 1027. Mahmud's raids destroyed and looted major Hindu temples at Mathura, Kanauj, and Somnath, and brought back to Ghazni great caravans of riches and slaves. The slower elephant-based armies of the Hindu dynasties in the northwest could not withstand the elite mounted archers of the Ghaznavid cavalry. Writing to the caliph at Baghdad, Mahmud boasted that his raids had killed 50,000 infidels and 50,000 Muslim heretics. He asked for (and received) the honor of being named a fighter in the cause of Islam.

The Ghaznavids looted cities in Iran and India, Muslim as well as Hindu. Their raids were needed to pay for their professional slave-based army. In addition, Mahmud used his plunder to bring Muslim scholars to Ghazni and establish a library there—the books were plundered from conquered Persian libraries—and to build a beautiful mosque. His dynasty was succeeded by the Ghurids, a dynasty of eastern Iranian origins, in 1151. The Ghurids were more ambitious than Mahmud, who had nominally extended his kingdom into the Punjab but had made little effort to control the lands he raided. By 1206 Ghurid rulers had conquered much of the north, controlling the cities of Delhi, Kanauj, and Varanasi (Benares), much of Rajasthan, and destroying the Sena dynasty in Bengal along with the Buddhist monasteries that the Senas supported.

South India (600–1300)

The flat farmlands of the northern Indo-Gangetic Plain invited the establishment of large agrarian empires. In regions south of the Narmada River, however, a more rugged geography enabled smaller, more regional clans and lineages to survive. The Chalukyas in Karnataka, the Pallavas in Kanchipuram, the Pandyas in Madurai, and the Cholas at Tanjore all struggled for power with one another and with even smaller kings and local rulers between the sixth and ninth centuries. The Chalukya control of the Deccan during the seventh century kept the North Indian emperor Harsha from expanding farther south. But by the eighth century Chalukya power was gone. In the far south, the Pandyas held on to their Madurai region by a series of ever-shifting alliances until the 10th century.

Unlike the Chalukyas, Pandyas, and Cholas—lineages that had fought one another for power since Mauryan times—the Pallavas were a new dynasty. One Tamil legend attributed their origin to a love match between a local prince and a Naga (snake) princess from the underworld. Contemporary historians link the Pallavas to an Iranian lineage (the Pahlavas, or Parthians) that briefly held power in the northwest during the first century B.C.E. Pallava kings controlled the eastern peninsula between the Krishna and Kaveri Rivers by the seventh century and remained powerful for the next 300 years. The last Pallava king died in the early 10th century.

THE TEMPLE AT SOMNATH

Mahmud of Ghazni's destruction of the Hindu Shaivite temple at Somnath provided later historians with an event that seemed a perfect symbol for the clash of religions on the subcontinent. Muslim historians, such as the 16th-century Qasim Hindushah Firishta, celebrated Mahmud's destruction of the temple as the act of a pious Muslim. In the 1840s, a British member of Parliament (wishing to prove the British better rulers than the Muslims) claimed that Mahmud's raids had created "painful feelings which had been rankling against the [Hindu] people for nearly a thousand years" (Thapar). In the 21st century, Hindu nationalists have also used Mahmud's attacks (and Muslim incursions into India in general) as examples of Muslim aggression that would leave "a split in India's national character" (Birodkar).

For historians, Somnath raises interesting questions. Earlier Muslim accounts emphasized the destruction of the Somnath temple idol; Mahmud of Ghazni was said to have struck off its nose and sent pieces to Ghazni, Mecca, and Medina. The temple was Shaivite, however, so the temple idol was not an image but a lingam—a solid stone object, with no features (and certainly no nose) to be struck off and probably no hollow inside either to hold (as in many stories) vast quantities of gold and diamonds (Embree et al.).

British and Hindu nationalist claims that the raid at Somnath had scarred contemporary Hindus deeply are also hard to demonstrate from 11th-century evidence. Jain texts from the region record the event but only to make the point that the Jain temple (protected by a stronger god) escaped unscathed. Sanskrit inscriptions at Somnath say nothing about the raid, although the inscriptions do register bitter complaints about the conduct of local Hindu kings, who, it seems, frequently looted pilgrims on their way to worship. "There are," historian Romila Thapar concludes after a survey of the historical evidence for the Somnath raid, "no simplistic explanations that would emerge from any or all of these narratives" (Thapar).

Source: Birodkar, Sudheer. "Hindu History: The Intervention of Alien Rule from 1194 C.E. up to 1947 C.E." Hindutva.org. 2004. Available online. URL: http://www.hindutva.org/landalienrule.html. Accessed March 31, 2005; Embree, Ainslie Thomas, et al., eds. *Sources of Indian Tradition.* Vol. 1: *From the Beginning to 1800.* 2d ed. (New York: Columbia University Press, 1988), p. 437; Thapar, Romila. "Somanatha and Mahmud." *Frontline* 16, no. 8 (April 10–23, 1999). Available online. URL: http://www.flonnet.com/fl1608/16081210.htm. Accessed July 26, 2005.

Iconographic representations of Hindu gods (among others) as pictured in Johann G. Heck's Iconographic Encyclopaedia of Science, Literature, and Art (New York: Rudolph Garrigue, 1851), volume IV, plate 2. Figure 1: The Trimurti [Brahma, Vishnu, Shiva]; 2: Vishnu and Shiva; 3: Vishnu as a fish; 4: Vishnu as a tortoise; 5: Vishnu as a boar; 6: Vishnu as a dwarf; 7: Vishnu asParam Rama; 8: Shiva; 9: Vishnu; 10: Vishnu as Krishna; 11: nymphs of the Milk Sea; 12: Vishnu as Kaninki or Katki; 13: Shiva as hermaphrodite [half man/half woman]; 14: Shiva on the giant Muyelagin; 15: Brahma and Saravadi; 16: Buddha; 17: Buddha-Surya; 18: Hindu solar system; 19: Mythic camel; 20: Hindu penitents; 21–24: Hindu sacrificial utensils; 25–30: Mongolian idols. (Library of Congress)

73

PLOWING FOR DEVOTION

I n this song of the Tamil saint Appar it is clear that farming and the worship of Shiva are completely intertwined.

Using the plow of truth
sowing the seeds of love
plucking the weeds of falsehood
pouring the water of patience;
They look directly into themselves
and build fences of virtue.
If they remain rooted in their good ways,
the Bliss of Shiva will grow.

Source: Prentiss, Karen Pechilis. *The Embodiment of Bhakti* (New York: Oxford University Press, 1999), p. 92.

By the ninth century, the ancient lineage of the Cholas had reemerged in the south. From the mid-ninth century to 1279, kings of the Chola dynasty controlled most of the Tamil-speaking south, including the region around Tanjore, the Coromandel Coast, and much of the eastern Deccan. Two Chola kings (Rajaraja I [985–1014] and Rajendra I [1014–44]) extended the Chola domains to the northern part of Sri Lanka, which remained a Chola tributary until the 1070s.

Bhakti Is Born

"I was born in Dravida [South India]," says the goddess Bhakti in a Puranic story about the origins of devotional Hinduism. "I was born in Dravida and grew up in Karnataka. I lived here and there in Maharashtra; and became weak and old in Gujarat" (Prentiss 1999, 31).

Although the concept of bhakti appears as early as the Bhagavad Gita (ca. first century C.E.), the first bhakti sects are not seen in South India until the seventh to 10th centuries. Bhakti was in North India by as early as the 10th century B.C.E., and bhakti devotional sects proliferated in the north during the 15th through 18th centuries. Bhakti sects were regional movements linking language, geography, and cultural identities in the devotional worship of a god—and sometimes blurring distinctions between Hinduism and Islam in the process.

Bhakti became the most popular form of Hindu worship, not so much replacing Vedic Hinduism as existing alongside it. The major bhakti gods were Vishnu (in any of his nine incarnations), Shiva, or a form of the Mother Goddess (Devi). Shiva was most popular in the south, Vishnu (particularly in his incarnation as Rama or Krishna) in northern India, and the Goddess in the east (Bengal). The choice of god, however, could also be a matter of personal preference, one brother in a family becoming a Vaishnavite (a devotee of Vishnu), while another was a Shaivite (a devotee of Shiva).

Sixty-three Shaivites (called the Nayanars) and 12 Vaishnavites (the Alvars) made up the earliest south Indian bhakti saints. "I have never failed to worship you," sang the Tamil saint Appar, "with flowers and incense and water, never failed to sing you in melodious Tamil songs" (Peterson 1998, 176). The saints sang to all castes and classes of society. They linked their songs to specific Tamil places and to the ordinary tasks of work and daily life.

Bhakti in South India

The Tamil bhakti movement was quickly linked to a temple-centered Hinduism in which *puja* (worship) rather than Vedic sacrifices was the central mode of veneration. As early as the Pallava dynasty, the songs of the itinerant saint-devotees were being sung in Hindu temples. Chola kings built temples to Shiva all across Tamil land, particularly in places identified in the bhakti saints' songs. By the 12th century, devotional songs were a regular part of the liturgy and worship of South Indian temples. The performance of temple rituals and sacrifices was still the unique provenance of Brahman priests, but now a special class of non-Brahman Shudra singers was attached to the temples to perform the bhakti songs.

Although South Indian Hindus recognized the four classes of the *varna* system, these four classes were not well represented in South Indian society. In much of the south the main distinction was between Brahman and non-Brahman classes, and most non-Brahmans were classified as Shudras. Thus the Vellala community of South India was technically classified as Shudras, although they were a dominant *jati* in regional society and in many places were major landowners. Despite their Shudra status the Vellalas were allowed to recite the Tamil saints' songs in temples.

In the same period as the South Indian bhakti movement, two South Indian Brahmans used the central insights of the Sanskrit Upanishads to develop different branches of a philosophy called Vedanta (the end of the Vedas). The first to do this was Shankara (ca. eighth–ninth century C.E.), who emphasized the unqualified monism in earlier Upanishadic teachings that the Brahman (universal spirit) and the atman (individual self) were one. Only when individual souls recognize that the world around them is illusion (maya), according to Shankara, can they recognize the identity of Brahman and atman and escape the cycle of reincarnation (samsara). Such liberation or release (*moksha*) was, for Shankara, the ultimate goal of Hinduism. Shankara's teachings were spread through the subcontinent by the monastic order (*matha*) he founded and by the missionaries his order sent out. A later philosopher, Ramanuja (d. ca. 1137 C.E.), also a South Indian Brahman, developed a school of Vedanta that emphasized the importance of devotion (bhakti) in attaining *moksha*.

Bhakti in North India

By the 15th century bhakti sects had spread throughout North India. By the 18th century these sects had appeared in virtually all Indian regions and vernaculars. In Varanasi (Benares) on the Ganges River, Kabir (1440–1518), an ex-Muslim weaver, sang of a god without attributes (*nirguna*), unlimited by Islamic sectarianism or Hindu caste. In the Punjab, Nanak (1469–1539) rejected the caste system of his Hindu birth and founded the Sikh religion, the devotional worship of a monotheistic *nirguna* god. In eastern India, the Bengali ex-Brahman Chaitanya (1485–1533) and his followers replaced caste and Hindu rituals with ecstatic public dances and songs of devotion to Krishna. Chaitanya's Krishna was a god with attributes (*saguna*), worshipped, not as the warrior-god of the *Mahabharata*, but as a naughty child or adolescent lover. Other 16th-century bhakti saints also sung of *saguna* gods. The North Indian Hindi speaker Tulsidas (16th–17th century) retold the story of Rama in the devotional *Ramcaritmanas* (Spiritual lake of the acts of Rama). Surdas, a blind saint from Mathura, and Mirabai, a woman devotee from Rajasthan—both dated by tradition to the reign of the Mughal emperor Akbar (1556–1605)—worshipped the god Krishna in their songs. In Maharashtra, Tukaram (1608–49) sang in Marathi to the god Vitobha (a form of Vishnu). As in the south, bhakti worship was incorporated into Hindu temples, but *bhajan maths* (singing halls) were also built in many North Indian towns where saints and their followers could meet, sing, and worship their god. Sang Surdas to the god Krishna (Hari):

> Songs to Hari work great wonders.
> They elevate the lowly of the world,
>   who celebrate their lofty climb with drums.

To come to the feet of the Lord in song
is enough to make stones float on the sea....(Embree et al. 1988, 362)

Mirabai Worships Krishna

One of the most popular of bhakti saints in North India was Mirabai. According to legend, she was a Rajput princess devoted to the god Krishna from childhood. Forced to marry, she nevertheless dedicated herself only to the god Krishna. In her in-laws' home she refused to bow to her mother-in-law or to the family's household goddess. In spite of her sister-in-law's pleas she spent her time with wandering holy men. When the *rana* (the king, and her father-in-law) tried to poison her, the god Krishna transformed the poison and saved Mirabai's life. She eventually left her in-laws' home to became a wandering saint; according to legend she disappeared, drawn into the Krishna image one day as she worshipped it.

Mirabai's devotion shows the unselfish devotion of the true wife. Her struggle to maintain this devotion reveals the many difficulties women faced in their in-laws' homes and shows a strength of character often found in popular Hindu goddesses:

> *Life without Hari is no life, friend,*
> *And though my mother-in-law fights,*
> *   my sister-in-law teases,*
> *   the rana is angered,*
> *A guard is stationed on a stool outside,*
> *   and a lock is mounted on the door,*
> *How can I abandon the love I have loved*
> *   in life after life?*
> *Mira's Lord is the clever Mountain Lifter:*
> *   Why would I want anyone else? (Hawley and Juergensmeyer 2004, 134)*

(In one legend, the boy-god Krishna holds aloft Mount Govardhan to shelter cows and cowherds from the anger of the rain-god Indra.)

Persecution of Jains and Buddhists

During the seventh to 12th centuries South Indian kings increasingly identified themselves as devotees (bhaktas) of particular Hindu gods. Kings of the Pallava, Pandya, or Chola dynasties incorporated the institutions and ceremonies of devotional Puranic Hinduism into their royal functions and used this new revived Hinduism to solidify their control over the peoples and territories they claimed. Kings built temples dedicated to the god with whom they identified, generously endowed those temples' operations, and gifted whole villages to temples, to Brahmans, or to Brahman communities. Kings gave these gifts in temple *pujas*, ceremonies that now replaced older Vedic rituals as the way a king legitimated his relationships. Such gifts left kings constantly searching for new sources of land or wealth. The more plunder a ruler had, the more subordinates (such as lesser kings, temple officials, and Brahman *jatis*) he could bring under his sway.

Where earlier rulers had given gifts and used ceremonies drawn from many different religions, South Indian kings were increasingly willing to consider the rivals and enemies of the Hindu sect they endorsed as their own rivals and enemies. Tamil bhakti saints sang of the differences among themselves (as devotees of Shiva) and the Buddhist monks or Jain ascetics with whom they competed for royal favor. "The Jains who expose their skulls," sang the saint Appar, "Conceal Shiva with their minds. / But is it possible to conceal him?" (Prentiss 1999, 72). After the Shaivite saint Appar converted the Pallava king Mahendravarman I (ca. 580–630 C.E.) from Jainism to Shaivism, a 12th-century Shaivite text tells us, the king attacked the Jains' temples and monks. According to another legend, after the Shaivite saint Campantar defeated the Jains in debate in the Pandya-ruled city of Madurai, 8,000 Jain monks were impaled on stakes (Peterson 1998, 180–181).

By the 13th century, as a result of these persecutions, Jain and Buddhist communities in South India had lost influence and power. The Jain religion survived in western India, where it retains a strong presence down to the present day. Buddhism, however, disappeared entirely from India. In North India Buddhism was incorporated into Hinduism, the Buddha appearing as one of the nine incarnations (avatars) of the god Vishnu. In the mountain regions farther to the north—the old centers of Gandharan culture—Buddhism disappeared as local populations converted to Islam.

The Delhi Sultanate

The Delhi Sultanate was not a single dynasty but a succession of five unrelated lineages: the Slave, or Mamluk, dynasty; the Khaljis; the Tughluqs; the Sayyids; and the Lodis. For more than 300 years (1206–1526) the sultans (rulers) of these lineages ruled a north Indian kingdom with its capital at Delhi. At its largest the sultanate controlled virtually all of India, but at its weakest it could barely rule its own capital and the encircling villages.

Sultanate lineages came from Turkish and Afghan military clans, initially forced into the subcontinent by tribal movements related to the expanding Islamic Empire. In theory the sultans governed as Muslims under the political authority of the caliph at Baghdad; in reality they were independent kings, most focused on wealth and glory. During the first two centuries of the sultanate, Delhi sultans faced the constant threat of attacks from the Mongol armies that swept across Central Asia and into Persia and Arabia. By 1258 the Mongols had destroyed the caliphate itself at Baghdad. Mongol power cut off local Turks and Afghans from their original homelands beyond the mountains, while, at the same time, making the sultan capital at Delhi an attractive refuge for Muslim elites fleeing south.

The Mongol Threat

The Mongols were a nomadic, pastoral people based in the arid grasslands north of China. Mongol tribes had been unified in the early 13th century under the leadership of Chinggis Khan, whose grandson would found the Yuan dynasty in China. In 1220 the killing of a Mongol emissary brought Mongol cavalry under Chinggis Khan to the Oxus River region north of the Indian subcontinent. A second Mongol invasion destroyed the Abbasid dynasty in Baghdad in 1258 and established Mongol rulers in territories that reached from the Mediterranean through Central Asia and into China.

As Mongol armies terrorized lands to India's north and west, successive sultans kept the Mongols from overrunning India by a combination of diplomacy, military skill, and luck. Attacks from Mongol forces between 1229 and 1241 overran the Punjab region but were stopped at the Mamluk dynasty's Indus border. During the Khalji dynasty, the Mongols made a series of attacks between 1299 and 1307, but each time the sultan's armies drove them back. Throughout the 13th and 14th centuries, the sultan's court at Delhi was a refuge for elite Muslims—scholars, religious leaders, and intellectuals—fleeing Mongol violence beyond India's borders.

At the end of the 14th century, the Turkish/Mongol ruler Timur (Tamerlane) based in Transoxiana (modern Uzbekistan, Tajikistan, and Southwest Kazakhstan) conquered Persia and occupied Russia. The violence of Timur's campaigns exceeded even the Mongol heritage he claimed as his own. In 1398–99 Timur's armies, already resident in the Punjab, occupied, sacked, and plundered Delhi, dragging back across the northern mountains wealth and thousands of slaves; behind him, in Delhi, Timur left towers made out of the skulls and bodies of slaughtered Delhi residents. Timur's invasion broke the power of the Tughluq dynasty, which was overthrown in 1413.

Sultanate Dynasties

The power of the Delhi sultans, as that of Indian kings before them, was based on constant warfare and on alliances with conquered lesser kings. Sultans also faced the constant threat of plots by sons, wives, relatives, and courtiers, all eager for their power. What was gained in one season might easily be lost in the next. As the sultans expanded their territories across north India, they appointed Muslim subordinates to govern regions they had conquered. In this way Muslim rule spread through north India, for when a region declared its independence from the sultan, the ruler who did so, more often than not, was also a Muslim.

The first dynasty of the Sultanate was the Mamluk, or Slave, dynasty, established by Qutbuddin Aybak (r. 1206–10/11), who proclaimed himself sultan of Delhi in 1206, when the last Ghurid ruler was assassinated. Qutbuddin was a Mamluk, a Turkish military slave bought as a child and trained to fight for his masters. Mamluks were widely used throughout kingdoms in Central Asia, Persia, and the rest of the Islamic Empire. They made fierce and skillful soldiers, particularly as cavalrymen, and were famed for their ability to fire their crossbows backward as they galloped away from an enemy. Qutbuddin, however, died in a polo accident. His military slave and successor, Shamsuddin Iltutmish (r. 1210/1211–36), secured the kingdom's northern frontier along the Indus River and expanded its territories into Sind, Rajasthan, and Bengal. The sultan pacified his Hindu subjects by granting all Hindus the status of *dhimmis*. His daughter Raziyya (r. 1236–39) briefly succeeded him on his death. Within three years she was deposed and then subsequently murdered by a coalition of palace guards (known collectively as "the Forty"), one of whom, Balban, later ruled as sultan between 1266 and 1287.

The Khalji dynasty, founded by Jalaluddin Firuz Khalji (r. 1290–96), had Turkish origins but had long been settled in the Afghan region. The second Khalji sultan, Alauddin (1296–1316), used gold gained from his raids in the Deccan to arrange his uncle's assassination and then to buy the loyalty of his nobles. Alauddin's army—funded through increased taxation—successfully repelled repeated Mongol raids and attacks between 1297 and 1307. When the Mongols withdrew, Alauddin sent his armies south under the command of Malik Kafur, a Hindu convert from Gujarat with whom the emperor was said to have a homosexual relationship. The Khalji forces conquered as far south as the city of Madurai, giving the sultan dominion over virtually all of India. By 1316, however, when Alauddin died, the empire was in disarray. Malik Kafur was killed by his own soldiers, and both Gujarat and Rajasthan had regained independence.

The Tughluq lineage was founded by Ghiyasuddin Tughluq in a revolt against the Khaljis in 1320. Both Ghiyasuddin and his heir died suddenly in 1325, when a pavilion collapsed, and another son, Muhammad (r. 1325–51), came to the throne. Muhammad's reign was characterized by plans to rebuild the empire and by idiosyncratic decisions that suggest he may have been mentally unstable. In 1327, in an effort to gain better control over conquered South Indian territories, he attempted to move the capital—his administration and all Delhi residents—500 miles south to the Deccan. Many died in the move, and heat and health conditions later caused the Deccan capital to be abandoned. In the same period Muhammad also introduced a new copper and brass currency, which had to be withdrawn several years later because of difficulties with forgeries. In 1335–42, when a severe drought caused famine and death in the Delhi region, the sultanate offered no help to the starving residents. The latter years of Muhammad's rule saw many regions of his empire in rebellion. In 1334 the provincial governor of Madurai declared himself an independent "sultan," and in 1338 Bengal became independent under a Muslim ruler. In 1346 the Hindu kingdom of Vijayanagar solidified its control over the southern half of peninsular India.

In 1351 Muhammad died from fever while in Sind trying to quell a rebellion. His cousin Firuz Shah (r. 1351–88) was the choice of court nobles and religious leaders. Firuz repaid these nobles and orthodox ulama for his appointment by returning previously confiscated estates and lands, building no fewer than 40 mosques, and through laws that required Brahmans (previously exempt) to pay the *jizya* (a tax on non-Muslims). After his death, the dynasty had no strong rulers and was finally destroyed at the end of the century by the invasion of Timur.

The Sayyids, a Turkish clan, took power in 1414 and remained in control until 1451. From this time on, regional Muslim rulers controlled most of what had once been sultanate lands. Sind, Gujarat, Malwa, the Deccan, and Bengal were all governed by independent Muslim rulers. The Hindu kingdom of Vijayanagar held the southern peninsula, and independent Hindu Rajputs ruled in Rajasthan. During the rule of the last Sayyid, Alauddin Alam Shah (1445–51), the Delhi Sultanate ruled over little more than the city of Delhi and its immediate surrounding villages.

The last dynasty was founded by a Sayyid provincial governor, Buhlul Lodi (r. 1451–89). The Lodis were descended from Afghans, and under their rule Afghans eclipsed Turks in court patronage. Buhlul's son Sikandar (r. 1489–1517) once again extended the sultanate control to the northern reaches of the Indus and southeast along the Ganges

River valley up to, but not including, Bengal. The last Lodi, Sikandar's son Ibrahim (r. 1517–26), antagonized his own Afghan nobles by assertions of the absolute power of the sultanate. They appealed for help to Kabul, where Zahiruddin Muhammad Babur, a Turkic descendant of both Timur and Chinggis Khan, had established a small kingdom.

Vijayanagar and the Bahmani Sultanate

In south India, in the 1330s and 1340s, five Hindu brothers of the Sangama family took advantage of rebellions against the Tughluq dynasty to establish the city and independent kingdom of Vijayanagar. By 1347 Harihara I (d. 1357), the first ruler of Vijayanagar, together with his brothers ruled a kingdom that included virtually all of the southern half of the peninsula. Vijayanagar rulers protected themselves by adopting Muslim tactics, cavalry, and forts. Vijayanagar kings developed tank-irrigated agriculture in their higher lands and made their coastal regions into a center of trade between Europe and Southeast Asia. Among Vijayanagar's greatest rulers were Krishnadevaraya (r. 1509–29) and its last powerful ruler, Aliya (son-in-law) Rama Raya, who held power from 1542–65.

Farther north in the Deccan, the Bahmani Sultanate was founded by a Turkish or Afghan military officer who declared his independence from the Delhi Sultanate and ruled under the name of Bahman Shah from 1347. Over the next 200 years, Bahmani rulers fought Vijayanagar kings over the rich *doab* (land between two rivers) on their border. In 1518 the sultanate split into five smaller ones: Admadnagar and Berar, Bidar, Bijapur, and Golconda. In 1565 these five kingdoms combined to attack and defeat Vijayanagar. All five Deccani sultanates were subsequently absorbed by the Mughal Empire.

The Mughal Empire

Babur, the ruler of Kabul, had dreamed for 20 years of conquering India. In 1526, when discontented Lodi nobles invited him to save them from their power-mad sultan, Babur invaded India. At Panipat in 1526 his mobile cavalry, matchlock-equipped infantry, and light cannon drove the sultan's larger army and war elephants from the field. A year later Babur's cavalry and firepower had a second victory, this time over a confederacy of Hindu Rajput kings with an army of 500 armored elephants.

Babur became the first ruler of the Mughal dynasty, which continued to rule powerfully and effectively for nearly 200 years (1526–1707) and then survived in a much weaker form through to the mid-19th century. At the height of the Great Mughals' rule the empire covered almost all of the subcontinent and had a population of perhaps 150 million. The wealth and opulence of the Mughal court was famed throughout the world. Even today the vibrancy of Mughal miniature paintings and the elegance of the Taj Mahal show us the Mughals' greatness. For Mughal contemporaries, Shah Jahan's Peacock Throne more than demonstrated the empire's wealth: Ten million rupees' worth of rubies, emeralds, diamonds, and pearls were set in a gold encrusted throne that took artisans seven years to complete.

No one could foresee this greatness, however, in 1530, when Babur died in Agra and his son Humayun (r. 1530–56) took the throne. Humayun, struggling with an addiction to opium and wine, soon found himself under attack from his four younger brothers and the even stronger ruler of Bengal, Sher Shah (r. 1539–45). Sher Shah drove Humayun out of India and eventually into refuge at the court of the Persian Safavids. There, to gain the court's acceptance, Humayun converted to the Shiite sect of Islam. In return the shah sent him back to India in 1555 with a Persian army large enough to defeat his enemies. Within a year, however, Humayun died from a fall on the stone steps of his Delhi observatory. His son, Akbar, was 12 years old at the time.

Akbar

Jalaluddin Muhammad Akbar became emperor 17 days after his father's sudden death in 1556. An accord among the regime's nobles placed the boy under the authority of a regent, Bairam Khan. By 1560 Akbar and his regent had expanded Mughal rule across the Indo-Gangetic heartland between Lahore and Agra. Within two decades, Akbar, now ruling on his own, extended the Mughal Empire into Rajasthan (1570), Gujarat (1572), and Bengal, Bihar, and Orissa (1574–76). By the late 1580s he would annex the provinces of Sind and Kashmir, and by 1601 he would take Berar and two other provinces in the Deccan Plateau.

Akbar's military expansion was accompanied by the use of both diplomacy and force. Over the 40 years of his reign, which ended with his death in 1605, Akbar diluted his own Turkish clan within the Mughal nobility and gave the high rank of emir (amir, that is, military officer or nobleman) to men of Persian, Indian Muslim, and Hindu (mostly Rajput) descent. At the same time, in the 1567 siege of the Rajput city of Chitor, Akbar demonstrated the high cost of resistance to

Portrait of Aged Akbar, *a 17th-century portrait of Akbar as an old man, attributed to Govardhan (ca. 1640–50). Govardhan was one of a number of artists at the emperor Jahangir's court who developed individual artistic styles.* (Govardhan [artist], Indian, active ca. 1600–56. Portrait of Aged Akbar, ca. 1640–50. Ink and gold on paper, 25.2 × 16.8 cm. © The Cleveland Museum of Art, 2004. Andrew R. and Martha Holden Jennings Fund, ID number 1971. 78)

RAJPUT MARTIAL CLANS

The Rajput (son of the king) military clans that first appear in the ninth and 10th centuries in northwestern and central India were probably descended from earlier Central Asian tribes and may not have had any hereditary connections to one another. Nevertheless, Rajput clans claimed ancient Hindu and Kshatriya status based on genealogies linking them to the Hindu solar or lunar royal dynasties and on legends connecting mythological Rajput founders with Vedic fire rituals.

Rajputs successfully maintained their independence through much of the Delhi Sultanate. Under the Mughals they were both defeated and incorporated into the Mughal nobility. Akbar defeated the great Mewar clan through sieges of its key cities, Chitor and Rathambor, in 1567–69. But he also encouraged the Rajputs to become part of his court. Akbar made his first Rajput marriage alliance in 1562, marrying a daughter of a minor Rajput chief of Amber. By 1570, all major Rajputs but the king of Mewar had accepted noble status and sometimes marriage alliances with Akbar. In these alliances Rajput kings kept control over their ancestral lands, but in all other ways came under Mughal authority. Under future emperors the Rajputs remained a key Hindu element within the Mughal nobility. As late as Shah Jahan's reign (the 1640s), 73 of the 90 Hindus in the higher *mansabdari* (Mughal service) ranks were Rajputs.

Under the emperor Aurangzeb, however, the percentage of Rajput nobles decreased, and new administrative rules limited the lands (*jagirs*) from which Rajputs could collect revenues. Aurangzeb's more orthodox Islamism also led him to attempt to place a Muslim convert on the Marwar clan's throne. All these changes led to the Rajput war of 1679 and to the Rajputs' support of Aurangzeb's son Akbar II in his unsuccessful effort to overthrow his father in 1781. Although Aurangzeb ended the Rajput rebellion and forced one Rajput clan, the Mewars, to surrender, and although his son's coup failed, the Marwar Rajputs remained in rebellion against the Mughals for a generation.

his will: His armies destroyed the fort itself, massacred its inhabitants, and killed 25,000 residents in the surrounding villages.

Akbar was a brilliant military commander and a man of great personal charisma and charm. Illiterate—and perhaps dyslexic (four tutors tried unsuccessfully to teach him how to read)—he was still curious and interested in history, religion, and philosophy. Above all, Akbar was a great leader of men not only on the battlefield but also within his own court and administration. It was the structures of Mughal organization and administration devised by Akbar and his Muslim and Hindu ministers that held the Mughal Empire together over the next century and a half.

After 1560 Akbar administered his empire through four ministers: one each for finance, military organization, the royal household, and religious/legal affairs. He reserved for himself control over the army, relations with other rulers, and appointments/promotions in rank. The Mughal system assigned all *mansabdars* (those in Mughal military service) a rank that specified status, salary, and assignment. Ranks were not hereditary; they could change as a result of service, great courage in battle, or the emperor's wish. Each *mansabdar* provided the Mughals with a fixed number of soldiers (determined by rank) and, in return, each received a salary. Higher-ranking *mansabdars* might also receive a *jagir* (the right to collect land revenues from a specified village or region).

The Mughal War Machine

War was the business of the great Mughals. Mughal emperors from Akbar through Aurangzeb spent fully one-half their time at war. Mughal wars were initially fought to bring the different regions of the subcontinent under Mughal authority, and then, subsequently, Mughal military power and warfare was used to maintain Mughal rule against unruly regional powers. As early as the end of Akbar's reign, the Mughal war machine was so powerful that local and regional rulers saw their only alternatives as surrender or death. The Mughals, however, never solved the problem of succession. The saying went, "*takht ya takhta*" (throne or coffin) (Spear 1963, xiii), and before and after the death of each emperor, contending heirs turned the great Mughal army viciously against itself.

Under the Mughal system, as it evolved, all *mansabdars,* whether noble or non-noble, military or bureaucratic, were required to recruit, train, command, and pay a fixed number of soldiers or cavalry for the emperor's armies. The number of soldiers varied from 10 to 10,000, with the lowest *mansabdars* providing the former and the highest nobles the latter. This system gave Mughal emperors a ready, well-equipped army, and they depended on these armies and their *mansabdar* leaders to extend and preserve the Mughal Empire. At the end of Akbar's reign, 82 percent of the regime's revenues and budget supported the *mansabdars,* their troops, and assistants.

The Mughal administrative system existed to funnel vast sums to its armies. As Mughal land revenues paid the *mansabdars*, Akbar's Hindu revenue minister, Todar Mal, ordered a survey of Mughal North Indian lands. Beginning in 1580 Mughal revenue officials determined land holdings, climate, soil fertility, and appropriate rent assessments at the district level. Annual assessments were set at approximately one-third the crop (lower than had been traditional or would be customary later). Taxes were to be partially remitted in years of bad crops. Local chiefs and zamindars (lords of the land) could keep only 10 percent of the revenues they collected each year. Unlike earlier tributary relationships between kings and subordinates, Mughal rule required local rulers to pay an annual tax based on crops and place all but lands personally occupied under Mughal fiscal and administrative control.

Such a military system required emperors to spend much of their time on the move. Akbar spent at least half of his long reign at war. He had capitals at both Agra and Lahore and at the city of Fatehpur Sikri, which he built outside Agra and which he used as a capital between 1571 and 1585. The emperor also took much of his court, wives, children, and servants with him on military campaigns. The Jesuit father Antonio Monserrate, who tutored Akbar's second son, accompanied the emperor on one such expedition into Afghanistan in 1581. The entire court lived in a great white city of tents, after the fashion of the Mongols. On the right, Monserrate wrote, "are the tents of the King's eldest son and his attendant nobles; these are placed next to the royal pavilion . . . [Behind the tents of the King's sons and nobles] come the rest of the troops in tents clustered as closely as possible round their own officers . . ." (Richards 1993, 42).

Akbar's Religion

The more intensive military, economic, and administrative control of the Mughal emperors was accompanied, in Akbar's reign at least, by greater religious freedom. Early in his reign (1563) the emperor abolished taxes on Hindu pilgrims and allowed Hindu temples to be built and repaired. In 1564, he abolished the jizya (the tax paid by all non-Muslim *dhimmis*). "Both Hindus and Muslims are one in my eyes," one imperial edict declared, and thus "are exempt from the payment of *jazia* [*jizya*]" (Richards 1993, 90). Land grants were still made to Muslims and the court *ulama*, but now they also went to monasteries, Zoroastrians (Indian followers of Iranian Zoroastrianism, later called Parsis), and Brahman priests. Cow slaughter was even prohibited late in Akbar's reign.

On a personal level, Akbar's religious convictions also changed. As a young man he had been a devotee of the Sufi saint Sheikh Salim Chishti (d. 1581), but by the 1570s he was developing more eclectic religious ideas. He invited representative Hindus, Jains, Parsis, Sikhs, and Christians to debate religious ideas in his Diwan-i-Khas (Hall of Private Audiences). He began to practice his own "Divine Faith," a form of worship centered on the Sun. High nobles were encouraged to become Akbar's personal disciples, agreeing to repudiate orthodox Islam and worship Allah directly.

Europeans in India

During the 16th–17th centuries, the Portuguese, Dutch, English, and French established trade with India, built "factories" (trading posts and warehouses) in various Indian ports, and hired independent armies to protect them. Trade was lucrative: Imports of black pepper to Europe in 1621 were valued at £7 million. Cotton textiles were the second most valuable commodity, with Indian silks, indigo, saltpeter, and other spices following behind. Unlike China or Japan in these centuries, Europeans could travel freely in Mughal India and had settled in most major cities by the end of the 17th century.

Trading wars (and actual armed conflict) between European companies in India were frequent. The Portuguese initially dominated Indian and Asian trade from their Goa settlement (1510). The Jesuit missionary Francis Xavier (1506–52) came to Goa in 1542, and as early as Akbar's reign Jesuits were in residence at the Mughal court, working both as Christian missionaries and to further Portuguese trading interests. Portugal's union with Spain (1580), however, the defeat of the Spanish Armada (1588), and Portuguese naval defeats in the Indian Ocean all reduced Portuguese dominance in India. Under a grant from Jahangir, the English established factories at Surat and Bombay (now Mumbai) (1612), Madras (now Chenai) (1639), and Calcutta (now Kolkata) (1690). By 1650 the Dutch controlled the Southeast Asian spice trade from their bases on Sri Lanka. In the late 1660s the French company established settlements at Surat and Pondicherry (south of Madras) and in Bengal upriver from Calcutta.

The Great Mughals

By Akbar's death in 1605, the Mughal military and administrative systems were well established and would remain, more or less unchanged,

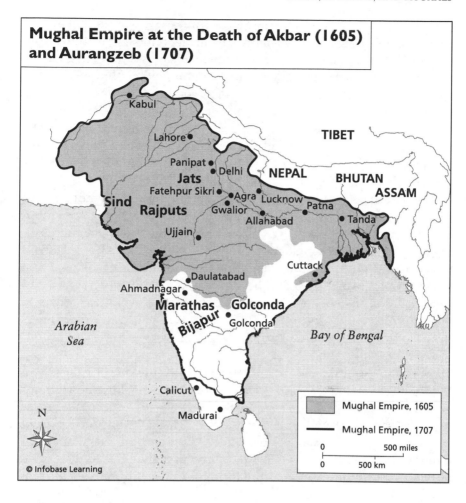

Mughal Empire at the Death of Akbar (1605) and Aurangzeb (1707)

through the reign of Aurangzeb (1658–1707), the last of what are called the "Great Mughals." Mughal military expansion was blocked to the far north by mountainous terrain and resistant hill tribes, to the east and west by the oceans, and to the south at the Kaveri River and—in spite of Aurangzeb's efforts—by Deccani resistance.

The Mughals maintained public order throughout this vast empire through constant military readiness and a well-organized infrastructure. Hindu service castes such as the Khatris and Kayasthas, as well as Brahmans, had learned Persian and staffed the provincial levels of Mughal government. An extensive road system, built and maintained by a public works department, connected the Agra-Delhi region to the provinces, allowing for the easy movement of troops and the securing of routes against roving bandits or local armies. A far-flung "postal system" of couriers relayed paper reports, news, orders, and funds back and forth from the imperial center to the *mofussil* (rural) periphery.

Trade flourished in markets, towns, and cities throughout the empire, and the manufacturing of traded goods was widely dispersed. Cotton textiles, such as calicoes, muslins, and piece goods, were the largest manufactured product, produced for both internal and external trade. Economically the Mughals were self-sufficient. Foreign traders found they needed gold or silver to purchase products desired in Europe or Southeast Asia.

This centralized, orderly, and prosperous empire did not survive Aurangzeb's reign. Its greatest problem was not the religious differences between Muslim rulers and Hindu populations; Muslim rulers adapted their religious convictions to the realities of governing a mostly Hindu land. The Mughals' great weakness was succession. From Babur through Aurangzeb and beyond, an uncertain succession pitted impatient sons against aging fathers, and brothers against brothers in violent, costly, vicious struggles that only escalated in destructiveness throughout the Mughal period.

Jahangir

Jahangir (r. 1605–27), Akbar's eldest son and heir, became emperor after a six-year struggle that began with his own attempt to overthrow his father in 1599 and ended with his own son Khusrau's attempt to usurp the throne. On his deathbed Akbar recognized Jahangir as emperor, and Khusrau was imprisoned and partially blinded. Khusrau's supporters, among whom was the fifth Sikh guru, Arjun, were all captured and executed.

Jahangir maintained with little change the lands he inherited from his father and continued Akbar's political alliances and his policy of religious tolerance. He allowed the Jesuits to maintain churches in his capital cities, and he treated both Hindu holy men and Sufi saints with reverence. Like his father Jahangir took a number of Hindu wives. Like Akbar he also encouraged court nobles to become his personal disciples. The mixture of Persian and Indian elements in Mughal court culture became more pronounced during his reign. Persian was now the language of court, administration, and cultural life throughout Mughal India. Court artists, both Hindu and Muslim, developed distinctively "Mughlai" styles of painting and portraiture.

In 1611 Jahangir married Nur Jahan (light of the world), the beautiful Muslim widow of one of his officers who was also the daughter of one of his high-ranking nobles. Nur Jahan, in conjunction with her father and brother, dominated court politics for the remainder of Jahangir's reign.

Shah Jahan

Jahangir died in 1627. His son Shah Jahan (r. 1628–58) assumed the throne at the age of 36, after a brief but bloody succession struggle that was resolved by the execution of two brothers and several adult male cousins. At the time, Shah Jahan was already a mature general in his father's armies. Over the course of his reign he maintained Mughal military dominance against challenges from Afghan nobles, through campaigns in Sind, and against regional rulers in Central India. He ruled

ORIGINS OF THE SIKH *KHALSA*

The Sikh religion was founded in the early 16th century by the first guru, Nanak (1469–1539). Guru Nanak taught a monotheistic, devotional religion that accepted Hindu ideas of reincarnation and karma but rejected caste. This religion proved popular among Hindu Jat peasants in the Punjab. Until 1708 the community was led by 10 Sikh gurus, and during this time the Sikh sacred scriptures (the Granth Sahib, or Adi Granth) were compiled in a special Sikh script, *gurumukhi* (from the Guru's mouth).

The third and fourth gurus were patronized by Akbar. But the fifth guru, Arjun (1563–1606), was tortured to death by Jahangir on suspicion of treachery. Arjun's son and successor, Hargobind, fled to the Himalayan foothills with armed followers. The ninth guru, Tegh Bahadur (1621–75), was executed by Aurangzeb when he refused to convert to Islam. The two young sons of the 10th and last guru, Gobind Rai (1666–1708), were executed by Aurangzeb's successors, and the guru himself was assassinated when he sought to protest their murder. At his death Gobind Rai declared himself the last of the gurus and vested his authority in the Adi Granth, which was to guide Sikhs in the future.

Constant Mughal-Sikh conflict during the 16th–18th centuries forged the Sikhs into a fighting force, a *khalsa* (an army of the pure). As signs of membership in this army, male Sikhs left their beards and hair uncut, always carried a comb and a sword, and wore a steel bracelet on the right wrist and knee-length martial shorts. The Sikhs remained a powerful military force in the Punjab into the mid-19th century.

Jama Masjid, New Delhi. Built by Shah Jahan in the 17th century, this is one of the largest and finest mosques in India. (courtesy of Judith E. Walsh)

a mature empire, enormous in size and wealth, where the revenues from a large district in Lahore or Agra brought in more than 1 million rupees each year.

Shah Jahan was a seasoned general, and his army overall was larger than it had been in Akbar's time. Yet he spent a smaller proportion of his wealth on military and government officials than had his grandfather. Instead he directed a series of spectacular building projects. For his coronation he had the Peacock Throne constructed. At the death of his favorite wife, Mumtaz Mahal, he commissioned the Taj Mahal as an eventual tomb for both their bodies. In 1639 he ordered a new capital city, Shajahanabad, to be built on a site just south of Delhi. When finished in 1648, the new city contained a great royal fortress and the largest mosque in India, the Jama Masjid.

During Shah Jahan's reign, prominent Sufi leaders were urging orthodox Sunni Muslims to adhere strictly to sharia laws. Perhaps this, as much as personal inclination, accounts for the more Muslim style of Shah Jahan's rule. He celebrated Islamic festivals with great enthusiasm and resumed sponsorship of a yearly pilgrimage to Mecca. Beginning in 1633 he enforced sharia laws forbidding the repair of churches or temples. In his relations with court nobles he abandoned the personal discipleship encouraged by his father and grandfather, emphasizing instead the long-standing familial ties Muslim nobles had with Mughal rulers. By the middle of his reign all 73 of the most elite nobles and 80 percent of higher-ranking *mansabdars* were Muslim.

Taj Mahal, Agra. The Taj was built by Shah Jahan as a memorial and resting place for his favorite wife, Arjumand Banu Begum (otherwise known as Mumtaz Mahal, "ornament of the palace"). They were married in 1612, and all 14 of Shah Jahan's subsequent children were hers. She died in 1631, at the age of 39, giving birth to her 14th child. Construction of the Taj, which would provide a tomb for the bodies of both Mumtaz Mahal and Shah Jahan, began in 1632. (courtesy of Judith E. Walsh)

Conflict among Shah Jahan's adult sons (and their court factions) preoccupied the last years of the emperor's reign. Dara Shukoh, the emperor's favorite and appointed heir, shared his great-grandfather's ecumenical interest in religion. He had had the Upanishads translated into Persian and believed that they reflected a monotheistic religious sensibility that was, at its core, Islamic. Dara attracted those at court who yearned for a return to Akbar's more religiously diverse court. At the opposite pole was Shah Jahan's third son, Aurangzeb. An excellent military commander and experienced administrator, Aurangzeb was a pious Muslim. "He pretended to be a faquir (*faqir*), a holy mendicant," observed an unsympathetic Italian at the court, "by which he renounced the world, gave up all claim to the crown, and was content to pass his life in prayers and mortifications" (Richards 1995, 153). Aurangzeb attracted those who wanted a court committed to Islam and the institution of a religiously orthodox state.

Aurangzeb

When Shah Jahan fell seriously ill in 1657, these two court factions turned the Mughal military inward upon itself. The struggle for succession lasted two years. It ended with Aurangzeb (r. 1658–1707) as emperor; his father, Shah Jahan, imprisoned; and all three of his brothers dead. Dara Shukoh was executed after the Delhi *ulama* convicted him of apostasy and idolatry.

Aurangzeb's rule inaugurated a more aggressively orthodox and Islamic court culture. The new austerity curtailed large building projects, ended Mughal patronage of musicians and painters, and banned wine and opium from court. The sharia, as interpreted by court *ulama*, was to provide the ideological basis for Mughal government. New temple construction was banned, and old temples and idols were often destroyed; new taxes were imposed on temple pilgrims and Hindu merchants; and in 1679 the *jizya* was again imposed on all Hindus. Aurangzeb also sought to increase the number of Muslims in Mughal service and to restrict Rajput access to the higher *mansabdari* ranks. When he learned that the ninth Sikh guru had converted Muslims to his religion, Aurangzeb had him arrested and put to death. His armies pursued the 10th guru for years in the Himalayan foothills.

The first 30 years of Aurangzeb's reign aimed at creating a more Islamic Mughal regime. But in 1681, in part because of the emperor's anti-Hindu policies, Rajput clans supported the efforts of a son, Akbar II, to usurp the throne. The attempt failed, and Akbar fled to the

Maratha kingdom and eventually to the court of the Persian kings. Aurangzeb, fearing a possible coalition of enemies at court with Rajputs, independent Deccani sultans, and Marathas, determined to bring the Deccan under his control. He marched south, taking with him his own army, the armies of his three sons, and those of his major generals. In 1685 he defeated the sultans of Bijapur (the Karnatak) and Golconda (Hyderabad). In 1689 his forces tracked down and killed the Maratha king Sambhaji. By then Mughal territories extended from the Himalayas to all but the very tip of the Indian peninsula.

But the Marathas refused to surrender. Aurangzeb spent the last 20 years of his life in the Deccan, much of it living in a giant tent city 30 miles in circumference, vainly attempting to bring the Deccan under his control. Even after Mughal troops killed Sambhaji's brother Rajaram in 1698, Rajaram's widow, Tara Bai, fought on as regent for her infant son. From 1700 to 1705 the Mughals repeatedly besieged and captured Maratha hill fortresses only to have the Marathas recapture them as soon as the Mughals withdrew. In the countryside, Maratha armies collected the land revenues before the Mughals could secure them.

In the north, Mughal administrative and fiscal systems were breaking down. The cost of the Deccan war was depleting the treasury even as the growing practice of "tax farming" (hiring a third party to collect revenues from a *jagir*) was reducing overall revenues. The old *mansabdari* military system was no longer honored—soldiers were either not provided or inadequately horsed and equipped. Rebellion, disorder, and disaffection were breaking out even in the Indo-Gangetic heartland. In the late 1680s, Hindu Jat peasants south of Agra plundered Mughal supply trains with such impunity that Aurangzeb had to send troops from the Deccan to stop them.

In 1705, old and ill, Aurangzeb abandoned his war and began a slow march north. Two years later he died, in his tent city outside Aurangabad. "My famous and auspicious sons should not quarrel among themselves and allow a general massacre of the people," he wrote in almost identical letters to his three sons and heirs shortly before his death. "My years have gone by profitless. . . . I have greatly sinned and know not what torment awaits me" (Smith 1958, 426).

Muslim Society

The Muslim society that developed across India over the centuries of Muslim rule was divided into elite, or *ashraf* (honorable), and nonelite households. *Ashraf* Muslims were urban, religious officials (*ulama*),

SHIVAJI AND THE MARATHAS

The term *Maratha* occurs early in Indian history (1st century C.E.) but originally only as a description of peoples who spoke the language of the region. During the 14th–17th centuries, with repeated Muslim invasions of the Deccan Plateau and the establishment of the Bahmani Sultanate, a distinct Maratha community, defined by martial, military, and administrative abilities, began to differentiate itself from other non-Muslim, non-Brahman, cultivating and pastoral castes of the Deccan Plateau. By the 17th century, Maratha clans were soldiers and administrators either within Deccani Muslim governments or in opposition to them. The most famous Maratha leader, Shivaji Bhonsle (1630–80), had begun to build his kingdom and his army of mobile guerrilla fighters out of competing Maratha clans by the age of 20. His exploits and the daring of his guerrilla forces became legendary in the Deccan. In 1659, surrounded by troops of the Bijapur Sultan, he disemboweled their general, Afzal Khan, with "tiger claws" strapped to his fingers, and his followers slaughtered the Bijapur forces (among whom were also Marathas). In 1666, offended by Aurangzeb's treatment, he escaped imprisonment in Agra (allegedly by hiding in a basket of sweetmeats) and returned to Maharashtra within a month, eluding capture by taking side routes through tribal areas east of Malwa. In 1674, after Brahman ritual specialists invested him with the sacred thread and

soldiers, and administrators. By the end of the Delhi Sultanate, independent Muslim rulers had established themselves throughout much of the subcontinent. Muslim elites settled along with these rulers in their capitals and trading centers. By the 15th century elite Muslims who claimed Arab ancestry were called Sayyids; from Central Asian ancestry, Mughals; and Afghan ancestry, Pathans.

Non-*ashraf* Muslims were urban artisans and rural cultivators organized into endogamous *jati* communities, some of which certainly had preexisted the Muslims. The first British census in the mid-19th century found that Muslims made up one-quarter of the population, concentrated in the largest numbers in the Punjab and Bengal. Conversions in Bengal probably date to Mughal efforts to expand deltaic farmlands under Aurangzeb and were carried out by Sufi masters who established mosques and Muslim religious centers in the eastern Bengal region.

Muslim elites and Muslim artisan *jatis* lived in the urban centers of India, in the prosperous trading cities and in the various provincial

Kshatriya status, Shivaji installed himself as ruler in an elaborate Vedic ritual employing thousands of priests and reputedly costing 5 million rupees. At the time of his death in 1680, Shivaji's Maratha kingdom extended the length of the Konkan hills in the west and included smaller domains to the southeast, the largest centered on Tanjore city.

Shivaji's heir, Sambhaji (ruled 1680–88), supported the failed coup of Aurangzeb's son Akbar II in 1681 and was hunted down, tortured, and killed by the Mughals in 1688—his body torn apart and thrown to dogs. But although the Mughal emperor annexed the Deccan the next year, neither he nor his successors could stamp out Maratha power. In 1719 the Mughals gave the Marathas all of Shivaji's earlier territories in return for a yearly tribute.

During the 18th century, a series of literate Chitpavan Brahman *peshwas* (prime ministers) shaped the Marathas into a powerful confederacy. Shivaji's grandson Shahu (1707–49) appointed Balaji Vishwanath (r. 1713–20) as the first *peshwa*; the position became hereditary with his son, Baji Rao I (r. 1720–40). *Peshwa* bureaucrats, based in Pune (Poona), used Mughal techniques to organize the confederacy and farm out its extensive land revenues. Marauding Maratha armies periodically swept across the North India plains in plundering raids that in 1742 reached the outskirts of Calcutta. By 1751 Maratha Confederacy territories extended north into Rajasthan, Delhi, and the Punjab and south into the Karnatak and Tamil land.

capitals and the capitals of independent, regional sultanates. The Bengal sultanate, for instance, had its capital in Gaur in the early 16th century. Gaur was a large and prosperous city. It had a population of 40,000 and stretched for several miles along the river. Its markets were full of cheap and plentiful food, and its streets and lanes were paved with bricks. A Portuguese traveler who visited it noted how crowded its streets had become: "The streets and cross-lanes are so full of people that [it] is impossible to move and it has reached the point where the high noblemen have taken to being preceded along the road to the palace by men carrying bamboo sticks to push people out of the way" (Eaton 1993, 98).

Purdah

The Qur'an places women and men in terms of absolute equality before God (Allah), but in social terms, Muslim women were subordinate to Muslim men. "Men are in charge of women," says the Qur'an, "because

97

LATER MUGHAL EMPERORS AND THE CAUSE OF THEIR REIGN'S END

Date of Rule	Emperors
1707–12	Bahadur Shah I (died)
1712–13	Jahandar Shah (murdered)
1713–19	Farukkhsiyar (murdered)
1719–48	Muhammad Shah (died)
1748–54	Ahmad Shah (deposed)
1754–59	Alamgir II (murdered)
1759–1806	Shah Alam II (died)
1806–37	Akbar Shah II (died)
1837–57	Bahadur Shah II (deposed)

Allah hath made the one of them to excel the other, and because they spend their property (for the support of women)" (Eaton 1993, 297). The Muslim practice of purdah (meaning literally "veil" or "curtain") required that women not be seen by men unrelated to them. Elite Muslim women lived in the zenana (women's quarters) of the home, away from all men but their husbands and closest male relatives. When they traveled, they did so in covered conveyances. Ancient Indian society had also developed practices that restricted women's social mobility and behavior, particularly in the early centuries C.E. Over the centuries in which Muslims ruled many sections of India, Muslim conventions intensified these Hindu practices, and by the 19th century purdah was the customary practice of high-caste Hindu and elite communities throughout India.

In Decline

The centralized Mughal Empire did not survive much past the last of its great Mughal leaders. Aurangzeb's ambition to control the Deccan forced him to spend long years there, to the detriment of his North Indian empire. Wars of succession, the one problem the Mughals never solved, tore them apart periodically during the time of the Great Mughals. After Aurangzeb's death, with administrative and revenue systems in growing disarray, succession struggles brought Mughal power more or less to an end. In the succession crisis that followed Aurangzeb's death in 1707, Bahadur Shah (r. 1707–12) killed his two competing brothers and became the sixth Mughal emperor. Between his death in 1712 and 1720, repeating wars of succession convulsed the Mughal court. By 1720 regional Mughal nobles were asserting their independent control over Punjab, Oudh, Bengal, Gujarat, and the Deccan. Rajput kings and the Marathas encroached on Mughal territories at every opportunity. By the mid-18th century the Mughals themselves controlled little more than the territory surrounding Delhi. It would only be under the next great empire—that of the British—that the centralization begun by the Great Mughals would reach its logical conclusion.

4

THE JEWEL IN THE CROWN
(1757–1885)

When, by the blessing of Providence, internal tranquility shall be restored, it is our
earnest desire to stimulate the peaceful industry of India, to promote works of
public utility and improvement, and to administer its government for the benefit
of all our subjects resident therein. In their prosperity will be our strength,
in their contentment our security, and in their gratitude our best reward.

■

Proclamation of Queen Victoria of Great Britain, 1858
(Muir 1969, 384)

In 1739 the Persian king Nadir Shah (r. 1736–47) raided the Mughal
capital at Delhi, destroyed the current emperor's army, killed more
than 30,000 Delhi residents, and returned to Persia with gold, jewels, and
Shah Jahan's Peacock Throne. The Mughal Empire was over—although
it would survive as a weakened shell for more than a hundred years. The
remaining competitors for Mughal power were local and regional Mughal
officials (nawabs and nizams), regionally dominant tribes and rulers
(Hindu or Muslim), and two foreign trading companies, one English and
one French, both relative newcomers to the Indian scene.

Of all of these, it was British East India Company that would replace
the Mughals as India's new paramount power—against the objections
of many in Great Britain itself. By 1876, when the British government
finally declared Queen Victoria empress of India, Great Britain had
made India the "jewel in the crown" of its worldwide empire and was
developing new ideologies—"Pax Britannica" and the "civilizing mission"—to justify British imperial rule.

Nawabs and Nabobs

The Mughals were so weak by the mid-18th century that they had
become, in effect, a regional power, controlling Delhi and its surround-

100

ing environs but little else. Their war machine was in ruins, and their land taxes were farmed out to the highest bidders. Regional nawabs (Mughal provincial governors) in Hyderabad, Oudh, and Bengal were now de facto rulers. They maintained a superficial deference to Mughal authority but sent no revenue and fought wars or sued for peace at their will. To the north, an Afghan-based empire that included Sind and much of the Punjab was ruled by Ahmad Shah Abdali (r. 1747–72).

To the south, the Marathas ruled homelands in the Deccan and adjacent centers in Tanjore and the Karnatak. By the 1750s the Maratha *peshwa* (prime minister) at Pune headed the Maratha Confederacy dominated by four Maratha ruling families, each with its own local domain: The Gaekwar dynasty controlled Baroda; Holkar controlled Indore; Scindia controlled Gwalior; and Bhonsle controlled Nagpur. The breakdown of Mughal authority left villages across North India unprotected and allowed Maratha armies to raid virtually unchecked across the subcontinent. Maratha horsemen rode up to the walled villages of the Indian plains, demanding gold and rupees—and killing those who did not have them. An 18th-century observer described the terror of these raids:

> . . . the bargis [Maratha horsemen] entered the villages. They set fire to the houses, large and small, temples and dwelling places. . . . Some victims they tied with their arms twisted behind them. Some they flung down and kicked with their shoes. They constantly shouted "Give us rupees, give us rupees, give us rupees." When they got no rupee, they filled their victims' nostrils with water and drowned them in tanks. Some were put to death by suffocation. Those who had money gave it to the bargis; those who had none gave up their lives. (Smith 1958, 466)

In 1742 Maratha raiders reached as far east as the outskirts of Calcutta before being turned back. Maratha hopes of installing their own candidate on the Mughal throne were destroyed in 1761, however, on the battlefield of Panipat, when Afghan armies helped the weak Mughal ruler to destroy Maratha forces.

As the Mughals' collapse became increasingly obvious, two European trading companies, one French and the other English, battled each other for commercial and political dominance along the Indian coasts. By the mid-18th century the India-Europe trade in textiles, indigo, saltpeter, tea, and spices was extremely lucrative. The French company was returning almost 25 percent on its investment to shareholders at home. The British East India Company's share in this trade was worth £2 million. As early as the late 18th century wealthy company "nabobs"—a

THE EAST INDIA COMPANY

The English East India Company was founded in 1600 as a private joint-stock corporation under a charter from Queen Elizabeth I that gave it a monopoly over trade with India, Southeast Asia, and East Asia. The company was governed in London by 24 directors, elected by its shareholders (known collectively as the Court of Proprietors). Profits from its trade were distributed in an annual dividend that varied during 1711–55 at between 8 and 10 percent. The company's trading business was carried on overseas by its covenanted "servants," young boys nominated by the directors usually at the age of 15. Servant salaries were low (in the mid-18th century a company writer made £5 per year), and it was understood they would support themselves by private trade.

Between 1773 and 1833 a series of charter revisions increased parliamentary supervision over company affairs and weakened the company's monopoly over Asian trade. In the Act of 1833 the East India Company lost its monopoly over trade entirely, ceasing to exist as a commercial agent and remaining only as an administrative shell through which Parliament governed Indian territories. In 1858 the East India Company was abolished entirely, and India was placed under the direct rule of the British Crown.

corruption of the Indian title nawab—had begun to return to England to live in "Oriental" splendor on their Indian riches.

The main French trading settlement was at Pondicherry (south of Madras), with smaller centers at Surat (north of Bombay), and Chandernagar (north of Calcutta on the Hugli River). After 1709 the British East India Company carried on trade from well-fortified settlements at Bombay, Fort St. George in Madras, and Fort William in Calcutta. Satellite factories in the *mofussil* (the Indian hinterland) were attached to each of these "presidency" centers.

The French East India Company was led at Pondicherry after 1742 by Joseph-François Dupleix (1697–1764), a 20-year commercial veteran in India. Dupleix's goal was to make himself and his company the power behind the throne in several regional Indian states. The English in Madras had much the same idea, and French and English forces fought the three Carnatic Wars (1746–49, 1751–54, 1756–63) over trade and in support of their candidates for nizam of Hyderabad and nawab of the Carnatic (the southeastern coast of India, from north of Madras to the southernmost tip). Robert Clive (1725–74), a company servant turned soldier, used English forces to place the British candidate on the Carnatic throne in 1752. Dupleix was recalled to France, and in the last Carnatic war the French were completely defeated. Chandernagore and Pondicherry remained nominally French, but French commercial, military, and political power in India had come to an end.

The Carnatic Wars showed servants of the British East India Company such as Clive the potential for political and economic power (and personal fortune) in India. The wars also demonstrated to both Indians and Europeans the military superiority of European armies. The disciplined gun volleys of a relatively small English infantry formation could defeat the charge of much larger numbers of Indian cavalry. This military superiority would be a critical factor in the company's rise to power.

The Battle of Plassey

In 1756 the young nawab of Bengal, Sirajuddaula (r. 1756–57), marched on British Calcutta to punish its citizens for treaty violations.

An 18th-century palki (palanquin). The palanquin was a common form of conveyance for both men and women in 18th- and even 19th-century India. East India Company servants (like the gentleman pictured within) could read as they were carried about on their business. This drawing is a detail from the Thomas Daniell (1749–1840) etching View of Calcutta, *ca. 1786–88. (courtesy of Judith E. Walsh)*

The British soldiers fled, and the nawab had the remaining English residents (either 64 or 146 in number) imprisoned overnight in a local cell (the "Black Hole"). The smallness of the cell, the heat of the June weather, and the shock of confinement killed all but 23 (or 21) by dawn. Clive marched north from Madras with 3,000 troops to avenge the disaster. Company forces defeated the nawab's army at the Battle of Plassey in 1757—a date often used to mark the beginning of British rule in India. Clive owed most of his victory, however, to a private understanding reached before the battle between Clive, the Hindu banking family of the Seths, and Mir Jafar, the nawab's uncle and the commander of his troops. Mir Jafar's soldiers changed sides during the battle, and Clive subsequently had Mir Jafar installed as nawab. Four days later Sirajuddaula was captured and executed by Mir Jafar's son.

The Battle of Plassey began a 15-year period during which the company's new political power allowed its servants to acquire great for-

OPIUM SCHEMES

In the years before the Battle of Plassey, there was little demand in India for European or English commodities (such as woolens), and the British East India Company had imported bullion to pay for its trade. After 1757 the company imported little bullion into Bengal. Bengal's land revenues, estimated at 30 million rupees per year, now funded a variety of company expenses, among which was the trade in opium. The company had a monopoly over opium cultivation in Bengal and Bihar, and beginning in 1772 land revenues were used to purchase the opium crop. The company shipped its opium through middlemen to China, where it was exchanged (illegally under Chinese law) for gold and silver bullion. That bullion, in turn, bought Chinese goods that were then shipped back for sale in England. Although this exchange never worked quite as planned, the opium trade was enormously profitable to the company.

This trade sent a steadily rising supply of opium into China: 1,000 chests a year in 1767, 40,000 chests in 1838, and 50–60,000 chests after 1860. By 1860 the British had fought two wars to force the Chinese government to legalize opium trading. The East India Company lost its commercial functions in 1833; nevertheless, opium remained a government monopoly in India until 1856, contributing up to 15 percent of the Indian government's income and making up 30 percent of the value of Indian trade. Opium imports into China continued into the 20th century, ending only in 1917.

tunes. Clive himself received £234,000 in cash at Plassey, in addition to a *mansabdari* appointment worth £30,000 per year (Wolpert 2008). For most company servants, wealth was why they had come to India. The saying was "Two monsoons are the age of a man"—so if a servant survived, his goal was to become rich and return to England as quickly as possible (Spear 1963, 5). After Plassey, servants trading privately in Bengal were exempt from all taxes and had unlimited credit. Posts in the *mofussil,* even quite modest ones, were now the source of lucrative presents and favors.

In the 1760s and 1770s company servants began to return to England with their post-Plassey wealth. Clive himself returned in 1760 as one of England's richest citizens and used his new wealth to buy a fortune in East India Company stock, hoping to forge a career in politics. Criticisms mounted in Parliament about nabobs who had pillaged Bengal's countryside and returned to live in splendor. In 1774 the censure became so intense that Clive, who had had earlier bouts of depression and attempted suicide, took his own life.

When the new nawab, Mir Jafar, took power in Bengal in 1757, he found himself saddled with huge debts from the Plassey settlement, and his tax coffers emptied by concessions made to company servants. Tired of his complaints, the British East India Company briefly replaced him with his son-in-law, Mir Qasim, only to return Mir Jafar to power in 1763. Mir Qasim, however, then looked for help to the Mughal emperor, Shah Alam. At the 1764 Battle of Baksar (Buxar) the Mughal emperor's army was defeated by a much smaller company force. In the 1765 peace negotiations, Clive (who had returned to India as governor of Bengal that same year) left political control in the office of nawab (to be held by an Indian appointed by the company) but took for the company the *diwani* (the right to collect the tax revenues) of Bengal.

From 1765 on, the East India company collected Bengal's tax revenues. Land taxes paid for company armies and were "invested" in company trade. Local company monopolies of saltpeter, salt, indigo, betel nut, and opium improved the company's position in international trade. That trade made Bengal potentially one of India's richest provinces. In theory, after 1757 and 1765, much of Bengal's wealth came under the direct control of the East India Company.

Regulations and Reforms

Between Plassey in 1757 and 1833 when the East India Company's commercial activities ended, company territory in India grew enormously.

By 1833 the company controlled directly and indirectly most of the subcontinent. This expansion, however, was accompanied by parliamentary objections and public outcry, often from the company's own directors.

Within India, most officials saw expansion as inevitable. The only way to secure company trade and revenues or to protect territories already conquered was to engage in the intrigues and warfare that characterized 18th- and 19th-century Indian politics. The military superiority of the East India Company armies gave the company an advantage, but it was the loyalty of company servants that made the greatest difference. Servants might (and did) put personal profit ahead of company interests, but they saw no future in siding with an Indian ruler in battle or in court intrigues. In a world where Indian rulers faced at least as much danger and treachery from their own relatives and courts as from external enemies, the loyalty of its servants gave the East India Company a great advantage. "The big fish eats the small fish," said the ancient Indian proverb. From the point of view of company officials in India the choice was either eat or be eaten.

From the perspective of England, however, the company's wars in India often appeared immoral, pointless, and extravagant. To the company's many parliamentary enemies it seemed immoral for a private corporation to own a foreign country. Countries needed to be under the guidance of those who would act, as the member of Parliament William Pitt (the Younger) put it, as "trustees" for their peoples. Even the company's own directors and its parliamentary friends had difficulty understanding why Indian territories should be expanded. Indian wars did not improve company dividends; more often than not they put the company further in debt. But India was six months away by ship from England, and London directives were often moot before they arrived. In the end it was the company's failure to pay its taxes after 1767—even as its servants returned with private riches—that forced the issue of government regulations.

The Regulating Act and Warren Hastings

In the years after Plassey and the East India Company's assumption of the *diwani* of Bengal, conditions in Bengal deteriorated rapidly. The company's servants used its political power for personal gain, the nawab's government had no funds, and the company's efforts to secure returns from the tax revenues were in chaos. In 1769–70 crop failures led to severe famine and the death of up to one-quarter of Bengal's population. The company took no steps to ameliorate famine conditions in these years, but its reduced revenue collections left it unable after 1767 to pay its taxes to the British Crown.

Parliament responded in 1773 with two acts. The first authorized a loan of £1.5 million to the company. The second—the Regulating Act of 1773—reorganized company operations. The company's London directors were to be elected for longer terms, and in India the three presidencies (Calcutta, Bombay, and Madras) were unified under the control of a governor-general based in Calcutta.

The first governor-general appointed under the Regulating Act was Warren Hastings (1732–1818), a 20-year veteran of company service in India who held the appointment from 1774 to 1785. As governor of Fort William in Bengal (Calcutta) Hastings had already brought the collection of Bengal taxes directly under company control. As governor-general he abolished the office of nawab, bringing Bengal under the company's direct political rule. He used East India Company armies aggressively: first to protect an ally, Oudh, from marauding Rohilla tribes; then to attack Maratha armies in the Bombay area; and finally against Haidar Ali Khan (1722–82) of Mysore. To refill his treasury after these military operations, he forced the dependent kingdoms of Oudh and Benares to pay additional tribute to the company.

Orientalists

Hastings's long residence in India had given him a deep interest in Indian society and culture. It was under his auspices that Sir William Jones, judge of the Calcutta supreme court, founded the Asiatic Society of Bengal in 1784. Jones had studied Latin, Greek, Hebrew, Arabic, and Persian at Oxford before turning to law. In India he also studied Sanskrit, a language almost unknown to Western scholars at that time. It was Jones who first suggested the link between Latin, Greek, and Sanskrit that began the comparative study of Indo-European languages.

The Asiatic Society began the European study of the ancient Indian past. Europeans in both India and Europe, Jones included, were more familiar with Muslim society and culture than with India. It required considerable work over the 18th and 19th centuries for men such as Jones and his Asiatic Society colleagues to translate India's ancient past into forms compatible with and comprehensible to European sensibilities and scholarship. In Bengal Jones and a successor, H. T. Colebrooke, compiled materials for both Hindu and Muslim personal law codes, basing the Hindu codes on pre-Muslim Brahmanical Sanskrit texts. In

Rajasthan James Tod compiled records and legends into his *Annals and Antiquities of Rajastan* (1829–32). In South India Colin Mackenzie collected texts, inscriptions, and artifacts in an extensive archive on South Indian history. These efforts, along with the great cartographic projects that reduced the physical features of empire to paper maps, constructed an India intelligible to Europeans.

Men such as Jones, Tod, and Mackenzie were loosely classed together as *Orientalists,* a term that to them implied a European scholar deeply interested in the Oriental past. In the late 20th century, the intellectual Edward Said gave this term a more negative gloss: "Orientalists," he pointed out, had often studied what was to them foreign and exotic in Middle Eastern and Asian cultures only to demonstrate the inherent superiority of the West (Said 1978).

Pitt's India Act and Lord Cornwallis

William Pitt's India Act was passed by Parliament in 1784 in a further effort to bring company actions in India more directly under Parliament's control. Under the act the East India Company's London directors retained their patronage appointments, including the right to appoint the governor-general, but a parliamentary Board of Control now supervised company government in India—and could recall the governor-general if it wished. When Warren Hastings in India learned of Pitt's act, he resigned his position as governor-general. Within two years Parliament had brought impeachment proceedings against Hastings, in part on grounds that he had extorted funds from Indian allies. The broader point was the issue of British "trusteeship" over India and the idea that political behavior considered immoral in Britain should also be immoral in India. After seven years Hastings was acquitted of all charges but financially ruined and barred from any further public service.

In 1785 the East India Company directors sent Charles Cornwallis (1738–1805) to India as governor-general, an appointment Cornwallis held until 1793. Lord Cornwallis, who had just returned from America where he presided over the surrender of British forces at Yorktown (1781), had a reputation for uncompromising rectitude. He was sent to India to reform the company's India operations. His wide-ranging reforms were later collected into the Code of Forty-eight Regulations (the Cornwallis Code). Cornwallis fired company officials found guilty of embezzling and made the servants' private trade illegal. He barred Indian civilians from company employment at the higher ranks and sepoys (Indian soldiers) from rising to commissioned status in the British army. He replaced regional Indian judges with provincial courts run by British judges. Beginning with Cornwallis, the "collector" became the company official in charge of revenue assessments, tax collection, and (after 1817) judicial functions at the district level. Where Pitt's India Act defined a dual system of government that lasted until 1858, Cornwallis provided administrative reforms that structured British government through 1947.

Cornwallis's most dramatic reform, however, was the "permanent settlement" of Bengal. Pitt's act required new tax rules for Bengal, and initially a 10-year settlement was considered. Bengali tax collectors under the Mughals had been the zamindars (lords of the land), an appointed, nonhereditary position. Over the centuries, however, zamindari rights had often become hereditary. In 1793, hoping to create a Bengali landowning class equivalent to the English gentry, Cornwallis decided to make the revenue settlement permanent. The "permanent settlement" gave landownership to Bengali zamindars in perpetuity— or for as long as they were able to pay the company (later the Crown) the yearly taxes due on their estates. The settlement's disadvantages became clear almost immediately, as several years of bad crops forced new zamindars to transfer their rights to Calcutta moneylenders. The Bengal model was abandoned in most 19th-century land settlements, in part because by then the government's greater dependence on land revenues made officials unwilling to fix them in perpetuity.

The Company as Paramount Power

By the early 19th century British wars in Europe against France had produced a climate more favorable to empire. From 1798 to 1828 governors-general in India aggressively pursued wars, annexations, and alliances designed to make the British dominant in India. Richard Colley Wellesley (1760–1842) was sent to India in 1798 with specific instructions to remove all traces of French influence from the subcontinent. As a member of the British nobility comfortable with the pomp of aristocratic institutions (much under attack by the French), Lord Wellesley assumed that uncontested British dominance in India would improve both company commerce and the general welfare of the Indian people. Consequently Wellesley took the occasion of his instructions as an opportunity to move against virtually all independent states in India. Wellesley also augmented the imperial grandeur of company rule

Government House, Calcutta, 1819. Lord Wellesley had Government House (Raj Bhavan) built in Calcutta between 1799 and 1803 to give himself and future governors-general a palatial dwelling appropriate for the empire they were creating in India. The East India Company directors in London only learned about the building (and its enormous cost) in 1804. The building's architect was Charles Wyatt (1759–1819), and the design was modeled on a Derbyshire English manor, Kedleston Hall, built in the 1760s. This drawing, A View of Government House from the Eastward, *is by James Baillie Fraser, ca. 1819. (courtesy of Judith E. Walsh)*

by building, at great cost, a new Government House in Calcutta. As an aristocratic friend said in defense of the expense of this undertaking, "I wish India to be ruled from a palace, not from a counting house; with the ideas of a Prince, not with those of a retail-dealer in muslins and indigo" (Metcalf and Metcalf 2006, 68).

In addition to war and outright annexation, Wellesley used the "subsidiary alliance" to expand British territories. Under this agreement a ruler received the protection of East India Company troops in exchange for ceding to the company all rights over his state's external affairs. Rulers paid the expenses of company troops and a representative of the company (called a resident) lived at their courts. Internally the state was controlled by the ruler; foreign relations—wars, peace, negotiations—were all the business of the company. The East India Company had used such alliances since at least the time of Robert Clive, but Wellesley made them a major instrument of imperial expansion.

The Anglo-Mysore Wars (1767–1799)

Wellesley's anti-French instructions led him first to attack Tipu Sultan (ca. 1750–99), the ruler of Mysore in south India. Both Tipu Sultan and his father, Haidar Ali Khan, were implacable foes of the British. Haider Ali had built up an extensive army of infantry, artillery, and cavalry on the European model and used it in a series of wars with the company. Haidar Ali had won an early contest with the British in 1769. Then in 1780, after a series of company treaty infractions, the Mysore king, in alliance with the Marathas and the nizam of Hyderabad, had sent 90,000 troops against the British at Madras. Warren Hastings sent Calcutta troops to defend Madras and sued for peace with Tipu Sultan, who had become ruler after his father's death. In the third Anglo-Mysore war (1790–92) the East India Company made alliances with the Marathas and Hyderabad against Mysore. These allied forces besieged Tipu at his capital at Seringapatam. In the surrender Tipu lost half his kingdom.

After his defeat in the third war, Tipu, who had reached a tentative alliance with the French on the Mascarene Islands, had shown his sympathy with the French Revolution by planting a "tree of liberty" in his capital, Seringapatam. This was considered enough to justify Wellesley's attack on him in 1799. The war ended in three months with Tipu's death in battle. In the subsequent division of the Mysore kingdom, the East India Company took half and gained direct access from Madras to the west coast. Wellesley installed a Hindu king over the small remaining kingdom, with whom he signed a subsidiary alliance. (Mysore would remain a princely state ruled by Hindu kings until 1947.)

Between 1799 and 1801, Wellesley also annexed a series of territories from rulers who had been company allies for some time. Tanjore (1799), Surat (1800), and Nellore, the Carnatic, and Trichinolopy (all in 1801) came under direct company rule. In Oudh, Wellesley forced the current nawab's abdication, and in the renegotiation of the kingdom's subsidiary alliance the company annexed two-thirds of Oudh's territory.

Maratha Wars (1775–1818)

Wellesley turned next to the Marathas. The Maratha Confederacy had fought British East India Company troops for the first time in 1775–82 in a struggle over company territorial expansion. But Nana Fadnavis, the peshwa's Brahman minister and his skilled diplomacy had kept the Marathas relatively united and the English at bay. After his death in 1800, however, the confederacy began to degenerate into a loose and

Mahadaji Scindia, ca. 1820. This picture (a modern hand copy of an 1820 painting) shows the Maratha ruler of the house of Scindia entertaining a British naval officer and military officer with a nautch (a performance by dancing girls). (courtesy of Judith E. Walsh)

feuding collection of clans, although the major Maratha houses were still powerful and controlled substantial territories in central India. The Scindias at Gwalior had long employed a French-trained military, and Wellesley used this limited French connection to justify a war against them. In 1802 Wellesley took advantage of internal Maratha conflicts to convince the *peshwa*, Baji Rao II (1775–1851), to sign a subsidiary alliance with the company. Wellesley used this treaty to justify attacks on the four Deccan Maratha clans; by 1805 new subsidiary alliances with the houses of Bhonsle and Scindia gave him direct control over additional lands in the Deccan and Gujarat, as well as over Orissa and the cities of Delhi and Agra (all of which had been under Maratha control).

Wellesley's campaign against the Marathas was interrupted when he was recalled to London in 1805. Between 1798 and 1806 Wellesley's military expansions had tripled the company's debt (Bayly 1988, 80). Neither the East India Company nor Parliament could justify the expense of additional Indian wars. Yet by 1805, even the prime minister, William Pitt, a frequent critic of company activities, supported the company's new supremacy in India. If Britain's war against France (and company indebtedness) momentarily required a halt to further Indian campaigns, all agreed that the future stability of British interests required Britain's unchallenged domination of India.

Wellesley's successors—Lord Cornwallis (who died in 1805, the year of his second appointment), Sir John Barlow, Lord Minto, Lord Hastings, and Lord Amherst—continued his policy of expansion. The company's charter was renewed in 1813 but only with new provisions allowing private traders (and missionaries) to travel to and work in company domains. Hastings forced the kingdom of Nepal to accept a subsidiary alliance in 1816 and the next year negotiated 19 subsidiary alliances with Rajput states. He then renewed company attacks on the Marathas; by 1818 the Marathas were defeated. A final settlement dismantled their Pune court, sending the *peshwa* into retirement and exile at Cawnpore (Kanpur) on the Ganges and making the Pune region part of the Bombay Presidency. The Maratha clans of Scindia, Holkar, Gaekwar, and Bhonsle all signed subsidiary alliances with the British. In 1824 Amherst began a series of wars against Burma that forced the kingdom into a subsidiary alliance in 1826. In India by 1833 the Sikh kingdom of Ranjit Singh in the Punjab was the only independent Indian state within a subcontinent otherwise completely under company control.

Land Revenues and Pax Britannica

British territorial gains in both North and South India led relatively quickly to new revenue settlements in these regions. Between 1790 and 1826 the company's twin goals were the reassessment of taxes in newly conquered territories and the pacification of villagers, peasants, and tribesmen to ensure the regular collection of those taxes. Whereas Bengal revenues had brought in £3 million, by 1818 the company's conquests and annexations had increased the total from Indian revenues to £22 million (Bayly 1988, 116). Land taxes underwrote the company's balance of trade with India and China and subsidized the cost of the East India Company's far-flung army. Company expenses in India were also remitted to Britain on an annual basis out of Indian revenues. Collectively called the "Home Charges," these charges included the cost of offices, salaries, pensions, and all other expenses associated with the running of Great Britain's Indian Empire. By 1820, according to one historian's estimate, these transfers had reached £6 million annually (Bayly 1988). Extravagant levels of official expenditures and the expenses of military campaigns, however, made serious inroads into Indian revenues. In 1828, a senior company official noted in a letter to the new governor-general Lord William Bentinck in 1828 that India "has yielded no surplus revenue. It has not even paid its own expenses" (Bayly 1988, 121).

Although Bengal's permanent settlement was extended to zamindars in Bihar and Orissa in 1802–05, British officials were already disillusioned with it. Instead of a reforming gentry, the settlement had produced only a class of wealthy absentee rent collectors. More important, as the company increasingly focused on revenues and tax collection, the disadvantages of a "permanent" settlement, under which taxes could never be raised, became increasingly obvious. In the Madras Presidency in the 1820s its governor-general, Sir Thomas Munro, devised a system to settle revenues directly on peasant cultivators (the *ryots*). Under this *ryotwari* system assessments were made with individual cultivators on the basis of small plots of land for periods of 30 years. Taxes took one-half the net value of the crop, a high assessment given that Mughal taxes had only taken one-third of the crop (and even that was not always collected). Munro's *ryotwari* system was later used in Bombay, Gujarat, and in the Deccan. In the Delhi region, in parts of Oudh, and in the Punjab, however, the land settlements made between 1833 and 1853 followed a variety of different models, sometimes settling revenues with village communities or village elders, usually for periods of 30 years.

Even as they mapped and catalogued revenue statistics, company officials were also trying to bring order to their new territories. To reduce the military capabilities of chiefs and petty rajas (princes or nobles) they awarded honors to some and used their armies against others. They attempted to award migrant tribes and forest peoples landholdings (and tax assessments) in marginal marsh and waste lands and on the peripheries of more settled regions—in part to fix their location. Company armies hunted down and eliminated marauding Maratha *pindari* (plunderers) tribes and Afghan Rohilla bands.

The British named their pacification of company lands the Pax Britannica. As had also been true during early Mughal rule, peace and stability brought renewed prosperity to many areas. Recycled Mughal rest houses along major routes helped farmers and merchants move goods to regional markets. In Delhi, urban property values almost tripled between 1803 and 1826, and interest rates fell sharply both in Delhi and throughout India. By the 1830s British armies had brought peace and order—and heavier taxation—to much of urban and rural India.

Lord Bentinck's Reforms

When Lord William Cavendish Bentinck (1774–1839) became governor-general in 1828, the warfare that had characterized the company's expansion was over. As a utilitarian, Bentinck believed in the rational organization of society, and during his time in office the restructuring of company expenditures turned a deficit of £1.5 million into a surplus of £0.5 million. The company's court system was also reorganized, making English, not Persian, the official language for the higher courts and for government business. Company armies and police eradicated the gangs of *thagi* (ritual thieves and murderers) from central and north India.

Bentinck's most dramatic act as governor-general was the abolition of sati. Sati was not widespread in either Bengal or India. It occurred mostly in the Gangetic region and (in a slightly different form) among Rajputs in central India. Nevertheless, for Christian missionaries and officials like Bentinck, an evangelical Christian, sati symbolized all that was evil and barbaric in an idolatrous Hinduism. Missionaries in Bengal had long campaigned against the practice, but British officials feared that interfering with a religious practice might provoke an uprising. In 1829 Bentinck signed Article XVII into law in company territories. The article made the burning or burying alive of a widow "culpable homicide"; if drugs or compulsion were used, the offense was murder. When the missionary William Carey was sent the new regulation for translation into Bengali, he was said to have jumped to his feet crying, "No church for me today! . . . If I delay an hour to translate and publish this, many a widow's life may be sacrificed" (Thompson 1928, 78). Bentinck's regulation provoked no mass protests or uprisings. The only protest came from a group of Calcutta Hindus, who sent an 800-signature petition to the Privy Council in England asking (unsuccessfully) for the law's repeal.

Toward the end of Bentinck's tenure, Parliament took further steps toward direct British rule in India. The Charter Act of 1833 abolished the East India Company's commercial functions, opening all of Asia to private trade and ending the company's existence as a commercial body. It left the company's government structures in place, however, as a bureaucratic shell through which Parliament would continue to govern India.

By 1833 Great Britain had become an industrialized country. English machine-woven cloth was exported to India as early as 1800. After 1815 the Bengal handloom industry—Bengal's most popular and lucrative industry since Mughal times—could no longer compete in either Europe or Asia with Lancashire woven cottons, and by 1833 Bengal's cotton industry had collapsed. Increasingly raw cotton was India's major export, and industrially produced finished goods were the imports British merchants wanted to sell in India. By ending the commercial functions of the old East India Company, Parliament signaled the end of the mercantile economy that had brought the English to India centuries earlier.

Against this background of changing political and economic relations between Great Britain and India, the government in Calcutta debated the question of Indian education. The debate was between two groups of British officials: the Orientalists, who believed Indians should be educated in their own indigenous languages, and the Anglicists, who argued that education should be in the superior and more useful language of English. The Anglicists' spokesman, the new law secretary Thomas Babington Macaulay (1800–59), summed up his arguments in 1835 in the famous "Minute on Education."

"I have no knowledge of either Sanscrit [sic] or Arabic," Macaulay wrote without apology, but "I have never found one among them [the Orientalists] who could deny that a single shelf of a good European library was worth the whole native literature of India and Arabia" (Macaulay 2001). The best and most responsible course the British could take in India was to educate a small elite group of Indians in the superior British language and traditions. By doing so they would create a group to serve as intermediaries between the British and the Indian masses—"a class of persons," Macaulay wrote, who would be "Indian in blood and colour, but English in tastes, in opinions, in morals and in intellect" (2001).

Behind the debate but largely unaddressed were some practical realities: English had just been made the official language for court and government business throughout India. In future years, government would need substantial numbers of local people literate in English to carry out its ordinary administrative functions. Probably for both ideological and practical reasons, the government committed itself to the financial support of English-language education for Indians. There were already English-language schools for Indians in Bombay, Calcutta, and Madras. However, government orders expanding college-level education throughout India would not be mandated for almost 20 years.

Dalhousie's Reforms and Annexations

If in Wellesley's time the British goal was for British power to dominate India, by the time James Andrew Brown Ramsay, the marquis of Dalhousie (1812–60), began his appointment as governor-general in 1848, the British were ready for an even more ambitious task: the creation of an empire. But as Dalhousie's regime saw the outlines of a modern British empire emerge in India, more than one Indian constituency found reasons to wish for an end to British rule.

Sikhs and Afghans

Dalhousie's first major effort was a simple war of expansion against the Sikhs, the last independent Indian kingdom on the subcontinent. Ranjit Singh (1780–1839) had ruled the Sikh Punjabi community from 1799 to his death in 1839. His army, made up of Sikh, Muslim, and Hindu soldiers, was organized on modern lines and trained by European officers. But when Ranjit Singh died in 1839, the British, began the first of their three Afghan Wars (1839–42, 1878–80, 1919). Fearing the Russians would attack through Afghanistan, the British tried to place their own candidate on the Afghan throne. In 1841, Afghan troops trapped 16,000 British troops in winter weather at Kabul and only one man survived the retreat back to British territories. By 1843, however, British armies had successfully annexed Sind, and troops had been massed on the Sutlej border, ready to move against the Sikhs. In the First Anglo-Sikh War (1845–46) the Sikhs lost the northeastern edge of the Punjab. In the Second Anglo-Sikh War (1848–49), fought under Dalhousie, the British destroyed the Sikh army and annexed the remaining Sikh lands. Dalhousie sent the Lawrence brothers, John and Henry, to pacify the region. John Lawrence established what became known as the "Punjab system," an approach that combined government investment in rural agricultural projects (irrigation, roads, bridges) with revenue settlements calculated after crops had been harvested and set as low as 25 percent of the harvest (Bayly 1988, 134).

"Lapse" and "Paramountcy"

The Dalhousie government used the administrative tools of "lapse" and "paramountcy" to expand British land and land revenues in India even further. Ignoring Indian adoption customs, "lapse" argued that where there was no biological male heir to a throne, the British could legally annex the kingdom. "Paramountcy" said that, as the British were the paramount power in India, they had responsibility for each ruler's behavior and could annex territories where rulers governed irresponsibly.

Relying on these doctrines, Dalhousie's government moved aggressively between 1849 and 1856 to eliminate royal titles and privileges and to annex states where the royal line had "lapsed" or where rulers governed "unwisely." The government eliminated the royal titles of the Carnatic and Tanjore—and the pensions of the families that held them. Officials attempted the same with the Mughal imperial title—its last holder, Bahadur Shah II, was living on a pension in Delhi—but the intervention of British aristocrats forced Dalhousie's regime to settle for a provision under which the title would die with the old man who held it. In the same way, the government used "lapse" to annex seven princely states in Bengal, central India, Rajasthan, and the Punjab— among which were the Rajput state of Udaipur (1852) and the Maratha states of Satara (1848), Jhansi (1853) and Nagpur (1854). Dalhousie also terminated the pension of the adopted son of the Maratha peshwa, living in British-imposed exile at Cawnpore. His government's last and most dramatic act was the annexation of Oudh in 1856. Oudh had been a subsidiary ally of the British since the days of Clive. British officials

THE GREAT INDIAN RAILROADS

The Indian railroads were built mostly by private companies with government land grants, government incentives, and profits guaranteed by the government. After the tracks were built, the government purchased and ran the lines. The major lines were laid between 1853 and the 1920s: the first 5,000 miles of track by 1869; 16,000 by 1890; 35,000 by 1920; and 40,000 by 1946. In 1946, 78 percent of the Indian countryside was no more than 20 miles from a rail line.

The government's initial intent was to connect the three great British capitals—Calcutta, Bombay, and Madras—by rail and to run a rail line up the Ganges River Valley into the Punjab. By the 1880s, a main trunk-line network connected Indian inland regions to the major port cities of Calcutta, Bombay, Karachi, and Madras. Freight carried by the rail lines increased from 3.6 million tons in 1871, to 42.6 million tons in 1901, to 143.6 million tons in 1945–46. The same tracks, of course, could also move troops in times of conflict and food in times of famine. By the 20th century the railroads had unified India's internal markets, producing cheaper prices and greater availability of goods even as they destroyed small-scale and local industries. Rail transport was popular and crowded from its very beginnings, despite prophecies that caste barriers would keep Hindus away. By 1927 government purchasing programs had given the government ownership of 72 percent of India's rail lines.

now argued that its rulers had misgoverned the state, and Dalhousie's government annexed it. Dalhousie's annexations brought in additional revenues at relatively little expense. The annexations of Satara, Jhansi, Nagpur, and Oudh alone added an estimated £10 million to the company's annual Indian taxes.

Railways, the Postal System, and Telegraphs

When he left India in 1856, Dalhousie noted that he had introduced the "three great engines of social improvement, which the sagacity and science of recent times had previously given to the Western nations—I mean, Railways, uniform Postage and Electric Telegraphs" (Muir 1969, 365). Dalhousie had overseen the development of Britain's railway system as president of London's Board of Trade. In India he did the same. The first railway line was laid out of Bombay in 1853 and ran 21 miles from the city to one of its suburbs. Subsequent lines followed in Calcutta (1853) and Madras (1856).

Dalhousie also oversaw the unification of India's mail system and the laying of its telegraphic lines. Where mail between Calcutta and Bombay had previously cost 1 rupee per letter, the new unified postal service delivered mail anywhere in British India at a cost of only a half-anna ($1/32$ of a rupee). Between 1851 and 1854, 2,500 miles of telegraph line connected all India's major cities. In 1855, post and telegraph were unified into a single, all-India system.

Dalhousie and his successor, Charles John Canning (1812–62), also saw the beginnings of a number of educational and social reforms with far-reaching consequences. In 1854, the Wood dispatch created three university centers at Calcutta, Bombay, and Madras to oversee college education in the English language. These universities had no teachers or classes but oversaw the curricula, examinations, degrees, and honors for affiliated, privately run English-language institutions. Throughout the provinces private English-language schools at the primary, middle school, and secondary levels would serve as feeder schools for the university system. This was not mass education—as the government specifically pointed out in 1858. This was an elite educational system, designed to create graduates with English-language skills and Western knowledge in every province in British India.

The government also passed several reforms contravening customary Hindu religious practices. The 1850 Caste Disabilities Act allowed Hindu converts to Christianity to inherit property, and a subsequent 1856 law allowed Hindu widows to remarry. In the same year Lord

Canning's government also passed a reform act directed at soldiers in the military. The 1856 General Service Enlistment Act ordered Indian soldiers to serve wherever the British government sent them, regardless of caste customs and concerns. (Four years earlier, 47 sepoys in a Bengal regiment had been executed for refusing to break caste customs and board ships bound for Burma.) Most of these measures had limited effect at the time they were passed. But, taken together, they showed a government more ready than ever before to create a British colonial state in its Indian territories—regardless of the concerns, prejudices, or religious practices of its Indian subjects.

Mutiny and Rebellion

When Dalhousie left office in 1856, turning over the government to Lord Canning, observers might have considered Dalhousie as the governor-general who had modernized British India. Within less than two years, however, as India was convulsed by the violent uprisings of 1857, it appeared that Dalhousie's regime might go down in history as responsible for bringing British rule in India to an end.

The uprisings of 1857–58 began as mutinies among Indian troops but spread quickly through northern India among states and groups recently disempowered by the British. The Sepoy Rebellion, or Indian Mutiny, began in the barracks at Meerut, 30 miles outside Delhi. New Enfield rifles had recently been introduced but to load them soldiers had to bite open the cartridges. The rumor spread that the cartridges were greased with pig and cow fat. When 85 sepoys at Meerut refused to use the guns and were put in irons, their comrades rebelled on May 10, killed several officers, and fled to Delhi. There they found the 82-year-old Mughal emperor, Bahadur Shah II, and declared him the leader of their rebellion. At Cawnpore, Nana Sahib, adopted son of the former *peshwa,* and at Jhansi, the Maratha rani (queen) Lakshmibai joined the uprising. At Lucknow in Oudh, Sir Henry Lawrence (1806–57) and the European community were besieged within a fortified and supplied residency. At Cawnpore the British general surrendered to Nana Sahib, and all but four of the 400 Englishmen, -women, and children were killed.

The rebellion spread through much of the central and northern Ganges River valley, centering on Lucknow (Oudh), Cawnpore, and Delhi. In central India, Rajput and Jat communities and in the Deccan, old Maratha centers were also involved. Opposition in Oudh was the most unified. Almost one-third of the Bengal army came from high-caste Oudh families, and there was widespread support for Oudh's

Sir Henry Lawrence, in a 19th-century drawing based on a photograph taken at Lucknow. In 1857 Lawrence organized and led the English community within the besieged Lucknow Residency. He died in July from wounds received in battle, but his planning enabled the English to hold out until the siege was lifted. In later years it became a point of pride that the flag was never lowered at the residency, and both Lawrence and the residency itself became part of the heroic memories Anglo-Indians attached to the period's events. (Frederick Sleigh Roberts. Forty-one Years in India, 34th ed., 1905)

deposed ruler, Wajid Ali Shah. Throughout the affected areas, local rajas and chiefs also took this opportunity to settle old scores or acquire the holdings of longtime enemies.

Despite widespread opposition to the British, the rebellion's main leaders never unified, and even in the Delhi, Oudh, and Cawnpore centers, court factions competed with and undercut one another. Delhi was recaptured by the British in September 1857. Bahadur Shah's sons were summarily executed, and the old man was exiled to Burma where he died the next year. The siege of Lucknow was lifted in November, and Cawnpore, recaptured in December. The Maratha city of Gwalior fell in 1858. The Rani of Jhansi died in battle, and Nana Sahib's main general, Tantia Tope, was captured and executed. The *peshwa* himself vanished into Nepal.

By July 1858 the British had regained military control. Although there were less than 45,000 English troops to somewhat less than 230,000 sepoys (and 200 million Indian civilians), the British had been unified. They had regained the north with Sikh troops from the Punjab,

THE WELL AT CAWNPORE

Of all the Sepoy Rebellion, or Indian Mutiny, stories that later circulated among British and Anglo-Indian communities, none was as famous as that of the well at Cawnpore (Kanpur). *Cawnpore*, a book written eight years after the 1857–58 mutiny, retold a bystander's account of the murder of British women and children well suited to the racialized feelings of the English in post-mutiny India:

The bodies . . . were dragged out, most of them by the hair of the head. Those who had clothes worth taking were stripped. Some of the women were alive. I cannot say how many. . . . They prayed for the sake of God that an end might be put to their sufferings. . . . Three boys were alive. They were fair children. The eldest, I think, must have been six or seven, and the youngest five years. They were running round the well (where else could they go to?) and there was none to save them. No: none said a word, or tried to save them.

Source: Embree, Ainslie T., ed. *1857 in India: Mutiny or War of Independence?* (Boston: D. C. Heath, 1963), p. 35.

English troops sent from overseas, and sepoys from south India—a region generally untouched by rebellion. Outside the Gangetic north, most of British India and many of the princely states had not actively participated in the rebellion.

In the aftermath of the rebellion, the British took their revenge. British troops and sometimes civilians attacked neutral villagers almost at random. Captured sepoys were summarily executed, often by being strapped to cannons and blown apart. Governor-General Canning's call for moderation won him only the contemptuous nickname "Clemency Canning."

The 1857–58 rebellion changed the nature of the Indian army and racialized British relations with Indians in ways that were never forgotten. The army had had its origins in the independent forces hired by the Bengal, Bombay, and Madras Presidencies. By 1857 the number of soldiers had grown to 271,000 men, and European officers were only one out of every six soldiers. After the rebellion, the army was unified under the British Crown. Only British officers were allowed to control artillery, and the ethnicity of regiments was deliberately mixed. In addition, the ratios of European troops to Indian troops increased. In Bengal there was now one European soldier for every two Indians; in Bombay and Madras, one for every three (Schmidt 1995). The army also recruited Indian soldiers differently after 1857. Where the pre-mutiny army had had many high-caste peasants from Oudh and Bihar, the post-rebellion army was recruited from regions where the rebellion had been weakest and among populations now (somewhat arbitrarily) identified as India's "martial races"—from Punjabis (Sikhs, Jats, Rajputs, and Muslims), from Afghan Pathans, and from Nepali Gurkhas. By 1875, half of the Indian army was Punjabi in origin.

In the later decades of the 19th century key mutiny locations were monumentalized by British imperialists and India's Anglo-Indian community. The well at Cawnpore received a sculpture of Mercy with a cross. The Lucknow Residency's tattered flag was never lowered. Windows in churches and tombs in graveyards were inscribed with vivid memories of the place and violence of mutiny deaths. The mutiny confirmed for the British their own "heroism . . . moral superiority and the right to rule" (Metcalf and Metcalf 2006, 107). But the violence of attacks on women and children and the "treachery" of sepoys and servants on whose devotion the British had thought they could rely also weighed heavily in later memories of events. The Sepoy Rebellion left the British intensely aware of the fragility of their rule.

Crown Rule Begins

The 1857–58 rebellion cost Britain £50 million to suppress in addition to monies lost from unpaid land and opium revenues. (Bayly 1988, 195). Many in Parliament blamed the archaic structures of the East India Company's administration for the loss and in 1858 Parliament abolished the company entirely, placing the Indian empire under direct Crown rule. The Government of India Act created a secretary of state for India, a cabinet post responsible for Indian government and revenues, together with an advisory 15-member Council of India. In India, Lord Canning kept the title of governor-general but added to it that of viceroy, in recognition of India's new place in Great Britain's empire. Queen Victoria herself would become empress of India in 1876.

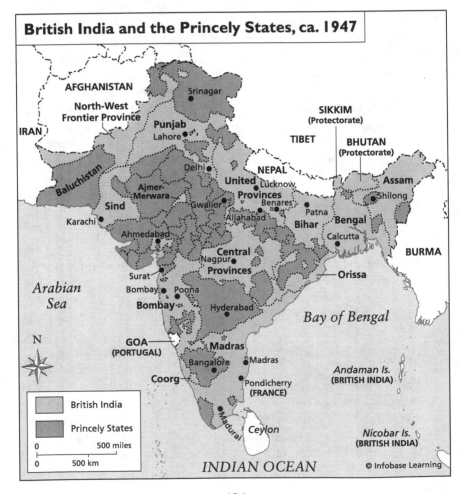

British India and the Princely States, ca. 1947

AFGHANISTAN

North-West Frontier Province

IRAN

Baluchistan

Punjab
Lahore

Srinagar

SIKKIM (Protectorate)

TIBET

BHUTAN (Protectorate)

Delhi

NEPAL

United Provinces
Lucknow

Assam
Shilong

Ajmer-Merwara

Sind

Gwalior

Benares

Allahabad

Patna

Bihar

Bengal

Karachi

Ahmedabad

Calcutta

Central Provinces
Nagpur

BURMA

Surat

Orissa

Arabian Sea

Bombay
Poona

Bombay

Hyderabad

Bay of Bengal

N

GOA (PORTUGAL)

Madras

Bangalore
Madras

Coorg

Pondicherry (FRANCE)

Andaman Is. (BRITISH INDIA)

Madurai

Ceylon

Nicobar Is. (BRITISH INDIA)

British India

Princely States

0   500 miles

0   500 km

INDIAN OCEAN

© Infobase Learning

Two rajas from the Central Provinces. Almost one-third of India was controlled by Indian princes who ruled their states under the watchful eyes of local British residents. The princes were among the strongest supporters of British rule after 1858. They ruled more than 500 to 600 princely states that ranged in size from territories as large as England to those cover-ing only several square miles. These two local rajas held territories of the smaller type in the Central Provinces during the late 19th century. (Andrew H. L. Fraser, *Among Indian Rajahs and Ryots: A Civil Servant's Recollections and Impressions of Thirty-Seven Years of Work and Sport in the Central Provinces and Bengal*, 3rd ed., 1912)

In November 1858, the Queen's proclamation—"India's Magna Carta" Indian schoolbooks later called it—announced these changes to the "Princes, Chiefs, and People of India" (Stark 1921, 11; Muir 1969, 384). The proclamation declared there would be no further religious interfer-ence in India. Dalhousie's doctrine of "lapse" was rejected, several former rulers were restored to their thrones, and the princes were assured that treaty obligations would be "scrupulously" observed in future. Aristocrats and princes were to be the new bulwark of the Crown-ruled empire; indeed, from 1858 to 1947 the territories ruled by Princely (or Native) States made up almost one-third of British India. The 500 to 600 Indian princes recognized by the British by the end of the century were, both individually and collectively, the staunchest supporters of British rule.

The Princely States were overseen by the governor-general/viceroy through his political department. The rest of British India was directly governed by the governor-general with the advice of a five-person Executive Council. The army was directly under the governor-general as were the provincial governments. At the district level, administration was through the Indian Civil Service (ICS), whose covenanted civil servants were appointed after 1853 on the basis of competitive examinations. The head of each district, variously called the "district magistrate" or the "collector," was an ICS officer. In 1861 the Indian Councils Act added members (up to the number of 12) to the governor-general's Executive Council for the purposes of legislation. Half of these additional members could be "non-officials," that is, Indians.

Economics of Imperial Expansion

The second half of the 19th century was a period of growth for India's economy and saw the increased exploitation of the empire's rural regions. The Indian government guaranteed foreign investors a rate of return whether or not their projects proved profitable, and under these arrangements British companies invested £150 million into railroads, hard-surfaced roads, and irrigation canals. Irrigation projects increased cultivated lands in regions such as the western United Provinces and in Andhra. Almost half of all new irrigation, however, was in the "canal colonies" of the Punjab where 3 million acres were added to cultivated lands by 1885 and 14 million by 1947. By the end of the century, rail routes and improved roads connected the Indian hinterlands to major sea ports, facilitating the movement of raw materials such as cotton and coal out of the country and British imports in. The opening of the Suez Canal in 1869 added further impetus to European and British commercial exploitation of the empire.

During the first 50 years of the 19th century, India had exported indigo, opium, cotton (first cloth and yarn, then later raw cotton), and silk. In the decades after the East India Company's monopoly on trade ended in 1833, private European planters developed tea and coffee estates in eastern and southern India. By 1871 tea plantations in Assam and the Nilgiri hills shipped more than 6 million pounds of tea each year. By 1885 South Indian coffee cultivation expanded to more than a quarter million acres. The jute industry linked jute cultivation in eastern Bengal to production mills in Calcutta in the late 19th century. European merchants also took control of indigo production in Bengal and Bihar; they treated their "coolie" workers so harshly that they precipitated India's first labor strike, the Blue Mutiny of 1859–60. Between 1860 and 1920, however, both the opium and indigo trades disappeared (Tomlinson 1993, 51–52). Opium exports declined from 30 percent of all Indian exports in the 1860s to nothing in 1920 as a ban on its trade came into effect. Indigo also disappeared as an export commodity, declining from 6 percent of Indian exports in the 1860s to zero in the 1920s.

THE INVENTION OF CASTE

The British were great critics of the Indian caste system, seeing it as a retrograde institution that caused the decline of India's ancient "Aryan" civilization and blighted India with its superstitions and restrictions. During British rule, however, the British government's analytic frameworks and survey practices—as well as British assumptions that caste was a fixed and unchanging social institution—politicized and changed how caste functioned. In the provincial gazetteers that were compiled beginning in 1865, caste was a major ethnographic category. In the census, the 10-year population surveys begun in 1871, caste was a core organizing principle. The 1891 census ranked castes in order of "social precedence," and in 1901 the census attempted to assign a fixed *varna* status to all castes.

From the 1880s through the 1930s, in part due to British census tabulations, hundreds of caste conferences and caste associations came into existence throughout British India. Although these regional organizations had multiple agendas and many were short lived, a common reason for organizing was to control how census tabulations recorded their caste status. Some groups met to define their status; others sent letters and petitions to protest census rankings. By 1911 many Indians believed that the purpose of the census was not to count the population but to determine caste ranks. By 1931 caste groups were distributing flyers to their members, instructing them on how to respond to census questions. Over a century of surveys and tabulations, British statistical efforts threatened to fix caste identities more permanently than at any other time in the Indian past. It is in this sense that some scholars have suggested that the British "invented" the caste system.

Source: Dirks, Nicholas B. "Castes of Mind." *Representations* 37 (Winter 1992): pp. 56–78; ———. *Castes of Mind: Colonialism and the Making of Modern India* (Princeton, N.J.: Princeton University Press, 2001).

Between 1860 and 1920, raw cotton, wheat, oilseeds, jute, and tea were the major exports of the imperial Indian economy. While the main export crops of the first half of the 19th century—opium, indigo, cotton, and silks—were traditional products, their export (with the exception of cotton) had depended largely on European enterprise and state support. The main export crops of the late 19th and early 20th century, however, were (with the exception of tea, a plantation crop) indigenous crops produced by rural peasant communities as part of the peasant crop cycle (Tomlinson 1993, 51). Raw cotton was the largest single export item. Before 1850 most Indian cotton was exported to China; after the 1870s, Indian cotton went to the European continent and to Japan. The export of Indian wheat and oilseeds (as well as rice grown in Burma) developed after the Suez Canal opened in 1869. By the 1890s about 17 percent of India's wheat was exported, and between 1902 and 1913 Indian wheat provided 18 percent of Britain's wheat imports. Jute, which provided the bags in which the world's grain exports were packed for shipment, was the most valuable Indian export during the early decades of the 20th century. Tea production began in the 1830s, and by the early 1900s Indian tea made up 59 percent of the tea consumed in Britain.

British business firms received most of the profits of India's late 19th- century export trade. British firms controlled the overseas trade in Indian export commodities and also their shipping and insurance. The secondary beneficiaries of the export trade were Indian traders, middlemen, and moneylenders. Such men facilitated the production of export crops at the rural level and usually profited regardless of export fluctuations. Of all the participants in the export trade, peasant cultivators took the greatest risks and made the least profits. Local farmers bore the brunt of the price and demand fluctuations of exporting to global markets, and as a result, rural indebtedness became a major problem in the late century. Well into the 20th century peasant cultivation, even of export crops, remained at the simplest technological level. As late as the 1950s, peasants' tools for agricultural production were still "bullocks, wooden ploughs and unsprung carts" (Tomlinson 1993, 83).

Although agricultural exports were the major reason for imperial India's economic growth, the second half of the 19th century also saw the beginnings of Indian industrial production if only on a small scale. The first Indian steam-powered cotton mill opened in Bombay in 1856. In the 1870s–80s the Indian textile industry in Bombay expanded in

Bullock cart technology. As this picture from Rajasthan in the late 1970s shows, bullocks and the carts they pulled remained a major technology of Indian farming well into the late 20th century. (courtesy of Judith E. Walsh)

earnest, as first 17 and then 79 mills opened there. Bombay cotton industries were often started by Indian traders in raw cotton looking to expand their business activities. In the Gujarati city of Ahmedabad, long a regional weaving center, indigenous banking families (shroffs) added the industrial production of cotton yarn as part of their dealings with cotton growers and handloom weavers. By 1900 Indian mill-produced yarn was 68 percent of the domestic market and also supplied a substantial export market to China and Japan. By 1913 Ahmedabad had become a major center for Indian mill-made cloth. Imported cloth, however, was half the cloth sold in India up to 1914, falling to less than 20 percent only by the 1930s.

In eastern India industrial production appeared first in the late 19th century in jute and coal businesses controlled by European and Anglo-Indian firms. Jute was manufactured by firms in Calcutta between 1880 and 1929. Coal production began in the 1840s, and by the early 1900s Indian railways used mostly local coal. In 1899 J. N. Tata, a Parsi businessman, began work on the organization of the Tata Iron and Steel Company (TISCO). The Tata family already owned cotton mills in western India and their family firm, Tata Sons and Company, was among India's largest iron and steel importers and dealers. Unable to finance their new company through London, the Tatas obtained funding from Indian investors in Bombay. In 1907 the company founded its first modern plant at Jamshedpur in Bihar.

The British in India

The long-term British residents of India, called Anglo-Indians in the 19th century, were only a small minority on the Indian subcontinent, never numbering more than 100,000, even at the height of the British Empire. The men in this community ran the upper levels of the Indian government and the Indian Civil Service and were often from families that could trace connections with India over several generations. Such connections gave Anglo-Indians as a whole both faith in their own authoritative knowledge about India and a strong vested interest in the continuance of British rule in India.

While during the course of the British Raj many Anglo-Indians made important contributions to our understanding of Indian history and culture, it is also true that the Anglo-Indian community was often the source of racist and supremacist ideas about India and its peoples. Anglo-Indians believed implicitly in the benefits of British rule in India and in what is sometimes called the "civilizing mission" of British imperialism—the belief, that is, that the British had a mission to civilize India by reforming its indigenous ways of life with the more "advanced" ideas, culture, and practices of Great Britain and the West. Such beliefs when combined with the dominant position of Anglo-Indians within British India itself often resulted in relations with Indians that were either overtly or covertly racist. And the ingrained conservative and racist attitudes of Anglo-Indian officials may also have contributed to the slowness of constitutional reforms during the late 19th and early 20th centuries.

There is some irony in the fact that while many 19th- and 20th-century British critics railed against Indian customs and caste practices, the Anglo-Indian community in India lived and worked in conditions that replicated many practices of indigenous caste or *jati* groups. Like members of Indian castes, the British ate and socialized only with each other. As in Indian castes, Anglo-Indians married only within their own community (or with people from "home"). They worshipped with and were buried by members of their own community

"IMPERIAL CHINTZ"

"The kitchen is a black hole, the pantry a sink," wrote Flora Annie Steel and Grace Gardiner in their late 19th-century manual for Anglo-Indian housewives, *The Complete Indian Housekeeper and Cook:*

> The only servant who will condescend to tidy up is a skulking savage with a reed broom; whilst pervading all things broods the stifling, enervating atmosphere of custom, against which energy beats itself unavailingly as against a feather bed. The authors themselves know what it is to look round on a large Indian household, seeing that all things are wrong, all things slovenly, yet feeling paralysed by sheer inexperience in the attempt to find a remedy. (Steel and Gardiner 1902, ix)

Like many in the late 19th century, Steel and Gardiner saw the English home in India as the local and domestic site of the more general confrontation between British civilization and Indian barbarism. By imposing proper practices of cleanliness, system, and order within their Indian homes, Anglo-Indian housewives could demonstrate both the

(continues)

Chalk Farm at Meerut, 1883. An Anglo-Indian bungalow home in Meerut, Bengal, complete with horses, dogs, and servants (harappa.com)

"IMPERIAL CHINTZ" (continued)

superior virtues of Victorian domesticity and that domesticity's ability to civilize India itself. Anglo-Indian wives who decorated their Indian homes with English chintz, grew English pansies in hill stations, arranged tea parties and croquet matches on Indian lawns, buried their children, and survived the Indian heat participated in a "public domesticity" of empire (George). They were seen (and sometimes saw themselves) as exemplars of a global and naturalized domesticity fundamental to civilization itself. The basic Anglo-Indian view that India was a decadent and uncivilized society much in need of British tutelage became specific and concrete through demonstrations of the superior virtues of the Anglo-Indian home. Anglo-Indian domesticity became an important part of the broader "civilizing mission" of British imperial rule in India.

Source: George, Rosemary Marangoly, ed. *Burning Down the House: Recycling Domesticity* (Boulder, Colo.: Westview Press, 1998), p. 51; Steel, F. A., and G. Gardiner. *The Complete Indian Housekeeper and Cook: Giving the Duties of Mistress and Servants, the General Management of the House and Practical Recipes for Cooking in All Its Branches.* 4th ed. (London: W. Heinemann, 1902), p. ix.

---

and according to its customs. And for those who broke Anglo-Indian social conventions, ostracism was as severe as for any indigenous Indian "outcaste."

The Anglo-Indian community in India developed slowly from the late 18th to the mid-19th century. In these decades it took six months to travel from England to India by way of the African cape. There were few European women in India, and company servants regularly kept Indian mistresses and socialized with local Muslim elites. In 1830, however, an overland route across Egypt shortened the journey somewhat, and in 1869 the opening of the Suez Canal cut the time for travel between England and India to just over three weeks. More Englishwomen accompanied their husbands to the subcontinent (or traveled to India in search of husbands). As a result Anglo-Indian society grew, becoming in the process both more elaborate and more restrictive.

Particularly after 1857, British urban settlements in India were physically separated from the surrounding Indian society. British cantonments (towns where armies were quartered) or provincial or district centers had sections set apart—the "Civil Lines" inhabited by Anglo-Indians and

St. Mary's in Madras. Churches were a standard feature of Anglo-Indian communities. St. Mary's Church in the city of Madras (present-day Chennai) was built in 1679. Often described as the Westminster Abbey of the East, it is the oldest British building in Chennai and the first Anglican church built in Asia. (courtesy of Judith E. Walsh)

133

Europeans. The bungalow-style residences of the Anglo-Indian officials and staff were located within these Civil Lines, as were their church, club, polo grounds, and cemetery. Army barracks were separate. And most towns and cities also had a "black town," a section for Indian residents and their businesses.

The demands and patterns of government service also bound together Anglo-Indian families and separated them further from indigenous Indian life. Anglo-Indian civilian life was extremely peripatetic, with officers and their families moving constantly from station to station over the course of a career. In addition, it was a government practice, inaugurated in the 1830s, to move officials and staff to the hills during the hot Indian summer season. The central government moved from Calcutta to the Himalayan town of Simla, while provincial governments developed their own local hill stations, such as Darjeeling for Bengal and Mahableshwar for Bombay. Not all memsahibs (wives of English officials, or sahibs) thought this was a good idea—or even necessary. Steel and Gardiner advised their readers to consider remaining in the plains with their husbands. "Don't give in to it," they said of the hot weather, "and it will give in to you" (1902, 204).

But whether in Civil Lines or in hill stations, Anglo-Indian society developed its own strict codes and customs. Just as Anglo-Indian men staffed the ICS and the upper levels of central and provincial governments, the law courts, and the military, Anglo-Indian society divided itself internally along these lines. One 20th-century Anglo-Indian joked,

> The Brahmins . . . were the members of the topmost Government service, the Indian Civil Service . . . below them were the semi-Brahmins, the various other covenanted services—the provincial civil services and so on. Then you had the military caste . . . [and the] British businessmen, very wealthy and powerful in places like Calcutta, but fairly low caste. (Allen and Mason 1976, 83)

Precedence for seating and for presentation at parties was defined by printed "civil lists." At the larger stations, dress codes were elaborate, and visiting customs, complex (Allen and Mason 1976, 68). "Dress becomingly," advised *The Complete Indian Housekeeper and Cook,* ". . . and never, even in the wilds, exist without one civilised evening and morning dress" (Steel and Gardiner 1902, 217).

The English writer Rudyard Kipling (1865–1936) wrote many stories chronicling Anglo-Indian life in India. Kipling himself came from an Anglo-Indian family. Born in Bombay, the son of Lockwood Kipling and Alice Macdonald, he had spent his early years in India, raised by Indian servants and speaking Hindustani with them. In 1871, as was common with Anglo-Indian families, he and his sister were sent "home" to England, where they boarded with a retired merchant captain and where Kipling attended school. When he returned to India in 1882, Kipling began work as a reporter for a Lahore newspaper. He was a bad reporter; he garbled facts and had no memory for details. But his stories of Anglo-Indian life began to be published, first in the local press and then as *Plain Tales from the Hills* (1888) in England. When he returned to England in 1889, he was already a popular and well-known author. He would write most of his later work, including the famous adventure novel *Kim* (1901), in either England or America, and in 1907 he would receive the Nobel Prize in literature, the first Englishman to win this honor.

Kipling's famous 1899 poem "The White Man's Burden," although written about U.S. involvement in the Philippines, nevertheless captured the Anglo-Indian community's own sense of its purpose and function in India:

> *Take up the White Man's burden—*
> *Send forth the best ye breed—*
> *Go bind your sons to exile*
> *To serve your captives' need. . . . (Howe 1982, 602)*

The self-sacrifice, honor, duty, and service that Kipling eulogized in this poem were qualities that defined, for Anglo-Indians, the meaning and purpose of their lives and work in India. The poem's assumption that all nonwhite peoples needed white "civilization" was also one with which Anglo-Indians would have agreed. For the most part neither the Anglo-Indian community nor British imperialists more generally gave much thought to the many ways British rule profited Great Britain and British citizens at the expense of India and Indian people.

Still, even in 1899 when Kipling wrote his famous poem, his views were not entirely unchallenged. The British daily, *London's Truth*, added this poetical coda to Kipling's poem:

> *Pile on the brown man's burden*
> *To satisfy your greed. (Bartlett 1992, 593)*

By 1899 there was already an audience in India that would have approved this critique of imperialism. Over the course of the 19th century English education had produced an elite class of Indians intimately familiar with the colonial modernity that British rule had brought to India. By the end of the century this Indian elite had begun to organize itself politically and was both ready and willing to add its own opinions of British greed and racism to the London paper's short coda.

5

BECOMING MODERN—THE
COLONIAL WAY (1800-1900)

To the memory of the British Empire in India which conferred subject hood
on us but withheld citizenship. To which yet everyone of us threw out
the challenge "Civis Britannicus Sum" because all that was good and living
within us was made, shaped and quickened by the same British Rule.

■

Nirad C. Chaudhuri, The Autobiography of an Unknown Indian
(1968, dedication)

As British armies consolidated imperial control across the subcontinent, British institutions and economic structures reshaped life in
towns and cities and in the countryside. British architecture redrew the
skylines of urban centers, while British technologies and administrative structures reorganized urban public spaces and public life. In rural
India a new focus on exports shifted from agricultural production for
local consumption and exchange to farm products to be sold across the
subcontinent and in world markets.

These changes had an enormous impact on Indians themselves. For
both urban and rural Indians Pax Britannica meant more than just foreign rule and India's political unity. For the high-caste sons of regional
Indian elites it meant attendance at new English-language colleges,
an introduction to the ideas and concepts of Western modernity, and
futures shaped by the need to succeed within the new occupations and
professions introduced into India along with British rule. As early as
the 1820s the members of the growing "English-educated elite" formed
literary clubs, debating societies, and religious and social reform groups
in which they debated the merits of India's past and their own and their
country's future. By the 1870s many members of this urban, middle-
class elite were joining regional political associations.

For rural Indians, however, current conditions posed more urgent problems than debates about the future. As farmers produced more crops for commercial export, substantial food shortages appeared in rural regions, particularly among poorer communities. Both famine and disease spread more quickly than ever before through India's now closely interlinked provinces. Over the last 30 years of the century major famines ravaged villages, towns, and cities, often followed closely by contagious diseases that further devastated already weakened populations. Sporadic protests during these years revealed undercurrents of local opposition to the changes brought by the new colonial regime.

Colonial Modernity

Over the course of the 19th century the British presence and power in India altered the physical, economic, social, and even domestic landscapes of urban towns and cities across the subcontinent, introducing into them the structures, ideologies, and practices of a British-mediated colonial modernity. Along with governmental and administrative offices, British rule brought to Indian cities law offices, hospitals, hotels, emporiums, schools and colleges, town halls, churches, learned societies, printers and publishers—the full panoply of 19th-century life as it existed in mid-century English or European cities. These changes were most dramatic in India's capital, Calcutta, but they also reshaped public and work spaces in most towns, cantonments, and cities throughout the Raj.

The use of English rather than Persian as the language of courts and government and the railroads, telegraphs, and unified post all contributed to the new urban British India. Along with these changes came European-style buildings and the institutional structures of Western-style office work and British administrative practices. In downtown Calcutta the old East India Company Writers' Building was rebuilt over the 1850s and 1870s into a vast Gothic brick building. Its endless corridors and offices made it the proper home for the reports, forms, receipts, officials, clerks, scribes, and peons (servants) of a colonial bureaucracy. Such workers and their array of paper procedures became the standard features of the businesses and other modern occupations introduced into India with British rule. By mid-century, office work and its routines and hierarchies defined daily life throughout urban British India.

Just as imperial-style buildings dominated public space in British India, British concepts of time, efficiency, and order organized life

Writers' Building, Calcutta, as it looked after being rebuilt in the 1850s and 1870s (courtesy of Ron Ellis, Derby, United Kingdom, and also with thanks to the Center for Study of the Life and Work of William Carey, D.D. [1761–1834], William Carey College, Hattiesburg, Mississippi)

within those spaces. Clock time (a concept almost equally new in industrialized England and Europe) structured daily public life. Office work began and ended at fixed times. Trains ran according to "time-tables," and streets were cleaned on schedule. "How the English appreciate the value of time!" wrote one Indian admiringly. "They work at the right time, eat at the right time, attend office at the right time, and play at the right time. Everything they do is governed by rules. . . . It is because of this quality that the English get the time to accomplish so much" (Chakrabarty 1993, 6). The pocket watch became an emblem of British colonial modernity for Westernized Indian men.

Printed books and newspapers were equally omnipresent signs of modern colonial life. Print culture and print capitalism—in both English and newly revitalized indigenous languages—grew quickly in the 19th century. Multiple newspapers and tracts addressed the diverse reading publics that coexisted in British Indian towns and cities. English-language newspapers for the Anglo-Indian community dated from the late 18th and early 19th centuries. The first vernacular newspaper, the *Bengali Gazette,* began in 1816. Bombay had its first Indian press in 1861; Madras had its first Indian-owned newspaper, the *Madras Mail,* in 1868. By mid-century literate Calcutta families were said to prefer printed almanacs to live astrologers. By the 1860s Indian-printed publications had become so numerous the government needed new laws to catalog and track them. Printing was the capital's second largest industry by 1911. Throughout the rest of India, as in Calcutta, a large and diverse Indian reading public consumed books of all types in both English and the many regional Indian vernaculars.

Hindu Renaissance in Bengal

The earliest urban Indian response to the ideas and practices of the English came in the 1820s from the Indian elites based in the city of Calcutta. By the 1820s Calcutta was already a "city of palaces," so named for its palatial European-style mansions. It was the capital of Britain's Indian empire and the second city of the world (after London) in Britain's global trading empire. Many well-known Bengali men in the city were descended from families grown rich either working for the East India Company or as zamindars under Bengal's permanent settlement (or sometimes as both). Dwarkanath Tagore (1794–1846), who founded the city's most famous family, built upon the fortune made by his family in Calcutta trade and then solidified that fortune through the purchase of extensive zamindari estates in eastern Bengal. Rammohan

Belvedere House, Calcutta. Belvedere and its 30-acre estate in south Calcutta was occupied during the 19th century by the lieutenant governors of Bengal. When the capital was moved to New Delhi in 1911, Belvedere became the Calcutta residence of the viceroy. Today it houses the collection of the National Library of India. (courtesy of Judith E. Walsh)

RAMMOHAN ROY

Rammohan Roy (1772–1833) was one of India's earliest public figures, a man whose interest in and response to Western ideas later won him the title of the "Father of Modern India." After retiring to Calcutta in 1815, Roy wrote and published newspapers in English, Persian, and Bengali. He was deeply opposed to idolatry, which he found in both Hinduism and in the Christian idea of the Trinity. He also opposed the Hindu custom of sati, which, it was said, he had once seen a member of his own family commit. In 1804 Roy wrote a tract in Persian denouncing image worship, and in 1818, a tract in English opposing sati. Another English publication, his 1820 "The Precepts of Jesus," praised aspects of Christianity. In 1828 Roy founded the Brahmo Sabha (later renamed the Brahmo Samaj, or "Society about the Absolute Being"). He based his new religious association on the ancient Hindu Upanishads; there he found a monotheism that demonstrated, as he put it, the "unity of the Supreme Being as sole Ruler of the Universe." In 1830 Roy traveled to England to visit English Unitarian friends in Bristol with whom he had long corresponded. He died in Bristol three years later, in 1833.

Source: Quotation from Kopf, David. *The Brahmo Samaj* (Princeton, N.J.: Princeton University Press, 1979), p. 14.

Roy (1772–1833), later called the "Father of Modern India," worked for the East India Company in various capacities before retiring to Calcutta as a wealthy zamindar in 1815. Gopimohan Deb, the father of the conservative Hindu Radhakanta Deb (1784–1867), had been Robert Clive's Persian secretary and *munshi* (clerk) and acquired large zamindari estates in the late 18th century.

In 1817 Tagore and the Debs (father and son), along with other locally prominent English and Indian men, founded Hindu College, a private English-language school for the boys of their own and other similar families in the city. Gopimohan Deb became the school's first director, and a year later Radhakanta Deb took over the directorship, a position he held through the 1830s. Rammohan Roy also approved of English education and supported the college—but not openly. He was already an anathema to many Calcutta Hindus because of his well-known opposition to Hindu idolatry and his interest in Christianity.

Jorasanko Thakurbari, Tagore family mansion in Calcutta. Jorasanko Thakurbari was a residence in north Calcutta—the "black," or Indian, part of town—but it was as palatial and grand as the European-style homes to the south. Today the building houses the Rabindra Bharati Museum. (courtesy of Judith E. Walsh)

In the late 1820s (the same period in which the government made sati illegal and Roy founded his Brahmo Sabha) students of the new Hindu College began to put their education's ideas into practice. The students had come under the influence of a young Eurasian teacher at the college, Henry Derozio (1809–31), who had lectured on rationalism, the European Enlightenment, and the French Revolution. Determined to demonstrate their opposition to what they now saw as the irrational superstitions of Hinduism, Hindu College students began to eat meals together that broke Hindu dietary and commensality laws and to attend public meetings at which they were heard shouting "Down with Hinduism! Down with orthodoxy!" (Bhattacharjee 1986, 113). In one scandalous and provocative incident several students threw beef bones into the courtyard of a prominent Brahman family.

The director of Hindu College, Radhakanta Deb, had already made his convictions on reform issues known by founding the Hindu Dharma Sabha (Hindu Association for Dharma), a group that had collected signatures for a Privy Council petition against the new anti-sati law. Blaming Derozio for the students' behavior Deb and his associates forced Derozio's resignation from the college. It made no difference. Over the next decade Hindu College students, graduates, and sympathizers—later collectively labeled "Young Bengal"—founded clubs and associations, started newspapers, and wrote tracts and plays, all with the goal of reforming and rationalizing Hindu religious and customary practices, or (as one participant put it) of achieving the "eradication of Hindu idolatry" (Bhattacharjee 1986, 139).

Later scholars would call this movement the "Hindu Renaissance" because of its participants' desire to see Hinduism "reborn," shorn of its idolatry and superstitions. But the Hindu Renaissance was as much about social and cultural reform—about adaptation to British colonial modernity—as it was about religion. While a strong Christian missionary presence in and around Calcutta in the 1830s shaped the language and rhetoric with which men such as Roy and the student reformers wrote and spoke, few Hindus actually converted to Christianity in this period. In the second half of the 19th century, as the ideas and practices of British colonial modernity became institutionalized in the routines of office work in Indian towns and cities and through the teachings of an expanding English-language educational system, later conflicts over reform and adaptation would take on a more secular tone.

The Hindu Renaissance was also, as many contemporaries pointed out, a generational struggle among the men of elite Calcutta families. Participants on both sides of the conflict, both "orthodox" men such as Radhakanta Deb and "reformers" such as Roy and the Hindu College students, were members of a Calcutta elite already substantially influenced by Western ideas and practices. What they disagreed over was the degree of adaptation, the degree to which reform ideas and practices should replace older customs and traditions. Later in the 19th century, as the Western-style employment of English-educated men became increasingly necessary for their families' economic well-being, the Western ideas and practices such men advocated would become more acceptable, even to more conservative family elders.

English Education

The Wood Dispatch of 1854 had established the outlines of an English education system in India with university centers at Calcutta, Bombay, and Madras. Over the next half century, as English-language education became a required credential for elite employment throughout British India, both the number of schools and their enrollments rose dramatically. In 1854 there were only 180 English-language schools at all levels (primary through college) in the country. By 1885 most provinces had English-language schools, and 78 colleges were affiliated to the three university centers. By 1902, 140 arts colleges enrolled 17,000 college-level students. Two years later, the system expanded to five universities with 200 affiliated colleges. By 1918 Calcutta University's 27,000 students made it the largest university in the world.

Although organized by region, the educational system was remarkably uniform both in structure and in content across British India. Regardless of region, students studied English, a classical language (European or Indian), mathematics, logic, physical science, geography, and history in their first two years. They were tested on these subjects through written examinations whose questions were set two years in advance and whose answers were to be factual and detailed, based on information in a recommended textbook. In history, for instance, exam questions might ask students to name "some of the chief of our liberties established by the Magna Carta," or ask "Who was the founder of the Mahratta [sic] dynasty? Give a brief account of his career" (Punjab University Calendar 1874, 195; Calcutta University Calendar 1861, 32).

The standard for passing was severe. At the Matriculation Examination (M.E.), required for entrance into the college curriculum, half the candidates regularly failed. At the B.A. level, the pass rate was even lower, just above 10 percent. Between 1857 and 1885, for instance, 48,000 candidates passed the M.E., but only slightly more than 5,100 obtained a B.A. degree. By the end of the century, Indians who had studied in the system but had failed their examinations took to appending "B.A. Failed" to their names on cards and publications as an indication of their English-language credentials.

The English-Educated Elite

The young Indian men who graduated from English education institutions were part of what contemporaries called the "English-educated elite." The numbers of such men were minuscule in relation to the wider Indian population, not even 1 percent of the total as late as 1900. Nevertheless this elite dominated Indian religious, social, and political movements throughout the late 19th and 20th centuries. It was the urban, middle-class English-educated elite who organized the religious and social reform movements of the late 19th and early 20th centuries; it was English-educated men who agitated for widow remarriage, against child marriage, and for women's literacy and education. In the last decades of the 19th century it would be the Westernized elite that provided the organizational base and the leadership for the Indian nationalist movement.

DEFINING THE MIDDLE CLASS

The English-educated elite were a wealthy select community, less than 0.3 percent of the total Indian population in the 1880s, according to one estimate (McCully). Nevertheless they were frequently referred to, then and now, as the "Indian middle class." There were two reasons for the use of this term. First, many 19th-century British and Indian writers assumed that there was an analogy to be made between the "respectable" educated classes of Indian society and the bourgeoisie of various European countries. And second, as urban professionals and/or office workers, the English-educated fell into no other category of Indian life: They came from the upper castes (usually defined as those linked with the Brahman, Kshatriya, or Vaishya *varnas*) but not from any one caste or *varna*. They were not a hereditary aristocracy, nor were they peasants.

The "Indian middle class," to the extent that it can be defined as such in the 19th century, lived professional lives structured by employment within the British Raj and had lifestyles broadly adapted to the ideas and practices of British colonial modernity. The men of such families were invariably literate, usually in both English and at least one vernacular language. Family backgrounds were generally those of high-caste Hindu or *ashraf* Muslim, and often these families had traditions of service within the courts and provincial centers of earlier Muslim rulers. In income, members could range from the wealthiest descendants of zamindars to impoverished office clerks.

Source: McCully, Bruce. *English Education and the Origins of Indian Nationalism* (New York: Columbia University Press, 1940), p. 177.

Although schooled in different regions and speaking different vernaculars, English-educated graduates had much in common. Most were Hindus, relatively high caste, and from families already literate in the languages of the Mughal Empire (Persian or Urdu) or in Sanskrit. The educational system through which they passed added to this shared background a common language (English) and a perspective shaped by common Western ideas and values of the time. Indian students, although living under the absolute imperial power of the Raj, memorized the "rights" given by the Magna Carta; they learned about science and scientific method; and they rehearsed the "Benefits of British Rule"—an obligatory chapter in many Indian history textbooks that listed the benefits of technology, peace, and prosperity that the British had brought to India.

School textbooks actively urged students to acculturate, to become Anglicized and Westernized, and to leave behind the decadent accretions of their indigenous pasts. After acculturation would come prominent positions within British India, schoolbooks promised; it was the British government's intention, as one text put it, "to offer a large share in the administration . . . to natives of India who were qualified by character and education" (Thompson 1908, 393). The educational system, however, taught more than a simple message of acculturation. It also taught schoolboys about India's "degenerate" past and their own "weak" and/ or "effeminate" natures. Caste, idolatry, the treatment of women, India's debilitating climate, and vegetarianism were, according to schoolbooks, responsible for India's backward and superstitious culture and its puny and small citizenry. The nationalist leader Mohandas K. Gandhi (1869–1948) recalled from his Gujarati youth a verse that ran

> Behold the mighty Englishman,
> He rules the Indian small,
> Because being a meat-eater
> He is five cubits tall. (1957, 21)

British racism was institutionalized within an educational system that simultaneously taught Indian inferiority and British superiority. These superior Western qualities and inferior Indian counterparts became base points of a core identity increasingly internalized over the 19th and 20th centuries in succeeding generations of English-educated families. After graduation, employment in British institutions or under British superiors introduced the educated elite to racial prejudices but in more personal circumstances. One English-educated Punjabi gentleman, for instance, worked as an engineer for the government in turn-of-the-century India and admired many qualities of his British employers, but at work he had the sense of being always "on test." The British, his son remembers the father saying, "could afford to relax because if things went wrong they managed to explain it to each other. . . . But when an Indian made a mistake the reaction, if an understanding one, was that the job, perhaps, was too difficult for him" (Tandon 1968, 210–211).

Religious and Social Reform Associations

"The Life of the Educated Native: What Should It Be?" This was the title of a student essay in the 1870s and a question many Western-educated Indians asked themselves in the second half of the 19th century. "Rationalism" and the "Enlightenment" were the keys to a modern future; just as caste, idolatry, and superstition were its anathema. But beyond schoolbook formulas lay the thornier realm of actual practice. The wearing of a sacred thread, prohibitions against eating beef, restrictions on commensality (sharing food across caste lines), prohibitions against the use of utensils for eating and against overseas travel, the ban on widow remarriage, and the customs of child marriage and of purdah—all were linked to social practices embedded in Hindu daily and domestic life. The changed conditions of life in British-ruled India politicized these practices (and many more), precipitating debates and conflicts within Westernized communities. The religious and social reform associations that formed over the latter half of the 19th century were the contexts in which the Western educated debated the degree to which they would adapt themselves, their religions, and the Indian past to the ideas and practices of British colonial modernity.

The Brahmo Samaj and the Prarthana Samaj

Originally founded by Rammohan Roy in 1828, the Brahmo Samaj expanded throughout the second half of the 19th century, gaining new followers and splitting several times over issues of practice. By the end of the century Brahmos functioned almost as a separate caste within Bengali Hindu society. They had their own religious beliefs and practices, their own "churches," and their own social rituals. Their children's marriages were arranged within the Brahmo community.

In the 1840s and 1850s Debendranath Tagore (1817–1905) renewed the Brahmo Samaj as a religious association committed to the monotheistic worship of a formless deity. Then in 1866 Keshab Chandra Sen (1838–84) left Tagore's society to found the Brahmo Samaj of India, a society in which members could aggressively practice their religious beliefs. Sen's Brahmos refused to wear the Hindu sacred thread or to perform Hindu rituals or death ceremonies, practices that provoked violence, ostracism, and disinheritance from converts' families. Sen established ashrams (hostels) for Brahmo converts who needed shelter, and his Brahmos traveled throughout Bengal and India as missionaries spreading the Brahmo faith. In 1878, however, when Sen ignored Brahmo reforms in order to marry his daughter to a Hindu prince, younger members left him to form the Sadharan Brahmo Samaj (the People's Brahmo Samaj), a sect with even more reformist practices particularly in regard to women. Sadharan girls wore petticoats under

The Sadharan Brahmo Samaj (the People's Brahmo Samaj) was formed by a split away from Keshab Sen's Brahmo group in 1878 over differences in the practice of the Brahmos' monotheistic faith. The building for the new sect was begun the next year, on Cornwallis Street (now Bidhan Sarani) in Calcutta. Debendranath Tagore, although himself still a member of the original Brahmo group (the Adi Brahmo Samaj), gave 7,000 rupees toward the building project. The new mandir (temple) opened in 1881. (courtesy of Judith E. Walsh)

their saris and ate at European-style tables using Western utensils; they studied math and science and were encouraged to go to college.

Sen's missionary lectures in Bombay inspired the founding there in the late 1860s of a West Indian religious reform group, the Prarthana Samaj (Prayer Society). One of its early leaders, Mahadev Govind Ranade (1842–1901), was a Chitpavan Brahman from the Konkan region who became a lawyer and later judge in the Pune region. The Prarthana Samaj shared Brahmo ideas on monotheism and on the desirability of reforming caste customs, particularly in regard to women, but, as elsewhere, orthodox pressure could make it difficult to translate these beliefs into practice. Ranade, for instance, spent much of his life working for social reform, arranging Bombay's first widow remarriage in 1862, founding the Society for the Encouragement of Widow Remarriage shortly thereafter, and later (1884) founding the Deccan Education Society to promote girls' education (Wolpert 1962, 11). But when his first wife died in 1873, he did not marry a Hindu widow, as he had long advocated and as he wished; instead he accepted the 11-year-old bride chosen for him by his father.

Muslim Education and Reform

Writing about conditions in India after the 1857 rebellion, the well-known Urdu poet Maulana Altaf Hussain Hali (1837–1914) said:

> We [Muslims] are not trusted by the government,
> Not are we among the prominent courtiers or the ruler
> Neither are we among the educated elite
> We have no share in trade or the industry
> Nor do you found [sic] us in the civil services
> Or among the businesses.... (Khalidi 1995, 52)

Muslim elites had been slow to enlist under the British rulers who had replaced them, and Muslim families had been reluctant to enroll their sons in English-language schools. But Muslim religious leaders were not unaware of the changed society around them. Northern Indian Muslim elites saw their control over positions in regional government services steadily declining in the second half of the 19th century, from 65 percent in 1857 to 35 percent by the early 20th century, as Muslims lost ground to English-educated applicants from Hindu trading, money lending, and professional communities.

The six years between 1868 and 1875 saw the founding of competing Muslim educational institutions in the towns of Deoband and Aligarh in northern India (modern Uttar Pradesh). These two institutions appealed to different levels of elite Muslim society and offered different responses to British rule in India. The Deoband Dar-ul-Ulum was a madrassa (religious seminary) founded in 1868 for the education of Muslim *ulama* (theologian-scholars). It took an orthodox approach to Islamic studies, attracted poorer but elite Muslim students, and produced teachers for local religious schools throughout its region. Deoband offered a traditional Islamic curriculum. But it taught in Western-style classrooms modeled on the British school system and used the North Indian language Urdu. In the 20th century Deoband's relatively anti-British politics would cause its teachers, students, and graduates to align themselves with the Indian nationalist movement.

The other school, the Muhammadan Anglo-Oriental College, was the first Muslim English-language college in India. It was founded at Aligarh in 1875 by the Muslim reformer (and later Muslim separatist) Sir Sayyid Ahmad Khan (1817–98). Sayyid Ahmad's family was highly placed within the Mughal nobility at Delhi, but he himself had worked many years under the British. He founded the Scientific Society in 1864 and a modern Urdu-language journal in 1870, hoping through these media to demonstrate to upper-class Muslims that Western science was compatible with and complementary to the teachings of Islam. Impressed by Western colleges on a trip to England in 1875, Sayyid Ahmad founded Aligarh (as the school came to be known) on the model of Cambridge University. The school taught classes in English and combined Western and Islamic subjects within a single curriculum. Sayyid Ahmad wrote in a letter at the time,

> *The adoption of the new system of education does not mean the renunciation of Islam. It means its protection. . . . The truth of Islam will shine the more brightly if its followers are well educated, familiar with the highest in the knowledge of the world; it will come under an eclipse if its followers are ignorant. (De Bary 1958, 745)*

Unlike Deoband, Aligarh's students were drawn from the wealthier Muslim landlord and service communities of northern India.

Aligarh's "reformist" religious attitudes, however, placed it and its founder in opposition to contemporaneous pan-Islamic movements from the Middle East. In the 1880s, one pan-Islamicist, Jamal al-Din al-Afghani, lived and lectured in both Calcutta and Hyderabad; al-Afghani's movement stressed the role of the Ottoman sultan as supreme leader of a worldwide Muslim community. In his speeches al-Afghani argued for Hindus and Muslims to unite against the British in India and abroad, a position the Deobandis found attractive, and British government officials, alarming. Aligarh had always received considerable government funding; Sayyid Ahmad's pro-British views had led the British to hope that the school would develop a new (pro-British) Muslim elite that would dominate Indian Muslim communities. In the 1880s the British further raised their economic support for the college, and this was one of the factors that led Aligarh to become the premier English-language institution for Muslim Indian students in India.

Arya Samaj

The North Indian religious reform association, the Arya Samaj, was founded in 1875 in Bombay and in 1877 in the Punjab. It shared many of the same reform concerns as the Bengal and Bombay associations but added to these an aggressively militant stance in relation to other North Indian religions. Dayananda Sarasvati (1824–83), the society's founder, was a Gujarati *sannyasi* (holy man) with little interest in English education. In his early career Dayananda dressed and lived as a holy man, spoke in Sanskrit, and debated orthodox Hindu priests. After a trip to Calcutta in 1872 during which he met Debendranath Tagore and other Brahmos, Dayananda abandoned his mendicant clothing and began speaking in Hindi, a language that allowed him to reach an audience of Western-educated professionals and trading communities (Jones 1989).

His teachings resonated with these groups, particularly in the Punjab and northern Indian regions where followers nicknamed him the "Luther of India." Dayananda traveled these regions debating competing religionists (Muslims, Sikhs, or Hindu Sanatanists, that is, orthodox Hindus). He based his "purified" Hinduism on the Sanskrit Vedas and rejected the popular Puranas, polytheism, idolatry, caste exclusivity, and customary restrictions on women. In Dayananda's Hinduism, *jatis* (local caste divisions) should be replaced by a *varna* system that would be fixed for boys and girls "according to merits and actions" (Jaffrelot 1996, 14).

In the 20th century both the Brahmo Samaj and the Prarthana Samaj remained focused on religious and cultural reform and subsequently declined in influence and membership. In contrast, the Arya Samaj switched its focus from reform and education to Hindu revivalism and nationalism and remained a vital and popular movement.

Theosophical Society

The theosophist movement of the late 19th century was also a religious reform society, but one that drew its membership primarily from

Europeans and Americans. The society was founded in New York City in 1875 by a Russian, Helena Petrovna Blavatsky, and an American, Colonel Henry Steel Olcott. The society's religious ideas were originally drawn from Jewish mysticism and Western occultist movements. In 1879, Madame Blavatsky traveled to India to meet Swami Dayananda Sarasvati, whose Arya Samaj movement greatly interested her. Within a few years the society based its religious ideas on Hindu and Buddhist concepts of karma and reincarnation. Madame Blavatsky established the Indian headquarters of the Theosophist Society in Madras in 1882.

The Women's Question

Throughout the second half of the 19th century the "women's question" encompassed a set of concerns debated in many Indian forums. For British critics Indian women's social conditions demonstrated the backwardness and decadence of Indian civilization. In public meetings and tracts Western-educated Indian men debated the need to reform practices such as the early age of marriage (child marriage), the seclusion of women (purdah), the ban on widow remarriage, and the Hindu religion's prohibition against women's literacy and education. At the same time young Western-educated Indian men read *Romeo and Juliet* in college classes and often wrote passionately of their desire for romantic love and companionate marriage.

Both to reform women's social conditions and to create wives more to their liking, young English-educated men founded numerous societies for women's social reform and education during the second half of the 19th century. Women's education grew rapidly in this period among urban elites. In the mid-19th century provinces such as Bengal had had only a small number of girls in school, but by the 20th century education was an accepted part of an urban middle-class girl's life. Many customary practices regarding women had changed or been adapted in urban and middle-class families: The age of marriage had risen, women appeared more frequently in public, and even widow remarriage had become marginally acceptable, especially for child widows, that is, girls whose "husbands" had died before the marriage was consummated. Two million girls were in schools in 1927, a small percentage of the total population of women but nevertheless a dramatic increase. Women's education was now identified with the general progress of Indian society: "Educating a girl," said one early 20th-century reformer, "means educating a family" (Chanana 1988, 97).

The Dance of the Emancipated Bengalee Lady by *Gaganendranath Tagore, ca. 1918–21.*
Tagore (1867–1938) was born at Jorasanko, the Tagore mansion in north Calcutta, and was
the nephew of Rabindranath Tagore. Well known as an artist, cartoonist, and social critic,
Tagore drew several versions of this cartoon. He titled this version Colour Scream, *noting*
"the times are changed and we are changed with them" and drawing his very liberated Indian
lady dancing with a rather red- (and pig-) faced English dancing partner. (Chandi Lahiri)

A GUJARATI WOMAN'S JOURNAL

The new wives desired by young Western educated men in the late 19th century were to be modern, literate, and educated. Equally important they were to bring new domestic skills to family and home life. During the late 19th and early 20th centuries many domestic magazines and manuals appeared in North Indian languages, specifically addressed to women (both Hindu and Muslim) and written to teach women the new skills needed for modern home management, cooking, account keeping, child care, hygiene, and married life. The manuals and magazines of the 19th century were almost all written or edited by English educated Indian men, but by the 20th century Indian women had taken over the production of these materials. The Gujarati-language journal *Stribodh* (Enlightenment of women) published from 1857 well into the 20th century, was part of this domestic literature. *Stribodh* encouraged women to use their leisure reading for domestic and self-improvement. Its issues profiled "An Inspiring Woman" (for example, Queen Victoria or Florence Nightingale) and offered instructions on sewing, embroidery, and drawing, advice on how to purchase and arrange furniture, how to hire servants, how to use Western eating utensils, and on the moral benefits of reformed practices like the wearing of shoes and socks. Of special concern was how a wife cared for a husband when he returned home after a hard day at the office. Here are a few of *Stribodh*'s suggestions:

   i. Arrange the house neatly and aesthetically.
   ii. Keep the children neat and disciplined.
   iii. Do not shout at children or beat them.
   iv. Dress in nice clothes, especially to receive him when he returns home in the evening.
   v. Manage the servants well but do not mix with them.
   vi. Never sit idle.
   vii. Do not sit with other women to gossip and make idle talk.
   viii. Do not complain to your husband about your children, mother-in-law, and sisters-in-law.
   ix. Do not complain to him about your problems in household management.
   x. Sing or play a musical instrument to help your husband relax when he returns home.
   xi. Speak to him in a soft and pleasant manner.
   xii. Do not ever nag him. (Shukla 1991, 65)

Source: Shukla, Sonal. "Cultivating Minds: 19th Century Gujarati Women's Journals." *Economic and Political Weekly,* 26 October, 1991, p 65.

Rural India

Even as British rule reshaped Indian towns and cities and the urban Westernized Indian elite explored the ideas and practices of colonial modernity, in the Indian countryside a much larger population struggled to deal with the consequences of higher land revenues, a more commercially oriented agriculture, famine, and disease. India was a rural and agricultural society throughout the 19th and 20th centuries. In 1901 there were only 2,100 towns and cities in British India; India's total population was 284 million, and villages held 90 percent of those people.

Although records for 19th-century village life are limited, scholars think villages were populated by multiple castes and subcastes in the north and in the south by castes and subcastes that identified primarily with the Brahman or the Shudra *varna*. Religious and social relations in northern villages were structured through local castes' and subcastes' *varna* identifications. Hereditary service relationships (called *jajmani* relations) bound village service and subordinate castes to the dominant caste of a village, that is, to the caste community that owned the greatest amount of the land surrounding the village.

During the 19th century, the British land settlements redefined rural life for the purpose of revenue collection by awarding land ownership to select categories of Indian peasants. In permanent settlement regions, such as Bengal, land ownership was awarded on the basis of prior zamindar (tax collector) status; in later settlements (particularly in south India), on the basis of land cultivation (*ryotwari*, or peasant, cultivation). In both types of settlement, however, landholdings became further subdivided over time, either as a result of divisions due to inheritance or because landowners subleased their lands to subordinate cultivators. Further, by the 20th century (if not earlier), large numbers of peasant households both owned land and worked as tenants on other families' lands. In the 1950s when the first direct surveys of land control were done, 75 percent of rural households held less than five acres of land and 23 percent owned no land at all.

Below village landowners, partial landowners, and tenants was the poorest rural class: the landless laborer. These workers had no rights in lands and survived only by working the lands of others. These workers and their families were often desperately poor; in 1881 one British official noted that this class permanently lacked sufficient food. By some estimates, landless laborers and their families numbered more than 52 million in 1901, almost 20 percent of the total Indian population. They came mostly from lower caste and tribal communities.

Commercialization of Agriculture, 1860–1920

During the second half of the 19th century Indian rural products became increasingly integrated into global markets, and Indian peasants shifted to growing raw materials for export to these markets. Peasant proprietors had an absolute need for cash funds both to pay land revenues and sometimes to buy seed crops. Money lenders, whether locals or outsiders (such as Marwari traders said to have come originally from Rajasthan), were the peasants' only source of funds. Local food crops grown for exchange within the village economy were less attractive than the commercial export crops—cotton, jute, wheat, oilseeds, tea, indigo, opium—that could be grown for cash.

From the 1860s to the 1920s the commercialization of agriculture reshaped rural India, altering the crops planted as well as patterns of rural relationships. Agriculture expanded from 1881 to 1931, and the number of agricultural workers rose 28 percent. But peasant economies, growing crops for export, could now also be destroyed by fluctuating world markets, and both rural indebtedness and loss of land became major rural problems in this period. During the 1860s and 1870s, for instance, the worldwide shortage of cotton caused by the American Civil War encouraged Indian peasants to increase cotton plantings. When the Civil War ended and cotton from the U.S. South reentered the world market, prices for Indian-produced cotton plunged. In addition, as Indian farmers switched to export crops, they lowered their production of food crops, particularly of the millets and pulses that fed poorer people in their economies. Between the 1890s and the 1940s commercial crops increased by 85 percent, but the overall production of food crops declined by almost 30 percent. More rigid contractual agreements and new transportation networks linking Indian regions and tying into a world market worked together to give local producers little flexibility in deciding where their crops would go.

Famine

Famine had been a regular feature of Indian life from at least the 12th century, usually caused by the failure or excess of monsoon rains and usually limited in impact to a single region. Severe famines had occurred during both the Delhi Sultanate and the Mughal Empire. Under East India Company rule, in 1769–70 a famine in Bengal killed one-quarter of the region's population.

From the 1860s into the early years of the 20th century, however, a new pattern of famine emerged in British India. The commercialization of Indian agriculture reduced supplies of locally consumed food crops, at the same time as railroads and roads tied even remote hinterlands into the wider Indian economy. Fixed contracts moved crops out of a region for sale elsewhere regardless of local conditions and even as local shortages mounted. Famines that once had been local or regional now spread more widely, affecting food supplies and causing deaths across several regions or even the whole country. Infectious diseases (bubonic plague in the 19th century, influenza in the 20th) often followed in the wake of these mass famines, attacking populations already weakened by starvation.

The first of this new type of famine was the 1866–67 "Orissa famine," a spreading series of food shortages and dearth that extended from the Ganges River valley down the eastern seacoast (well past Orissa) through the Madras Presidency and west into Hyderabad and Mysore. The Orissa famine caused 800,000 famine deaths and affected more than 3 million people. ("Famine deaths" are calculated by subtracting the number of deaths normally expected in a region or period from the number of deaths that occur.)

Orissa was followed over the next several decades by an almost continuous series of regional or multiregional famines. In 1868–70 a second famine caused 400,000 deaths in the western Ganges, Rajasthan, central India, and the northern Deccan; 1873–74 saw severe famine in Bengal and eastern India; 1875–76 in the Deccan; 1876–78 in the Ganges region and in the cities of Madras, Hyderabad, Mysore, and Bombay. At the end of the century two devastating India-wide famines occurred one after the other: The 1896–97 famine affected 96 million Indians and caused more than 5 million famine deaths; the 1899–1900 famine affected 60 million Indians, also causing 5 million deaths.

Initially the British Indian government attributed the increased famines to monsoon failures and bad weather and argued that government intervention would only make conditions worse. But during the viceroyalty of Edward Robert Bulwer-Lytton (Lord Lytton) in the late 1870s, public outcry in Great Britain forced some government intervention. In 1883 a more Liberal viceroy, George Frederick Samuel Robinson, Lord Ripon, passed the Famine Code, a series of regulations to guide government interventions in famines and food shortages. The code prescribed methods for the early determination of shortages, declaring states of scarcity and famine, and using railways and shipping to move grain into famine regions. By the early 20th century the Famine Code, in conjunction with more aggressive food relief and public health measures, had all but eliminated mass famine deaths from India.

Rural Protests

After 1857 there was never again a regional uprising that threatened British dominance in India. Nevertheless British land revenue pressures, peasant indebtedness, and widespread famines produced a series of smaller, regional, tribal, communal, and caste uprisings during the second half of the 19th century. Before 1857 local uprisings were most likely to be organized by regional rulers, chiefs, or zamindars dispossessed by an expanding British authority. After 1857, however, surviving princes and zamindars became staunch supporters of the Raj. Rural rebellions and social protests, some of the most important of which are described below, came mostly from lower-caste and -class communities and were not always directed against the British.

Tribal Rebellions

Tribals, or Scheduled Tribes, were forest-dwelling communities linked by kinship rather than caste and found throughout the subcontinent wherever cultivated lands met unexploited forests. By the late 19th century tribals still made up perhaps 10 percent of the total Indian population. British laws gave land and tenancy rights to peasant farming populations that paid land revenues but not to tribal communities that used the forests for hunting and gathering or for shifting cultivation but paid no revenues for this use.

Throughout the 19th century the British government made repeated efforts to force the tribal communities of northeastern Bengal, Bihar, central India, Gujarat, and Madras into cultivation (and the payment of land taxes) wherever possible. Violent protests against these pressures from the 1850s to the 1920s came from the Santhals in northeastern India (1855), from Naikda tribes in Gujarat (1868), and from several different communities in Madras Presidency (1879–80, 1886, and 1900). The largest tribal uprising, however, was the 1899–1900 Ulgulan (great tumult) of the Munda tribespeople of southern Bihar. By the 1890s Munda traditional lands had been seized by Hindu migrants from the plains and encroached on by the British government itself. Birsa Munda (ca. 1874–1900), a sharecropper convert to Vaishnavism with some missionary education, became the leader of the Munda movement in 1899. Claiming to be a new prophet Birsa Munda urged his followers to kill Hindus, Muslims, and Christians, telling them that the weapons of the British police would magically melt into water once fighting began. Between December 1899 and January 1900 the Birsaites attacked churches and police stations in Ranchi district before being captured and imprisoned. Birsa Munda himself died in jail, and 350 Mundas were tried, three of whom were hanged and 44 transported for life.

Moplah Rebellions

Along the Malabar Coast, a Muslim community called the Moplahs (Mappilas) had developed out of mid-seventh to ninth-century Arab trading settlements. When the British took over the region in the early 19th century, they gave landlord rights to Hindu upper-caste groups. A series of violent conflicts between the Moplahs and their Hindu landlords erupted, occurring in 1836, 1854, 1882–85, 1896, and 1921. In these uprisings small bands of Moplahs attacked high-caste Hindu landlords and moneylenders, desecrated temples, and led suicide attacks against local police.

Peasant Protests

Peasant groups in the Deccan and in eastern India used a combination of violence, mass meetings, and legal challenges to seek relief from high land revenues and rural indebtedness in the decades after 1870. In 1875 the Deccan was torn by riots following the fall of cotton prices after the American Civil War. Villagers facing bankruptcy and the loss of lands joined together in attacks on the Marwari moneylenders to whom they were in debt. One of the Deccan's worst famines followed on the heels of riots, and the combination drove many peasants into banditry. Vasudeo Balvant Phadke (1845–83), a Chitpavan Brahman petty clerk in Pune, led a multicaste *dacoit* (bandit) gang in this period. Phadke declared himself the new minister to Shivaji II (an 18th-century descendant of Shivaji) and led a series of robberies to finance what he hoped would be a more general rebellion against the British. Captured in 1879, Phadke was sentenced to transportation for life and died four years later.

In eastern Bengal, Assam, and Bombay, peasant movements turned to organization and legal actions to protest the imposition of higher land revenues. In 1873 in Pabna district in eastern Bengal, prosperous peasants organized protest meetings, rent strikes, and legal challenges to fight zamindar rent increases. In two districts of Assam in 1893, village assemblies and local elites used rent strikes to protest higher revenue settlements. In the region surrounding Bombay city, the famine of 1896–97 led to the looting of grain stores and to general demands for the remission of revenues. When the Bombay government refused these demands, a Pune political association, the Sarvajanik Sabha, sent representatives out to the villages to inform peasants of their rights to rent remissions under British famine law. In the later famine of 1899–1900 "no revenue" movements also appeared in Surat and Ahmedabad.

Jyotirao Phule's Non-Brahman Movement

Not all protest was anti-British, however. In 1873 Jyotirao Phule (1827–90), whose family was part of a relatively prosperous but low in status *mali* (gardener) caste in Pune, founded the Satyashodhak Samaj (Truth Seeking Society), an organization whose purpose was to unify the lower castes. Having completed his secondary education in English at a Pune school run by missionaries of the Free Church of Scotland, Phule read works on the lives of Shivaji II and the first U.S. president, George Washington, as well as the writings of the 18th-century revolutionary Thomas Paine. He wanted to bring together what he called the *bahujan samaj* (the masses, the multitude) to free them from upper-caste oppression. In Phule's reading of Indian history the low castes and Untouchables, the original inhabitants of India, had been forced into "Brahmin thralldom" by invading foreign Aryans (Jaffrelot 2003, 153). For Phule the British were liberators, come to India to free "the disabled Shudras from the slavery of the crafty Aryas" (Wolpert 1962, 7). Phule's movement developed into a 20th-century Marathi protest movement that was village-based and anti-Brahman.

Second Afghan War, 1878–1880

The small revolts in the Indian interior that occurred after the 1857 rebellion could be easily contained by police and armies. But in the 1870s slow Russian advances into the Central Asian region of Turkistan renewed the fears of British officials in London that Russia might attack India through the Afghan country to the northwest. To ensure a sympathetic Afghan regime, the viceroy, Lord Lytton, deposed the Afghan ruler, Sher Ali, in 1878, replacing him with one of his sons, Yakub Khan; however, in September 1879 the British political resident and his entire staff were massacred at Kabul in a popular uprising. British armies retaliated with great brutality. The cost and the violence of the war provoked public opposition in Great Britain. With the fall of the Conservative government and the appointment of the Liberal Lord Ripon as viceroy, the Indian government sued for peace. They supported Abdur Rahman Khan, a nephew of the deposed Sher Ali, as emir (ruler) of Kabul, providing him with an annual subsidy on the sole condition that he have no relations with any foreign powers except Great Britain. By 1881 Abdur Rahman had gained control over all of Afghanistan, which he ruled until his death in 1901. (In 1919 a third, one-month war forced the British to concede the Afghans' rights to conduct their own foreign relations.)

Vernacular Press Act

To forestall Indian public criticism over the expenses of the Second Afghan War, Lord Lytton's government passed the Vernacular Press Act of 1878. The act required Indian-language presses (but not those that published in English) to post bonds for their conduct with the government, with the clear threat that such bonds would be forfeited if what the presses published displeased the government. The act provoked angry objections from both press owners and their Indian readers. It became the occasion for political organizing in Calcutta, Pune, and Bombay, where newly formed political associations arranged protests and wrote petitions demanding its repeal. At a public meeting in Pune to oppose the act, speakers from the Sarvajanik Sabha (Public Association) denounced the act for infringing on that "freedom of thought and speech [which] is a right to which all subjects of the British Crown are entitled by their birth and allegiance" (Wolpert 1962, 12).

Regional Political Associations

By 1878 politics was a major interest of urban Indian elites. Indians began forming regional political associations in the late 1860s and early 1870s. The religious or social reform associations of the century focused inward on questions internal to indigenous Indian society: religious practices, women's social conditions, caste interactions. Political associations, in contrast, looked outward, focusing their activities on the policies and actions of the British Indian government.

English-educated Indians organized their regional political associations along "modern" lines, using contemporary political forms and practices, and framed their concerns using the language and concepts of British constitutional democracy. Political associations elected officers, collected dues and subscriptions, kept minutes of their activities, and held Town Hall meetings to debate and publicize their issues. They petitioned regional governments on issues of concern to English-educated and middle-class communities that supported them. Key issues were access to ICS (civil service) examinations, broader (middle-class) Indian participation in the government's Legislative Councils, the excessive expenses of the Afghan wars, and government inaction during famines.

Pune

One of the earliest and most successful of the regional associations was Pune's Sarvajanik Sabha. Founded in 1870 out of several smaller groups, Pune's political association regularly organized public meetings, debates, protests, and petitions on the issues of the day. It provided an early and regional context for the political development of three of India's most famous nationalist leaders.

The three men were Mahadev Govind Ranade (1842–1901), a leader of the Prarthana Samaj in Bombay, Gopal Krishna Gokhale (1866–1915), and Balwantrao Gangadhar Tilak (1856–1920). All came from Maharashtra, from the elite Chitpavan Brahman community, and all three were English educated: Ranade and Gokhale at Elphinstone College in Bombay and Tilak first at Pune's local Deccan College and then later at Elphinstone. Ranade, the eldest of the three, was a lawyer and judge, college teacher, historian, and above all else, social reformer. He founded in 1887 the National Indian Social Conference. Gokhale, Ranade's disciple, was a founding member of Pune's Fergusson College, where he taught for 20 years. He was committed to secular social reform, founding the Servants of India Society in 1905, an organization of full-time volunteers dedicated to welfare work. In contrast, Tilak was the editor and publisher of two popular Pune newspapers: the English-language *Mahratta* and the Marathi-language *Kesari* (Lion). In his newspapers and speeches Tilak rejected the idea of social reform. He preferred to direct his energies toward the revival of Hinduism and the use of Hindu religious images and festivals for political organizing in the region. Over the years, from the 1870s until their deaths in the 20th century, the two younger men, Gokhale and Tilak, fought out their opposing views—first on social reform and religion, later on politics—both within Pune's Sarvajanik Sabha and later on the national stage.

Bombay

In Bombay city, the English educated came from commercial and trading communities, one of the most visible of which was the Parsis. Descended from 10th-century Zoroastrian migrants from Iran, the Bombay Parsis had been early supporters of English-language education. Their most famous member in the 19th century, and one of India's earliest nationalist writers, was Dadabhai Naoroji (1825–1917). Naoroji was an early graduate of Elphinstone College who had founded one of the first Indian business firms in London and Liverpool in the 1850s. Traveling frequently between England and India, he wrote on British-Indian economic relations and became a mentor in England to Indian boys sent abroad for education. In the 1890s he became the first Indian elected to the British Parliament. Another politically prominent Parsi was Pherozeshah Mehta (1845–1915), a prominent Bombay lawyer. Mehta began his long career in regional and national politics in the late 1870s, when he was drawn into local efforts to protest the Vernacular Press Act. He and other members of Bombay's urban elite formed a local political association, the Bombay Presidency Association, in 1885.

Madras

In the 19th and early 20th centuries Madras Brahmans dominated the local English-educated community, and local Brahman communities

Annie Besant, shown here in a sari on a street in India, 1926. Annie Wood Besant (1847–1933) had been the wife of an Anglican clergyman and associate of an English atheist and social reformer before she converted to theosophy in 1889 and moved to Madras (now Chennai), India. Besant, who was the international president of the Theosophical Society from 1907 until her death, lived at the society's headquarters in Madras and lectured and wrote extensively on theosophy and on educational and humanitarian issues in India. She became a strong supporter of Indian independence, founding the Home Rule League during World War I and serving as the first woman president of the India National Congress in 1917. (Library of Congress)

competed for control over the city's political activities. G. Subramaniya Ayyar and M. Viraghava Charia, joint publishers of the leading Madras newspaper, the *Hindu,* initially founded a local political association, the Madras Native Association, in 1878. When disagreements split that association during the 1883–84 Ilbert Bill controversy, the original founders reformed it as the Madras Mahajana Sabha (Great Peoples' Association). Madras politics were further complicated after 1893, when the English Socialist Annie Besant (1847–1933) moved to the city. Besant, who became the Theosophical Society's president in 1907, actively involved herself in regional (and national) politics on the side of Indian political self-determination.

Calcutta

Bengal was home to what was probably the oldest political association in the country. The British Indian Association was a loyalist organization of princes, zamindars, and, later, industrialists founded in the 1840s. In 1875 a new political organization, the Indian League, was founded by members of the English-educated Bengali community who worked in the city's new professions of law, education, and journalism. After a year, it was supplanted by the newly formed Indian Association, founded by Surendranath Banerjea (1848–1926), a former ICS officer who had been fired from the service and had turned instead to college teaching and journalism. Under Banerjea's leadership the Indian Association aggressively pursued public issues of interest to its members, among other things helping to organize a multiregional protest by Indian elites against the 1878 Vernacular Press Act.

The Ilbert Bill

The return of a Liberal government to power in Britain had brought the marquis of Ripon to India as viceroy in 1880. Ripon began his term in a mode popular with Westernized Indians by repealing the Vernacular Press Act of 1878. He also encouraged the growth of primary and secondary schools and created governing boards in municipalities and districts that elected two-thirds of their members. But in 1883 he aroused the fury of the Anglo-Indian community when his law member, Sir Courtney Ilbert, proposed modifying an 1873 law to allow certain cases involving Europeans to be tried by Indian judges. At well-organized public meetings and in newspaper ads, the Anglo-Indian community declared the Ilbert Bill "intensely distasteful and humiliating to all

Europeans" (Metcalf and Metcalf 2006, 120). In blunter language, Anglo-Indian associations denounced the idea that "nigger natives" could be considered their "peers or equals" (Wolpert 1989, 257). In 1884 Ripon's government gave in and amended the bill to mandate that if a European's case was to be tried by an Indian judge, his jury must be at least half Europeans. For Anglo-Indians this was a great victory. For Westernized Indians, both the process and the resolution demonstrated the fundamental racism of Anglo-Indians and the Indian government in which they served. The bill also demonstrated to the Indian elite the power and effectiveness of organized public protest.

By the time of the Ilbert Bill controversy, British rule in India had transformed many aspects of Indian society. The British Raj had introduced British administrative structures and the ideas and practices of the West to a newly forming urban Indian elite. British economic structures had transformed Indian agricultural production even as government-subsidized railroads and roads bound the subcontinent more tightly together. In rural India, these changes left peasants more vulnerable than ever both to the economic fluctuations of the global marketplace and to the spread of calamitous famine and disease. In urban India, over the course of the 19th century the new elites of British Indian towns and cities had adapted themselves to the office work, administrative structures, and Western practices of the British Raj. By the late 19th century these elites had begun to change their focus. From earlier preoccupations with religious and social reform, acculturation, and self-improvement, they now wrote and spoke more about the revival and protection of indigenous religion and culture, about finding ways to participate in India's imperially controlled government, and even about nationalism, independence, and *swaraj* (self-rule).

6

TOWARD FREEDOM
(1885–1920)

This is the first and most essential thing to learn about India—
that there is not, and never was an India, or even any country of India,
possessing, according to European ideas, any sort of unity, physical, political,
social or religious. . . . That men of the Punjab, Bengal, the North-Western
Provinces and Madras, should ever feel that they belong to
one great Indian nation, is impossible.

∎

Sir John Strachey, India, 1888 (Embree 1972, 3)

The men who participated in the Indian nationalist movement from its beginnings in the Indian National Congress in 1885 to Mohandas Gandhi's assumption of leadership in the 1920s all came from the English-educated elite. They agreed broadly on the issues that most affected them as a class—the need for greater access to the ICS and for middle-class appointments to the Legislative Councils—and they agreed on the terrible effects of "the drain" of Indian wealth to Great Britain. But on the questions of whether the nationalist movement should work for social reform or Hindu revivalism or whether its members should see themselves as Her Majesty's loyal opposition or as freedom fighters, they had no such easy answers. Early nationalists spent as much energy fighting one another over these matters as they did in fighting the British.

In the decades between 1885 and 1920, in response to nationalist pressures British rulers offered a series of constitutional concessions, giving Indians marginal participation in India's government while conceding as little real power as possible. At the same time, British officials worked to "divide and rule." To preserve British power, officials encouraged minority constituencies to define themselves in opposition to one another, as Muslims against Hindus, Dravidians against Aryans, or Untouchables against Brahmans.

In the end, however, despite all their efforts, it was the British themselves who brought about the unity of Indian nationalists. Unbridled demonstrations of imperial power and British racism in both 1905 and in 1919 brought elite urban Indians not only into unity but looking outside their own elite class for broader support for their movement against the British.

The Indian National Congress

In December 1885, 73 mostly self-appointed delegates from all over British India met in Bombay for a three-day conference. This was the first meeting of the Indian National Congress. It had originally been scheduled to meet in Pune, for Ranade and Pune's Sarvajanik Sabha were among its leading organizers, but an outbreak of cholera forced its relocation to Bombay. Its delegates represented every province of British India; 54 delegates were Hindu (most of whom were Brahman), two delegates were Muslim, and the rest came from the Parsi or Jain communities. All were English educated. "Congress," as it came to be called, began its existence as a supraregional political association, a three-day yearly forum through which middle-class Indian men could petition and memorialize the Indian government, just as regional associations had already been doing but now on a wider basis.

The immediate impetus for the meeting came from Allan Octavian Hume (1829–1912), a retired ICS official who believed, as he told the viceroy, Frederick Hamilton-Temple-Blackwood, Lord Dufferin (1826–1902), that such a gathering would stabilize the English-educated elite. Hume helped organize the first meeting of Congress, circulating letters to English-educated graduates to encourage their support and serving as its first secretary. But many Congress attendees already knew or knew of each other before the first meeting. Surendranath Banerjea, W. C. Bonnerji (the first Congress president), Romeshchandra Dutt, Pherozeshah Mehta, and Badruddin Tyabji had all come under the influence of Dadabhai Naoroji while in England in the 1860s and 1870s. Leaders of regional political associations in Pune, Bombay, Madras, and Calcutta knew of each other from shared protests against the 1878 Vernacular Press Act. And Banerjea's Indian Association had already organized two national conferences, one in 1883 and one held at the same time as the Bombay meeting in 1885.

Until Gandhi reorganized it in the 1920s the Indian National Congress met for only three days each year, each meeting organized by members from the region in which it was held. It had limited funds, and for its first nine years its only full-time officer was Hume, its general secretary. In its first years, Congress grew quickly: from 73 delegates in 1885 to 600 in 1887 and almost 2,000 in 1889. Through Hume's efforts, Muslim participation grew to almost 14 percent of the delegates by 1887. Attendance at the 1887 and 1888 sessions was particularly broad based, with more than half the delegates traveling to the meeting from outside the region in which it was held.

Congress delegates came from every British Indian province and spoke many dialects, but they shared the elite status and high-caste background common to the English-educated elite. They agreed (as did the English educated generally) that Indians needed greater access to the ICS and that middle-class Indians should serve on the government's Legislative Councils. The ICS was the premier service in India; appointment within the civil service gave Indians the only direct governmental power they could have in British India. ICS appointments were chosen by open competitive examinations, but the exams were held only in England, and the maximum age for examinees (in 1876) was 19. As late as 1880 the 900-member ICS had only 16 Indians. In a similar way, the Legislative Councils also offered Indian members a voice, if not in government decisions, at least in the debates that preceded them. But while the councils had had appointed Indian members since the 1860s, in practice only Indian princes and zamindars were ever nominated.

Seven successive years of Congress oratory and petitions succeeded in 1892 in having the maximum age for taking the ICS exams raised to 23. In the same year the Indian Councils Act provided for indirect elections to the central and regional Legislative Councils in Bengal, Bombay, and Madras. Through an elaborate procedure local municipal boards, universities, and landowners' associations (among others) submitted lists of elected representatives to the government for final selection. Nevertheless the process brought prominent regional leaders such as Banerjea and Tilak onto their respective regional councils and moderate Congress members, such as Mehta and Gokhale, onto the central Legislative Council. Despite constant Indian pressure, however, the ICS examinations, the key to Anglo-Indian dominance within the service, would not be held in India until the 1920s.

While Congress petitions on English-educated issues brought some limited success, escalating conflicts between social reformers and religion revivalists split the English-educated elite in the 1890s, and violent

THE DRAIN

From the perspective of British imperialists, all the expenses of the British Empire in India went toward services and projects that improved India itself. "England receives nothing from India," wrote Sir John Strachey, "except in return for English services rendered or English capital expended" (Sarkar 1983, 27). But for Indian nationalists nothing was farther from the truth. Against the backdrop of the widespread famines, sickness, and poverty of late 19th-century rural India, nationalist leaders such as Dadabhai Naoroji and Romeshchandra Dutt put forth their economic theory of "the drain."

Dadabhai Naoroji was from the Parsi community of Bombay (now Mumbai). He was educated at Elphinstone College in that city before traveling abroad to England where he established himself in business and even won election to Parliament in 1892. Naoroji mentored many Indian students who traveled to England to study in the late 19th century, and his economic theories about the British Empire—especially his theory of "the drain"—shaped the views of several generations of Indian nationalists. (R. P. Patwardhan, ed., Dadabhai Naoroji Correspondence, Vol. 2, Part 1: Correspondence with D. E. Wacha, 1977)

Far from benefiting India, they argued, British rule was draining India's wealth away from her. Yearly home charges (funds sent to Great Britain) drained revenues from India to pay for the high salaries and pensions of British civil servants in India and for the exorbitant expenses of an Indian army used by Great Britain throughout the world. British rule, said nationalist economists, had replaced a prosperous, indigenous Indian economy with an imperial economic network that benefited foreigners (and Great Britain itself) at the expense of indigenous Indians.

Modern scholars have continued to debate "the drain." Some argue that railroads, technology, and export agriculture benefited India's economy in the end. Others assert that the

(continues)

THE DRAIN (continued)

British Empire drained off as much as 4 percent of India's national income in the later decades of the 19th century (Tomlinson 1993, 14).

Sources: Sarkar, Sumit. Modern India 1885–1947 (Madras: Macmillan India, 1983), p. 27; Tomlinson, B. R. The Economy of Modern India, 1860–1970 (Cambridge and New York: Cambridge University Press, 1993), p. 14.

---

communal clashes divided the broader Indian society. These conflicts took their toll on Indian political associations. Interest in both Congress and regional political associations declined in the 1890s, and Muslim attendance at Congress sessions was cut almost in half. Annual Congress meetings began attracting fewer delegates from outside the state where they were held and making up the difference with more local members.

Hindu Race/Hindu Nation

As was true of much of 19th-century society, early Indian nationalists imagined "the nation" using two different and often contradictory sets of ideas and images. One strand of 19th-century thought conceived of the nation in terms of citizenship and constitutionalism. Nations, in this view, were composed of individual citizens living within a territorial state, their political obligations and rights defined by a constitutional contract between each citizen and that state. Congress and regional political leaders known collectively to their contemporaries as the "moderates," men such as Ranade, Gokhale, Mehta, or Banerjea, advanced this concept of the nation, citizenship, and constitutionalism. They spoke the language of British constitutional democracy and presented themselves as the government's "loyal opposition," as leaders of India's citizenry struggling to obtain for them their inalienable rights.

Comfortable themselves with a style of life, dress, and habits adapted to British colonial public life, these leaders enjoyed their new elected or appointed positions within British government and their status within elite urban Indian society. They looked forward to middle-class Indians making gradual gains in influence and power within British-ruled India but were not troubled by the idea that such gains might be far into the future. They frequently (if not always) supported social reforms;

THE SCIENCE OF NOSES

The leading exponent of "race science" in India was H. H. Risley (1851–1911), a British ethnologist who served in India in the Indian Civil Service from 1873 to 1910. Risley was the census commissioner in 1901, and after his retirement in 1910, he was elected president of the (British) Royal Anthropological Institute. Following the anthropometric techniques of the French anthropologist Paul Topinard, Risley used a "nasal index" (a ratio of the width of a nose to its height) to divide Indians into two races—a dark-skinned Dravidian race and a fair-skinned Indo-Aryan race. Using this nose science, he proved (to his own satisfaction and that of contemporaries) the existence of a seven-caste racial hierarchy in India, with Dravidians at the "primitive" bottom and Indo-Aryans at the "civilized" top. "The social position of a caste," he once said, "varies inversely as its nasal index" (Trautmann). Race, not occupation, he concluded, was the true basis of the Indian caste system. For late 19th-century "race scientists" such as Risley, this type of physiological measurements served to confirm the distinct racial essences they believed existed within the Indian population (and more generally in the larger world).

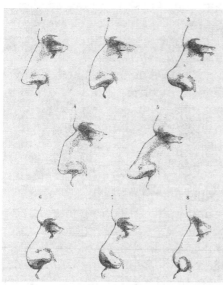

The "science" of noses. H. H. Risley drew his ideas on nose measurements from the work of a contemporary, 19th-century French scholar Paul Topinard. Writing in his 1885 Elements of General Anthropology (Éléments d'anthropologie générale), Topinard developed a "nasal index" (a ratio of the breadth of the nose to its height) that enabled him to classify noses (and their owners) into a series of nose types. Narrow noses, said Topinard, characterized the Europeans (types 1 through 5); medium noses characterized the "yellow races" (type 6); and broad noses belonged either to Africans (type 7) or to Melanesians and native Australians (type 8). (Paul Topinard, Éléments d'anthropologie générale, 1885)

Source: Trautmann, Thomas R. Aryans and British India (New Delhi: Vistaar, 1997), p. 203.

these would, as they saw it, modernize Indian society, ridding it of the degraded practices of the past.

But there was a second way of imagining "the nation" current in the 19th-century world. Nationhood, as social anthropologist Susan Bayly has pointed out, "was widely regarded both in India and elsewhere as an expression of collective moral, spiritual, and racial essences" (1999, 156). This second view conceived of the nation as a unit bound together by racial ties of blood and ethnic ties of culture. The language of race itself was in constant use in whatever was said or written in this period about Indian communities. Writers frequently referred to the Hindu or "Mohammedan" races and talked of castes (*varnas* or *jatis*) as racial entities. Both Westernized social reformers and Hindu cultural revivalists used "race" without self-consciousness to describe the deeper ties that might bind a religion, a caste, or a regional community together. Ranade could describe how social reforms would benefit the "chosen race" of the Hindus as easily as Arya Samajis could describe the rituals through which Muslims and/or Untouchables might reenter the "Aryan race" (Bayly 1999, 175).

By the late 19th century, the linkage of "race" and "nation" was commonplace, with both British and Indians referring interchangeably to an Aryan or Hindu "race" or an Aryan or Hindu "nation." But at the turn of the century some Indian leaders, beginning with Tilak in Pune, began to place this more general sense of a Hindu race/nation in a deliberately and more explicitly political context, linking anticolonial protests to a Hindu communal identity through the religious language and symbols of Hinduism. Contemporaries labeled Tilak, along with such men as Lajpat Rai (1865–1928) in the Punjab and Bipin Chandra Pal (1858–1932) in Bengal, as "extremists," not for their evocation of a Hindu cultural identity, but because they questioned the inevitability of Indian self-government and were willing to use a variety of means, including violence, to bring Indians closer to self-rule.

Hindu Revivalism

Up to the 1890s Western-educated Indians had supported social and religious reforms. They founded movements such as the Brahmo Samaj in Bengal or the early Arya Samaj in North India and used such organizations to move contemporary caste practices and Hindu customs regarding women's education and social behavior closer to the norms of British colonial modernity. But at the turn of the century, even as such adaptations became well integrated into middle-class urban lifestyles, a

RAMAKRISHNA AND VIVEKANANDA

The Hindu saint Sri (meaning "respected") Ramakrishna (1836–86) was a Brahman priest at a temple of the goddess Kali in north Calcutta. Ramakrishna had little formal education and could read and write only in Bengali. He attained mystical ecstasies by worshipping the goddess through a variety of religious forms and idioms: as the Mother Goddess, as Krishna, as Muhammad, and as Jesus Christ. Discovered by the Brahmo Samaj leader Keshab Sen, Ramakrishna became popular among young men from Calcutta's Indian elite in the 1870s and 1880s. To these Westernized followers, Ramakrishna's mystic bhakti (devotion) to the Mother Goddess was more vibrant than the Westernized worship of Brahmo "churches." Ramakrishna's religious teachings and mystical experiences seemed to demonstrate the "oneness" of all religions and the inherent superiority of a Hinduism that could acknowledge this universality.

Narendranath Datta (1863–1902) was one of the middle-class men who visited Ramakrishna in his temple. Narendranath came from a family of Calcutta lawyers, was Western educated, and had joined the Brahmo Samaj. He was planning to study law abroad when he first went to visit Ramakrishna in 1882. By 1886, the year of the saint's death, Narendranath had dedicated himself to the life of a religious holy man, a *sannyasi*. Under the name Vivekananda, he became Ramakrishna's best-known disciple. In 1893 in a famous speech at the First World Parliament of Religions in Chicago, Vivekananda spoke of Hinduism as the mother of all religions, a religion that could recognize and incorporate within itself the truths of all religions. Vivekananda saw his religious movement as a contemporary form of Vedanta. His Chicago speech gained him an international audience that kept him traveling and lecturing in the United States and England for the next four years. Returning to India in 1897, he founded the Ramakrishna Mission in Calcutta, an institution of Hindu monks dedicated to Ramakrishna's religious insights and teachings and to social service.

renewed interest emerged in what contemporaries called "Hindu revivalism," that is, the maintenance of extant Hindu beliefs and practices and the defense of such practices from further erosion.

In Calcutta young English-educated men turned away from the "male" worship of the Brahmo Samaj churches to become fascinated with the mystic visions of Ramakrishna, a semi-illiterate priest in a north Calcutta temple. In novels and newspaper pieces writers discovered anew the inspiring bravery and devotion of the sati. Women's literature and manuals denounced the denaturalizing effect of higher education on women— for, as one manual writer noted in a common joke of the period, "If a girl can become a 'bachelor', what else does she need to become a man?" (Gupta 1885, 23). The Arya Samaj had long stood uncompromisingly for social and religious reform in northern India. Now it split in the 1890s. One sect continued the old work of education and reform, but a second and larger group committed itself instead to the revival of the "Aryan race," to the conversion of orthodox Hindus, Muslims, Sikhs, and Untouchables to the Samaj through new *shuddhi* (purification) ceremonies, to proselytizing for the use of Hindi and the Sanskritic Devanagari alphabet in north India, and the protection of the cow.

Cow Protection Riots

Cow protection riots, pitting Hindus against Muslims, occurred repeatedly across northern India during the 1880s and 1890s, from Bombay and Maharashtra in the west to the Bengal in the east. The earliest riots were in the Punjab in 1883, followed by large-scale communal riots from 1888 to 1893 in the United Provinces, Bihar, Bengal, and even Rangoon. In 1893–95 violent riots broke out in the city of Bombay and in the wider Maharashtra region.

At issue was the Muslim slaughter of cows for meat, particularly as part of religious festivities such as Bakr-Id (the festival in the last month of the Islamic calendar). Such slaughter demonstrated to Hindu revivalists how contemporary society failed to protect Hindu religious practices and the Hindu way of life. Linked with cow protection were campaigns to replace Urdu written in the Perso-Arabic script with Hindi written in the Sanskrit-based Devanagari script and the Arya Samaj's use of "purification" rituals to bring converts into the Arya Samaj fold.

The founder of the Arya Samaj, Dayananda Sarasvati, had himself written a pamphlet urging the protection of cows in 1881. From the late 1880s cow protection societies appeared among Hindu populations in northern India. These societies emphasized long-standing Hindu customs venerating the cow, held meetings protesting cow slaughter, and even petitioned the government to prohibit this slaughter on hygienic grounds. They were funded by a range of local elites, including zamindars, middle-class lawyers, and even, in Bombay, a Gujarati mill owner.

Regional politicians, such as Tilak in Bombay, helped organize such meetings and participated in their protests.

Bitter competition between local Hindu and Muslim elites for government employment helped fuel the communal riots that grew out of cow protection conflicts. In different regions, class and cultural conflicts helped the violence to escalate. In the Punjab the cow protection riots built on long-standing conflicts between Muslim peasants and Hindu traders and moneylenders. In the United Provinces multiple social tensions supported the riots: in rural regions conflicts between Muslim landlords and Hindu peasants and in urban towns between Hindu bankers and Muslim artisans and workers.

Cow protection conflicts merged easily with more general violence over religious festivals and processions. Although in prior decades Hindus and Muslims had participated in each other's religious festivals, by the late 19th century the two communities were openly split along religious lines. "What boon has Allah conferred upon you," went one turn-of-the-century Maharashtrian song, "That you have become a Mussalman today? The cow is our mother, do not forget her" (Sarkar 1983, 60).

Age of Consent Act, 1891

Controversy over the 1891 Age of Consent Act gave public expression to the feelings of many middle-class Hindus that the protection of Hindu customs and a Hindu identity was now of much greater urgency than the reform of social customs. The immediate cause for the act was the death in Calcutta of an 11-year-old girl, Phulmoni Bai, from lacerations caused by intercourse with her 35-year-old husband. As the law set the age of statutory rape at 10 for girls, the husband could not be prosecuted. The Age of Consent Bill raised the age of statutory rape for girls from 10 to 12 years old. Although proposed by the government, the reform had long been sought by Indian reformers, and the act was supported by an Indian National Congress dominated by its moderate faction.

In both Bengal and western India, however, opposition to the bill was virulent. By custom Hindu marriages were consummated immediately following the wife's first menstruation. Under the bill, for girls who menstruated before the age of 12 the custom would now be criminalized. "The Hindu family is ruined," wrote *Bangabasi*, the conservative Bengali newspaper that spearheaded opposition in Calcutta (Sarkar 2002, 234). In west India, Tilak opposed the bill in his newspaper *Kesari*. In both regions opponents of the bill held mass meetings and sent petitions. In Pune young Hindu men broke up a meeting attended by social reformers and wrecked the hall in which they met.

The bill became law in 1891 despite substantial Indian opposition. In the aftermath of the controversy social reformers were vilified in Bengal and Bombay as Western turncoats who had betrayed their own religion. Every year since its founding in 1887, Ranade's Indian National Social Conference had held its annual meetings at the same time as the Congress session and under Congress auspices. Now in 1895 Hindu revivalists threatened to boycott the next meeting of Congress if Ranade's conference met under the Congress banner. To pacify the revivalists, Ranade's conference was barred from the session. Disagreements over social reform issues would not be allowed to divide the Congress. Congress would include, said its president Surendranath Banerjea, both "those who would reform their social customs and those who would not" (Wolpert 1989, 263).

Although they lost their struggle, opponents of the Age of Consent Bill still profited from their efforts. Bengali newspapers that supported the protests turned from weekly to daily papers on the strength of their increased circulation. In Pune, Tilak's opposition to the act made him a hero to lower-middle-class Hindus in Deccan towns and *mofussil* regions and gained him increased financial support from wealthy Hindu conservatives.

The Marriage of Religion and Politics

The Age of Consent controversy showed Bal Gangadhar Tilak the role religion might play in political organizing. In the decade after 1891 Tilak and others organized two festivals that used Hindu religious icons and images for political ends: In 1893 a new festival began celebrating the birthday of the elephant-headed Hindu god Ganesh, and in 1895 a second festival celebrated the memory of Shivaji. Both festivals became Hindu community events, with songs, dances, scriptural readings, and (in the Shivaji celebration) a religious procession led by huge portraits of Shivaji and his Brahman guru. The Ganesh festival was deliberately timed to draw Hindus away from the Muslim festival of Mohurram, which both communities had previously celebrated. Both new festivals encouraged Hindus to see themselves as a distinct community separate from Muslims or Christians: By 1895 Tilak's opposition to the Age of Consent Act combined with his role in organizing the new festivals had made his faction strong enough to take over Pune's political association, the Sarvajanik Sabha.

Ganesh (Ganapati), Bhubaneswar, Orissa. Ganesh (Ganapati in western India) is the elephant-headed son of the Hindu gods Shiva and Parvati. He is widely worshipped throughout
India as a god able to overcome (or to help his worshippers overcome) obstacles in life. His
image is frequently found installed in stores and businesses. The celebration of Ganesh's
birthday became a central religious/political festival of western India beginning in the late
19th century. (courtesy of Judith E. Walsh)

177

Tilak encouraged his followers to use violence against social reformers, Muslims, and the British. He himself had ties to revolutionary societies now organized in Maharashtra. His supporters threw rocks at Pune social reformers; his followers paraded noisily in paramilitary fashion past Muslim mosques; in *Kesari* Tilak used references to the Bhagavad Gita to justify the use of violence, arguing that violence committed with no thought of gain or reward was not morally wrong. "Shrimat Krishna," he said in comments at the time of the Shivaji festival of 1897, "preached in the *Gita* that we have a right even to kill our own *guru* and our kinsmen. No blame attaches to any person if he is doing deeds without being actuated by a desire to reap the fruit of his deeds" (Wolpert 1962, 87).

In June 1897 bubonic plague spread through Maharashtra. Pune's plague commissioner, Walter Charles Rand, took drastic measures to combat it. Rand ordered British troops to fumigate and lime all houses where plague was suspected. The soldiers forced all inhabitants (including women in purdah) out of their homes and took anyone thought infected to an isolation camp outside the city. Often family members only saw their relatives when told to come and collect their dead bodies. The measures provoked fury among Pune's residents and failed to contain the plague. As the plague raged, Pune's Anglo-Indian elite organized an elaborate gala to celebrate Queen Victoria's jubilee. Two brothers, Damodar and Balkrishna Chapedar, assassinated Rand and one other officer as they left the celebrations. Both the Chapedar brothers were subsequently caught and hanged.

The brothers were followers of Tilak, and rumors linked him with the assassinations. Based on articles written for *Kesari* Tilak was arrested in July and tried for sedition. The six Europeans on his jury found him guilty; the three Indians said he was innocent. Tilak was sentenced to 18 months' imprisonment in Bombay but released after one year on grounds of ill health. From this time on Tilak acquired the unofficial title of "Lokamanya" (revered of the people).

Bengal Partition

If the Age of Consent controversy revealed deep divisions among elite Hindu communities, the British government's partition of Bengal in 1905 overrode many of those divisions. Bengal's partition provided the context for India's first national protest against British actions and united many in support of the nationalist cause.

The partition was planned during the 1899–1905 viceroyalty of George Nathaniel Curzon (1859–1925). In some ways Curzon was fortunate, taking office as new government procedures brought the 19th-century mass famines under control and as a more stable Indian rupee began to lower the growth rate of "home charges." During his term as viceroy, Curzon oversaw the overhaul of government bureaucracy, the building of more than 6,000 miles of new railroad tracks, and the passage of several land measures designed to protect cultivators from eviction for debts (including the Punjab Land Alienation Act in 1901).

Curzon's imperious and autocratic character, however, created conflicts. His resignation in 1905 resulted from an internal political dispute in which he ultimately refused to follow orders from his superior in London, the secretary of state for India. His arrogance and racism made him contemptuous of English-educated Indians—he once called the Indian National Congress an "unclean thing"—and his government took a number of actions that antagonized elite Indians (Sarkar 1983, 104), including reducing the number of Indians on the municipal boards of cities and passing the Universities Act in 1904, a series of measures that tightened government controls over universities and their affiliated colleges in order to control student protests.

Curzon's most provocative government action, however, was undoubtedly the partition of Bengal. With 78.5 million people in 1901, Bengal was India's largest province and an unwieldy administrative unit (Schwartzberg 1992, 217). Its partition was planned for almost two years within Curzon's administration and formally announced in July 1905. The division created two provinces. One of approximately 38 million people was made by combining predominantly Muslim eastern Bengal with the smaller province of Assam. The second was a somewhat larger western province of almost 55 million people that merged Bengali-speaking regions north and west of Calcutta with Hindi-speaking Bihar and Oriyan-speaking Orissa. One benefit of the plan, from the perspective of British officials, was that it offered Muslims a separate province in which they were a majority. A second advantage was that in both new provinces Bengali-speaking Hindus were in the minority, thus enabling the government, as one official wrote in a private memo, "to split up and thereby weaken a solid body of opponents to our rule" (Sarkar 1983, 107).

Swadeshi

British officials anticipated mass meetings and memorials to protest the division, but they were unprepared for the sustained political protest that occurred or for the new forms that protest took. Partition protests lasted several years, spreading beyond Bengal to Bombay, the Punjab, and Madras and involving substantial numbers of English-educated students, professionals, and their families. Initially even Congress moderates supported the protest, although as violence broke out, they quickly withdrew their support. Antipartition leaders called for the boycott of British goods and the support of *swadeshi* (the native country's) products. Schools and shops closed. Public bonfires burned imported cotton goods. Schoolchildren sang "Bande Mataram" ("Hail to the motherland")—a slogan and song from an 1880s Bengali novel. Processions chanted the slogan and shouted out in unison the names of the three most popular "extremists" who led them: "Lal, Bal, Pal"— Lala Lajpat Rai from the Punjab, "Bal" Gangadhar Tilak from Pune, and Bipin Chandra Pal from Bengal. Terrorist cells sprang up in Bengal, as they had in Maharashtra earlier, and their members planted bombs and attempted the assassination of several British officials.

The *swadeshi* boycotts were surprisingly effective, demonstrating the degree to which Indian middle-class tastes had already shaped British imports. By 1906 Calcutta customs officials had noted substantial decreases in imported products: a 22 percent decrease in cotton fabrics, a 44 percent decrease in cotton threads, a 55 percent fall in imported cigarettes, and a 68 percent drop in imported boots and shoes. By 1908 imports were down overall by 25 percent. Indian merchants and textile producers raised both prices and profits (Wolpert 2009, 285). In Bombay, the Tatas, a Parsi industrialist family loyal to the British, launched India's first indigenous steelworks, thus reducing the Indian government's need for imports of Belgian steel.

The government attempted to stop the protests by arresting middle-class students, banning public meetings, and imprisoning protest leaders. In London, the new Liberal government considered offering constitutional reforms in the hope that this would undercut further protest.

Muslim League

Whether and to what extent elite Muslims would join the Indian National Congress was an open question throughout the late 19th and early 20th centuries. As early as 1869 the prominent Muslim leader (and British loyalist) Sir Sayyid Ahmad Khan had declared Hindus and Muslims to be two separate communities and urged Muslims to work independently on their own society. For Sayyid Ahmad, the different "nationalities of India—the Muslims, the Marathas, the Brahmins, the

"BANDE MATARAM"

The poem that became the song and slogan of the 1905 Bengal partition protests was written in 1875 by the popular Bengali novelist Bankim Chandra Chatterji (1838–94) and later incorporated into his 1882 novel, *Anandamath* (Monastery of bliss). Set at the end of the 18th century, *Anandamath* told the story of a band of patriotic, armed sannyasis, devoted to the Mother Goddess (Durga/Kali), who traveled the region fighting local Muslim rulers and the East India Company for the protection of Bengal's 70 million people. In Chatterji's novel, the "Mother" stood for both the goddess and the land of Bengal, a land ruled illegitimately by foreigners. Sedition laws were part of the reason Chatterji made Muslims rather than the British the villains in his novel. The novel used vivid Hindu imagery and strong anti-Muslim rhetoric. Modern 20th-century enthusiasts have often wished Chatterji's novel had a more "national" focus. At least one recent translation has accomplished this by removing the original novel's regional and anti-Muslim references, turning Chatterji's Bengali motherland into "Mother India" and morphing his long-bearded Muslim kings into the British (Chatterji 1992).

"Bande Mataram" (Bow to the Mother)
Bow to the Mother!
Watered by swiftly flowing rivers,
Rich with abundant fruits,
Cooled by lovely southern breezes,
Dark with harvest crops, the Mother . . .
When 70 million voices roar out your call,
And twice 70 million hands hold sharp, unwavering swords,
Why, Mother, do they call you weak!

. . . In every temple it is your image enshrined.
For as Durga, with ten weapons in ten hands,
As Lakshmi, dallying in the lotuses,
As Saraswati, the giver of wisdom,
I bow to you . . .
Bow to the Mother,
Dark-hued, guileless, smiling, bejeweled and adorned,
The earth that supports us, the succor of us all, the Mother.
(Chatterji 1989)

Sources: Chatterji, Bankim Chandra. *Anandamath* (New Delhi: Orient Paperbacks, 1992), pp. 38–41; ———. *Bankim Racanabali* (Collected works of Bankim). 13th ed. (Calcutta: Sahitya Sangsad, 1989), p. 674.

Kshatriyas, the Banias, the Sudras [sic], the Sikhs, the Bengalis, the Madrasis, and the Peshawaris" could never become a single homogeneous nation (De Bary 1958, 747).

Nevertheless, by 1887, largely due to the efforts of Allan Octavian Hume, Muslim attendance at Congress sessions had risen to almost 14 percent of the delegates. But after 1893, as communal conflict escalated in north India, revivalist Hindu groups demanded cow protection and the Hindi language, and political festivals in Maharashtra defined Hindus as a separate communal and political entity, Muslim willingness to support a Hindu majoritarian institution such as the Indian National Congress declined. Muslim participation in Congress dropped to just over 7 percent of the delegates for the years from 1893 to 1905. Protests against the partition of Bengal only alienated Muslim leaders further as many east Bengali Muslim leaders could see great benefits for themselves and their communities in a separate Muslim majority province.

In 1906 at the height of partition conflicts, as rumors circulated of possible new British constitutional reforms, a deputation of 35 elite Muslims, most from landed United Province families, met the viceroy, Gilbert John Elliot-Murray-Kynymound, Lord Minto (1845–1914), at Simla. Their leader was Aga Khan III (1877–1957), the spiritual head of the Nazari Ismaili Muslim community and one of the wealthiest men in India. If there were to be reforms involving elections to the Legislative Councils, the deputation told Minto, they must include separate electorates for Muslims. (Separate electorates gave a community a special electoral category in which only that community could vote.) Only separate electorates could guarantee Muslims a voice among elected representatives, the delegates insisted. As the Hindus were the majority, they would vote only Hindus into office. Neither Muslim interests nor the Indian Muslim population, the Simla delegation insisted, could be adequately represented by non-Muslim candidates.

Many scholars have pointed to the 1906 Simla conference as the beginning of an explicit British policy of "divide and rule" in India. By encouraging Muslims to see themselves as a separate political entity— one defined in opposition to Congress—the British hoped to prolong British rule. In 1906 the viceroy assured the Simla deputation that Muslim interests would be considered in any new reforms. Encouraged by this support, the Simla delegates and an additional 35 Muslims from all provinces in India met at Dacca several months later and founded the All-India Muslim League. Only Muslims could become members of this league, whose specific purpose was defined as the advancement of Indian Muslims' political rights. Modeling themselves on the Indian

National Congress, the Muslim League met annually over the Christmas holidays. With its inception Muslims had a nationwide political organization that paralleled that of the "Hindu-dominated" Congress.

The Surat Split

The credibility of Congress moderates was badly damaged by their inaction during the swadeshi movement. While Gokhale (Congress president in 1905) initially supported the boycott, he and other moderates withdrew their support within a month from fear of government reprisals. Instead the moderates hoped that the new Liberal government in Britain, and especially its pro-Indian secretary of state, John Morley, would withdraw the partition.

In 1906, however, as protests continued, the moderates maintained control over the Congress session only by endorsing (if somewhat belatedly) the *swadeshi* movement. Even the 81-year-old Dadabhai Naoroji now declared that *swaraj* (self-rule) was the goal of Congress. In 1907 at Surat, however, the extremist faction was again frustrated in their attempt to elect Lajpat Rai as Congress president. Someone threw a shoe at the moderate president-elect as he attempted to speak, and the session dissolved in chaos. The moderates walked out of the meetings and in the aftermath of the Surat debacle effectively shut the extremist faction out of Congress.

In 1907 the Liberal British government and its India appointees escalated their efforts to shut down the *swadeshi* movement. Police attacked and arrested student picketers. Officials threatened colleges supporting the protests with the withdrawal of their grants, scholarships, and affiliations. Public meetings, assemblies, and strikes were banned; *swadeshi* committees became illegal; even schoolchildren were prohibited from singing "Bande Mataram." Extremist leaders were arrested, charged with sedition, or exiled. In 1907 Lajpat Rai was deported without trial to Mandalay in Burma. In 1908 the Bengali extremist Aurobindo Ghosh, who had led Bengali protests through his English-language weekly, *Bande Mataram,* was jailed and charged with sedition. (Two years later, in 1910, fearing further imprisonment Ghosh would flee Calcutta for the French colony of Pondicherry where for 40 years he would head a religious ashram.) In Pune the government arrested Tilak in 1908, charging him with sedition on the basis of editorials supporting Bengali terrorism. Tilak's sentence to six years' imprisonment prompted a violent general strike in Bombay that left 16 people dead. The arrest and imprisonment of extremist leaders gave the moderates full control over Congress but no access to the substantial Indian public now in sympathy with extremist aims.

Morley-Minto Reforms

Long-rumored constitutional reform became official in 1909 with the announcement of the Morley-Minto reforms, officially known as the Indian Councils Act of 1909. Although written by Liberal officials in London, the act was announced by the viceroy, Lord Minto, in Calcutta to give a great impression of government unity. The reforms put additional Indian members on the Legislative Councils, both at the center and in the provinces, and more important, they changed the method of selection for the councils to "direct elections" from the various constituencies—municipalities, district boards, landowning groups, universities, and so forth—from which recommendations for the councils had come since 1892. The act also established separate electorates for Muslims: six within the landlord constituencies of the Imperial Legislative Council and others in the provincial councils. The Imperial Legislative Council was not a voting body: Its members only commented on government policies when official (British) members of the council introduced them for discussion. The 1909 act, however, gave council members greater freedom to ask questions during such discussions.

Morley himself, the Liberal secretary of state for India, denied that the reforms would in any way lead to self-government in India. In the context of Indian nationalist politics where extremist calls for *swaraj* were now common, the Morley-Minto reforms offered little. But to moderates, who had long interested themselves in elections and appointments, the reforms were attractive.

In 1911, two years after the Morley-Minto reforms became law, the British celebrated a great durbar (the Persian name for a grand court occasion) in Delhi to celebrate the coronation of the British king George V. At a spectacle calculated to demonstrate the permanence of British rule, the British made their real concession to the power of the *swadeshi* movement. They revoked the 1905 partition and reunited Bengali-speaking Indians with a smaller, new province of Bengal. (At the same time Bihar and Orissa became separate provinces and Assam a separate territory.) At the same durbar, however, the British also took their revenge on Bengal and Bengalis: The viceroy announced the transfer of the capital to Delhi. The government would now be closer to the summer Simla capital and further from the troublesome political

activities of Bengali babus (gentlemen). "New Delhi," the British section of Delhi, would be designed by the architects Edward Lutyens and
Herbert Baker.

Bengal's reunification embittered Indian Muslims without satisfying
Indian nationalists. "No bomb, no boons" was one Muslim slogan in
Dacca and eastern Bengal (Wolpert 1989, 286). At the 1912 ceremonies
to open the new capital, the viceroy, Charles Hardinge (1858–1944),
was almost killed by a bomb. His assailants were never found, and terrorist violence continued in the Punjab. In 1913 the Muslim League
moved significantly away from its former loyalist position when it
adopted self-government as its goal.

World War I

When Great Britain declared war on Germany on August 4, 1914, the
Indian viceroy, Lord Hardinge, was at once informed that India was
also at war. Indian nationalists of all factions supported Great Britain
in World War I, assuming that support for Britain in a time of crisis
would translate later into significant self-government concessions.
Tilak, released from prison in 1914, raised funds and encouraged enlistment in the army. The lawyer and nationalist Mohandas K. Gandhi
(1869–1948), who was returning to India from South Africa by way of
England, also urged support for the war.

During World War I the Indian army expanded to more than 1.2 million men. Indian casualties were high. Within two months of the war's
start 7,000 Indian troops were listed as dead, wounded, or missing in
action in Europe. Fighting in 1916 in the Persian Gulf, thousands of
Indian soldiers died from lack of adequate food, clothing, mosquito
netting, and medicines. By 1918 more than 1 million Indians had
served overseas, more than 150,000 had been wounded in battle, and
more than 36,000 had died.

Within India the war brought increased income taxes, import duties,
and prices. From 1916 to 1918 Indian revenues increased approximately 10 to 15 percent each year. Increased amounts of Punjabi wheat
were shipped to Great Britain and its Allies during the war, with the
result that in 1918, when the monsoon failed, food shortages increased
and food prices rose sharply. The war also cut off India from its second
largest export market; prewar Indian exports to Germany and Austria-
Hungary in 1914 had a value of £24 million. Products from the Central
Powers (the countries allied with Germany) were also among India's
most popular imports. The war was a boon, however, to indigenous

Indian industries such as cotton cloth, steel, and iron. In all these industries production grew more quickly in the absence of European competition.

Lucknow Pact, 1916

Anticipating possible constitutional concession at the end of the war, nationalist leaders looked for ways to renew the movement. In 1916 both Annie Besant in Madras and Tilak in Pune founded "home rule leagues," organizations that argued for Indian self-government (on the model of Canada) within the British Empire. Within a few years the movement had hundreds of chapters and 30,000 members. In 1916 at a meeting at Lucknow, the newly reunited Indian National Congress joined with the Muslim League in the Lucknow Pact (otherwise known as the Congress-League Scheme of Reforms). The joint pact called for constitutional reforms that would give elected Indian representatives additional power at the provincial and the central levels. All elections were to be on the basis of a broad franchise. The principle of separate electorates for Muslims was accepted, and the percentage of such electorates was specified province by province. Half the seats on the viceroy's Executive Council were to be Indians. India Office expenses were to be charged to British taxpayers.

New Leaders

Both the reunification of Congress and the Lucknow Pact were made somewhat easier by the natural passing of an older generation of nationalist leaders and the rise to prominence of younger ones. Gokhale and Pherozeshah Mehta died in 1915, Lokamanya Tilak in 1920, and Surendranath Banerjea in 1925. Two younger men appeared who would dominate Congress throughout the 1920s–40s: Mohammed Ali Jinnah (1876–1948), a successful Muslim lawyer and Congress politician, joined the Muslim League in 1913; and Gandhi, already known in his homeland for leading Indian protests against the British in South Africa, returned to India in 1915.

Mohammed Ali Jinnah

Jinnah was born and educated in Karachi, the son of a middle-class merchant of the Muslim Khoja community who had migrated to Sind from Gujarat. Sent to England for university and law education in

1892, Jinnah was drawn into nationalist politics during his first year in London when he worked for the parliamentary election of Dadabhai Naoroji. Back in India, he rapidly established a successful law practice in Bombay, became a delegate to the 1906 Congress, and was elected (under Morley-Minto provisions) to the Imperial Legislative Council in 1910. Jinnah impressed Indian politicians and British officials alike with his intelligence, his skill in argument, his anglicized habits, and his fastidious dress and appearance. When the Muslim League declared its goal to be self-government in 1913, Jinnah joined. He initially hoped to bring the Muslim League and the Indian National Congress into unified opposition to British rule.

Mohandas K. Gandhi

Gandhi, like Jinnah, was born in western India, in the small Princely State of Porbandar (now a district in the modern state of Gujarat). His father served there as *dewan* (minister) before moving on to another small state nearby. Also like Jinnah, Gandhi was educated first in India and then sent in 1887 by his family to study law in London, an experience that anglicized him, too. When Gandhi returned to India in 1890 he wore British-style frock coats and trousers, insisted that his wife and children wear shoes and socks, and wanted his family to eat oatmeal regularly. Unlike Jinnah, however, Gandhi did not succeed as a lawyer, either in Gujarat or Bombay. After several years of trying to establish himself in practice there, he accepted a legal assignment with an Indian Muslim business firm in Natal, South Africa.

From 1893 to 1914 Gandhi lived and worked in South Africa. It was in South Africa that he discovered his avocation as a political organizer and his religious faith as a modern Hindu. The diverse South African community was made up of Hindus, Muslims, Parsis, and Christians who came from regions as different as Gujarat and south India. Gandhi led this multiethnic, multireligious community in a variety of protests against British laws that discriminated against Indians. He developed the nonviolent tactic of satyagraha (literally "truth-firmness" or "soul force") that he would later use in India. "I had . . . then to choose," he would later remember, "between allying myself to violence or finding out some other method of meeting the crisis and stopping the rot, and it came to me that we should refuse to obey legislation that was degrading and let them put us in jail if they liked" (Hay 1988, 266). He led nonviolent campaigns in 1907–08 and 1908–11 and a combined strike and cross-country march in 1913–14.

Mohandas K. Gandhi in South Africa, 1903. Gandhi lived and worked as a lawyer in South Africa from 1893 until 1914, eventually (by 1907) developing his ideas on nonviolent protest and on religion. Here he is seated in front of his South African law office with several employees. The woman is Miss Schlesin, the daughter of Russian immigrants to South Africa, who worked in Gandhi's office. To Gandhi's right is his clerk, H. S. L. Polak. (photo by Keystone/ Getty Images)

It was also in South Africa that Gandhi developed the religious and ethical ideas that merged the Western education of his youth with the beliefs and principles of his family's Hindu religion. By the age of 37, Gandhi had simplified his diet according to strict vegetarian rules, had taken a Hindu vow of celibacy (*brahmacharya*), and had exchanged his Western dress for a simpler Indian costume, a dhoti (a long cloth wrapped around the lower body), shawl, and turban. In South Africa and later in India Gandhi's political philosophy would rest equally on the Jain principle of *ahimsa* (nonviolence) and on the conviction that the means by which a political goal was achieved was fully as important as its end result. In India Gandhi would undertake fasts to the death on several occasions, a form of personal satyagraha by which he hoped to win over the hearts of his opponents.

In 1915 when Gandhi returned to India, he was already famous there. The diversity of the South African Indian community had given him a broader background and experience than that of most nationalist leaders with their more limited regional bases. Nevertheless, Gandhi was not an immediate success in India. His simple dress of dhoti, shawl, and turban made him seem idiosyncratic to Westernized audiences. He spoke too softly and tended to lecture his listeners on the need for Indian self-improvement. His initial speeches to Congress and the Home Rule League were not well received.

After his return to India, Gandhi made his base in the city of Ahmedabad, Gujarat, founding there an ashram and traveling by third-class railway coach throughout British India. In the first years of his return he organized a satyagraha against indigo planters in Champaran district in the foothills of the Himalayas, campaigned for a reduction of land revenues in Kheda district in Gujarat, and fasted to compel his friends and financial supporters, the industrialist Sarabhai family, to pay their workers higher wages. These campaigns gained Gandhi visibility and sympathy within India. But to the more anglicized nationalists he may still have seemed as incomprehensible as he did to Edwin Montagu (1879–1924), the British secretary of state for India, who met Gandhi on a tour in 1917. He "dresses like a coolie," Montagu wrote in his diary, "forswears all personal advancement, lives practically on the air, and is a pure visionary" (Wolpert 2009, 308).

The Amritsar Massacre

The end of World War I brought with it a new offer of constitutional reforms from the British government, but the reforms themselves were broadly disappointing to almost all factions of Indian nationalists. The Montagu-Chelmsford reforms (or the "Montford reforms," as they are sometime abbreviated) were promised as a move toward responsible government. They were announced in 1917 and implemented two years later in the Government of India Act of 1919. The Montford reforms offered Indians "dyarchy" (or dual government) at the provincial level; under this plan the government transferred responsibility for some governmental departments—education, public health, public works, agriculture—to elected Indian ministers, while reserving other departments—land revenue, justice, police, irrigation, and labor—to ministers appointed by the British. Indian legislative members would continue to be elected into these provincial governments through the various constituencies established in earlier reforms.

From the British perspective the Montford reforms had the advantage of bringing elected Indian officials into collaboration with the existing British Indian government, even as they cut off those same officials from the more extreme wing of the nationalist movement. From the nationalist perspective, the reforms ceded little if any real power to Indians. They gave Indian ministers the responsibility for traditionally underfunded departments, while giving them no control over or access to the revenues through which the departments were funded. Congress leaders split over how to respond. Jinnah proposed rejecting Montford outright. Tilak and Besant feuded over the wording and extent of their rejections. The remnants of the old moderate faction considered founding a separate party to allow them to accept the reforms.

But the unity that factions in the Indian National Congress could not find among themselves, British officials created for them. During World War I the Defense of India Act (1915) had created temporary sedition laws under which, in certain circumstances, political cases could be tried without juries and suspects interned without trials. In 1918 when the Rowlatt Committee recommended that these laws become permanent, the Indian government immediately passed the Rowlatt Acts, ignoring the unanimous objections of all Indians on the Imperial Legislative Council. Jinnah resigned his council seat in 1919 when the acts became law. Gandhi called for a nationwide *hartal* (strike) to protest them.

When the strikes in Delhi and North India turned into riots and shooting, Gandhi immediately ended the *hartal*, calling it a "Himalayan miscalculation" (Fischer 1983, 179). But in Amritsar, the sacred city of the Sikhs in the Punjab, the government responded to the city's *hartal* by deporting Congress leaders and prohibiting all public meetings. On April 13, Brigadier General Reginald Dyer (1864–1927), the commander in charge of the city, heard that a gathering was to take place at Jallianwalla Bagh (Jallianwalla Garden). Dyer posted his troops at the entrance to the walled garden where some 10,000 people had already gathered. Without warning, he ordered his troops to fire. A later parliamentary report estimated that 1,650 rounds of ammunition were fired, killing 379 people and wounding another 1,200. In the months following the Amritsar massacre, Dyer maintained rigid martial law. At one site where a British woman had been attacked, he ordered Indians who passed to crawl. Those who refused were to be publicly flogged.

Dyer was subsequently forced to resign from the military, and the Indian Hunter Commission condemned his actions. But in Great Britain he was a martyr. The pro-imperial House of Lords refused to censure Dyer, and on his return to England a British newspaper raised £26,000 for his retirement.

In India, public outrage brought Indians together in opposition to the British. Rabindranath Tagore, who had been knighted after receiving the Nobel Prize in literature in 1913, renounced his knighthood. The 1919 session of Congress was moved to Amritsar. The 38,000 people attending demonstrated that Congress was united as never before. In the 1920s Gandhi would move nationalism to a new level. By building up the Congress organization in Indian villages, Gandhi would make the Congress Party a mass movement.

7

GANDHI AND THE
NATIONALIST MOVEMENT
(1920–1948)

Even a handful of true satyagrahis [followers of soul force], well organized and disciplined through selfless service of the masses, can win independence for India, because behind them will be the power of the silent millions.

■

Mohandas K. Gandhi, "Satyagraha: Transforming Unjust Relationships through the Power of the Soul" (Hay 1988, 269–270)

Mohandas K. Gandhi led India's nationalist movement from the 1920s to his death in 1948. Gandhi made nationalism a mass movement in India bringing rural Indians into the Congress Party through his unique combination of Hindu religiosity, political acumen, and practical organizing skills. Between 1920 and 1948 Gandhi led a series of campaigns against the British—the 1921–22 noncooperation movement, the 1930 Salt March, the 1942 Quit India movement—successfully mobilizing masses of urban and rural Indians in opposition to British rule. Gandhi's 1921–22 campaign was a coalition of Hindus and Muslims, but in the late '20s and '30s communal violence, conservative Hindu intransigence, and Congress's own misjudgments split Mohammed Ali Jinnah and the Muslim League from the Congress movement.

In the end, it was as much the expense of World War II as Gandhi's nationalist campaigns that ended British rule in India. But neither the British nor Congress or the Muslim League was able to devise a government scheme for a free India that would maintain a strong central government (an essential Congress demand) and yet provide protection within a majoritarian democratic system for India's Muslim minority (the Muslim League demand). This failure meant that with independence in 1947 also came partition. The division of British India into India and Pakistan may have caused as many as 1 million deaths and made 10 million Indians refugees. Even as other Indian leaders participated in the detailed negotiations of Britain's 1947 transfer of power, Gandhi worked tirelessly to stop Hindu-Muslim violence. He was assassinated in 1948 by a right-wing extremist who believed Gandhi to be too pro-Muslim.

The Economic Aftermath of World War I

World War I created economic hardships in India that lasted into the 1920s and were worsened by a poor monsoon in 1918 and an influenza outbreak that killed more than 12 million Indians. Prices rose overall by more than 50 percent between 1914 and 1918 (Sarkar 1983, 170). During 1920–22, rural conditions grew so bad that the Indian government passed legislation capping rents to protect large landowners from eviction. Poorer farmers received little help. Villagers on the edges of the Himalayas set forest preserves on fire in protest. Throughout the Ganges River valley peasants founded Kisan Sabhas (Peasant Societies) through which they organized protests and rent strikes against landlords. Congress took no action in these matters, unwilling to intervene in conflicts that might prove internally divisive while at the same time fearing to antagonize a middle landlord constituency that was a major source of support.

Labor strikes were also frequent in the early 1920s. Congress founded the All-India Trade Union in 1920, the same year that the Communist Party of India was founded by Manabendra Nath Roy (1887–1954). The Communist Party began to organize unions in India's cloth, jute, and steel industries. There were more than 200 strikes in the first half of 1920 and almost 400 in 1921. By 1929 there were more than 100 trade unions in India with almost a quarter million members.

Gandhi and the Khilafat Movement

The noncooperation movement of the 1920s marked the start of Gandhi's leadership of the Indian nationalist movement. After his return to India, Gandhi had attended Congress sessions annually, but his real entrance into Indian nationalist politics came only after the Amritsar massacre, the British violence that followed it, and with his support of the Khilafat movement in the 1920s.

The Khilafat movement began after World War I. British (and Allied) plans to carve up the old Ottoman Empire gave rise to a worldwide pan-Islamic movement to preserve the Ottoman sultan's role as caliph (that is, as leader of the global Islamic community) and Islamic holy places in the Middle East. In India, the leaders of the Khilafat (the name derived from the Arabic word for "Caliphate") movement were the Ali brothers, Muhammad and Shaukat. The younger, Muhammad Ali (1878–1931), had graduated from Oxford in 1902.

By 1920 Gandhi was president of the Home Rule League. He and other Congress leaders had reluctantly agreed to participate in the elections mandated by the Montagu-Chelmsford reforms, only to be outraged by the Amritsar massacre and the subsequent British violence in the Punjab. In 1920 the release of a British report on that violence further offended Congress leaders, offering, as Gandhi put it, nothing but "page after page of thinly disguised official whitewash" (Sarkar 1983, 196). When an Indian branch of the pan-Islamic Khilafat movement formed in 1920, Gandhi was interested. At a meeting in June 1920 with Gandhi and several nationalist leaders in attendance, the Khilafat leaders adopted a plan for noncooperation with the British government in India. The plan called for the boycott of the civil services, the police, and the army and for the withholding of tax revenues. Gandhi was ready to put his Home Rule League behind it. "I have advised my Moslem friends," he wrote the viceroy, Frederic John Napier Thesiger Lord Chelmsford (1868–1933), "to withdraw their support from Your Excellency's Government and advised the Hindus to join them" (Fischer 1983, 189).

The noncooperation movement began without the sanction of Congress. At an emergency September session of Congress held in Calcutta, delegates overrode the objections of longtime Congress leaders such as Jinnah and Chittaranjan (C.R.) Das (1870–1925) from Bengal, to approve a modified noncooperation plan that included the surrender of titles and the boycott of schools, courts, councils, and foreign goods. By the regular December Congress session, only Jinnah—who preferred constitutional and moderate forms of protest—remained opposed. His objections were shouted down, and he quit Congress in disgust. Congress, now firmly under Gandhi's leadership, declared its goal to be "the attainment of Swaraj [self-rule] . . . by all legitimate and peaceful means" (Brecher 1961, 41). Against the background of a worsening economy, widespread *kisan* (peasant) protests, and labor strikes—all of which contributed to the general sense of upheaval and change—noncooperation began.

Reorganization and Change

Under Gandhi's leadership the 1920 meeting reorganized Congress, making it a mass political party for the first time. The new regulations set a membership fee of four annas ($^1/_{16}$ of a rupee) per person. A new 350-person All-India Congress Committee (AICC) was established with elected representatives from 21 different Indian regions. The election system was village based, with villages electing representatives to districts, districts to regions, and regions to the AICC. The 15-person Working Committee headed the entire Congress organization.

Organizing for noncooperation brought new and younger leaders to prominence, the most important of whom was Jawaharlal Nehru (1889–1964). Nehru was the son of Motilal Nehru, an Allahabad (United Provinces) lawyer and Congress member who had grown so wealthy and anglicized from his profession that, it was sometimes joked, his family sent their laundry to be washed in Paris. The son was raised at Allahabad within the aristocratic Kashmiri Brahman Nehru family and educated in England at Harrow and Cambridge. He returned to India in 1912 after being called to the bar in London.

Nehru was drawn to Congress as the Mahatma (a title meaning "great soul") took control in the 1920s, deeply attracted to Gandhi's philosophy of activism and moral commitment. Nehru's second great political passion, socialism, also began about this same time. In the early 1920s Nehru spent a month traveling with a delegation of peasants through a remote *mofussil* region of the United Provinces. The experience, probably Nehru's first encounter with rural poverty, filled him with shame and sorrow—"shame at my own easygoing and comfortable life," he later wrote, and "sorrow at the degradation and overwhelming poverty of India" (Brecher 1961, 40).

Nehru shared his leadership of younger Indian nationalists with a contemporary, Subhas Chandra Bose (1897–1945). Bose was also the son of a wealthy lawyer, although his Bengali father had practiced in Cuttack, Orissa. Unlike Nehru, Bose had had a stormy educational career. He was expelled from an elite Calcutta college in 1916 because he and his friends beat up an Anglo-Indian professor said to be a racist. Bose then finished his college education at a Calcutta missionary college and was sent to England by his family to study for the ICS examinations. In 1921, however, having passed the exams and on the verge of appointment to the service, Bose gave it all up. "I am now at the crossways," he wrote to his family, "and no compromise is possible" (Bose 1965, 97). He resigned his candidacy to return to India and join the Congress movement full time. Working under the Bengal politician C. R. Das and supported economically for most of his life by his lawyer brother Sarat, Bose (along with Nehru) became the leader of a young socialist faction in Congress. In 1921 during the noncooperation movement he was imprisoned, released, and then deported to Burma, accused by the British of connections with Bengali terrorists. In 1927 on his return to Calcutta, he was elected president of Bengal's branch of the Congress Party.

A third young man, Abul Kalam Azad (1888–1958), later known as Maulana Azad, also joined the Congress movement at this time. Maulana Azad came to India at the age of 10, the son of an Indian father and an Arab mother. He received a traditional Islamic education but turned to English education after being convinced of the value of Western education by the writings of Sir Sayyid Ahmad Khan. He took the pen name Azad (which means "freedom") while publishing an Urdu journal in his youth. Interned by the British during World War I, he joined both the Khilafat movement and the Congress during the 1920s. He would become one of the staunchest Muslim supporters of Congress in the years leading up to and following independence and partition, serving as Congress president in 1940 and as minister of education after independence.

Noncooperation Campaign (1921–1922)

Gandhi predicted at the 1920 Nagpur Congress session that if noncooperation was carried out nonviolently, self-government would come within the year. By July 1921 the movement was fully under way, with Congress calling for the boycott of foreign goods and supporters burning foreign clothes in public bonfires. Only 24 Indians turned in their awards and titles, Gandhi among them, and only 180 lawyers, including Motilal Nehru and C. R. Das, gave up their legal practices. But support among students was said to be very strong with the claim that new nationalist schools and colleges had enrolled 100,000 students by 1922. The boycott of British goods was also effective: The value of imported British cloth dropped by 44 percent between 1922 and 1924.

Gandhi traveled the country by rail for seven months, addressing public meetings, overseeing bonfires of foreign cloth, and meeting with village officials to organize new Congress branches. He wrote a weekly column in English for *Young India* and in Gujarati for *Navajivan* (New life). Everywhere he went he urged supporters to spin and wear *khadi* (hand-loomed cloth)—hand-spun and hand-loomed cloth would replace foreign imports—and he designed a Congress flag with the *charkha* (spinning wheel) at its center.

GANDHI'S SOCIAL VISION

pinning and wearing *khadi* (homespun cloth) were part of a broader belief Gandhi held that India should abandon all aspects of Western industrialization. He first expressed this view in *Hind Swaraj (Indian Home Rule)*, a book he wrote in South Africa in 1909. In it Gandhi described his vision of an India stripped of all the changes brought by the West—no railroads, telegraphs, hospitals, lawyers, or doctors. As he wrote to a friend in that same year,

> India's salvation consists in unlearning what she has learnt during the past fifty years. The railways, telegraphs, hospitals, lawyers, doctors, and such like have all to go, and the so-called upper classes have to learn to live conscientiously and religiously and deliberately the simple peasant life, knowing it to be a life giving true happiness (Gandhi).

(continues)

Gandhi at his spinning wheel, 1931. Released from jail following the 1931 Salt March and en route to London aboard the S.S. Rajputana to attend the Round Table Conference, Gandhi maintained his daily practice of spinning. (Library of Congress)

GANDHI'S SOCIAL VISION (continued)

India, Gandhi believed, would be revitalized by a return to village society, although the village societies he wanted would be shorn of communalism and discriminatory practices against Untouchables. In India Gandhi emphasized the wearing of *khadi*. He himself spun for some time each day, and he urged all nationalists to do the same. Such acts would help free Indians from an overreliance on the West and its industrial technology and would revitalize Indian national culture.

Source: Gandhi, Mohandas K. "Gandhi's Letter to H. S. L. Polak." 1909. The Official Mahatma Gandhi eArchive & Reference Library. Available online. URL: http://www.mahatma.org.in/books/showbook.jsp?id=204&link=bg&book=bg0005&lang=en&cat=books&image.x=11&image.y=9. Accessed January 10, 2005.

The combined Khilafat and Congress movement brought British India to the edge of rebellion. By the end of 1921, an estimated 30,000 Indians had been jailed for civil disobedience, most for short periods (Brecher 1961, 43). The government had banned all public meetings and groups. The Ali brothers and all major Congress leaders, old and young, were under arrest, including C. R. Das, Motilal Nehru, Lala Lajpat Rai, Jawaharlal Nehru, and Subhas Bose.

Gandhi remained at large throughout 1921 and into 1922, but he was no longer in control of the movement. By 1921–22 the combined force of noncooperation protests, worker and peasant strikes, and communal riots had moved India close to a state of absolute upheaval. Muslim Khilafat leaders began to talk of abandoning nonviolence. On the Malabar Coast, Muslim Moplahs declared a jihad to establish a new caliph, attacked Europeans and wealthy Hindus, and forced poorer Hindu peasants to convert to Islam. Edward, the Prince of Wales's visit to India in November 1921 was boycotted by Congress, and everywhere he went he was met by strikes and black flags. In Bombay city riots broke out on the occasion of the prince's visit and lasted five days. Although pressed by Congress leaders, Gandhi refused to sanction a mass civil disobedience campaign, agreeing only to a small demonstration campaign in Bardoli, a Gujarati district of 87,000 people. But before even that could start, in February 1922 reports reached Gandhi that a nationalist procession in Chauri Chaura (United Provinces), seeking revenge for police beatings, had chased a group of police back to their station house, set it on fire, and hacked 22 policemen to death as they fled the blaze.

Gandhi immediately suspended the Bardoli movement and to the disbelief of Congress leaders, declared noncooperation at an end. "I assure you," he wrote to an angry Jawaharlal Nehru, still in jail, "that if the thing had not been suspended we would have been leading not a non-violent struggle but essentially a violent struggle" (Nanda 1962, 202). Congress leaders watched helplessly as their movement collapsed around them. "Gandhi had pretty well run himself to the last ditch as a politician," the viceroy Rufus Daniel Isaacs, Lord Reading, told his son with satisfaction (Nanda 1962, 203).

One month later Gandhi was arrested and tried for sedition. He made no attempt to deny the charges against him: "I am here, . . ." he told the court, "to invite and cheerfully submit to the highest penalty that can be inflicted upon me. . . . I hold it an honor to be disaffected towards a government which in its totality has done more harm to India than any previous system" (Fischer 1983, 202–203). The judge sentenced him to six years' imprisonment.

Both during and immediately after the noncooperation campaign, British officials authorized several reforms that had long been sought by urban middle-class Indians. The India Act of 1921 made the viceroy's

GANDHI'S "EXPERIMENTS WITH TRUTH"

Mahatma Gandhi's autobiography, *The Story of My Experiments with Truth*, was one of the most influential nationalist books of the 20th century. Written in 1925, when Gandhi was 56, the autobiography appeared in weekly installments in a Gujarati newsletter and was subsequently translated into English by Gandhi's nephew. Its chapters covered episodes Gandhi knew would resonate with young Westernized Indians, recalling Gandhi's early "experiments" with eating meat, his exploration of an anglicized lifestyle while living in England, and his return to Hindu religious practices (celibacy, strict vegetarianism) in South Africa. Gandhi's quest for a personal and religious identity demonstrated to readers the ultimate "truth" of Hindu religious principles and practices even for Indians living in the modern 20th-century world.

Legislative Council a bicameral parliament with elected membership. A new Tariff Board in New Delhi in 1923 gave the Indian government the beginnings of fiscal autonomy. And in the same year, for the first time, the ICS examinations were simultaneously held in India and England. In the provincial and municipal elections of 1923–24 Congress candidates gained control of provincial ministries in Bengal and Bombay. A number of Congress leaders became elected mayors or heads of towns and cities: C. R. Das became mayor of Calcutta, Jawaharlal Nehru of Allahabad, and a west Indian Gandhi supporter, Vallabhbhai (Sardar) Patel (1875–1950), was elected the municipal president of Ahmedabad.

Gandhi was released from jail in 1924 for an appendicitis operation but refused to consider further campaigns against the government. Although he accepted the presidency of the 1925 Congress session, his focus was on relief projects and village work. "For me," he said in this period, "nothing in the political world is more important than the spinning wheel" (Fischer 1983, 232). He traveled for much of 1925, now by second-class carriage, raising funds for Congress, promoting spinning and hand-loom weaving, and leading a campaign in Travancore to open a temple road to Untouchables. In 1926 he began a practice he would continue to the end of his life: For one day in the week he maintained complete silence. It was not until 1928 that he would again be willing to reenter active political life.

Post-Khilafat Communal Violence

The worldwide Khilafat movement ended in 1924 when the modernizing ruler of Turkey, Kemal Atatürk, abolished the Ottoman caliphate. In India, Hindu-Muslim unity did not survive the end of the movement. With the collapse of Khilafat, local Muslim leaders in several provinces declared themselves "caliphs" and led movements to protect Islam, organize Muslim communities, and spread religious propaganda among them. Both Hindu and Muslim groups escalated their provocations of each other in these years, Hindu groups demanding an end to cow slaughter and Muslim groups responding violently when processions or loud music disturbed prayers at a mosque. Electoral politics also contributed to communal tensions in these years; separate electorates heightened the awareness of religious divisions. And elections encouraged Hindu candidates to court the majority Hindu vote. In Bengal even leftist Calcutta politicians, such as Subhas Bose, took strongly pro-zamindar positions to the irritation and disgust of Muslim peasants and tenants.

Beginning with the Moplah rebellion in 1921 and escalating between 1923 and 1927, communal riots erupted across northern India. The United Provinces had 91 communal riots in the 1923–27 period. The cities of Calcutta, Dacca, Patna, Rawalpindi, and Delhi all had riots. As the violence increased, the last remnants of Hindu-Muslim political unity vanished. The Khilafat leader Muhammad Ali had campaigned with Gandhi during the noncooperation movement and served as Congress president in 1923, but by 1925 Ali had broken his association with Gandhi. In the same vein, the Muslim League met separately from Congress in 1924 for the first time since 1918.

The Hindu Mahasabha and the RSS

In the years after 1924, communal associations flourished in northern India linking religious populations across class lines and allowing economic and social tensions to be displaced onto religion. The north Indian Hindu association, the Mahasabha, had been founded in 1915 by the United Provinces Congressite Madan Mohan Malaviya (1861–1946) and was originally a loose alliance of Hindu revivalists working for cow protection, language reform, and Hindu social welfare in the United Provinces and the Punjab. The Mahasabha had been inactive during the Khilafat and noncooperation movements, but in the increasingly hostile communal atmosphere of 1921–23 it revived. The organization gained new members in the northern Gangetic regions of United Provinces, Delhi, Bihar, and the Punjab. In a shared front with the older Arya Samaj it used many of the older society's tactics, forming Hindu self-defense corps, demanding that Hindi replace Urdu, and using purification and conversion to bring Muslims and Untouchables into Hinduism.

By 1925 the Mahasabha had spawned a paramilitary offshoot and ally: the Rashtriya Swayamsevak Sangh (National Volunteer Force, or RSS). Founded at Nagpur in 1925 by Keshav Baliram Hedgewar (1889–1940), the RSS was a paramilitary religious society along the lines of an *akhara* (a local gymnasium where young men gathered for wrestling and body-building). RSS members took vows before the image of the monkey-god Hanuman, drilled in groups each morning, often in uniform, and pledged themselves to serve the RSS "with [their] whole body, heart, and money for in it lies the betterment of Hindus and the country" (Jaffrelot 1996, 37). By 1940 the RSS had spread from Nagpur into the United Provinces and the Punjab; its membership numbered 100,000 trained cadres.

V. D. SAVARKAR AND "HINDUTVA"

Vinayak Damodar Savarkar (1883–1966) became the Hindu Mahasabha's most prominent spokesman during the 1930s and is today considered the ideological founder of Hindu nationalism. By 1911, because of his associations with terrorist groups from his native Maharashtra, Savarkar had received two life sentences and had been transported to the Andaman Islands. By 1922, through the intervention of Congress leaders, Savarkar was back in India in a prison at Ratnagiri in Maharashtra. There he wrote *Hindutva: Who Is a Hindu?*—the earliest attempt to describe a Hindu national identity and one written in part as response to the pan-Islamicism of the Khilafat movement. Savarkar, who described himself as an atheist, insisted that "Hindutva" or Hinduness, was not the equivalent of Hinduism. Hinduism was only one part of Hinduness, and not necessarily the most important part. Instead Savarkar defined "Hindutva" as made up of the geographic, racial, and cultural ties that bound Indians together. "These are the essentials of Hindutva," he wrote, "a common [geographical] nation (Rashtra), a common race (Jati), and a common civilization (Sanskriti)" (Savarkar 2005, 116). Hinduness rested on these three: first, on residence within the geographical territory/nation

Congress leaders maintained friendly relations with Mahasabha members during the 1920s, and in this period prominent politicians, such as Malaviya himself, were members of both organizations. But in 1926 Malaviya and Lajpat Rai organized the Independent Congress Party, a political group through which Mahasabha candidates could contest elections. In the 1926 provincial elections Congress candidates lost badly to Mahasabha candidates. And in Muslim separate electorates, where Congress Muslim candidates had previously been able to win, in 1926 they won only one Muslim seat out of 39 contested.

All Sons of This Land

In 1927 the British government appointed Sir John Simon (1873–1954) as head of a parliamentary commission that would tour India and make recommendations for future political reforms. From the start, however, the Simon Commission provoked opposition because it included no of India from the Indus to the Bay of Bengal, the sacred territory of the Aryans as described in the Vedas; second, on the racial heritage of Indians, all of whom, for Savarkar, were descendants of the Vedic ancestors who had occupied the subcontinent in ancient times; and third, on the common culture and civilization shared by Indians (the language, culture, practices, religion) and exemplified for Savarkar by the Sanskrit language. The Hindus, Savarkar wrote, were not merely *citizens* of an Indian state united by patriotic love for a motherland. They were a race united "by the bonds of a common blood," "not only a nation but a race-*jati*" (Jaffrelot). Indian Muslims and Christians, however, were not part of Hindutva. Even if they lived within the geographical territory of India and even if they were descended from the ancient ancestors of India, the Islamic and Christian religions they worshipped were foreign in origin and therefore not part of the "civilization" that was essential to Hinduness.

Released from prison in 1924, Savarkar was kept under house arrest until the 1930s. Once free he became the president of the Mahasabha for seven years in a row. "We Hindus," he told a Mahasabha convention in 1938, "are a Nation by ourselves" (Sarkar 1983).

Sources: Jaffrelot, Christophe. *The Hindu Nationalist Movement in India* (New York: Columbia University Press, 1996), p. 28; Sarkar, Sumit. *Modern India 1885–1947* (Madras: Macmillan India, 1983), p. 356.

Indians. Demonstrations followed its members wherever they went, and Congress, the Muslim League, and all but two minor Indian political groups boycotted its inquiries.

To counter any Simon Commission proposals, Motilal Nehru headed an All-Parties Conference in 1928 to which Congress, the Muslim League, and the Hindu Mahasabha sent members. The conference was to develop a separate, Indian plan for constitutional reform. Its members agreed that the overall goal should be commonwealth status within the British Empire, But they could not agree on how minorities would be represented within this government. Jinnah, representing the Muslim League, was willing to give up separate electorates for Muslims; in return, however, he wanted one-third of the seats in the central legislative government to be reserved for Muslim candidates, and he also wanted reserved seats in the Muslim majority provinces of Bengal and the Punjab in proportion to the Muslim percentage of the population in each. (Reserved seats were seats set aside for candidates of a single community but voted on in elections by all Indians.) The Hindu Mahasabha delegates, however, led by the Bombay lawyer Mukund Ramrao (M. R.) Jayakar (1873–1959), absolutely refused seat reservations in the Muslim majority regions. In desperation Jinnah took his proposal to the December session of Congress. "If you do not settle this question today, we shall have to settle it tomorrow," he told the Congress meeting. "We are all sons of this land. We have to live together. Believe me there is no progress for India until the Musalmans and the Hindus are united" (Hay 1988, 227–228). Again Hindu Mahasabha delegates blocked the proposal, refused all pleas for compromise, and Congress leaders ultimately yielded to them.

The constitutional plan that resulted from these debates was not itself significant. Within a year it had been overturned. Gandhi, who had finally yielded to Congress entreaties and reentered political life, arranged to have Jawaharlal Nehru elected President of Congress in 1929. Nehru and Subhas Bose had formed the Socialist Independence for India League in 1928, and Gandhi wanted to draw Nehru and his young associates back into the Congress fold and away from the growing socialist and radical movements. Under Nehru's leadership, however, Congress abandoned the goal of commonwealth status, replacing it with a demand for *purna swaraj* (complete independence). Preparations began for a new civil disobedience movement that would begin under Gandhi's leadership the next year.

But the Congress's acquiescence in the Mahasabha's intransigence in 1928 was significant for the effect it had on Jinnah. Jinnah left the Congress session and immediately joined the parallel All-India Muslim Conference meeting in New Delhi. The Muslim Conference then declared its complete and irrevocable commitment to separate Muslim electorates. Muslim political leaders were now split off from the Congress movement. By 1930 Muhammad Ali, Gandhi's former ally, would denounce Gandhi as a supporter of the Hindu Mahasabha. Indian Muslims would remain on the sidelines in the 1930s civil disobedience movement. It was, as Ali told a British audience in London in 1930, "the old maxim of 'divide and rule.' . . . We divide and *you* rule" (Hay 1988, 204).

Non-Brahman Movements in South and West India

During the 1920s and 1930s, even as Hindu Muslim conflicts in northern India split the nationalist movement, lower-caste and Untouchable leaders in South India were defining Brahmans as their main political opponents. In Madras, E. V. Ramaswami Naicker (later called "Periyar," or "the wise man," 1880–1973) founded the Self-Respect Movement in 1925. Periyar's movement rejected Sanskritic Aryan traditions, emphasizing instead *samadharma* (equality) and the shared Dravidian heritage of Tamils. For Periyar and his followers the Brahman-dominated Gandhian Congress stood for social oppression.

Another leader who rejected high-caste Sanskritic traditions was Bhimrao Ramji Ambedkar (1891–1956), an Untouchable leader from the Mahar community of Maharashtra. Ambedkar had received a law degree and a Ph.D. through education in both England and the United States. Returning to India in the 1920s he organized a Mahar caste association and led regionwide struggles for the rights of Untouchables to use village wells and tanks and to enter temples. For Ambedkar caste was not a racial system. It was a socially mandated system of graded inequalities whose internal divisions kept lower castes from opposing the top. "All," Ambedkar wrote, "have a grievance against the highest [caste] and would like to bring about their downfall. But they will not combine" (Jaffrelot 2003, 21). By the late 1920s Ambedkar and his followers were publicly burning copies of the Laws of Manu to symbolize their rejection of high-caste practices and traditions.

The Great Depression and Its Effects

The worldwide depression that began in 1929 with the stock market crash destroyed India's export economy and changed Great Britain's economic relationship with India. Before 1929 Indian imports to Great Britain were 11 percent of all British imports. Indian exports, in fact, were so lucrative that they maintained Britain's favorable balance of trade in world markets. At the same time private British-run businesses in India remained strong, particularly in the mining, tea, and jute industries.

But the Great Depression cut the value of Indian exports by more than half, from 311 crores (1 crore = 10 million rupees) in 1929–30 to 132 crores in 1932–33. Indian imports also fell by almost half, from 241 crores to 133 crores. (Within India, agricultural prices were also devastated, falling by 44 percent between 1929 and 1931 and increasing tax pressures on peasant landlords, particularly at the middle levels.) The Indian government could no longer pay the home charges through revenues drawn from Indian exports; it now had to pay these charges through gold. Private British companies found direct investment in India less profitable than before 1929 and began to develop collaborative agreements with Indian businesses instead. Yet India's economy remained tied to the empire: The value of the Indian rupee was still linked to British sterling, and India continued to pay home charges—the old nationalist "drain"—to the British government throughout the 1930s.

If the worldwide depression weakened older imperial business structures, it strengthened Indian capitalists. In the 1930s Indian industry spread out from western India to Bengal, the United Provinces, Madras, Baroda, Mysore, and Bhopal. By the 1930s Indian textile mills were producing two-thirds of all textiles bought within India. The growth in Indian-owned business enterprises even affected the nationalist movement, as new Indian capitalists contributed money (and their own business perspective) to Congress in the 1930s.

Despite the gains of Indian industrialists, stagnation and poverty characterized the Indian economy in the late 1930s. The global depression produced agricultural decline and increased India's need to import food from other countries. Even though the Indian population grew slowly between 1921 and 1941, from 306 million to 389 million, food produced for local consumption in those years did not match this growth. The per capita national income (the yearly income for each Indian person) was estimated at 60.4 rupees in 1917 and 60.7 rupees in 1947. Over 30 years, the average Indian income had grown less than one-half of a rupee.

Salt March

Gandhi's 1930 Salt March was the most famous of all his campaigns. It drew participants from cities, towns, and villages all across British India and gained India's freedom struggle worldwide attention and sympathy. At its end, by Congress estimates, more than 90,000 Indians had been arrested. Despite these successes, however, the Salt March did not achieve Indian independence.

Congress leaders, such as Nehru, were initially dismayed at Gandhi's choice of focus for the campaign—the salt tax—but salt was necessary for life, and British laws made it illegal for any Indian to manufacture salt or even pick up natural sea salt on a beach without paying the tax. The salt tax touched all Indians, the poor even more aggressively than the rich. It illustrated the basic injustice of imperial rule. This focus on an issue that combined the political and the ethical was characteristic of Gandhi's best campaigns.

The march began on March 12 when the 61-year-old Gandhi and more than 70 *satyagrahis* (practitioners of satyagraha) left Gandhi's ashram at Sabarmati on foot. It ended on April 6 after marchers had walked 240 miles over dusty dirt roads and reached Dandi on the

Salt March crowds, 1930. Gandhi's second nationalist campaign drew huge crowds in India and worldwide attention. This photograph was taken on the banks of the Sabarmati River in Gujarat as Gandhi spoke to a crowd. (AP/Wide World Photos)

Gujarati seacoast. "Ours is a holy war," Gandhi told one of many crowds that gathered along the way:

> It is a non-violent struggle. . . . If you feel strong enough, give up Government jobs, enlist yourselves as soldiers in this salt satyagraha, burn your foreign cloth and wear khadi. Give up liquor. There are many things within your power through which you can secure the keys which will open the gates of freedom. (Tewari 1995)

When the march reached the coast, Gandhi waded into the sea, picked up some sea salt from the beach, and by so doing broke the salt laws. He urged Indians throughout the country to break the salt laws and boycott foreign cloth and liquor shops.

Civil disobedience now occurred in all major Indian cities. In Ahmedabad, 10,000 people bought illegal salt from Congress during the movement's first week. In Delhi a crowd of 15,000 watched the Mahasabha leader Malaviya publicly buy illegal salt. In Bombay Congress workers supplied protesters with illegal salt by making it in pans on their headquarters' roof. Nehru, the Congress president, was arrested on April 14; Gandhi on May 4. The former Congress president Sarojini Naidu (1879–1949) took Gandhi's place leading a march of 2,500 nonviolent volunteers against the Dharasana Salt Works. Row after row of marchers advanced on police guarding the works, only to be struck down by the policemen's steel-tipped *lathis* (long bamboo sticks). "Not one of the marchers even raised an arm to fend off the blows," reported a United Press reporter (Fischer 1983, 273–274).

In some places the campaign grew violent, but this time Gandhi, who had perhaps learned from the disastrous end of his earlier campaign, made no effort to stop it. In Bombay Gandhi's arrest led to a textile workers' strike, and crowds of protesters burned liquor shops and police and government buildings. In eastern Bengal, Chittagong terrorists seized and held the local armory through five days of armed combat. In the Northwest Frontier Province, peaceful demonstrators in Peshawar were killed by police fire, and the army had to be called in to stop the rioting that followed. In Sholapur, Maharashtra, news of Gandhi's arrest led to a textile strike and rioting that lasted until martial law restored order.

The 1930 campaign was much larger than the earlier noncooperation movement, reflecting the larger mass basis developed by Congress during the 1920s. The campaign involved fewer urban middle-class Indians and more peasants. Participation in it was also a greater risk. Police violence was brutal, even against nonviolent protesters, and property confiscations were more widespread. Nevertheless the movement saw at least three times as many people jailed as in 1921, more than 90,000 by Nehru's estimate, the largest numbers coming from Bengal, the Gangetic plains, and the Punjab.

Organizing Women

Women were active participants in the 1930 civil disobedience movement. Women's visibility in the campaign was itself a testament to the changes that had reshaped urban middle-class women's lives over the past century. Women's active involvement also demonstrated that support for independence was not limited to male family members. Sarojini Naidu was arrested early in the campaign, and Gandhi's wife, Kasturbai, led women protesters in picketing liquor shops after her husband's arrest. In Bombay, where the numbers of women protesters were the greatest, the Rashtriya Stree Sangha (National Women's Organization) mobilized women to collect seawater for salt, picket toddy shops, and sell salt on the street. In Bengal middle-class women not only courted arrest but also participated in terrorist activities. In Madras the elite Women's Swadeshi League supported spinning, the wearing of *khadi,* and the boycott of foreign goods, if not public marches. In the North Indian cities of Allahabad, Lucknow, Delhi, and Lahore, middle-class women, sometimes 1,000 at a time, participated in public demonstrations, even appearing in public on occasion without veils. Not all husbands approved their wives' activities, however. In Lahore one husband refused to sanction the release of his jailed wife; she had not asked his permission before leaving home.

The Round Table Conferences (1930–1932)

Civil disobedience coincided with the opening of the first Round Table Conference in London. Facing a new Congress campaign and under pressure from a new Labor government, the viceroy Edwin Frederick Lindley Wood, Baron Irwin (1881–1959), later known as Lord Halifax, invited all Indian political parties to a Round Table Conference in London in 1930. Gandhi and the Congress refused, but 73 delegates came, including the Indian princes, Muslim leaders, Sikh leaders, and representatives of the Hindu Mahasabha. British officials thought that a federated Indian government with semi-autonomous provinces might still allow the preservation of substantial British power at its center. Federation and provincial autonomy also appealed to many constituencies attending the first Round Table Conference. For the Indian princes (who controlled collectively about one-third of the subcontinent), such a federated government would allow the preservation of their current regimes. For Muslim leaders from Muslim majority regions (the Punjab or Bengal, for instance), provincial autonomy was an attractive mechanism through which they might maintain regional control. Even the Sikh representatives and those from the Hindu Mahasabha saw provincial autonomy as an opportunity to preserve local languages and regional religious culture—although whose languages and which religious cultures was never debated.

Only Jinnah of the Muslim League at the conference and Congress leaders jailed far away in India were opposed to the plan. Jinnah wanted a strong centralized Indian government, but one within which Muslims (and he as their representative) were guaranteed a significant position. Congress was entirely opposed to federation. They wanted to replace the British in India with their own government, not struggle for political survival in provincial backwaters while the British ruled at the center.

Gandhi and Nehru (in separate jails but in communication) had previously refused to end the civil disobedience movement, but now Gandhi suddenly reversed himself, perhaps from fear that the Round Table talks might resolve matters without the Congress or perhaps because enthusiasm was waning by 1931 both among demonstrators in the field and within the Indian business community. Gandhi met Irwin and reached a settlement: the Gandhi-Irwin pact. Civil disobedience would end; he would attend the Round Table Conference; jailed protesters would be released; and Indians would be allowed the private consumption of untaxed salt. Indian business leaders—the Tatas in Bombay, the Birlas in Bengal—approved the agreement. For Nehru, Subhas Bose, and the Congress left wing it was a betrayal, an abandonment of the campaign in exchange for no constitutional gains at all. Still if Gandhi's pact with Irwin won no concessions, his meeting with the viceroy served to irritate British conservatives and proimperialists. In Britain Winston Churchill (1874–1965), then a member of Parliament, expressed his disgust at the sight of "this one-time Inner Temple lawyer, now seditious fakir, striding half-naked up the steps of the Viceroy's palace, there to negotiate and to parley on equal terms with the representative of the King-Emperor" (Fischer 1983, 277).

The second Round Table Conference, however, made it clear that no Indian government could be designed without an agreement over how power at the center would be shared. The delegates deadlocked (as in 1928–29) over the question of how and to whom separate electorates should be awarded. In 1932 Gandhi returned to India to rekindle a dispirited civil disobedience movement. The new Conservative viceroy Freeman Freeman-Thomas, Lord Willingdon (1866–1941), however, immediately ordered the movement shut down. The Congress Party was declared illegal, its funds confiscated, and its records destroyed. Within months more than 40,000 Indians, including Gandhi and the entire Congress leadership, were in jail. The leadership would remain in jail for the next two years.

The Poona Pact

With no agreement from the Round Table Conference and with Congress leadership in jail, the British made their own decision on communal awards. They awarded separate electorates to Muslims, Sikhs, Indian Christians, Europeans, women, and the "Scheduled Castes" (that is, Untouchables). At the second Round Table Conference, Gandhi had refused to consider such awards. Ambedkar, a delegate to the conference, had been willing to accept reserved seats for Untouchables, but Gandhi had been adamant. Untouchables (or Harijans—"children of god"—as Gandhi had taken to calling them) were Hindus and could not be split off from the Hindu community.

When the 1932 awards were announced, Gandhi began a fast to the death in protest. Between September 18 and September 24 he took neither food nor water, as Congress leaders, Ambedkar, and British officials scrambled to define a new agreement before Gandhi died. The Poona Pact, signed on September 24, replaced separate electorates with reserved seats for Untouchables. Ambedkar, who had held out against great pressure and had feared that all Untouchables might be blamed for causing Gandhi's death, now commented only that if Gandhi had accepted seat reservation at the Round Table Conference, "it would not have been necessary for him to go through this ordeal" (Fischer 1983, 317).

After the Poona Pact Gandhi increased his interest in and activity on Hindu Untouchability. He founded a weekly newspaper, *Harijan,* toured Untouchable communities in 1933–34, and encouraged his followers to work for the opening of wells, roads, and temples to Untouchable communities. His 1932–34 speeches to Untouchable groups were disrupted by Sanatanists (orthodox Hindus), and in Pune there was a bomb attack on his car. Gandhi's relations with members of the Hindu Mahasabha also cooled in this period, particularly with Malaviya with whom he had been close in the 1920s. In the longer term his increased involvement with Untouchable concerns created loyalties toward Congress among Untouchable communities that lasted well into the postindependence period.

Government of India Act, 1935

In Great Britain, Parliament passed the Government of India Act of 1935, in spite of opposition from both sides: Conservatives such as Churchill thought it a covert attempt to grant India dominion status; Laborites such as Clement Attlee saw it as an effort to invalidate the Indian Congress. The act continued British efforts to preserve their power over India's central government, even while ceding Indian provinces almost entirely to elected Indian control. It created a Federation of India made up of 11 provinces, all the princely states, and a small number of territories. The provinces were to be run by elected Indians and the princely states by the princes. At the act's center was the "steel frame" that would preserve British control over India: The viceroy and his administration remained in control of the central government with a separate, protected budget and authority over defense and external affairs (Jalal 1985, 17). Two central legislative houses were also included in the act but never functioned, rejected for different reasons by both the princes and the Congress. Provincial autonomy, however, began in 1937 after nationwide elections that enfranchised 35 million Indians (about one-sixth of India's adult population).

Congress in Power

The Congress Party swept the provincial elections of 1937, winning 70 percent of the total popular vote and the right to form governments in

Birla Mandir, New Delhi. The Lakshmi Narayan Temple (commonly known as the Birla Mandir, or "temple") was built by the industrialist B. D. Birla in the late 1930s. The Birlas were major financial supporters of Mohandas Gandhi, and Gandhi himself dedicated the temple at its opening in 1938. The ornate, pink-colored temple was dedicated to Vishnu (Narayan) and his wife Lakshmi. Among the marble designs on its inside are panels illustrating the Bhagavad Gita. (courtesy of Judith E. Walsh)

eight out of 11 provinces: Madras, Bombay, Central Provinces, Bihar, United Provinces, Northwest Frontier, Orissa, and Assam. Regional parties won control of three out of the four Muslim majority provinces: Bengal, Punjab, and Sind. (Congress had won the fourth, the Northwest Frontier.) The Muslim League, in contrast, won only 5 percent of the total Muslim vote—109 seats out of 482 Muslim contests—and none of the Muslim majority provinces.

In their provincial governments and coalitions, winning Congress politicians made few concessions either to Muslim representatives or to Muslim sensibilities. In the United Provinces, Congress officials told Muslim League representatives that they could participate in the government only if they left the league and joined the Congress Party. Congress-dominated provincial assemblies sang "Bande Mataram," and regional Congress discourse extolled the virtues of the cow, the Hindi language, and the Devanagari script. For Jinnah, working later in the 1940s to rebuild the Muslim League, Congress provincial governments provided a clear illustration of the dangers Islam and Indian Muslims would face in an India ruled by a Hindu-dominated party.

On the national level, Gandhi and the Congress "old guard" faced a challenge from the party's left wing. In 1938 Subhas Bose won election as Congress president, supported by leftist and socialist Congress members. He was opposed by Gandhi, Congress businessmen, and more moderate Congress politicians. Bose and Gandhi had been opponents within the Congress, disagreeing on economic policies and political tactics. Unlike Nehru, however, Bose was unwilling to yield to Gandhi's overall leadership. Gandhi tolerated Bose as Congress president for the first term, but when Bose narrowly won reelection the following year, Gandhi engineered the resignations of most Working Committee members. Bose worked alone for six months before giving up and resigning the presidency. He and his brother Sarat resigned also from the Congress Working Committee and returned to Bengal to form their own party, the Forward Block, a left-wing coalition group.

Pakistan

After the losses of the 1937 election, Jinnah had to rebuild the Muslim League on a more popular basis. To do so, by the 1940s he was advocating the idea of "Pakistan" and stressing the theme of an Islamic religion in danger. At the 1940 Lahore meeting of the Muslim League, Jinnah declared—and the League agreed—that Muslims must have an autonomous state. "No constitutional plan would be workable in this country or acceptable to the Muslims," the League stated in its 1940 Lahore Resolution, unless it stipulated that "the areas in which the Muslims are numerically in a majority . . . should be grouped to constitute 'Independent States' in which the constituent units shall be autonomous and sovereign" (Hay 1988, 228). The idea of a separate Islamic Indian state had been expressed 10 years earlier by the Urdu poet Muhammad Iqbal (1877–1938). The imagined state had even been given a name by a Muslim student at Cambridge in 1933: He called it "Pakistan," a pun that meant "pure land" and was also an acronym for the major regions of the Muslim north (P stood for the Punjab, a for Afghanistan, k for Kashmir, s for Sindh, and tan for Baluchistan).

The difficulty with the idea of Pakistan was that it did not address the political needs of most Indian Muslims. Most Muslims were scattered throughout India in regions far from the four northern Muslim majority provinces. Minority Muslim populations needed constitutional safeguards within provincial and central governments, not a Muslim state hundreds, even thousands, of miles from their homes. Jinnah himself had worked throughout his career to establish just such safeguards within a strong centralized government. Some scholars have suggested that his support for Pakistan in the 1940s began as a political tactic—a device to drum up Muslim support for a more popularly based Muslim League and a threat to force concessions from Congress leaders, particularly from Gandhi for whom the idea of a divided India was anathema.

The idea of a state ruled by Islamic law where Muslim culture and life ways could reach full expression had great appeal to Indian Muslims. Muslims in majority regions imagined Pakistan as their own province, now transformed into an autonomous Muslim state. Muslims in minority provinces (always Jinnah's strongest constituency) thought of Pakistan less as a territorial goal than as a political identity—a Muslim national identity—that would entitle Indian Muslims to a protected position within any central Indian government. Even as late as 1946–47, Muslims in minority provinces supported the idea of Pakistan with little sense of what it might mean in reality. As one Muslim, a student in the United Provinces at that time, later recalled,

> Nobody thought in terms of migration in those days: [the Muslims] all thought that everything would remain the same, Punjab would remain Punjab, Sindh would remain Sindh, there won't be any demographic changes—no drastic changes anyway—the Hindus and Sikhs would continue to live in Pakistan . . . and we would continue to live in India. (Pandey 2001, 26)

Quit India!

On September 3, 1939, the viceroy, Victor Alexander John Hope, Lord Linlithgow (1887–1952), on orders from Britain, declared India at war with Germany. This time, however, the Indian National Congress offered cooperation in the war only on condition of the immediate sharing of power in India's central government. In April 1942, in an attempt to win over Congress leaders, the British government flew Sir Stafford Cripps (a personal friend of Nehru's) to India. With British prime minister Churchill completely opposed to any concessions to Indian independence, even as a possible Japanese invasion loomed on India's eastern borders, Cripps offered Congress leaders only a guarantee of dominion status (a self-governing nation within the British Commonwealth) at the end of the war. Gandhi called Cripps's offer "a post dated cheque" (Brecher 1961, 109).

With Cripps's mission a failure, Gandhi and the Congress opened a new civil disobedience campaign: "Quit India!" The government immediately imprisoned all major Congress leaders. Nevertheless, an uncoordinated but massive uprising spread throughout the country leading to more than 90,000 arrests by the end of 1943. Protests were marked by sporadic violence and included attacks on railways, telegraphs, and army facilities. The British responded with police shootings, public floggings, the destruction of entire villages, and, in eastern Bengal, by aerial machine-gun attacks on protesters.

Beginning in 1942 and lasting through 1946 a terrible famine erupted in Bengal. The famine was caused not by bad weather but by the conjunction of several other factors: the commandeering of local foods to feed the British army, the wartime stoppage of rice imports from Burma, profiteering and speculation in rice, and perhaps also a rice disease that reduced crop yields. By 1943 tens of thousands of people had migrated into Calcutta in search of food and an estimated 1 million to 3 million people had died from famine-related causes.

Independence

At the end of World War II, with a new Labor government in place, huge war debts to repay, and a country to rebuild, the British wanted to exit India. The combined costs of war supplies and of an Indian army mobilized at 10 times its normal strength had more than liquidated India's debt to Great Britain. Instead of home charges, it was now Great Britain that was in debt to India. British officials in both London and New Delhi knew Britain could no longer maintain its empire in India.

215

The biggest obstacle to British withdrawal, however, was the politicized communal identities that had grown up over the 20th century, fostered by Indian nationalists and politicians and by the British themselves through their "divide and rule" tactics. Such identities divided Muslims and Hindus, but they also existed among Sikhs, South Indian "Dravidians," and Untouchables. The problem was how to reunite all these political groups within the majoritarian electoral structures of a modern democratic state, while simultaneously protecting their minority interests.

The Congress Party won 91 percent of all non-Muslim seats in the winter elections of 1945–46 and was returned to power in eight provinces. By the 1940s Congress had built an all-India organization with deep roots throughout the country and with a unity and identity developed over its more than 50 years of struggle against British rule. The party's goal was a strong, centralized India under its control. For Congress socialists, like Nehru, such centralization would be essential if India was to be rebuilt as an industrialized, prosperous state. Minority groups' fears over such centralization, meanwhile, were an irritant for Congress. From the Congress perspective political differences between Hindus and Muslims could wait for resolution until *after* independence.

BOSE'S INDIAN NATIONAL ARMY

In 1941 Subhas Bose's arrest for sedition was imminent in Calcutta, and he fled India, seeking sanctuary with the Nazi government in Germany. In 1942 he was taken to Japan by the Germans and then to Singapore, now under Japanese control. In Singapore, Bose formed the Indian National Army (INA), drawing his recruits from the 40,000 Indian prisoners of war interned in Japanese camps. His new army fought with the Japanese against the British in Burma.

Many Indians identified with the INA and saw it as a legitimate part of the freedom struggle against Great Britain. In 1945, the same year that Bose died in a plane crash, the British government put several hundred captured INA officers on trial for treason in New Delhi. Both Congress and the Muslim League protested against the trials, but it was only after two students were killed by police in Calcutta riots against the trials that charges against most defendants were dropped.

Mohammed Ali Jinnah and Mohandas K. Gandhi both joined the Indian nationalist movement around the time of World War I. They would be political opponents for the next 30 years, differing not only on issues of political substance but also (as the photo shows) on questions of style and personal demeanor. By 1948 both men would be dead: Gandhi from an assassin's bullet and Jinnah from disease and ill health. This photo dates to 1944 and a meeting at Jinnah's house on September 9 to discuss Hindu-Muslim conflicts in Bombay city. (AP/Wide World Photos)

In contrast to Congress, Jinnah's Muslim League existed mostly at the center. The league was a thin veneer that papered over a wide range of conflicting Muslim interests in Muslim majority and minority regions—a veneer that Jinnah used, nevertheless, to justify the league's (and his own) claims to be the "sole spokesman" of Indian Muslims (Jalal 1985). By 1945 Jinnah's advocacy of an independent Muslim state and his campaign of "Islam in danger" had rebuilt the Muslim League. It had also completely polarized the Muslim electorate. In the winter elections of 1945–46 the Muslim League reversed its losses of eight years earlier, winning every Muslim seat at the center and 439 out of 494 Muslim seats in the provincial elections. The politicized atmosphere of the 1940s destroyed long-established communal coalition parties and governments in both Bengal and the Punjab, replacing them with Muslim League governments. For Muslims, religious identity was now the single most important element of political identity. For the league (and more broadly for the Muslim electorate) that identity needed political protection through constitutional safeguards *before* independence arrived.

A British cabinet mission, sent to India after the 1945–46 elections, was unable to construct a formula for independence. Jinnah refused to accept a "moth eaten" Pakistan, a Muslim state that would consist of parts of Bengal and parts of the Punjab (Sarkar 1983, 429). Congress refused a proposal for a loose federation of provinces. Plans for an interim government foundered on arguments over who would appoint its Muslim and Untouchable members. As the Congress left wing organized railway and postal strikes and walkouts, Jinnah, intending to demonstrate Muslim strength, called for Muslims to take "direct action" on August 16, 1946, to achieve Pakistan.

Direct Action Day in Calcutta triggered a series of Hindu-Muslim riots throughout northern India unprecedented in their ferocity and violence. Between August 16 and 20 Muslim and Hindu/Sikh mobs attacked one another's Calcutta communities killing 4,000 people and leaving 10,000 injured. Rioting spread to Bombay city, eastern Bengal, Bihar, the United Provinces, and the Punjab. In Bihar and the United Provinces Hindu peasants and pilgrims massacred at least 8,000 Muslims. In the Punjab Muslims, Hindus, and Sikhs turned on one another in rioting that killed 5,000 people.

As public order disintegrated, Clement Attlee, the British prime minister, declared the British would leave India by June 1948. When Lord Louis Mountbatten (1900–1979), India's last British viceroy, reached India in March 1947, the transfer of power had already been

Prime Minister Jawaharlal Nehru, 1947. Newly installed as prime minister, Nehru holds a gold mace presented to him on the evening of Indian independence, August 14, 1947. The white markings on his forehead were made by a priest during an earlier puja (prayer service). (AP/Wide World Photos)

advanced to August of that year. The British moved peremptorily to make their final settlement of political power. When Nehru privately rejected "Plan Balkan"—so named because it transferred power to each of the separate Indian provinces much as had occurred in the Balkan States prior to World War I—the British settled on a plan that granted dominion status to two central governments, India and Pakistan (the latter to be composed of a partitioned Bengal and Punjab, plus the Northwest Frontier Province and Sind). Congress, the Muslim League, and Sikh leaders agreed to this plan on June 2, 1947. The British Parliament passed the Indian Independence Act on July 18 for implementation August 15.

India became independent at midnight on August 14, 1947. The transfer of power took place at Parliament House in New Delhi. "Long years ago we made a tryst with destiny," Nehru said in his speech that night,

> *and now the time comes when we shall redeem our pledge, not wholly or in full measure, but very substantially. At the stroke of the midnight hour, when the world sleeps, India will awake to life and freedom. A moment comes, which comes but rarely in history, when we step out from the old to the new, when an age ends, and when the soul of a nation, long suppressed finds utterance. (Brecher 1961, 137)*

Nehru became India's first prime minister. Lord Mountbatten, at the invitation of Congress, served as governor-general of the Indian Dominion through June 1948. Regulations governing the new state devolved from the Government of India Act of 1935.

Partition

Two secret British commissions, directed by the British barrister Sir Cyril Radcliffe, drew the boundaries that would separate India from

THE PRINCES

The British made no provision for the Indian princes in the transfer of power, the viceroy simply informing the princes that they must make their own arrangements with one or another of the new states. Vallabhbhai (Sardar) Patel oversaw negotiations for India with the princes, offering generous allowances in exchange for the transfer of their states. By 1947 all but three states—Junagadh, Hyderabad, and Kashmir—had transferred their territories, most to India. Both Junagadh on the Kathiawad peninsula and Hyderabad in the south were Hindu-majority states ruled by Muslim princes. By 1948 the Indian government and its army had forced both princes to cede their states to India.

Kashmir, in contrast, was a Muslim-majority state bordering both India and Pakistan but ruled by a Hindu king, Hari Singh. In October 1947, faced with a Muslim uprising against him, Singh ceded his kingdom to India. At this point Kashmir became the battleground for Indian and Pakistani invading armies. A January 1949 cease-fire, brokered by the United Nations, drew a boundary within the province, giving India administrative control over two-thirds of the region and Pakistan the remaining one-third. Under the terms of the cease-fire India agreed to conduct a plebiscite in Kashmir that would determine the region's political fate. India's subsequent refusal to conduct the plebiscite caused Kashmir to remain in turmoil and a source of Indian and Pakistan conflict into the 21st century.

east and west Pakistan. The boundaries were not announced until August 17, two days after independence. It was only then that the real impact of partition began to be felt, as majority communities on both sides of the border attacked, looted, raped, and murdered the remaining minorities. Within a month newspapers were reporting 4 million migrants on the move in northern India. One nine-coach train from Delhi, crammed with refugees, crossed the border into Pakistan with only eight Muslim survivors on board; the rest had been murdered along the way (Pandey 2001, 36). Estimates of people killed in partition violence ranged from several hundred thousand to 1 million. The entire population of the Punjab was reshaped in the process. By March 1948 more than 10 million Muslims, Hindus, and Sikhs had fled their former homes on either side of the border to become refugees within the other country.

Gandhi's Last Campaign

During 1945–47 Gandhi took no part in the final negotiations for independence and partition. He could neither reconcile himself to the division of India nor see an alternative. Instead he traveled the villages of eastern India attempting to stop the spreading communal violence. In Calcutta in 1947 Gandhi moved into a Muslim slum, living with the city's Muslim mayor and fasting until the city's violence ended. In January 1948 he conducted what would be his last fast in Delhi, bringing communal conflict to an end in the city and shaming Sardar Patel, now home minister of the new government, into sending Pakistan its share of India's prepartition assets. On January 27, 1948, Gandhi addressed Delhi Muslims from a Muslim shrine. Three days later, on January 30, 1948, the elderly Mahatma was shot to death as he walked to his daily prayer meeting. His murderer, Naturam V. Godse, was a right-wing Hindu with ties to the paramilitary RSS. Gandhi's assassination had been planned by a Brahman group in Pune that thought Gandhi dangerously pro-Muslim. Godse was ultimately tried and executed for his act. Revulsion against Gandhi's assassination provoked anti-Brahman riots in the Mahasabha strongholds of Pune, Nagpur, and Bombay and caused the RSS to be banned for a year.

Gandhi had not attended the ceremonies marking independence and partition, nor had he asked for or accepted any role in the new government. The nationalist movement he had led since 1920 concluded with India's independence but also with a division of Indian lands, homes, and people more terrible than anything imagined. Yet Gandhi had raised no objections to the final settlement. The viceroy, Lord Mountbatten, hearing that Gandhi opposed partition, had called for a meeting. "It happened to be a day of silence [for Gandhi]," Mountbatten later recalled, "for which I was grateful. In retrospect I think he chose to make that a day of silence to save him the embarrassment of accepting the Partition. For he had no other solution" (Brecher 1961, 141). Less than a year later Gandhi was dead, the most famous victim of partition violence and upheaval. It would now be his heirs and successors in the new government of India who would take on the responsibility of shaping the newly independent Indian state.

8

CONSTRUCTING THE
NATION (1950–1996)

WE, THE PEOPLE OF INDIA, having solemnly resolved to constitute
India into a SOVEREIGN SOCIALIST SECULAR DEMOCRATIC REPUBLIC
and to secure to all its citizens:
JUSTICE, social, economic and political;
LIBERTY of thought, expression, belief, faith and worship; EQUALITY of status
and of opportunity; and to promote among them all FRATERNITY assuring
the dignity of the individual and the unity and integrity of the Nation;
IN OUR CONSTITUENT ASSEMBLY this twenty-sixth day of November,
1949, do HEREBY ADOPT, ENACT AND GIVE TO OURSELVES
THIS CONSTITUTION.

■

Preamble to the Indian Constitution, 1949, and as amended in 1976
(Hay 1988, 335–336)

After independence and partition came the work of creating the
new Indian nation. For more than 50 years the Congress Party had
fought India's British rulers; now Congressites had to re-create themselves and their party and build a modern state within the context of a
free and independent country. Almost 30 years of provincial elections
had already accustomed Indian leaders to competing for power through
the ballot box. Not surprisingly then, the Indian Constitution, accepted
in 1949 to take effect in 1950, defined India as a democratic republic.

India's first leaders also defined the new republic as both socialist and
secular, although this was not written into the constitution until 1976.
Years of British imperialism had convinced Jawaharlal Nehru and many
like him that only a socialist state, with a commitment to social and
economic justice and an emphasis on centralized state planning, could
ameliorate the deep poverty of India's people. The need for a secular

223

state, a second absolute commitment of the early Indian republic, had been underscored by partition's violent communal conflicts. For almost 20 years, from 1947 to his death in 1964, Nehru worked with his Congress colleagues to build India within these three defining rubrics: democratic, socialist, and secular.

The decades from Nehru's death to the end of the 20th century, however, would see substantial challenges raised to all three of these early commitments. In the decades after 1947, events demonstrated that electoral politics, far from uniting Indians, also had the potential to tear them apart. With Indira Gandhi's (1917–84) defeat at the polls in 1977 and the subsequent defeat of her opposition in 1980, it also became clear that the voters of the largest democratic system in the world would not always necessarily return elected officials to power. Similarly, socialist state planning was challenged as early as the late 1960s and 1970s as it became clear that neither central economic planning nor the absence of home charges would immediately transform India's economy. Finally, the decades after independence, and particularly the last 20 years of the 20th century, demonstrated frequently and dramatically the difficulties inherent in fitting India's castes, religions, regional cultures, and linguistic divisions into the conceptual framework of a secular state. The 1980s and 1990s saw the rise of an aggressive Hindu nationalist movement that by 1996 looked able, not only to take power, but also to challenge the basic premise of Indian secularism.

From Dominion to Republic

The caretaker dominion government of 1947 was headed jointly by Nehru as prime minister and Sardar Patel as deputy prime minister. Nehru's public pronouncements reflected his and the Congress left wing's secular and socialist convictions; however, Patel, who came from the more conservative and communalist wing of Congress, said less in public but controlled the Congress organization. By 1948 Patel and his faction had forced all socialists out of Congress, causing them to form the Praja Socialist Party in 1952. Patel's sudden death in 1950, however, left Nehru back at the center of government functions and essentially unopposed.

The work of writing the new constitution was directed by B. R. Ambedkar, now minister of law in the cabinet, and approved by the Constituent Assembly in 1949. The constitution became law on January 26, 1950. Its preamble guaranteed all Indian citizens justice, liberty, equality, and fraternity. A section on "fundamental rights" granted citizens a wide range of basic civil liberties (such as freedom of speech, assembly, travel) and abolished the practice of Untouchability "in any form" (Hay 1988, 336–337). Under British Indian law, separate legal codes had existed for the personal law of both the Hindu and the Muslim communities. At Patel's insistence the constitution left these separate legal codes intact.

The constitution established a parliamentary form of government, modified by the addition of an independent Supreme Court modeled on that of the United States. Asked by Gandhians in the Constituent Assembly why the government was not based on indigenous village systems, Ambedkar bluntly replied, "village republics have been the ruination of India. . . . What is the village but a sink of localism, a den of ignorance, narrow-mindedness and communalism?" (Hay 1988, 341).

The Republic of India was a federation of regional state governments joined together within a central union government. The union government was parliamentary. It had two houses: The Lok Sabha (People's Assembly) was the lower house, based on proportional representation with no more than 550 members directly elected to five- year terms; the Rajya Sabha (States' Assembly) was the 250-member upper house elected by provincial legislative assemblies for six-year terms. In the Lok Sabha, a prime minister and cabinet headed a government that was formed by whichever party could command an absolute majority of the elected seats. In addition, a president and vice president, whose powers were largely ceremonial, were elected through an electoral college.

The state governments included the nine former provinces of British India, nine former princely states, 10 other states administered by the center, and five new administrative territories. Relations between the union government and the states were based on the Government of India Act of 1935 with specific lists defining the areas over which each might legislate and 47 areas of shared jurisdiction. The union government controlled (among other areas) foreign affairs, defense, and communications, while provinces controlled the police, law courts, health, and education.

Under the constitution all Indians, male or female, over the age of 18 had the right to vote. The constitution eliminated separate electorates but maintained a provision of the Government of India Act of 1935 that allowed the reservation of seats for Scheduled Castes (Untouchables) and Scheduled Tribes. The first elections for the Lok Sabha were held over six months during the winter of 1951–52. As more than 85 percent of India's eligible voters were illiterate, each party was allotted a symbol; 17,000 candidates competed for more than 3,800 seats at the center and in the state assemblies and an estimated 60 percent of the 176 million eligible voters turned out at the polls (Tharoor 2003).

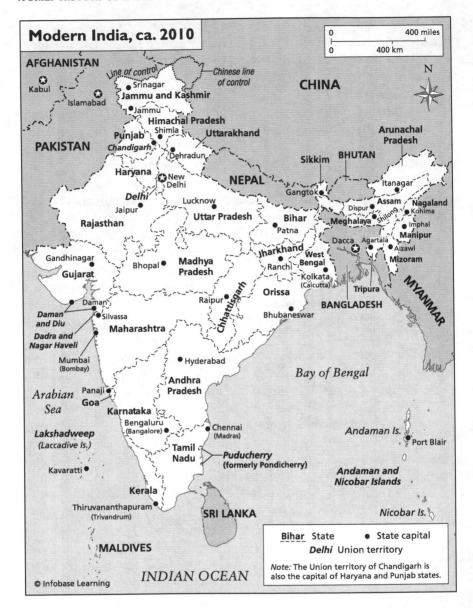

Modern India, ca. 2010

AFGHANISTAN

Kabul

Islamabad

Line of control — Chinese line of control

CHINA

N

Srinagar
Jammu and Kashmir
Jammu

Himachal Pradesh
Shimla

Punjab *Chandigarh*
Haryana
New Delhi
Delhi
Jaipur
Rajasthan

Dehradun

Uttarakhand

Sikkim

BHUTAN

Arunachal Pradesh

PAKISTAN

NEPAL

Lucknow
Uttar Pradesh

Gangtok

Itanagar

Bihar
Patna

Dispur
Shilong

Assam

Nagaland
Kohima

Meghalaya

Imphal
Manipur

Gandhinagar
Gujarat

Bhopal

Madhya Pradesh

Raipur

Jharkhand
Ranchi

West Bengal

Dacca

Agartala
Aizawl

Mizoram

Daman
Daman
and Diu
Silvassa
Dadra and Nagar Haveli

Maharashtra

Chhattisgarh

Orissa

Kolkata
(Calcutta)

Tripura

BANGLADESH

Bhubaneswar

MYANMAR

Mumbai
(Bombay)

Hyderabad

Andhra Pradesh

Bay of Bengal

Arabian Sea

Panaji
Goa

Karnataka

Bengaluru
(Bangalore)

Chennai
(Madras)

Andaman Is.
Port Blair

Lakshadweep
(Laccadive Is.)

Tamil Nadu

Puducherry
(formerly Pondicherry)

Andaman and Nicobar Islands

Kavaratti

Kerala

Thiruvananthapuram
(Trivandrum)

SRI LANKA

Nicobar Is.

MALDIVES

INDIA OCEAN

© Infobase Learning

0 — 400 miles
0 — 400 km

Bihar State   • State capital
Delhi Union territory

Note: The Union territory of Chandigarh is also the capital of Haryana and Punjab states.

The Nehru Era

Nehru traveled more than 30,000 miles in campaigning for the 1951–52 elections. Congress won an overwhelming majority of seats in the Lok Sabha, 364 of 489 possible seats, and emerged with majorities in all states except four (and even in those four it had the largest number of seats). Congress formed India's first government under the new constitution with Nehru as prime minister. It is worth pointing out, however, that in this election as in many since, Congress benefited from the "first past the post" style of Indian voting. This allowed the candidate with the largest number of votes to win the seat, even if that candidate did not have an absolute majority of all votes. Thus even in this first 1951–52 election, where Congress overwhelmingly dominated the results, it did so with only 45 percent of the popular vote.

During its years as a nationalist movement Congress had sought to incorporate as many Indian constituencies within it as possible. It had the support of wealthy professionals in the cities and a strong grass-roots organization among the upper levels of the rural peasantry. Its dominance of national elections for the first 10 years of the republic was so strong that the party always won a majority of Lok Sabha seats and most of the time controlled the state legislatures as well. At the state level, Congress bosses used the support (and votes) of upper-level peasants to dominate the state party apparatus. As a result, in the first decades after independence, important political and policy struggles took place within the Congress Party itself rather than among competing political parties.

Language Politics

During the nationalist movement Gandhi and the Indian National Congress had emphasized and encouraged the use of indigenous languages, seeing them as more authentic expressions of Indian culture than the foreign language of English. After independence it was natural for regional groups to agitate for provincial reorganizations on a linguistic basis. Nehru himself hated the idea of linguistic divisions, which he believed encouraged the kind of separatism seen in partition violence and Hindu communalism, but when a leader from the Telegu-speaking region of Madras Presidency died during a protest fast in 1952, the government immediately agreed to carve a new Telegu-speaking state—Andhra Pradesh—out of the old Madras Presidency.

In 1956, on the recommendation of a commission, linguistic divisions were carried further, dividing India into 14 language-based states: Kerala was created for Malayam speakers, Karnataka for Kannada speakers, and Madras (present-day Tamil Nadu) for Tamil speakers. In 1960 the old Bombay Presidency was divided into a Gujarati-speaking Gujarat and a Marathi-speaking Maharashtra, with the city of Bombay going to Maharashtra. The movement of refugees during partition had given the Sikhs, a religious community whose members spoke Punjabi, a majority presence in the western Punjab. In 1966 the old province of the Punjab was also divided into a Punjabi-speaking (Sikh) Punjab and two smaller states, Himachal Pradesh and Haryana. Over the next 40 years, regional campaigns for additional language-based states continued to appear and to be successful, so that, by 2009, the number of Indian states had grown from the original 14 to 28 (with seven union territories).

Secular Law

Hindu customary law (as codified by the British and carried over into Indian law) made marriages between castes illegal and women's status before and after marriage dependent on the male heads of their families. In 1949 the Hindu Marriage Validating Act removed intercaste barriers to marriage. Ambedkar wanted a broader reform, but Nehru, whose personal commitment to secularism was absolute, deferred to more conservative Hindus in the cabinet, and Ambedkar quit the cabinet in disgust in 1951. The 1955 Hindu Marriage Act subsequently raised the minimum age of marriage to 18 for men and 15 for women and gave women the right to divorce polygamous husbands. A year later the Hindu Succession Act and the Adoption and Maintenance Act gave women the same claim as men over paternal property and equalized the adoption status of female children. Finally, in 1961 it became illegal to demand a dowry. All these laws, however, applied only to Hindu women because Muslim personal law was defined by a separate legal code.

In 1955 the government also passed the Untouchability (Offences) Act, providing penalties for discrimination against Untouchable individuals or communities. At the same time the government established quotas for Scheduled Castes and Scheduled Tribes, reserving seats in the Lok Sabha and provincial legislature, educational institutions, and government departments for these groups.

Central Planning

From the early 1920s, despite his wealthy background, Nehru had been a socialist, believing that government ownership of crucial industries combined with state planning for economic growth were the keys to Indian economic progress and social justice. Beginning in 1950 Nehru's government used the newly formed National Planning Commission (headed by the prime minister himself) to design three successive five-year plans, economic blueprints for government and private activity over each five-year period.

A BUDDHIST SOLUTION

In 1951 after resigning from Nehru's cabinet, B. R. Ambedkar returned to Aurangabad in western India to work locally on social reform and education for his community. Five years later he turned his back on Hinduism forever and converted to Buddhism. "Even though I was born in the Hindu religion, I will not die in the Hindu religion," Ambedkar said at his conversion on October 14, 1956, recalling a vow he had made earlier to himself. Buddhism, which removed Untouchables from the obligations of Hindu dharma, offered an alternative escape from Hindu customary obligations and restrictions. "There is no equality in the Hindu religion," Ambedkar said on the same occasion. "Only one great man spoke of equality, and that great man is the Lord Buddha." At the Nagpur ceremony, the oldest Buddhist monk in India initiated Ambedkar into Buddhism, and Ambedkar in turn converted other Untouchables, by some estimates as many as 500,000 people. Ambedkar died within two months of his conversion, but Buddhism drew an estimated 4 million Indian converts over the next few years, most from Untouchable communities.

Source: Hay, Stephen, ed. *Sources of Indian Tradition.* Vol. 2: *Modern India and Pakistan,* 2d ed. (New York: Columbia University Press, 1988), p. 348.

Mass conversions to Buddhism, New Delhi, November 2001. A Buddhist monk shaves off the mustache of Ram Raj, chair of the All-India Confederation of Scheduled Castes/Scheduled Tribe Organisations (AICOSCSTO), as part of a ceremony in which he converted to Buddhism. Ram Raj and the thousands of other low-caste Hindus who chose Buddhism in this mass ceremony were following a practice initiated more than 40 years earlier by the famous Untouchable leader Dr. B. R. Ambedkar. (AP/Wide World Photos)

The goal of the First Five-Year Plan (1951–56) was economic stability. The costs to the Indian government of World War II, the wartime famine in Bengal, the violence and upheaval of partition, as well as the costs of the political and economic changes brought by independence had almost destabilized India's economy. Severe food shortages forced the Indian government to begin importing food grains in 1951, imports that would continue for the next 20 years. The plan directed 27 percent of its modest 20-billion-rupee expenditure toward agriculture, 18 percent to transport, 4.4 percent to industry and minerals, and 2.7 percent to power (Tomlinson 1993, 177). The Planning Commission established government controls over a range of business activities: industrial licensing, foreign exchange, imports, exports, food prices, and food grain movements. By 1956 the Indian economy had recovered from the worst instabilities of the late 1940s. National income had risen 18 percent. Good monsoons and new irrigation works had increased the agricultural production of food grains from 52 to 65 million tons. During this first period, India also secured international aid and was able to draw on the funds owed to it by Great Britain. The gains of the First Five-Year Plan were modest, but in contrast with the disrupted economic conditions of the late 1940s, they appeared dramatic.

Rural Reform

The Kisan Sabhas (Peasant Assemblies) and peasant agitations had played major roles in nationalist protests before independence, and from the 1930s the left wing of Congress had advocated major land reform. As absentee zamindars and landlords were thought responsible for the inefficiency of rural agriculture, politicians in the United Provinces and the Telegu-speaking (Andhra) region of Madras had produced plans, even before 1947, to abolish the zamindari (tax farming) system that existed in almost half of India and place restrictions on the amount of lands held by landlords throughout the country. By the end of the First Five Year Plan (1956), state governments had eliminated the zamindari system in most of India.

The new Congress government, however, showed little interest in more far-reaching land reform that might have guaranteed "land to the tiller" (Brecher 1959, 210). Instead the First Five Year Plan authorized the Community Development program (which continued in the second and third five-year periods) to help villages reorganize and to provide technical assistance for agricultural improvements. The officials responsible for overseeing rural development programs were those of the old

230

ICS, now renamed the Indian Administrative Service. In 1959 the government launched a new rural development program, the Panchayati Raj plan. Under it, Panchayats (five-person village councils) were to organize agricultural and village development work and send representatives (through a hierarchy of elections) to a district committee. By 1964 the Panchayats had spread to most Indian states. They were successful in involving dominant landed castes in each region in development work but tended to funnel available funds and programs to these same caste communities. In general both the Community Development programs and the Panchayats were most successful at helping wealthier, upper-caste peasants, while doing relatively little to improve the lives and working conditions of the poorest rural inhabitants.

In a related effort the Gandhian disciple Vinoba Bhave (1895–1982) began his Bhoodan (gift of land) movement in 1951. Bhave traveled by foot through rural India, asking wealthier peasants and rich landlords to donate lands to landless laborers. Within a decade Bhave's movement had collected more than 1 million acres for landless laborers, although the acreage donated was sometimes scrubland that could not be farmed.

Second and Third Five-Year Plans

The First Five-Year Plan's success encouraged planners to be more ambitious in subsequent ones. Believing that the key to long-term economic growth was industrialization, the Second (1956–61) and Third (1961–66) Five-Year Plans divided industries into the public and private sectors and focused aggressively on developing key public-sector industries, such as electricity, iron, and steel. Import substitution—that is, the substitution of goods produced in India for those imported from abroad—was also emphasized to make the Indian economy more self-sufficient and protect Indian businesses from foreign competition.

The second and third plans produced substantial industrial development. Indian industrialization grew 7.4 percent annually between 1950 and 1965, making India the world's seventh most industrially advanced country in 1966. By 1966 steel factories produced 7 million tons annually; electrical plants, 43 billion kilowatt-hours a year; Indian cement factories, 11 million tons of cement; and chemical factories, 0.5 million tons of chemical fertilizers every year.

The second and third plans emphasized industry at the expense of agriculture. Farming production lagged in these years, not only behind industrial growth, but in relation to India's now rapidly growing population. Although total food-grain production rose from 50.8 million tons in 1950 to 82 million tons in 1960, in the same period the Indian population grew from 361 to 439 million people. As population growth negated most of the increased food production, India was forced to import more food. Total food imports rose from 4.8 million tons in 1950 to 10.4 million tons in 1960. During 1965–68, as severe droughts increased scarcity and drove food prices higher, India was forced to import more than 11 percent of the food grains its people consumed, much of it from the United States.

Nonalignment

Rather than commit India to the United States or the Union of Soviet Socialist Republics (USSR) at the start of the cold war. Nehru advanced a plan for "nonalignment" at a 1955 Indonesian meeting of Asian and African nations. He envisioned a coalition of "third world" countries, newly emerging from colonization and with India at its head, whose members would pledge themselves to peaceful coexistence and mutual territorial respect. A year earlier India and China had signed a treaty that Nehru hoped would be the model for such relations; the treaty recognized Tibet as part of China and pledged the two countries to respect each other's territorial integrity. "Hindi-Chini Bhai Bhai" (India and China are brothers) was the slogan in India when it was signed.

The treaty, however, did not determine the actual boundary between the two countries, in part because much of the 2,640-mile-long border was remote and unmapped. Between 1955 and 1959 the Chinese made repeated military incursions into territories claimed by India. In 1959 India granted political asylum to Tibet's Buddhist religious leader, the Dalai Lama. In fall 1962, after repeated talks had failed to resolve the boundary disputes, Nehru ordered the Indian army to take back the territories held by China. The Chinese easily defeated India's army. They took and kept the Karakoram Pass in the north, a route to Tibet that lay through Indian Kashmir, and marched into Assam virtually unimpeded before withdrawing on their own in November.

In May 1964, after a year of serious illness, Nehru died of heart disease. On the international scene his nonaligned policy was in tatters, damaged by India's invasion and seizure of Portuguese Goa in 1961 and then destroyed by the Sino-Indian War of 1962. The defeat of India's army by the Chinese had also badly damaged his prestige at home. In India evidence was mounting that the three five-year plans had failed to remake the Indian economy. It was a sad ending to the career of a dedicated freedom fighter and statesman.

232

Lal Bahadur Shastri

Lal Bahadur Shastri (1904–66), a former Gandhian and political moderate from the United Provinces, had served in Nehru's place during the prime minister's last illness. In 1964, on Nehru's death, Shastri was elected head of the Congress Party and became prime minister. Shastri's brief tenure in office (1964–66) was marred by an escalating food crisis as poor monsoons produced increasing food shortages and prices soared. His government also faced South India protests against a government plan to make Hindi the official language of India; his government ended the protest by resolving that each province could use three languages: English (as an associate language), a regional language, and Hindi. Finally, a three-week war with Pakistan in September 1965 over India's refusal to conduct a plebiscite in Kashmir saw Indian troops victoriously driving back Pakistani forces almost to Pakistan's capital at Lahore. A 1966 truce, mediated by the USSR at a meeting in Tashkent, returned Kashmir to the status quo before the fighting started.

Indira Gandhi

Prime Minister Shastri died suddenly of a heart attack in January 1966 just at the conclusion of the Tashkent meetings. The "Syndicate," the nickname for the four Congress bosses from different states who had controlled the Congress Party since Nehru's last years, chose Jawaharlal Nehru's only child, Indira Gandhi (1917–84), to be the next prime minister. At the time Indira Gandhi was a 48-year-old widow with two sons. Her husband, Feroze Shah Gandhi, who was not related to Mohandas Gandhi, had died suddenly in 1960. Indira Gandhi had spent much of her adult life, even while her husband was alive, as her father's hostess and housekeeper. In January, the Syndicate bosses chose her over Morarji Desai (1896–1995), the irascible 69-year-old leader of Congress's right wing, because of her family connections and because they believed they could more easily bend her to their will.

The Green Revolution

Indira Gandhi came to power in 1966 as successive monsoon failures and severe droughts brought sections of the country to near famine conditions. To gain food aid from the United States and the International Monetary Fund (IMF) she had to agree to devalue the rupee and to loosen government restrictions on foreign investment. Dependence on foreign grain and foreign aid limited her government's

---

A WOMAN IN OFFICE

For more than 15 years Indira Gandhi was India's prime minister, holding her country's highest political office at a time when many village women were still not allowed to read or write. Gandhi was made prime minister by Congress Party bosses (the so-called Syndicate) who believed that, as a woman, she would be pliable and easily managed. Syndicate bosses soon learned otherwise. Gandhi also learned, as she matured as a politician, how to use her age and gender to advantage with Indian voters, presenting herself, on occasion, as a compassionate, self-sacrificing mother struggling to maintain peace within a fractious extended family. As she told one crowd during the 1967 election,

> Your burdens are comparatively light, because your families are limited and viable. But my burden is manifold because crores [tens of millions] of my family members are poverty stricken and I have to look after them. Since they belong to different castes and creeds, they sometimes fight among themselves, and I have to intervene especially to look after the weaker members of my family, so that the stronger ones do not take advantage of them.

Source: Frank, Katherine. *Indira: The Life of Indira Nehru Gandhi* (Boston: Houghton Mifflin, 2002), p. 303.

---

ability to plan long term, and for three years (1966–69) the five-year plans were abandoned, and budgets were only year to year. Even after 1969 the ambitious centralized planning of the Nehru years was largely abandoned.

By the mid 1960s new strains of wheat (and later rice) had been developed in Mexico and the Philippines that when used with intensive irrigation, chemical fertilizers, and pesticides produced much higher crop yields. Beginning in 1965 these new strains of wheat were used in northern India from the Punjab and Haryana to western Uttar Pradesh. Over the next four years India used loans from the IMF and the United States to fund an intensive program of investment in new agricultural technologies. Crops increased dramatically, particularly in the Punjab, and by 1970 India was growing five times as much wheat as in 1960. By the 1970s Indian food production had made the country a net exporter of agricultural products. In the 1980s new strains of high-yield rice were introduced into India, doubling production of that crop.

Food Production Growth, 1950–2000						
	1950	1960	1970	1980	1990	2000
Food grain production (in millions of tons)	50.8	82.0	108.4	129.6	176.4	201.6
Food grain imports (in millions of tons)	4.8	10.4	7.5	.8	0.3	–
Food grain reserves (in millions of tons)	–	2.0	–	15.5	20.8	40.0
Population (in millions)	361.0	439.0	548.0	683.0	846.0	1,000.0

Source: INSA (2001, 215).

Note that the 2001 census report summarizing population growth over past censuses reported the population (in millions) for the year 1991 at 843.

The "Green Revolution," as the switch to high-yielding crops was called, made Punjabi farmers the wealthiest in the nation. By the 1970s Punjab's peasant families earned twice as much as peasant households in other parts of India. The increase in Indian food production was dramatic. Nevertheless, the Green Revolution had some disadvantages. It increased Indian dependence on chemical fertilizer dramatically and made farmers rely on strains of wheat and rice that later showed themselves to be more susceptible to disease and drought. Nor could Green Revolution innovations be used throughout India; only regions where landholdings were relatively large and peasants prosperous enough to invest in new tech nologies could use the new crops. Finally, the overall benefits for Indians consumers were somewhat undercut by continuing population increases, which used up much of the greater availability of food.

Indira Gandhi Moves Left

Despite the Syndicate's belief that she would defer to their advice and leadership, Gandhi quickly emerged as a powerful and independent politician. In the election of 1967, held as India's food crisis worsened, Congress retained its majority by its smallest margin ever: 20 seats. It lost seats to opposition parties on the right—the free-market Swatantra Party and the Hindu communalist Jana Sangh—and on the left—communist parties in West Bengal and Kerala. In Madras an anti-Brahman party, the Dravida Munnetra Kazhagam (Party for the Progress of Dravidam, or

DMK), took power. In the new (1966) state of the Punjab, the Sikh party Akali Dal took control. In Uttar Pradesh (formerly the United Provinces), Chaudhuri Charan Singh withdrew from Congress, formed a new peasant-oriented party, and became chief minister of the state.

To regain political popularity and against the advice and wishes of Syndicate leaders, Gandhi moved to the left. Between 1967 and 1973 she gathered around her a "Kashmiri mafia." These new advisers were leftist in their political convictions, often from Kashmiri Brahman backgrounds and, as former supporters of her father, saw her as his successor (Frank 2002, 312). Chief among these was her private secretary and longtime friend, Parmeshwar Narain (P. N.) Haksar. With Haksar's help, Gandhi proposed an ambitious economic plan that included land reform and ceilings on personal income, property, and corporate profits. In 1969 she nationalized 14 of the country's private banks—among them the Bank of India—an immensely popular move in rural areas where private banks had long refused to open branches. In 1970 she used a presidential order to abolish the privy purses awarded to former

THE END OF THE PRINCES

In 1970 there were 278 princes in India collecting annual tax-free privy purses ranging from $25 to $350,000 but totaling altogether more than $6 million. Indira Gandhi's first attempt at ending the princes' purses passed the Lok Sabha but was defeated by one vote in the Rajya Sabha, Parliament's upper house. She then used a presidential proclamation to strip the princes of their purses, privileges, and titles. In 1971 the courts declared the proclamation illegal, but by then Gandhi controlled Parliament. She had the Lok Sabha amend the Indian Constitution to give the lower house the power to alter the fundamental rights granted to citizens under the constitution and to exclude such alterations from judicial review. The Lok Sabha then passed another constitutional amendment, the 26th, abolishing the princes' privy purses and their privileges.

Like Gandhi's nationalization of the private banks, the abolition of the privy purses was enormously popular and enhanced her standing with left-wing groups but carried little political risk. Neither princes nor bank owners commanded sufficient political constituencies to act against her.

Indian princes at independence. When state ministers opposed her proposals for land reforms, Gandhi called for elections.

By the elections of 1971 Gandhi had been expelled from the old Congress Party, which split into the Congress (O), led by Morarji Desai, and her own Congress (R). (The R stood for "requisitioned." Gandhi had inaugurated her branch of Congress by sending around a requisition asking her supporters to meet. The O in Desai's Congress stood for "organization"—the assumption being that the Syndicate controlled the original regional Congress organization.) Gandhi ran for elections under her own party against the old Congress bosses. Her platform consisted of a leftist program of goals and economic reforms. One campaign slogan was *"Garibi hatao"* (Abolish poverty) (Frank 2002, 325). Her election speeches called for slum clearance, the building of better dwellings for slum residents, and the settlement of landless laborers on their own property. Her campaign was a spectacular success, giving Gandhi's Congress (R) Party 325 seats in the Lok Sabha and an overwhelming two-thirds majority of the popular vote.

Bangladesh and the 1971 Indo-Pak War

By 1970 Pakistan had discovered that religion alone was not sufficient to hold together two regions 1,000 miles apart with opposing economic interests, different languages, and distinct cultural traditions. East Pakistan had 60 percent of the country's population but found itself dominated economically and politically by West Pakistan. These conflicts came to a head in 1970 when the East Pakistani leader Mujibur Rahman (1920–75) and his political party won Pakistan's first parliamentary election but was not allowed by Pakistan's president, Agha Mohammad Yahya Khan (1917–80), to form a government. President Yahya Khan imposed martial law on East Pakistan, so on March 25, 1971, Sheikh Mujib, as he was called, declared independence for East Pakistan, present-day Bangladesh (Bengal country). West Pakistani troops entered East Pakistan and burned, looted, and murdered its citizens in cities, university centers, and bazaars across the province. Sheikh Mujib was arrested and jailed. By December 1971, 10 million East Pakistanis had fled across the border into India.

The U.S. government under President Richard Nixon supported West Pakistan. To gain support against the United States, Prime Minister Gandhi broke India's tradition of nonalignment to sign a 20-year treaty with the USSR in which each country agreed to aid the other in case of attack. At the same time India covertly supported the Bangladeshi uprising with funds, training, and equipment. In retaliation Pakistan declared war on India in December, bombing Indian airfields in the west. The Indian army entered East Pakistan, completely overwhelming the Pakistani army, which surrendered in mid-December 1971. India then declared a cease-fire, and Bangladesh was declared an independent country. Gandhi's military victory over Pakistan was wildly popular in India. In the 1972 state assembly elections the Congress (R) Party won 70 percent of the seats; her party was now incontestably dominant in both the center and the states.

The Emergency

Gandhi's political fortunes reached their zenith in the 1971 elections. The years following 1972 brought economic disasters and with them political crisis. Three years of monsoon failures (1972–74) again brought food shortages, rising food prices, and near famine to many Indian regions. The Arab-Israeli war of 1973 raised the cost of oil-based chemical fertilizers and, with it, the price of Indian foods. Inflation reached 20 percent per year. The government imposed curbs on salaries and incomes and cut expenditures. Strikes became commonplace, and factories closed throughout the country. In 1974 Gandhi received an emergency loan from the IMF but only on condition that the government retreat from its aggressive economic policies and curtail government expenditures even further. Not only had Gandhi not abolished poverty in her years in power; under her government economic conditions had worsened for virtually all classes of Indian citizens.

Even before the crises of 1972–76, Gandhi had wanted absolute loyalty from the members of her central government and from Congress (R) ministries in regional states. Over the years since 1967 she had abandoned internal party democracy, filling party positions by appointment from above rather than by elections. She had undercut her party's grassroots organization by systematically replacing regional Congress state leaders who had their own independent local networks with people loyal to and dependent only on her. She created a pyramid-like decision-making structure both in Congress and the government to ensure that all matters, even if regional, would be decided in New Delhi. A provision from the 1935 Government of India Act allowed the central government to take over a state under emergency conditions. By 1972 Gandhi was routinely using this provision to proclaim "president's rule" in any state that opposed her. By 1976, as one observer noted at the time, all dissent, whether outside Congress or within, was

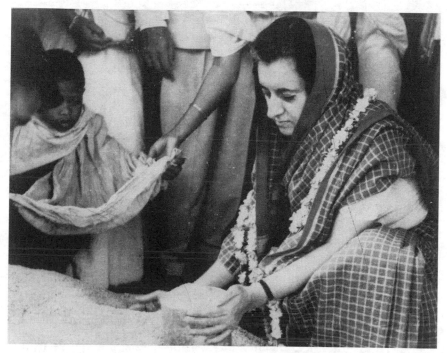

Indira Gandhi distributes food, 1966, scooping rice into containers for distribution to children at a food distribution center in Calcutta (now Kolkata). Repeated food shortages (1966, 1972–76) marked the first decade of Gandhi's tenure in office. During the decade from 1966 to 1976, Gandhi learned how to present herself politically to the Indian electorate through the image/metaphor of a mother feeding her nation/children. She adopted slogans and programs aimed at ameliorating the lives of the poorest Indians ("Garibi hatao"— Abolish poverty). Even during the Emergency of 1975–77, Gandhi's government took actions aimed at curbing the abuses of rural landlords, black-market operators, and smugglers. But after her return to power in 1980, she abandoned this earlier agenda and instead used appeals to communalism and religion to keep herself in power. (Library of Congress)

interpreted as "anti-party, anti-national, and traitorous, or even foreign-inspired" (Kochanek 2002, 100).

Gandhi's centralization of Congress worked against her in several ways. It made her programs more difficult to implement at state and local levels because her appointees there had only weak local support. Centralization also put government patronage and licensing regulations directly into the hands of Gandhi's close associates, making her government more vulnerable to corruption. Government corruption was among the main complaints against her government; Gandhi's younger son, Sanjay (1946–80), was among those most frequently rumored to be using government influence and connections to obtain quasi-legal loans and land deals.

Opposition to Gandhi and her government in 1973–74 crystallized around food shortages, rising prices, and corruption. Not even the detonation of an underground nuclear device on May 18, 1974, which made India the world's sixth nuclear power, could distract the Indian public from escalating inflation, strikes, and protests. In Bihar, Jayaprakash (J. P.) Narayan (1902–79), a Gandhian and founder of the Socialist Party, came out of retirement to take over a growing protest movement and invite peasants to join in protests against official corruption and Gandhi's authoritarian rule. In Gujarat students rioted over the 30 percent annual inflation rate and government corruption. A massive strike of railway workers paralyzed the nation for 20 days in mid-1974, ending only after the government jailed 30,000–40,000 striking workers. By 1975 Narayan's movement had become national as he and Morarji Desai brought protesters together with opposition parties—among them Congress (O), the Jan Sangh, and the Swatantra Party—to form the Janata Morcha (People's Front).

In June 1975 the Allahabad High Court in Uttar Pradesh found Gandhi guilty (on a technicality) of corrupt elections practices in the 1971 elections; the court invalidated her election to Parliament and barred her from office for six years. In New Delhi as Sanjay Gandhi tried to organize rallies in his mother's defense, the Janata Morcha held a mass rally at which Narayan urged the police and the army to join in a national satyagraha against government corruption. "We intend to overthrow her," Gandhi's old enemy Desai had told an interviewer some days before, "to force her to resign. For good. The lady won't survive this movement of ours" (Frank 2002, 374).

Faced with the imminent loss of both her office and her political career, Gandhi had the president of India issue an official proclamation "that a grave emergency exists whereby the security of India is threatened by internal disturbances" (Jayakar 1993, 199). Using Article 352 of the Indian Constitution, which authorized the government to suspend civil rights and take all necessary steps to preserve order, Gandhi declared a national emergency on June 25, 1975. She jailed her opponents and took complete control of the government. Narayan, Desai, 600 opposition members of Parliament, and tens of thousands of local party workers were detained without trial. Censorship laws closed all news outlets. Parliament, now composed only of Gandhi's supporters, nullified the election charges against her, and Gandhi postponed scheduled parliamentary and state legislative elections indefinitely.

The Emergency, as it is referred to, lasted until January 1977. Gandhi banned the Hindu nationalist RSS group—which had provided strong local support for the Janata movement—along with a range of communalist and terrorist groups. The Maintenance of Internal Security Act (MISA) and the Prevention of Smuggling Activities Act gave the government broad powers to arrest and detain individuals. Strikes were banned, bureaucrats were ordered to work harder, black-market operators and smugglers were jailed, tax evaders were arrested, and in rural areas the power of the wealthiest landlords was curbed. Industrial production grew an average of 8 percent per year. "She stood between Chaos and Order," declared one of many Emergency posters (Wolpert 2009, 419). Between 1975 and 1977, stringent government policies (with help from a good monsoon) brought the prices of essential commodities down to 1971 levels.

During the Emergency Sanjay Gandhi, the prime minister's younger son, became her closest adviser and an active political figure. A college dropout with a reputation for using threats, smears, and organized violence in his business dealings, Sanjay Gandhi resurrected the Youth Congress (now made up, according to one contemporary, of "dropouts, drifters, and roughnecks") to help implement his plans (Malhotra 1989, 177). He pursued what his supporters called urban beautification and family planning among the poorest Indians in urban slums and rural villages. Under his program the *bustees* (slums), small shacks, and storefronts of the poor—the very Muslims, minorities, and low-caste voters who had been his mother's strongest supporters—were bulldozed in urban cities such as New Delhi, Calcutta, and Varanasi and their tenants forced to move elsewhere. In the Turkaman Gate section of Old Delhi the destruction of 150,000 shacks and the forcible relocation of 70,000 slum dwellers caused riots that put the area under a 24-hour curfew. Sanjay Gandhi's family planning initiatives were equally harsh. Government workers were given sterilization quotas to meet in order to collect their salaries. Vasectomy tents were set up in cities, and sterilization vans roamed the countryside. Over two years more than 10 million sterilizations were performed, many, according to rumors, under compulsion.

Janata Government

In January 1977 Prime Minister Gandhi suddenly announced that new elections for Parliament would be held in two months. She ordered well-known political prisoners released and suspended press censorship. Narayan and Desai reformed the Janata coalition to fight in the election. Shortly before the voting began, Jagjivan Ram, an Untouchable politician who was Gandhi's minister of irrigation and agriculture, resigned his office, left Congress (R), and joined the Janata coalition.

Observers later speculated as to why Gandhi called for elections, whether in the mistaken belief that Emergency reforms had restored her earlier popularity or because she could no longer endure her role as a dictator. In any event Congress (R) lost the elections. In Uttar Pradesh both Gandhi and her son Sanjay were defeated. Janata candidates won 299 seats (with 43 percent of the popular vote), while Congress (R) won 153 seats (and 35 percent of the vote). Gandhi resigned as prime minister immediately, and in March 1977 Morarji Desai became India's first non-Congress prime minister. Charan Singh (1902–87), whose peasant proprietor constituency had joined Janata, became home minister; Atal Bihari Vajpayee of the Jana Sangh was foreign minister; and Jagjivan Ram became minister of defense. The Janata government appointed the Shah Commission (named for former Supreme Court justice J. C. Shah who headed it) to investigate the Emergency, and by 1978 the commission had produced a three-volume catalogue of Emergency abuses. Over the next two years the Janata government filed 35 criminal cases against Sanjay Gandhi. In 1978 when Indira Gandhi won election to Parliament from Karnataka, the Janata majority expelled her from the Lok Sabha and jailed her for one week.

Apart from their pursuit of the Gandhis, however, Janata leaders had no unified political program. Prime Minister Desai showed interest in promoting his own personal Brahman regimen (which included complete vegetarianism and the drinking of his own urine daily), and Desai had his government pass laws banning alcohol and the eating of beef. The Janata government also endorsed programs for encouraging Gandhian village industries. But otherwise Janata leaders did little more than feud with one another, in the process revealing the corruption of some of them. The end of the Emergency, meanwhile, brought rising prices and black marketeering. Inflation rates again reached double digits by 1978. The surplus of food grains and the $3 billion foreign exchange built up during the Emergency were gone within two years. In 1979 the socialists abandoned the coalition, and the government fell.

Indira Gandhi's Communal Turn

Indira Gandhi was returned to power in the elections of 1980 under the slogan "Elect a Government that Works!" (Wolpert 2009, 429). Her Congress (I) Party (I for "Indira") won 351 seats, or two-thirds of the Parliament, and both she and her son Sanjay won election to

Parliament. Sanjay Gandhi had selected almost half of Indira Gandhi's Congress (I) members of Parliament and was now widely viewed as the newest addition to the Nehru-Gandhi political dynasty, but in June 1980 Sanjay died in a private airplane accident in New Delhi. Within a year of his death, Sanjay's elder brother, Rajiv Gandhi (1944–91), an airline pilot for Indian Airlines with an Italian-born wife, Sonia Gandhi (1946–   ), and no prior interest in politics, had yielded to his mother's wishes, entered politics, and won a seat in Parliament.

Indira Gandhi returned to power shorn of the left-wing "Kashmiri mafia" that had guided her before the Emergency. She no longer presented herself as the secularist, socialist fighter for the Indian poor. Her government offered few new legislative initiatives and no longer showed interest in central state planning. Unchanged, however, was the demand for loyalty, Gandhi's highest priority in political associates. Was she to blame, she asked in an interview of the time, if she entrusted sensitive jobs not to bureaucrats who would not "move a little finger to help me" but to "men who may not be very bright but on whom I can rely?" (Malhotra 1989, 228).

As the ideological difference between Congress (I) and most opposition parties narrowed in these years, Gandhi turned to communal and/or religious appeals to maintain herself in power. She courted the Hindu vote and in her relations with regional parties adopted whatever communalist strategy—whether anti-Hindu, -Muslim, or -Sikh—seemed likely to benefit her. In Kashmir her government attempted to weaken a regional Kashmiri party by appealing to the fears of Hindus in southern Kashmir. In Assam, where large numbers of Muslim immigrants from Bangladesh now outnumbered indigenous Assamese Hindus, Gandhi courted the Muslim vote. One effect of Gandhi's turn toward communalism, political scientist Christophe Jaffrelot has suggested, was that communal themes replaced secular themes as the accepted language of political discourse.

In the Punjab Gandhi's communal manipulations produced disaster. The main Congress opponent in the Punjab was the Akali Dal, a relatively moderate Sikh party that had supported Janata during the Emergency and that wanted the Punjab to become the autonomous Sikh state of Khalistan (land of the Sikh *khalsa*). To undercut the Akali Dal, Sanjay Gandhi and his associates had promoted the rise of a militant Sikh holy man, Jarnail Singh Bhindranwale (1947–84); however, by 1983 Bhindranwale and his followers were carrying on a campaign of assassination and terror designed to drive non-Sikhs out of the Punjab. To avoid capture they barricaded themselves in the Sikh community's holiest site, the Golden Temple at Amritsar. Bhindranwale refused to leave the temple until the Punjab became completely autonomous. In June 1984 Indira Gandhi approved "Operation Bluestar"; the army invaded the Sikh temple, killing Bhindranwale and 1,000 Sikhs in a two-day battle that destroyed the sacred inner sanctum of the temple and its library of ancient Sikh scriptures.

Hindu Society Under Siege

As Gandhi's political manipulations and communal campaigns fueled tensions in several Indian states, the conversion of a large number of Untouchables to Islam raised fears of a Hinduism in danger. In 1981 1,000 Untouchables in Meenakshipuram, Tamil Nadu, converted to Islam in a ceremony organized by the Muslim League. In the next several months numbers of Untouchables, estimated between 2,000 and 22,000, also converted to Islam. These conversions, like those in the 1950s to Buddhism, were motivated both by the converts' desire to escape the stigma of untouchability and by the attraction of Islamic egalitarianism and freedom from caste distinctions. Press reports at the time, however, claimed that the conversions had been funded by Muslim organizations in the Arab states and focused on the danger such conversions posed to the Hindu majority within India. "International Islamic Conspiracy for Mass Conversion of Harijan [Untouchables]" was the headline of a 1981 *Times of India* story, while an RSS newspaper ran a story titled "Hindu Society under Siege" (Jaffrelot 1996, 341, 343). One Indian newspaper published statistics showing that Hindus could become a minority community in India by as early as 2231.

The Sangh Parivar and Its Members

The desire to increase Hindu solidarity against the possible threat of future Muslim conversions spurred the RSS (Rashtriya Swayamsevak Sangh) Hindu nationalist group into increased activity during the years of Indira Gandhi's return to power. After independence, the RSS had created several affiliated organizations, and all these groups were known collectively as the Sangh Parivar (Association Family, or RSS Family). Now the RSS added several new organizations to the Sangh Parivar and revitalized others. In the 1980s the Sangh Parivar's chief organizations were the RSS itself, the VHP (Vishwa Hindu Parishad, or World Hindu Party), the Bajrang Dal (Strong and Sturdy Faction), and the BJP (Bharatiya Janata Party, or Indian People's Party). Allied with the Sangh Parivar in the 1980s but not technically one of its members was the Maharashtrian political organization, the Shiv Sena (Shiva's or Shivaji's Army).

Unlike modern religious organizations labeled as "fundamentalist" today, the goal of these RSS organizations was not to revive Hinduism as it had existed in the past but to adapt, modernize, and politicize it for the future. The RSS groups wanted to create a unified Hindu religion to compete with the world religions of Islam and Christianity and wanted a mobilized Hindutva-oriented Indian public that would vote cohesively and function effectively in the political arena. "Hindus must now awaken themselves," said Balasaheb Deoras, head of the RSS, in 1979 so that "the politicians will have to respect the Hindu sentiments and change their policies accordingly" (Jaffrelot 1996, 346). But if RSS organizations were not fundamentalist, they were, nevertheless, communalist. Their targets were two: (1) Indian Muslims and Christians, demonized by RSS propaganda as "foreigners" whose ways of life were alien to the Hinduness shared by other Indians; and (2) secularism, an idea and set of practices that, in the view of Sangh Parivar groups, kept India's Hindu nationalism in check and made it impossible to create a strong India.

The RSS

The RSS was the key organization of the Sangh Parivar and often provided directions for and lent its members to other organizations. Founded in 1925 as a paramilitary organization of "volunteers" (*swayamsevaks*) dedicated to the protection of Hinduism and Hindus, the RSS by the 1980s had a single head presiding over an elite corps of celibate *pracharaks* (preachers), who in turn supervised a larger number of full-time *swayamsevaks*. At the end of the 1980s there were 700,000 full-time party activists, or *swayamsevaks*, working throughout India.

The VHP

The VHP was initially founded in 1964 as the religious and social wing of RSS activity. It was revived in the 1980s with the task of transforming Hinduism into a unified world religion, one that could compete successfully for converts with the more centralized religions of Christianity and Islam. Hinduism was to be given theological unity by having a central sacred text (the Bhagavad Gita). Its organizational unity would come through two related groups—a council of spiritual leadership (the Central Margadarshak Mandal) and a religious parliament (the Dharma Sansad), both of which were to guide the development of the religion, its practices, and of VHP activities. During the 1980s the VHP organized movements for counterconversions into Hinduism, a symbolic pilgrimage for Hindu Oneness (the 1983 Ekatmata Yatra), and

DAILY RITUALS OF THE RSS

From 1990 to 1995 Vijay Moray was in charge of recruiting and training new RSS members in the tribal Dang region of Gujarat. Moray subsequently left the RSS, and he described his recruits' daily rituals in 1999:

It happened from 6:00 a.m. to 7:00 a.m. daily. There could be fifteen to 150 boys at a time, as young as pre-school children, ages five and six, up to college age and above. We did prayers. We stood in a circle and gave statements. We talked about pre-independence Hindu politicians. We also taught pride to the children. "We are Hindu, we have to protect our nation," things like that. Then we sang patriotic songs and performed a sun prayer. Then we did training with lathis [batons] and training on how to protect the Hindu nation. Outside of the meetings, the trainers would say that the Christians are toeing the American line, that Muslims are toeing the Pakistan line, and that eventually Hindus would be kicked out of their own country. "There is no other Hindu country for us to go to," they would say.

Source: Human Rights Watch. *Politics by Other Means: Attacks Against Christians in India.* October 1999. Available online. URL: http://www.hrw.org/reports/1999/indiachr/. Accessed September 26, 2004.

the many activities around the 1984–92 Ramjanmabhoomi campaign to recapture the god Rama's purported birthplace in Ayodhya.

Bajrang Dal

The Bajrang Dal (Strong and Sturdy Faction) was founded in 1984 specifically to mobilize young people for the Ayodhya Ramjanmabhoomi campaign. Bajrang Dal members did not undergo the same discipline or daily drills as RSS volunteers but were expected to attend training camps where they would learn "how to be bold" (Jaffrelot 1996, 363). The group, which operated under different names in several Indian states, was implicated in communal violence during and following the Ramjanmabhoomi campaign.

RSS daily rituals, 2000. Volunteers at a three-day camp held at the RSS National Security Camp in Agra demonstrate the daily drills and paramilitary practices that are a regular feature of RSS life. This camp was organized in celebration of the 75th anniversary of the RSS, and more than 75,000 volunteers were said to have attended. (AP/Wide World Photos)

The BJP

The Jana Sangh political party came under RSS control in the mid-1950s and functioned as the political wing of RSS efforts through the 1970s. The Jana Sangh was part of the Janata coalition, and in the 1980s in an effort to maintain Janata's popular appeal and to lose the party's negative communalist identity, the Jana Sangh was dissolved and subsequently reborn as the Bharatiya Janata Party (BJP). The new party was headed by Atal Bihari Vajpayee (1924–   ), a former RSS member who had worked his way up through the ranks. The BJP focused more on social and economic issues—"Gandhian socialism"—and less on Hinduism—the word *Hindu* did not appear in the party's constitution—and forged coalitions and alliances with other opposition parties. These tactics, however, did not bring the BJP much electoral success. In the 1984 elections the party won only two Lok Sabha seats, and in the state assembly elections after 1984, its seat total fell from 198 to 169. These election reversals raised questions about the party's new identity. As a result Lal Krishna Advani (ca. 1927–   ), another RSS leader, replaced Vajpayee as the party's head and returned the BJP to a more aggressive Hindu communalism.

Shiv Sena

Although not part of the RSS-controlled Sangh Parivar, the Shiv Sena in Maharashtra was allied with it in ideology and tactics. The Shiv Sena was founded in 1966 by Bal Thackeray, a former cartoonist and Marathi-language journalist turned Maharashtrian Bombay politician. Thackeray's party grew to regional power by combining a reputation for violence in dealing with opponents with a strong grassroots organization that offered local constituents job bureaus, unions, and access to local social workers. In the 1980s the party adopted a Hindu nationalist ideology and harshly anti-Muslim rhetoric. Allied with the BJP in elections after 1990, the Shiv Sena won seats in the Bombay region in both the central and state elections up to 2000. Its members were repeatedly involved in communal riots and conflicts in the Bombay region.

The Ramjanmabhoomi (Rama's Birthplace) Campaign

In 1983 the VHP organized a spiritual pilgrimage for Hindu Oneness (the Ekatmata Yatra) that crisscrossed India, north to south and east to west, to the accompaniment of huge crowds. At the meeting of the VHP's religious parliament following this event, members decided that the Babri Masjid issue should become the organization's next focus. The Babri Masjid was a mosque in Ayodhya said to have been built in the early 16th century on Babur's order atop an earlier Hindu temple. Today many scholars question whether such a temple ever existed, but from at least the late 18th century, Hindu pilgrims traveled to the mosque to worship at what they believed was the site marking the Hindu god Rama's birthplace. Conflict over the site had erupted several times during the 19th century and again in 1949. From 1949 to 1984 the mosque was locked, as a lawsuit over which religious community was entitled to worship on the site remained unresolved.

The VHP's decision was to campaign to restore the site as a holy place marking it as the birthplace of Rama. Their militant youth wing, the Bajrang Dal, was to be the main strike force in this campaign. On July 27, 1984, a VHP procession set off from Bihar to Ayodhya in Uttar Pradesh, with carts carrying statues of the god Rama and his wife Sita. After Ayodhya the procession marched to the state capital, drawing a crowd of 5,000–7,000 people, and from the capital it headed for New Delhi. The organizers planned to arrive in New Delhi just before the January 1985 elections. Instead they arrived in the midst of the violence and chaos that followed Indira Gandhi's assassination.

Rajiv Gandhi

On October 31, 1984, two of Indira Gandhi's Sikh bodyguards, Beant Singh and Satwant Singh, shot her to death as she walked from her residence to her offices in New Delhi. Her son Rajiv, already the head of the Congress (I) Party, was immediately sworn in as prime minister in her place. For three days, with the collusion of officials and the police, mobs attacked New Delhi's Sikh population, killing at least 1,000, burning businesses and homes, and forcing 50,000 Sikhs to flee to refugee camps outside the city. The army was called out to end the violence only on November 3, the day of Gandhi's funeral.

Rajiv Gandhi immediately called for new elections. In the election campaign, in order to undercut the appeal of Hindu nationalist groups like the new BJP, Gandhi courted the Hindu vote, refusing either to criticize or disavow the RSS or its support. Campaign ads played on Hindu fears of Sikhs and portrayed opposition parties as weak and antinational: "Between order and chaos, Give Order a Hand" was one Congress ad (Manor 2002, 456). (The open hand was the Congress [I]

"Mr. Clean," 1984. Running for reelection in 1984, shortly after his mother Indira Gandhi's assassination, Rajiv Gandhi stressed his own incorruptibility and his ability to maintain order, as this hand-painted New Delhi sign indicates. The Congress (I) symbol—"I" for Indira— was the open hand pictured on the sign. (courtesy of Philip Oldenburg)

election symbol.) In the 1984–85 elections Congress won 404 out of 514 Lok Sabha seats (Election Commission of India online).

In Rajiv Gandhi's initial months as prime minister he reached political agreements that seemed to resolve regional conflicts in the Punjab, Assam, and in the tribal region of Mizoram. In the Punjab Accord, for example, signed with the Akali Dal in 1985, Gandhi agreed to give the Punjab the disputed city of Chandigarh and greater access to river waters shared with Haryana. In Assam and Mizoram, Gandhi's government gave leaders of rebellious regional political parties control over their regions, making them chief ministers virtually overnight. Mizoram became a state in 1987.

Gandhi and his government preferred free-market rhetoric and faith in technocratic expertise to the socialist rhetoric and faith in government planning of his grandfather Jawaharlal Nehru's era. Transfer permits and licensing procedures were cut short to allow the entrance into India of computers, televisions, and videocassette recorders (VCRs). Taxes on wealth and inheritance were cut with the argument (borrowed from followers of U.S. president Ronald Reagan) that these would lead to faster economic growth.

During the 1980s the Indian economy began to grow at a faster rate, although economists still disagree on why. From 1950 to 1980, the Indian economy grew at an average rate of 3.5 percent per year, a rate of growth considerably undercut by population growth, which averaged 2.2 percent each year. In the years between 1980 and 1988, however, the economy grew by an estimated 5 percent per year, most of the growth coming from industry, which itself was growing at a rate of 7.6 percent. Some economists suggest the 1980s growth was the long-term result of investments in industry, roads, and electricity begun in Nehru's time. Others attribute the growth rate to the rise of a consuming Indian middle class and/or to the lowering of food prices because of the Green Revolution. Whatever the cause, from the 1970s through the 1980s the percentage of poor people in India unable to afford basic food and shelter declined.

Despite the good economic news, within three years of Rajiv Gandhi's installation as prime minister, his early political agreements had begun to fall apart. Violence forced the government to send Indian troops back into Assam in 1990. Punjabi Sikh terrorists expanded their attacks on Hindus and moderate Sikhs beyond the Punjab into Haryana, Rajasthan, Uttar Pradesh, and New Delhi. Within the Punjab 520 civilians were killed in 1986, 910 in 1987, and 1,949 in 1988. By 1987 the Punjab was under president's rule and close to civil war.

In 1985 Gandhi, faced with demands from conservative Muslims on one side and Hindu nationalists on the other, attempted to conciliate each constituency in turn—a "package deal," as one adviser called it. That year the Indian Supreme Court had awarded alimony to a divorced Muslim woman in the *Shah Bano* case, a decision that was contrary to Islamic custom and against the Muslim personal law code. Gandhi appeased conservative Muslims and had Parliament pass the Muslim Women's (Protection of Rights on Divorce) Act, which made sharia, until then only orthodox Muslim practice, secular law.

At the same time, Gandhi's government yielded to the VHP's new Babri Masjid demands and orchestrated a court decision to allow the Babri Masjid grounds to be opened for Hindu worship. The decision inflamed the Ayodhya situation further. A national Muslim committee was established to contest the opening of mosque grounds. On the Hindu side the VHP demanded the right to build a giant Hindu temple at the Babri Masjid site. The VHP began a worldwide campaign to raise funds for the new building, inviting donors to fund Ram *shilas*, or bricks for the building inscribed with the name of Rama. At the third VHP religious parliament in 1989 a crowd of 50,000 heard a resolution pass to build the Ram temple in Ayodhya.

BHOPAL DISASTER

On December 3, 1984, just before the Indian elections, a gas tank at a Union Carbide pesticide factory in Bhopal, Madhya Pradesh, burst, spreading a combination of lethal gases through a city of 1 million people. The Bhopal gas explosion was the worst industrial accident in world history. Between 7,000 to 10,000 people died within three days, some immediately, some shortly after from illness or from injuries in stampedes as people tried to escape. Amnesty International has estimated that at least an additional 15,000 people died between 1985 and 2003 from the aftereffects of exposure, bringing the total death toll to well over 20,000.

The plant had been built in 1977 and operated under a joint agreement between the multinational corporation Union Carbide and its local Indian affiliate, Union Carbide India Ltd. Union Carbide denied responsibility for the accident but ultimately settled all lawsuits by paying $470 million to the Indian government. The Indian government used the compensation payment to distribute settlements of up to $2,000 to some individuals injured by the accident and unable to work. As a result of a Supreme Court order, the final dispersal of funds was made only in 2004. At a torchlight vigil on December 3, 2009, to mark the 25th anniversary of the disaster, activists demanded action on still pending Indian and U.S. criminal cases against former Union Carbide executives. Newspaper reports noted that the water and soil surrounding the disaster site remain contaminated causing birth defects, cancer, and other chronic diseases among the 30,000 people still living in areas around the factory.

Source: Amnesty International. "Clouds of Injustice: Bhopal Disaster 20 Years On" (2004). Available online. URL: www.amnesty.org/er/library/info/ASA20/015/2004. Accessed February 10, 2010.

During the late 1980s Gandhi's government also tried unsuccessfully to intervene in the civil war of Sri Lanka, an island off the southeastern coast of India. In 1986 war had broken out between the island's two largest communities, the Sinhalese Buddhist majority and the Tamil/Hindu minority. The Liberation Tigers of Tamil Eelam (LTTE), funded covertly by Hindu supporters in the Indian state of Tamil Nadu, were demanding a separate Tamil *eelam* (nation) in the north and east of the island. In July 1987 Sri Lanka's president, Junius Richard Jayewardene

(1906–96), signed the Indo–Sri Lanka Peace Agreement with India, allowing the Indian army to enter northern Sri Lanka as a peacekeeping force. From 1987 to 1990 the Indian army fought against the Tamil Tigers, losing almost as many soldiers as the guerrilla group and finally withdrawing in 1990 without having achieved a resolution.

V. P. Singh's Anticorruption Campaigns

Although Gandhi had based his 1984–85 election campaign on his personal reputation for incorruptibility ("Mr. Clean"), between 1987 and 1989 his government was besieged with charges of corruption. The most damaging charges came from Vishwanath Pratap (V. P.) Singh (1931–2008), Gandhi's defense minister and the former chief minister of Uttar Pradesh. Singh found evidence that kickbacks had been paid by the Swedish firm Bofors to gain a 1986 $1.3 billion government weapons contract. Gandhi forced Singh to resign in April 1987 and subsequently expelled him from the Congress (I) Party. Singh founded a new opposition party, the Janata Dal (People's Faction). It was modeled on the earlier Janata coalition and founded with the hope that it, too, could use allegations of corruption to topple a government.

In the by-elections of 1988 voters defeated Congress in four out of six state elections: Haryana, Jammu and Kashmir, Gujarat, and Uttar Pradesh. By 1989, in an effort to win Hindu votes, Gandhi's government allowed the VHP to hold a foundation ceremony for the proposed new temple at the Babri Masjid site. Nevertheless, in the November 1989 general elections, in which more than 60 percent of India's more than 498 million registered adults voted, Congress (I) lost its majority in Parliament, winning only 197 seats of 529 seats in the Lok Sabha (down from its 1984 tally of 404 out of 515). The National Front, meanwhile—composed of Singh's Janata Dal and four minor parties—won 143 seats in the Lok Sabha. Singh became prime minister with support from the various communist and socialist parties and with 85 seats from the BJP.

V. P. Singh and the OBCs

But whereas the BJP wanted to organize (Hindu) Indians into a cohesive Hindu majority, Singh's party, a coalition of smaller socialist and peasant-oriented groups, had pledged itself to help lower-caste communities in their struggle against the Hindu upper castes. Singh had committed his party, if elected, to attend to the "special needs of the socially and educationally backward classes" by immediately implementing the 1980 Mandal Commission reforms (Jaffrelot 2003, 337).

Janata Dal supporter. This villager from western Uttar Pradesh squats in front of a wall bearing a poster for the Janata Dal in the 1989 election. The man pictured in the poster is Ajit Singh, son of Charan Singh, whose peasant constituency supported the Janata Dal coalition. (courtesy of Philip Oldenburg)

254

From the early 1950s Indian officials had repeatedly considered actions to improve the economic and social conditions of communities that were neither Untouchable nor tribal but were, nevertheless, extremely poor. The means for improvement was to be the extension of government reservations to the "Other Backward Classes," or OBCs, as these communities were called. In 1979 the Janata government, under Morarji Desai, had appointed B. P. Mandal, a low-caste leader, to head a commission to review the issue. At the time, OBC communities held only 12.5 percent of central government jobs. The 1980 Mandal Commission Report subsequently identified "3,248 castes or communities comprising 52.4 percent of the population of India, roughly 350 million people" who should be given preferential treatment in order to improve their economic and social conditions (Brass 1994, 251).

No action was taken on the Mandal report until 10 years later when Singh's government came to power. Believing that positive discrimination would improve the conditions of OBCs (who were among Singh's strongest supporters) and that intercaste conflict might damage the growing popularity of the BJP's Hindu nationalism, Singh announced in August 1990 that the Mandal recommendations were going to be implemented. The implication of this decision was that 27 percent of all jobs under the direct control or influence of the central government would be reserved for people from OBC communities, a reservation that raised quotas for government and public-sector employment to almost 50 percent. (In absolute terms, however, the number of jobs reserved for OBCs would have totaled slightly more than 55,000.) "We want," V. P. Singh said in an interview at the time, "to give an effective [voice] here in the power structure and running of the country to the depressed, down-trodden and backward people" (Jaffrelot 2003, 339).

Mandal Protests

Opposition to the reforms from upper-caste Hindu communities was widespread and dramatic. In North India, upper-caste students and professors at such schools as Delhi University organized opposition to Mandal. More dramatic were the attempted suicides of a number of young people. Graphic news magazine coverage reported the efforts of more than 300 young upper-caste students to kill themselves, 152 by setting themselves on fire. Legal challenges postponed the implementation of the Mandal reforms for several years. The 27 percent reservations were finally put into effect in 1993, long after Singh's government had fallen. By then the Indian economy had already begun its dramatic

255

CASTE IN THE INDIAN CENSUS

The Census of 1931 was the last Indian census to publish statistics on caste. After 1947 government officials rejected caste categories as too divisive. Information on religious communities continued to be collected, but the only data collected on caste was information on Scheduled Castes and Scheduled Tribes. From the 1950s, however, all commissions that studied the Other Backward Classes (OBCs) issue pointed out the need for caste statistics. During the 1980s' and 1990s' debates on the Mandal Commission reservations, Untouchable and OBC leaders charged that the "government unwillingness to collect caste data [was] a deliberate move to preserve the status quo." Nevertheless, as late as the Census of 2001 caste information was still not included in census tabulations.

Source: quotation from Sundar, Nandini. "Caste as Census Category: Implications for Sociology." *Current Sociology* 48 (2000): 117. Available online. URL: http://csi.sagepub.com/cgi/reprint/48/3/111.pdf. Accessed February 10, 2010.

recovery, opening new private-sector jobs for upper-caste employment and dampening opposition to the reservations.

Mobilizing for Hindutva

The majority of the BJP's support in 1990 (as today) came from the upper castes, so Prime Minister Singh's decision to implement the Mandal reforms put the party, as part of the Janata Dal coalition, in a difficult position. L. K. Advani was a BJP member of Parliament from New Delhi, where a number of suicides and attempted suicides had taken place. According to him, "Parents used to come to my place daily: 'Why are you supporting this government? Withdraw your support!'" (Jaffrelot 1996, 416). The BJP could not support the Mandal recommendations, but neither could it afford to alienate 52 percent of Indian voters. The BJP leaders chose to move aggressively to support the VHP's new Ayodhya campaign; they could then use Singh's opposition to the Ramjanmabhoomi campaign as their justification for withdrawing from his government's coalition.

After months of unsuccessful negotiations with Muslim groups and Singh's government, the VHP had declared that construction of the Ram temple at Ayodhya would start in October 1990. In September of that year Advani began a 6,200-mile *rath yatra* from the Somnath temple in Gujarat to Ayodhya in Uttar Pradesh to demonstrate BJP support for the Ayodhya campaign. In October the BJP announced it would withdraw from V. P. Singh's government if the government attempted to stop the temple movement. Singh at that point ordered the chief minister of Bihar to arrest Advani in Bihar, halting his procession before it could reach Ayodhya. With Advani's arrest the BJP withdrew its support from the coalition government, new elections were called for May–June 1991, and construction plans were halted.

End of a Dynasty

By May 1991 Singh's government had collapsed, and Rajiv Gandhi was campaigning for reelection in Tamil Nadu. A young woman, later thought to be a member of the Sri Lankan Tamil Tigers, bent at his feet in a traditional gesture of respect and exploded a bomb concealed around her waist, killing herself, Gandhi, and 16 bystanders. In the aftermath of Gandhi's death, the Congress Party found itself for the first time without an adult heir to the Nehru-Gandhi dynasty. Congress (in one form or another) had governed India for more than 40 out of the 44 years since independence, and Nehru or his progeny had ruled the governing Congress Party for all but two of those 40 years. For better or for worse India had become a mature modern democratic state under the joint tutelage of the old nationalist party and the Nehru-Gandhi family.

By the 1980s and 1990s, however, both Indian political parties and Indian voters had changed. Congress, which had so easily dominated elections during the early years after independence, had lost much of its grassroots base during the centralizing regimes of Indira Gandhi and her son Rajiv. In addition, according to many political observers, Indian politics had become increasingly fragmented and regionalized over the decades after independence. Up to 1967, Congress had contained within itself the most important political factions in the country and had dominated elections in the various states. But the 1967 election marked the end of Congress dominance in state governments, and 10 years later the eighth national election (1977) marked the end of Congress dominance even at the center.

During the 1980s Congress became just one among an endlessly proliferating series of combining and dissolving political parties. Parties formed and dissolved as their leaders (and their aggregates of supporters) switched allegiances or left one coalition to join another. Few parties had defining ideologies by the 1980s—the Communists in Bengal and Kerala and the Jana Sangh–BJP–RSS network being major exceptions. Voters, too, were now more willing than in the republic's early years to switch from party to party.

Even with Rajiv Gandhi's assassination in May 1991 and no Nehru-Gandhi family leader for the first time since independence, Congress (I) still won 220 seats in the Lok Sabha elections, achieving a plurality that enabled it to form a coalition government with the support of Tamil Nadu's non-Brahman DMK party, Muslim League representatives, and the Communist Party of India (Marxist), or CPI (M). P. V. Narasimha Rao (1921–2004), who had been foreign minister in both Indira Gandhi and Rajiv Gandhi's governments became prime minister.

The BJP, which had campaigned aggressively on Hindutva and Babri Masjid issues, became the second largest party at the center, with 120 seats. The party had losses in regional elections in Bihar, Haryana, and Maharashtra, although it maintained control over state governments in Himachal Pradesh, Rajasthan, and Madhya Pradesh. In Uttar Pradesh, however, the BJP won the elections and formed the next state government.

Globalization of India's Economy

Even as the Mandal crisis grabbed headlines and the VHP's Ramjanmabhoomi campaign gathered support, the Congress (I) government of 1991 authorized the liberalization of India's economy. The United States's Persian Gulf War in 1991 had caused oil prices to rise in India (and worldwide), sending food prices higher and forcing many Indians working in Gulf states to return home unemployed. When India almost defaulted on its international debt in 1991, Prime Minister Rao appointed Manmohan Singh (1932–   ), a Harvard- and London-educated economist, as finance minister. Singh made severe cuts in government spending and devalued the Indian rupee in return for several billion dollars in World Bank and IMF loans. He aggressively courted foreign investment and cut bureaucratic restrictions on foreign businesses. The short-term effects of these changes were an increase in unemployment and a 15 percent inflation rate, which weakened Rao's coalition government severely.

Within five years, however, Manmohan Singh's economic program was being hailed as an economic miracle. India's economy grew faster in the years between 1991 and 1996 than it had in most years after

Indian independence. Foreign investment totaling more than $10 billion poured into India, and exports grew by 20 percent per year. Western companies long banned in India—Coca-Cola, Pepsico, IBM, Xerox, Kentucky Fried Chicken—opened businesses in urban centers. The city of Bangalore flourished as India's computer science and software center. By the end of 1995 inflation had fallen to below 6 percent per year and urban middle-class Indians were experiencing a surge in prosperity. Meanwhile the contrast between the 30 percent of India's population experiencing the new prosperity and the 30 percent of the population who were landless laborers and urban slum dwellers was as stark as at any time in the past.

Demolition of the Babri Masjid

The BJP's Uttar Pradesh victory left the party caught between its role as a state government (whose voters wanted stability and order) and its commitment to Hindu nationalism (whose supporters wanted the Babri Masjid razed and the Ram temple built). The situation remained stalemated through 1991 as negotiations between the VHP, the Congress (I) central government, the Uttar Pradesh government, and Muslim protest groups failed to reach any agreement. In October 1992 the VHP announced that construction would start on December 6. The Supreme Court declared the construction illegal and the Rao government moved 195 paramilitary companies into the Ayodhya region. At the same time armies of VHP *kar sevaks* (volunteer workers) from different parts of India began to converge on Ayodhya. By December their numbers were estimated at 150,000.

On December 6, 1992, with Advani, Murli Manohar Joshi, and numerous other RSS and VHP leaders present, volunteers broke into the Babri Masjid grounds and began to dismantle the mosque. Neither the state police nor the central government's paramilitary forces attempted to stop them. (Observers later attributed the central government's failure to act to the general reluctance of the already-weak prime minister, Rao, to interfere with a popular Hindu movement.) Within five hours the three domes of the mosque had fallen and the building was in ruins. A temporary temple for Hindu religious images was constructed on the mosque site by the *kar sevaks*. As the demolition was under way volunteers attacked press crews and local Muslims and burned Muslim homes in Ayodhya. The BJP later officially described the events as an "uncontrollable upsurge of [a] spontaneous nature" (Jaffrelot 1996, 455), but some observers at the time thought Sangh Parivar leaders had planned the demolition in advance.

TWO BJP LEADERS

L al Krishna Advani and Atal Bihari Vajpayee are often presented as holding opposing positions within the BJP and RSS hierarchies: Advani the "hard-liner" versus Vajpayee the "moderate." Yet the two men had worked together in the Jana Sangh and the BJP for years without major ideological disagreements. Their more recent differing political stances, some observers suggest, are more tactical than substantial.

Vajpayee (ca. 1924–) was born in Gwalior in Madhya Pradesh. He had earned an M.A. in political science at DAV College in Kanpur before dropping out of law school to join the RSS as a *swayamsevak* (volunteer) in the early 1940s. A dedicated *pracharak* (preacher) Vajpayee was assigned in the 1950s to organize and develop the Jana Sangh party along RSS lines. He became general secretary of the Jana Sangh in Uttar Pradesh during that decade, was first elected to Parliament in 1957, and served as foreign minister in the Janata government in 1977. He helped found the BJP in 1980 and was its first president before being replaced by Advani when the BJP's election results proved disappointing. In 1992 he was one of the few Sangh Parivar leaders to denounce the Babri Masjid demolition. In 1996 and again in 1998 he became prime minister in BJP coalition governments.

Like Vajpayee, Advani (ca. 1929–) also rose through the RSS ranks. Born in the port city of Karachi in Sindh, he joined the RSS in 1942, becoming a *pracharak* in the Karachi RSS in 1947. During Partition Advani and his family (along with 1 million other Sindhi Hindus) fled to India. In India Advani worked for the RSS in Rajasthan and then in New Delhi, becoming secretary of the Delhi Jana Sangh in 1958, president of the national Jana Sangh in 1973, and minister of information and broadcasting in the Janata government of 1977. Advani was also one of the BJP's founders and became its president in the late 1980s as the party turned from accommodation to a more militant political stance.

Rioting began in Ayodhya during the mosque demolition and continued through December and January in North Indian cities. On some occasions riots were started by Muslims protesting the mosque demolition; more often they were sparked by Hindu nationalist victory celebrations and aided by complicit local police. In the first week after the demolition 1,200 people were killed, most in Maharashtra, Gujarat, Uttar Pradesh, and Madhya Pradesh and somewhat fewer in Delhi and Rajasthan. In

Bombay rioting lasted into January 1993, instigated by Shiv Sena and BJP activists and aided by police. Shiv Sena processions chanted "*Pakistan or kabristan*" [Pakistan or the cemetery], a reference to where Muslims should now go (Jaffrelot 1996, 459). In Bhopal a week of riots led by Bajrang Dal and VHP activists forced almost 17,000 residents (two-thirds of them Muslim) to flee to refugee camps.

In Bihar there was little violence. The state's OBC chief minister, Laloo Prasad Yadav (1948–   ), had demanded quick action from local district magistrates and police. Outside the North Indian Hindi belt, riots were fewer and less deadly: 73 people died in Karnataka, 35 in West Bengal, 100 in Assam, 12 in Kerala, 12 in Andhra Pradesh, and two in Tamil Nadu.

If the Ayodhya demolition showed the potency of Hindutva issues, it also created new difficulties for a BJP that wanted to present itself as a responsible political party. Advani resigned as leader of the opposition in Parliament and Kalyan Singh as chief minister of Uttar Pradesh. Atal Bihari Vajpayee, a BJP leader who was not in Ayodhya on December 6, 1992, described the demolition as his party's "worst miscalculation" (Jaffrelot 1996, 457). The Congress (I) prime minister, Rao, widely

Demolition of the Babri Masjid, 1992. Volunteers of the RSS and related Hindu national-ist groups climb onto one of the three domes of the Babri Masjid after breaking into the mosque grounds on December 6. In hours the ancient Muslim house of worship had been razed to the ground. (AP/Wide World Photos)

criticized for failing to defend the mosque, ordered the arrest of six prominent Hindu nationalists, among them Advani and the head of the VHP, on charges of inciting communal violence. Rao's government banned the RSS, the VHP, and the Bajrang Dal, sealed their offices, and prohibited any further activities. The Congress (I) imposed president's rule in Uttar Pradesh, Madhya Pradesh, Rajasthan, and Himachal Pradesh, dismissing all their BJP state governments.

But Rao's coalition government was already weak, and his determination to punish participants in a popular Hindu cause had only a limited duration. All the Hindu nationalist leaders were released by mid-January 1993. Fewer than 4,000 Sangh Parivar participants were arrested nationally, among them 1,500 RSS, VHP, and Bajrang Dal members in Uttar Pradesh and almost 1,000 in Madhya Pradesh. Within weeks of the center's orders banning the Sangh Parivar groups, state courts began to modify them. In 1993 the Delhi High Court lifted the ban on the RSS and Bajrang Dal (while maintaining it on the VHP for two years because of its members' inflammatory speeches). By January 1993 the Allahabad High Court was allowing Hindu worshippers to enter the mosque grounds to view images in the makeshift temple there. A nationwide opinion poll in January 1993 showed that among North Indians more than 52 percent approved the mosque's demolition. In South India, in contrast, only 17 percent approved the demolition, while 70 percent approved the arrest of the BJP leaders and the banning of their organizations.

As the Babri Masjid campaign drew to an uneasy close, the Indian political scene was focused on the BJP's growing challenge to the assumption of secularism at the core of the nation. As parties prepared for the 1996 national elections, it seemed possible that Indian citizenship might soon apply only to those who could embrace a Hindutva identity. At the same time, however, low caste and Dalit communities at the "bottom" of urban and rural society were becoming increasingly politicized. Politicians had already discovered, with something of a shock, that OBC communities alone made up more than half of the Indian electorate. In coming elections they would contend with an increasingly visible *bahujan* (the many people, the masses). At the same time, all of India would have to contend with the repercussions of the liberalization and increasing globalization of the Indian economy.

These new political configurations and conflicts, however, also had their origins in the many changes that had reshaped Indian society during the decades between 1947 and the 21st century. These changes, demographic, social, and cultural, established the foundation for the movements of the late 1990s and after.

9

BOLLYWOOD AND BEYOND
(1947–2010)

When the koel birds sing in the spring, it's time again for memories
When the koels sing in the spring, it's time again for memories
It's time for swinging under the boughs,
Come home, stranger, your country calls you back
Come home, stranger, your country calls you back.

■

"Ghar aaja pardesi" (Come home, stranger), Hindi song from the film Dilwale
Dulhania Le Jayenge *(The lover will carry away the bride), 1995*

In the years between 1947 and 2009 Indian society changed greatly, not only politically but in terms of numbers of people, where they lived, the forms of their popular culture, and that culture's influence, even on older religious festivals and holidays. While the India of 1900 was almost entirely rural and agricultural, by 2009 India had a mixed economy and, if still agricultural, was growing steadily more urban. Urban India had been defined by an office-centered lifestyle since the 19th century, but in the years after 1947 its hybrid cultural mix became even more diverse. By the 21st century both urban and rural India were tied into a countrywide and globally connected economy. In rural areas older service relationships among village castes shifted into money exchanges, and in urban cities displays of caste commensality rules or pollution practices all but disappeared from public life. The consumer-oriented middle class that appeared in the 1980s and 1990s (variously estimated at between 55 and 250 million Indians) was at least as willing to define itself by its possessions as by its *jati* or *varna* classifications.

Life in Indian cities and villages was now shaped by refrigerators, buses, bicycles, and scooters. Indian culture throughout the country was knit together by new forms of popular culture—by movies, records, and, after the 1980s, cassette tapes and television. Initially these new media were highly centralized and their range of cultural expression limited. But by the end of the 20th century cheap cassette technology and a growing number of satellite networks gave regional and local popular culture new avenues for expression.

Population Growth

Although India's population began to increase in the 1920s and 1930s, the country's greatest population growth occurred in the decades after 1947. In the 1920s, as inoculations and new medicines began to take effect, the birthrate far exceeded the death rate. At first, India's population grew slowly, about 11 percent per decade in the 1920s, then 14 percent in the 1930s, and 13 percent in the 1940s. But from 1951 to 2001 the Indian population grew much faster: from 361 million people to 1.27 billion people, an average rate of increase of more than 23 percent every 10 years.

Population Growth		
Year	Total Population	Growth over Preceding 10 Years (%)
1881	250,160,000*	
1901	283,870,000*	
1951	361,088,090	
1961	439,234,771	+21.64
1971	548,159,652	+24.80
1981	683,329,097	+24.66
1991	843,387,888	+23.86
2001	1,027,015,247	+21.34
July 2009 (estimated)	1,156,897,766	

*Population figures for the years 1881 and 1901 are for prepartition India.

Sources: Schmidt (1995, 131), Census of India 2001 "Provisional Population Totals" (2001, 4), CIA World Factbook 2010 (for July 2009 estimate).

Note that these figures are from the census figures as of 2002. The 2001 census figures now given on the census Web site (dated 2007) lists the total population for 2001 as 1,028,737,436. The changed figures include some estimated figures for provinces where counts did not take place in 2001.

India's Urbanization		
Year	Percent of Urban Population	Percent of Rural Population
1881	9.3	90.7
1901	10.84	89.15
1951	17.29	82.71
1991	25.72	76.66
2001	27.78	72.22
2008 (estimated)	29	71

Sources: CIA. "India: The World Factbook." Available online. URL: www.odci.gov/cia/publications/factbook/geos/in.html. Accessed February 12, 2010. Schmidt, Karl J. *An Atlas and Survey of South Asian History* (London: M. E. Sharpe, 1995), pp. 134–135.

By the 2001 Census, India's most populous states were Uttar Pradesh, Maharashtra, Bihar, West Bengal, and Andhra Pradesh: Almost half of India's population lived in these five states, more than 500 million people. Three of these states (Uttar Pradesh, Bihar, and West Bengal) plus Delhi and the southeastern state of Kerala were also among the most densely populated states in the country, with more than 500 people living in each square kilometer (or 0.39 sq mi). In contrast, regions such as the northeastern Himalayans and the hills of the Deccan peninsula remained sparsely populated.

Urban India

From 1881, when census tabulations first give reliable information on urban and rural populations, to the present, India has slowly and steadily been growing more urban. Whereas in 1881 less than 10 percent of the population lived in towns and cities, in 2001, 27.8 percent did so and by 2008 that percentage was estimated to have grown to 29. (Since 1881 the Indian census has defined an urban area as one with a population of at least 5,000 inhabitants, a density of population of at least 1,000 people per square mile, and with at least 75 percent of its male workers in nonagricultural labor.) India's urban towns and cities (as a percentage of the whole) increased 20 percent between 1881 and 2008, from 9 percent in 1881 to 29 percent in 2008.

If India's overall urbanization has been slow but steady, the growth of its largest cities has been more dramatic. Cities with more than

Urban shack, ca. 1978. Modern Indian cities (like cities everywhere) offer sharp contrasts between rich and poor. Here a family makes its home in a makeshift shack along a street in northern Calcutta. (courtesy of Judith E. Walsh)

100,000 people in the 19th century have grown the fastest: Bombay (officially renamed Mumbai in 1995), for instance, had a population of only 821,764 in 1891 but by 2001 had grown to 11,914,398 within the Mumbai official city limits and to 16.3 million people within the city's larger "urban agglomeration" (UA). By 2001 according to the census, 27 cities and 35 urban agglomerates had crossed the "million plus" population mark. The urban population in the eight states and union territories of Delhi, Chandigarh, Pondicherry, Goa, Mizoram, Lakshadweep, Tamil Nadu, and Maharashtra was higher than 40 percent.

The same migrations from the countryside that brought people into the large cities, also created those cities' large urban slums. In the 27 Indian cities with populations greater than 1 million in 2001, almost one of every four Indians (23 percent) was a slum dweller. That same year almost half of Mumbai's 12 million people lived in slums; in contrast, Bangalore, a city whose growth as India's new software and computer center has been more recent, had a population well over 4 million people, but only about 345,000 slum dwellers.

Urban India dominates the country, spreading its lifestyle even into rural India through movies, radio, cassettes, and now television. Western visitors might find India's urban apartment buildings, shopping malls, traffic jams, bicycles, scooters, taxis, buses, superhighways, crowds, and slums familiar. Wealthy and middle-class urban Indians may maintain caste and food restrictions within their homes, but in the daily coming and going of urban city life—people shopping or jammed into buses, encounters between office clerks and people they wait on— older caste restrictions and pollution practices are rarely if ever seen. As in the West, however, Indian cities can offer stark contrasts between rich and poor. Luxury hotels, high-rise apartments, and walled or gated compounds house the wealthiest residents of the cities of New Delhi, Mumbai, or Kolkata, while burlap-covered huts or the streets themselves are the homes of the poor.

Secularization of Caste

Caste relationships and practices have changed from the early decades after independence, particularly (although not exclusively) in urban towns and cities. Castes have become what sociologist D. L. Sheth terms *de-ritualized*, separated from the religious rituals, beliefs, customs, and practices that in the past organized caste communities and their interactions. Desirable occupations are more likely to be defined by income rather than by ritual purity or appropriateness to one's *varna* status. In urban areas caste rules regarding food are now virtually inoperable outside the family home. Within caste communities economic differences have increased. Households of the same caste but with different occupations, educations, and/or income levels often identify more easily across caste boundaries with others from the same economic and social status, even if from different castes.

At the same time castes that previously held the same ritual status (such as Brahmans) but were divided ritually and/or by marriage rules into smaller *jatis* and subcategories are now more willing to see themselves as a single community. Marriages, for instance, which were earlier performed only within endogamous caste groupings, now more frequently occur either within much more broadly defined caste communities or by matching brides and grooms by educational, professional, or economic status. Caste communities have also broadened their self-definitions by links with wider ethnic or linguistic identities, such as "Dravidian" in south India, or through political and electoral categories, such as "Scheduled Castes" (Untouchables, or Dalits) or "OBCs" (Other Backward Classes). Hindu nationalist groups (in theory) have offered the broadest reclassification of caste categories—at the expense of Muslim and Christian Indians—by suggesting that the most meaningful category within which Indians should see themselves is as Hindus.

Village India

Despite the growth of urban areas and the dominance of urban life-styles, India remains today both rural and agricultural. In 2001, 72 percent of India's population lived in 638,588 small villages; in fact, even in the 21st century 58 percent of all Indian workers (about 234 million people out of a total of 402 million identified as workers) still lived by farming—32 percent by cultivating their own lands and 27 percent by working as laborers on the lands of others.

As has been true since independence, the villages these farmers and laborers live in are small; most have less than 1,000 residents. Village homes are nucleated (that is, crowded together, often sharing walls with adjacent houses) and within easy walking distance of surrounding farmlands. Although most villages in northern and central India are multicaste, the homes of different *jatis* are usually built close together. Untouchable homes, however, are often located apart, in separate neighborhoods or on the outskirts of the village. In south India, where many villages often have only Brahman and non-Brahman castes, Brahman homes are likely to be set apart.

In 2001 most rural families (61 percent) had from six to nine members. The homes of these 138,271,559 village households were simple. Most families (70 percent) lived in one- or two-room homes with mud floors, thatch or tile roofs, and walls of baked or unbaked brick. Fancier homes had cement floors and metal or concrete roofs. Amenities were basic: As late as 2001 less than 25 percent of village households got their drinking water from a tap. Almost all homes were lit with either kerosene or electricity, with the majority using kerosene. More than 77 percent of rural households had no bathroom or latrine facility within their homes.

Rural Caste Relations

In the 1950s, '60s, and '70s economic relations between different village castes (particularly in north India) were structured by the *jajmani* system, a hereditary system through which castes exchanged goods and services. Members of the dominant landowning caste in a village might enter into *jajmani* relationships with members of local service castes—with a barber, for instance, carpenter, sweeper, or washerman. In exchange for agricultural goods, usually provided at harvest time, the service caste member would provide his services to a specific landowning household. These relationships were hereditary, and their obligations were mutual (neither side could break them simply at will).

Even if *jajmani* relations existed among a variety of village castes—and although most villagers farmed in addition to whatever services they performed for others—it was the dominant village caste, the caste that owned most of the village lands, that used most of the services provided through *jajmani* relationships. Dominant landownership gave such power to the village caste that all other castes deferred to that caste. In villages where a non-Brahman caste owned the majority of land—such as in northern Indian villages dominated by the Jats, a major peasant caste—even Brahmans deferred to that caste. And other castes who wanted to raise their ritual status within the village might do so by imitating the customs and practices of whichever caste dominated their village, a variation on Sanskritization in which economic power trumped ritual *(varna)* status.

Dominant castes in a village used their economic power (and sometimes physical force) to resolve village conflicts and to maintain lower castes in their subordinate status. Castes also policed their own members, for if families in a village caste did not maintain proper caste customs, fellow caste members in other villages might not marry their daughters or loan seeds, when needed, at planting time. The threat of being outcasted was powerful: Individuals or families without caste connections had no means of earning their food, marrying their children, or burying their dead. Thus a complex system of economic dependence and hierarchy maintained order among village castes and tied each village into a system of interdependence with other villages.

Changes in Rural Relationships

Rural castes and their relationships changed a great deal during the final three decades of the 20th century. Villages became economic units within an all-India (and global) network of food production and distribution and were increasingly defined by state and central government tax and administrative structures. Religious, service, and trading caste communities now often served rural villages from residences in nearby towns. Older complex *jajmani* relations therefore have been increasingly simplified into economic and monetary exchanges between landowners (or their overseers) and laborers.

Conflicts over the maintenance of older social obligations and forms of deference owed by lower castes and/or Untouchables to higher castes have often sparked violence in recent years. In the 1960s the authority of dominant rural castes was unlikely to be challenged by lower-caste villagers, but in recent decades, as low-caste and Untouchable communities have become more politicized and more assertive, rural intracaste violence has increased. Between 1990 and 1995 the Untouchable political party Bahujan Samaj Party (Majoritarian Party, or BSP) became increasingly visible and active in Uttar Pradesh, raising statues of B. R. Ambedkar in villages throughout the state. Atrocities against Untouchables also dramatically rose in Uttar Pradesh from 1,067 in 1990 to 14,966 in 1995. (Some of this intercaste violence occurred between Untouchables and lower-caste groups immediately above them in the village hierarchy.) Despite the increased violence, Uttar Pradesh Untouchables experienced the change from earlier years as overwhelmingly positive. As one villager told a reporter in 2003, "When I was young, no Dalit could wear a shirt. We didn't have shoes. We would be beaten up if we tried. . . . Today our children go to school. And they have to comb their hair, wear clean clothes, put covers on their books" (Sheth 2004, 50–51).

Urban v. Rural

However much caste and economic relations have changed within rural India in recent years, the economic differences between town and village have grown ever sharper. Urban India has been the largest beneficiary of the economic prosperity that came with the globalization of India's economy in the 1980s and 1990s. Life in present-day India's 53,692,376 urban households looks particularly good when compared with life in its far more numerous (138,271,559) village households.

Urban families are slightly smaller than rural families, with most households (64 percent) having between four and eight members. While most urban families (65 percent) live, as do rural families, in only one or two rooms, their homes are of better quality, with cement or tiled floors, baked brick walls, and concrete, metal, or tiled roofs. Almost 88 percent of urban homes have electricity available,

Urban and Rural Amenities, 2001		
Basic Amenities Available	Percent of Urban Population	Percent of Rural Population
Electricity	87.6	43.5
Tap water	68.7	24.3
Latrines inside home	73.7	21.9

Source: Census of India, 2001. Office of the Registrar General. January 7, 2004. Available online. URL: http://www.censusindia.net. Accessed January 11, 2010.

69 percent get their water from a tap (although only 75 percent have that tap in their home), and almost 74 percent have latrines inside their homes. It is worth noting that while almost one-quarter of the residents of India's largest cities are classified as slum dwellers, the overall conditions of urban life are significantly better than those in rural India.

The New Consumer Indian Middle Class

In the 1990s the rapid growth of India's economy led to the expansion of its middle class. In the 19th and early 20th century this term referred to a tiny elite, less than 1 percent of Indian society in the 1880s. By the 1990s, however, it referred to a group variously defined as anywhere between 55 and 250 million people (that is, approximately 6 to 26 percent of India's population). This enlarged middle class was defined not by caste or location but by its consumption. Middle-class Indians had sufficient wealth to purchase refrigerators, cars, motor scooters, or color television sets. During the 1980s and 1990s sales of these consumer products escalated in India. The number of new cars sold each year increased five times in the 1980s. Sales of televisions went from

Mama Mia's ice cream parlor. Middle-class suburbs, such as this one in south Delhi, were centers for consumer purchases of all kinds in the 1970s and 1980s. Even larger malls have now sprung up in urban centers such as New Delhi. (courtesy of Judith E. Walsh)

Assets in Urban and Rural Households, 2001		
Assets	Percent of Urban Households	Percent of Rural Households
Radio, transistor	44.5	31.5
Television	64.3	18.9
Telephone	23.0	3.8
Bicycle	46.0	42.8
Scooter, motorcycle, moped	24.7	6.7
Car, jeep, van	5.6	1.3
None of these assets	19.0	40.5

Source: Census of India, 2001. Office of the Registrar General. January 7, 2004. Available online. URL: http://www.censusindia.net. Accessed January 11, 2010.

2 million in 1981 to 23.4 million in 1990. Packaged consumer goods increased 220 percent between 1984 and 1990.

The 2001 census tabulations confirm that it is urban Indians, not villagers, who buy most of the consumer products made possible by India's new prosperity. In 2001, bicycles were almost equally present in city and country households, but in the ownership of all other assets city dwellers trumped villagers. While 65 percent of urban households owned a television and 45 percent a radio, in the villages only 19 percent had a television and 32 percent some type of radio. While 30 percent of urban households had some kind of motor conveyance (a car, scooter, or moped), in the villages only 8 percent of households owned any at all. Village India was also home to many more of India's most impoverished citizens. Some households had no major assets whatsoever: 19 percent of urban households and 40.5 percent of village households.

Predictions of a growing—and consuming—Indian middle class that could number as many people as the populations of many Western countries began to appear through media and news outlets in India and the West as early as the late 1990s. For some, such as the author of *The Great Indian Middle Class,* consumerism meant growing middle-class selfishness and the end of empathy for (or even interest in) the plight of India's poorest citizens (Varma 2007). For others, the prospects of a large middle class and the increased liberalization of India's economy meant vast potential riches for all: Thus, the 2007 McKinsey Global Institute analysts predicted in *Bird of Gold: The Rise of India's Consumer Market* that

More than 80 percent of Indians own bicycles. The bicycle is one commodity found in almost equal numbers in rural areas and urban cities. (courtesy of Judith E. Walsh)

"Indian incomes will almost triple over the next two decades" and these rising incomes would "lift 291 million out of poverty and create a 583 million–strong middle class" by 2025 (McKinsey 2007, 10–11).

By the turn of the century, analysts were acquiring a firmer grasp on the potential size and composition of the new middle class. Based on household surveys done at the turn of the century, the National Council of Applied Economic Research (NCAER, a New Delhi economic and marketing research firm) produced a *Market Information Survey of Households*

Size of the New Middle Class (as determined by yearly household income)		
Households with Yearly Incomes	Estimated Size of Middle Class (in millions of people)	Percent of Total Indian Population
Above Rs. 140,000	55 million	6%
Above Rs. 105,000	115 million	12%
Above Rs. 70,000	248 million	26%

Source: Sridharan, Dr. E. "The Growth and Sectoral Composition of India's Middle Class: Its Impact on the Politics of Economic Liberalization." *India Review* 3, no. 4 (October 2004): 413–414. Figures are for 1998–99.

DEFINING THE MIDDLE CLASS BY POSSESSIONS

The National Council of Applied Economic Research's (NCAER) 1998–99 household survey enables analysts to estimate the new middle class by income levels. An earlier survey in 1996 used self-identification, education, and consumption to estimate the size of the new middle class and identify its composition. In 1996 the Centre for the Study of Developing Societies (CSDS) in New Delhi surveyed 9,614 Indian men and women drawn from every state except Jammu and Kashmir. The survey assumed an individual was middle class if he or she met the following criteria: 1) The individual identified him- or herself as "middle class" and 2) The individual also possessed two of the following four characteristics: (i) 10 years or more of formal education; (ii) ownership of three out of four specified assets (a motor vehicle, a television, an electric generator or pump, and non-agricultural land property); (iii) residence in a house built of brick and cement; (iv) a white-collar job.

By these standards approximately 20 percent of the CSDS's interview subjects were middle class. Members of the upper castes (the three highest *varnas*) and/or dominant landowning castes made up only 25 percent of those surveyed but were nearly 50 percent of the survey's middle class. More surprising, however, was the discovery that the other 50 percent of the survey's middle class came from lower castes, Untouchables, tribals, or religious minorities. Low ritual or religious status had not stopped these respondents either from acquiring middle-class assets or from thinking of themselves as middle class.

(MISH) that has been used by many analysts as the basis for estimating the current size and composition of the new middle class. Unlike early data that focused exclusively on consumption, the MISH data (published in 2003) included income information from a sample of 300,000 urban and rural households taken between 1998 and 1999. The survey divided the Indian population into five groups of households based on income (rupees per year) as reported by household heads. The highest group had incomes above Rs. 140,000; the upper middle group had incomes between Rs. 105,001–Rs. 140,000; the middle group had incomes above Rs. 70,000 to 105,000; the lower middle group, from above Rs. 35,000 to Rs. 70,000; and the lowest group had incomes up to Rs. 35,000.

The size of the new middle class depends on the criteria used to define it. Using NCAER data, Dr. E. Sridharan estimated in 2004 that the size of the middle class fell between 55 million and 248 million people, depending on which category of income one used to define it. The most restrictive definition of the middle class included only households with yearly incomes above Rs. 140,000, or about 55 million Indians; the next estimate of the middle class included all households making more than Rs. 105,000 each year, or about 115 million people; finally, the largest estimate of the middle class included members of all households making above Rs. 70,000 each year, or about 248 million people (Sridharan 2004, 414). Whatever definition is used to define (and count) the new Indian middle class, however, Sridharan points out that its emergence has changed India's class structure "from [an earlier] one characterized by a sharp contrast between a small elite and a large impoverished mass, to one with a substantial intermediate class" (Sridharan 2004, 405).

The assumption, fairly widespread in news stories, that this emerging middle class comes entirely or even in the majority from India's higher castes or communities is challenged by an earlier 1996 survey conducted by the Centre for the Study of Developing Societies (CSDS) in New Delhi. This survey estimated the middle class (as defined by self-definition, education, and possessions) at about 20 percent of its survey sample but noted that nearly half of its members now came from groups traditionally defined as among the lower castes (OBCs, Untouchables, tribals, or religious minorities).

Indian Popular Culture

It was after independence and in the context of rapid population growth, an urbanizing society, and (in the late 1980s and 1990s) a growing consumer-oriented middle class that Indian popular culture took its current form. A vibrant hybrid of old and new characterizes today's Indian films, television serials, and audiocassette music. This new popular culture has also marked India's festivals and religious cycles; in their new urban, middle-class forms, Indian holidays can seem as much about consumerism as about religion.

For most of the 20th century Indian popular culture was dominated by domestic films and film music. Indian radio began in 1927 but as a government monopoly used mostly for educational programs. Only in 1957 did All-India Radio (AIR) develop a new (and immediately immensely popular) channel on which film songs were played. The

Indian record industry was too expensive to serve more than a tiny minority who could afford its record players and albums. Television (also founded as a government monopoly in 1959) offered only a limited schedule, mostly of news and educational programs, until 1982.

Cinema tickets were much cheaper than televisions, record players, or even radios. Films became the entertainment medium of choice for Indian men in the decades after 1947. (Poor or lower-class Indian women particularly from rural areas did not go to see films although they knew the songs from radio broadcasts.) Films were shown in theaters in towns and cities and in traveling screen shows in villages. Even the tiny television system broadcast a Hindi film each week. For 40 years, from the 1930s to the 1970s, film and film music dominated Indian popular culture, influencing musical tastes, fashion, speech, and the worldviews of several hundred million viewers. Film songs were the major—virtually the only—popular music in India.

The expansion of Indian television began in 1982–83: Doordarshan, the government's television organization, began to use Indian communication satellites to broadcast in color a new set of programs, including the Asian Games of 1982 and the National Programme, sent from New Delhi to stations throughout India. In 1982 Doordarshan's 16 transmitters reached less than 8 percent of Indian people, but in 1983 the Sixth Five-Year Plan committed 869.5 million rupees to increase transmission facilities. By 1991 Doordarshan had 523 transmitters broadcasting programs to 35 million TV sets and with the potential to reach almost 80 percent of the population. The expansion of Indian television added a new video culture to that of Indian films. Portable black-and-white TVs (selling for 3,500 rupees) became a growing consumer product. By 2001 more urban Indian households (64 percent) owned televisions than owned radios (45 percent). Even in rural India, almost 19 percent of households owned a television by 2001.

At the same time a new and inexpensive medium—audiocassette tapes and players—suddenly made many different kinds of music and audio programming cheaply available to Indian consumers. This new technology created what ethnomusicologist Peter Manuel calls the "cassette culture" of the 1980s and 1990s. Cassettes were produced for a great variety of regional, local, and genre music, from regional folk music to religious *bhajans* (Hindu devotional songs), popular *ghazals* (Urdu poetry), obscene Punjabi truck driver songs, women's liberation songs, and Hindutva organizing songs. By the 1990s Hindi film songs had plummeted from 90 percent of Indian recorded music to less than 40 percent.

Film posters compete for space on the wall of Mumbai's (Bombay's) Victoria Station. Films (and film music) were virtually the only form of national popular culture until the advent of cassette tapes and television serials in the 1980s. (courtesy of Judith E. Walsh)

Bollywood

Film was first introduced in India in 1896 when six silent motion pictures were shown in Bombay. But only after 1931, when the first Indian sound film was produced, did the commercial Indian film industry begin. The movies were made in Bombay production studios—called Bollywood, a combination of Bombay and Hollywood—and in regional film centers in southern and eastern India. (Technically the largest number of films are made in Chennai, formerly known as Madras; however, the south Indian languages used in these films limit their distribution.) Bollywood films are shown in cities, towns, and villages throughout India. As of 2009, according to the annual report of the Ministry of Information and Broadcasting, Indian filmmakers produced more than 1,200 feature films each year, making the Indian film industry the largest in the world. On average, 11 million Indians attend the cinema every day, down from 15 million in 1993 due to competition from satellite television and TV serials. Still on average, 4 billion Indians go to the movies each year.

Most Bollywood films are musicals and follow a well-established format, with naturalistic dialogue scenes interspersed with five or six song sequences and at least three dance numbers. The song and dance numbers make the films popular with viewers even outside the

A MASALA HIT

The 1975 film *Sholay* (Flames) was so unusual in style and content for Bollywood that its failure was widely predicted. Instead, the movie became one of Bombay's most successful. Released during the early days of Indira Gandhi's Emergency, its stylish cinematography and story of violence and social disorder struck a chord in receptive Indian audiences. *Sholay* introduced the concept of the masala (spicy) film, a genre that added action, adventure, and violence to the basic Bollywood formula of romance and family conflict. Set in the harsh plateau lands of the northern Deccan, *Sholay* was one of Bollywood's first "curry Westerns." In a relatively dark parable of the erosion of traditional order, its story followed two outlaw adventurers, Veeru and Jai, as they struggled to take revenge against a villainous *dacoit* (bandit) who had maimed their patron, a local *thakur* (landlord/official), and killed his sons.

Sholay sold out movie houses in major cities for more than two years and set ticket records for profitability that held for almost 20 years. Not just its songs, but even its dialogues were sold on audiocassettes and memorized by devoted fans throughout India.

Source: Quotation from Lutgendorf, Philip. "Sholay." Philip's Fil-Ums: Notes on Indian Popular Cinema. 2002. Available online. URL: http://www.uiowa.edu/~incinema/. Accessed February 10, 2010.

North Indian Hindi language belt. Most stories are contemporary and domestic; only about 10 percent are mythological. Beginning in the mid-1970s Bollywood began to produce action-oriented films, filling them with murder and mayhem, but most plots still contained conflicts with romantic love set in the Westernized, modern upper-class world of urban India. Characters frequent night clubs, drive sports cars, drink alcohol, and wear Western clothing (if men) or fashionable versions of traditional Indian clothing (if women). They struggle to resolve conflicting attachments to romance on the one hand and family obligations and loyalties on the other. Although for many years censorship rules barred kissing in films, filmmakers circumvented these restrictions with voluptuous dance sequences and the famous "wet sari" sequences. Endings are virtually always happy as romance triumphs over misunderstandings, family, dowry, and caste or class distinctions.

Indian filmmakers deliberately strive to create a fantasy world in Bollywood films, a rich, upper-class Indian world in which all types of consumer products are lavishly displayed. As one lower-class village youth told an interviewer, "Ninety percent of the people I know want everything they see in films" (Manuel 1993, 266). Critics complain that this Bollywood fictional world not only is elitist and upper middle class but also is one in which the fairness of basic economic relationships in Indian society is never questioned (nor, for that matter, is the dominance of men within Indian families). Peasant characters, even when impoverished, appear clean, well fed, and well clothed. Rural settings bear little relation to actual villages. Bollywood films have yet to

BOLLYWOOD ABROAD

The 1995 hit *Dilwale Dulhania Le Jayenge* (The lover will carry away the bride) uses London, Europe, and the Punjab as the backdrop for its story of middle-class romantic love thwarted by family elders. In it Baldev Singh, an Indian émigré to London, returns home to the Punjab to marry his daughter (betrothed at birth) to the son of his best friend. She, unknown to him, is already in love with a brash but decent Indian boy from England who follows her to the Punjab to win her as his bride. The film explores the conflicts of elders in the Indian diaspora who long to return home—the song "Come home, stranger, your country calls you back" is frequently reprised—and of a younger expatriate generation eager to make its own way in life.

Dilwale Dulhania Le Jayenge sold out not only in India but among Indian diasporic communities in Great Britain and North America. Economically Bollywood's interest in the nonresident Indian (NRI) audience made sense, for although the NRI community is small by Indian standards (approximately 4 million potential viewers in Great Britain and North America), ticket prices are much higher in these countries, and the resulting profits substantial. The popularity of Hindi films in the overseas diaspora continued to grow during the 21st century. In 2000 four Hindi films were among the top 20 releases of the year in the United Kingdom. In 2003 *Time* magazine reported that the worldwide audience for Indian films (approximately 3.6 billion people) was more than 1 billion greater than the audience for Hollywood films (Guha).

Source: Guha, Ramachandra. India after Gandhi: The History of the World's Largest Democracy (New York: HarperCollins, 2007), p. 730.

approach the realistic (and empathetic) portraits of village India drawn, for example, in the 1950s–80s films of the world famous Bengali director Satyajit Ray.

Even though Bollywood production studios turn out a large number of films each year, Bollywood's "star system" ensures that only a small number of producers, directors, actors, and singers work on these films. Bollywood films have involved fewer than 70 such "stars" since the 1940s. The fees for these men and women can make up 65 percent of a film's budget, and films can sometimes take three years to complete because stars may work in as many as 50 films at one time.

Film Music

Hindi film songs dominated the Indian music industry from the 1940s to the 1970s. Unlike the West where popular music has long been generated by independent artists in concerts or in recordings, in India the only popular music until very recently was film music. Older Indian folk music had a wide range of subjects and styles; it wove regional culture into its songs through references to local customs, costumes, foods, jewelry, and spices. In contrast, Hindi film songs presented a homogenized all-India culture shorn of regional characteristics. Tunes had to be "so simple they can be hummed by everybody," in the words of one music director (Manuel 1993, 50).

Film music was (and is) studio art. Songs are performed in the studio by "playback singers," whose singing provides the vocals while film actors mouth the words on screen. As in Bollywood more generally, only a small number of musicians work in film songs. In the 1980s and 1990s some seven or eight music directors produced virtually all Bollywood film music; an equally small number of musicians wrote the scores and between five and six "playback" singers recorded them. The most famous of these singers was (and is) Lata Mangeshkar (1929–   ). Her high-pitched falsetto has been featured in several thousand film songs over the course of her career, especially from the 1940s through the 1980s, so much so that she was featured in the *Guinness Book of Records* as the singer of the most recorded songs in the world. Mangeshkar and her sister Asha Bhosle (1933–   ) together established the female style of film singing that dominates Bollywood films even today.

As Hindi film music grew in popularity over the 20th century, Indian folk songs began to make use of its music, style, and even of the songs themselves. Hindu festivals such as the yearly Ramlila (the celebration

WOMEN'S LIB AND HINDUTVA

In the 1990s two specialized but very different producers of cassette tapes were the women's liberation organizations of India and the Hindutva Ramjanmabhoomi organizers. In 1990 the New Delhi women's organization Jagori distributed three tapes of songs and speeches on women's issues. Jagori was one of perhaps 100 women's groups that worked on issues such as women's education, domestic abuse, dowry murder, and female infanticide by organizing at the grassroots level in urban and rural settings. The songs Jagori taped were set to folk tunes, film song melodies, and Muslim religious music, and the tapes were either directly distributed or were used by organizers in workshops and song sessions. One such song, set to a Rajasthani folk tune, began

> Hear how together with other women we can gain our rights
> Brother got freedom, we got the four walls
> Why don't we smash these walls?
> First we'll demand our rights at home, and then outside as well.
>   (Manuel, 240)

In the same period organizers for the Ramjanmabhoomi movement published four tapes of songs, chants, poetry, and speeches as part of their campaign to build support for the demolition of the Babri Masjid in Ayodhya. Officially the tapes were banned, but they were still easily available in North Indian cities. One tape featured Uma Bharati, a woman BJP member of Parliament, urging followers to embrace violence to build both the Ram temple and a stronger Hindu India:

> May our race not be blamed, and may our mothers not say that
>   when we were needed, we weren't ready.
> If there must be a bloodbath then let's get it over with
> Because of our fear of a bloodbath before
> Our country was divided [in partition]
> Since their [the Muslims] arrival until today, they have killed so many
>   Hindus
> We tried to appease them, but there was bloodshed after all
> Instead of having it simmer slowly, it's better to have it burst with a big flame
> If they don't understand our words, then we'll make them understand
>   with kicks;
> If there must be a bloodbath, then let it happen! (Manuel, 253–254)

Source: Manuel, Peter. *Cassette Culture: Popular Music and Technology in North India* (Chicago: University of Chicago Press, 1993).

of the god Rama's victory over the evil Ravana) have used both film tunes and the style of the singers in their celebrations. In 1991 Peter Manuel found local snake charmers using a theme song from a popular 1950s film to call their snakes (1993, 267).

"Cassette Culture"

In the 1980s the low-cost technology of audiocassette tapes and players ended the hegemony of Bollywood film music and allowed the emergence of a cottage industry in cassette recordings, one that catered to the specific interests of local and regional markets. This cassette culture allowed different forms of popular music to emerge, from regional folk music and nonfilm "pop" music to devotional music and music used for consciousness raising or political organizing.

By 1989, 500 indigenous Indian companies were involved in the consumer electronics industry. Cassette music sales boosted sales of Indian recorded music from $1.2 million in 1980 to $21 million in 1990. Indian consumers were purchasing 2.5 million cassette players each year by the 1990s. In 1991 Indian-made cassettes sold 217 million per year, making India the second largest producer of cassette tapes in the world.

Doordarshan

Doordarshan's new television programming gained Indian television a large audience in the 1980s and 1990s. Beginning in 1982, Doordarshan's National Programme included sponsored shows and new entertainment serials. The serials were set in India and focused on the conflicts and situations faced by modern Indians in the course of their lives. The first serial broadcast was *Hum Log* (We people), a family drama that told the story of a lower-middle-class urban family struggling to survive. Another, *Buniyaad* (Foundation), followed a postpartition family of middle-class Punjabi refugees as they began new lives in India. The series *Param Veer Chakra* (Medal for highest military heroism) told tales of nationalist and military martyrs. By 1987 40 serials had been telecast. These serials were so popular that movie attendance was ultimately cut in half; in New Delhi between 1984 and 1985 money from movie ticket sales declined by 25–30 percent.

After the success of *Hum Log,* Bollywood professionals also began to produce serials for Doordarshan. Among the television serials later produced by Bollywood directors were the made-for-television versions of the *Ramayana* and the *Mahabharata*. The *Ramayana* was shown in 78 weekly episodes that ran from January 1987 into 1988. The *Mahabharata* was televised from September 1988 through July 1990. Both shows drew enormous audiences: 80–100 million for the *Ramayana* and 200 million for the *Mahabharata*.

Hum Log and Maggi Noodles

Hum Log was the first Hindi-language television serial to be broadcast on Doordarshan. It centered on the struggles of an alcoholic carpenter, his long-suffering wife, and their five children in a small two-room flat in a lower-middle-class urban neighborhood. The series consisted of 156 episodes that ran over 17 months during 1984–85. Each episode ended with a commentary by the elderly Hindi film star Ashok Kumar pointing out that episode's moral and answering viewers' letters.

Hum Log's plots were didactic, emphasizing the importance of family planning, the dangers of alcohol, the damage done by dowry demands, the danger of disobedience to elders, and the importance of education. One story line, for instance, detailed the fall of the second daughter, Majhli, whose efforts to become a Bombay starlet (against her parents' wishes) led to her sexual exploitation. The series' moral hero was the family patriarch, the grandfather, a traditional and sympathetic old man whose continued efforts to help his family made a sharp contrast with the selfish behavior of his modern, alcoholic son.

Hum Log was not only a success with audiences, it was also successful in promoting its main sponsor's new product, Maggi Noodles, a foreign food being manufactured in India by a subsidiary of Nestlé. To give its product greater visibility, the subsidiary underwrote the serial's production costs. During *Hum Log's* 1984–85 run, Maggi Noodles commercials were shown to an estimated audience of 50 million people. Noodle sales jumped from 1,600 tons in 1983 to 5,000 tons in 1984. The product's success changed Indian advertisers' minds about television commercials. By 1985 there were 15 potential advertisers for every prime-time Doordarshan slot. Between 1985 and 1988 Doordarshan raised its advertising charges three times. In 1990 one estimate put Doordarshan's advertising revenues at the equivalent of $104 million.

Satellite Networks

Competition to Doordarshan's monopoly on television came in the form of transnational satellite television. In 1991 the U.S. Cable News Network's

CONSUMING DOWRIES

I t was in the mid-1980s that newspapers worldwide reported on the increasing incidence of "dowry deaths" in India. These were deaths in which a young woman was killed by her husband or in-laws (often in a kitchen fire made to look like an accident) because the dowry she had brought to the marriage was considered too small. In the late 1980s dowry deaths were reported mostly in northern India, but by the 1990s they were being reported throughout India. In 1986 the government of India made dowry deaths a new kind of crime in order to facilitate prosecutions. In 2000, according to a UNICEF (United Nations Children's Fund) report, dowry deaths numbered 5,000 a year. By 2007, according to the Indian National Crime Records Bureau (NCRB) the number of dowry deaths had risen to 8,093. Even this number, however, may not reflect the full scope of violent dowry deaths. In a 2009 article in the British medical journal the *Lancet,* researchers estimated that in 2001, 106,000 fire-related deaths had occurred among women aged 15 to 34, three times more than had occurred among men of the same age—and many more than police records indicated.

Some observers have linked the growing incidence of dowry murder to the rise of a consumer-oriented culture in India. Dowry has long been a feature of Indian marriage, with gold jewelry, saris, and other traditional objects accompanying a bride to her in-laws' home. But in recent decades dowry demands have escalated, leading even lower-middle-class families to expect refrigerators, electric generators, cars, and color televisions on the marriage of their sons. Dowry deaths occur most often among lower-middle-class urban families in which the desire for the consumer goods or the need for cash can be acute. As one New Delhi working-class Muslim woman told an interviewer in 1992, "We Muslims never had dowry deaths. . . . Now our culture is changing. People see all sorts of things on TV; people are getting greedy; people are losing respect for women" (Mankekar).

The need to provide escalating dowries for daughters may be one reason for the declining birthrate of girls relative to boys on the subcontinent. Demographers estimate that the normal, worldwide "sex ratio at birth" (or SRB) of males to females is between 104–105 male births to every 100 female births. Rising SRB values suggest human intervention before or after pregnancy, such as the abortion of a fetus before birth or infanticide (or neglect) after birth. In India, census information from 1981 to 2001 shows a rising SRB of male infants to 100 female infants. (India computes its sex ratio as the number of female children age 0–6 per every 1,000 male children aged 0–6, but here the information is given following international usage.)

Year	Total	Rural	Urban
1981	104.0	103.8	107.4
1991	105.8	105.5	107.0
2001	107.9	107.1	110.4

(Guilmoto)

Thus the sex ratio at birth has risen in all of India through the censuses of 1991 and 2001. While the Indian 2001 SRB is not as high as in countries such as China (where the SRB in 2005 was 120.5 boy infants to 100 girl infants), it is a significant change from the previous 20 years. Census data indicates significantly higher SRBs in some Indian states (such as the Punjab and Haryana), among urban residents and residents with more education, and for specific religious communities (Hindus, Jains, and Sikhs in particular).

Analysts attribute this changing ratio to the growing use of ultrasound tests to determine the gender of a fetus, followed by abortion if the test shows the fetus to be female. Although abortion because of gender is illegal in India, such tests and abortions have become common. In an article in the British medical journal the *Lancet* (2006), authors estimated that as many as 10 million female fetuses had been aborted over the past 20 years by families seeking to secure the birth of sons. As one (now illegal) advertisement for an ultrasound test reportedly put it: "Spend 500 Rupees Now, Save Five Lakhs [50,000 rupees] Later" (Rajan). In 2008, in a speech to a national conference on this problem, Prime Minister Manmohan Singh denounced the abortion of female fetuses as a "national shame" but made no specific suggestions for the increased implementation of laws forbidding this practice *(New York Times)*.

Sources: Gentleman, Amelia. "Indian Prime Minister Denounces Abortion of Females." *New York Times,* 29 April, 2008; Guilmoto, Christophe Z. "Characteristics of Sex-Ratio Imbalance in India, and Future Scenarios." In *4th Asia Pacific Conference on Reproductive and Sexual Health and Rights* (Hyderabad, India: United Nations Population Fund, 2007), p. 5; Mankekar, Purnima. *Screening Culture, Viewing Politics: An Ethnography of Television, Womanhood, and Nation in Postcolonial India* (Durham, N.C.: Duke University Press, 1999), p. 45; Rajan, V. G. Julie. "Will India's Ban on Prenatal Sex Determination Slow Abortion

(continues)

CONSUMING DOWRIES *(continued)*

of Girls?" 2003. Hindu Women's Universe. Available online. URL: http://www.hinduwomen.org/issues/infanticide.htm. Accessed October 9, 2004; Sanghavi, Prachi, Kavi Bhalla, and Veena Das. "Fire-Related Deaths in India in 2001: A Retrospective Analysis of Data." *Lancet* 373, no. 967 (2009). Available online. URL: http://www.thelancet.com/journals/lancet/article/PIIS0140-6736%2809%2960235-X/fulltext#article_upsell. Accessed January 26, 2010; Sheth, Shirish, Prabhat Jha et al. "Low Male-to-Female Sex Ratio of Children Born in India: National Survey of 1-1 Million Households." *Lancet* 367, no. 9,506 (2006): 185–186, 211–218.

Network's (CNN) satellite broadcast of the Persian Gulf War spurred wealthy Indians to purchase satellite dishes for their homes. By 1992 an estimated 1.28 million middle- and upper-class urban households were watching Star TV (Satellite Television for the Asian Region). By 1997 many transnational satellite networks were available to Indian homes, among them Star and Star Plus, Zee TV, the BBC, Jain TV, Sun TV, Asianet, and ATN. By 2010 households in cities such as New Delhi had as many as 515 channels available to them.

As Doordarshan began to lose its core middle-class audience to the satellite networks, it expanded the channels it offered to provide more programming and more regionally focused programs. It also added 11 vernacular language channels to broadcast in regional languages and focus on regional politics and issues.

Festivals

As India is a secular society, its three national holidays are secular and celebrate days or heroes significant in India's struggle for independence: Republic Day on January 26 was first declared a holiday in 1930 by the Indian National Congress. Today it is the occasion for a televised parade in New Delhi, a showcase for both Indian military units and for floats celebrating the cultural traditions of the many regions that make up the Republic of India. Independence Day on August 15 celebrates the date on which India gained independence, and Mahatma Gandhi's Birthday on October 2 is a day set aside for tributes to India's greatest nationalist.

Traditional religious festivals are celebrated by all of India's major faiths and have many regional forms and variations. Over the last 50

KAUN BANEGA CROREPATI?
SLUMDOG MILLIONAIRE

In 2000 and again from 2005 to 2006, the well-known film star Amitabh Bachchan hosted a popular STAR TV game show *Kaun Banega Crorepati?* (literally, Who will be a ten-millionaire?—a crore being equal to 10 million rupees). This quiz show was based on the British TV show *Who Wants to Be a Millionaire?* Amitabh's catchy Hindi phrases—such as "lock kiya jaye?" (is your answer final, locked?)—enlivened the TV contest and entered popular Hindi speech. The show stopped in 2006 when Amitabh fell ill and was continued for an additional year in 2007 with a substitute host. At that point four contestants had won one crore (that is 10,000,000 rupees).

KBC (as the show was known) was the inspiration for the 2008 Oscar-winning movie, *Slumdog Millionaire.* Based on the diplomat Vikas Swarup's 2005 novel, *Q & A,* the movie told the story of Jamal Malik, an 18-year-old orphan from Mumbai's slums and criminal world, who (however improbably) succeeds in moving to the top of the movie's version of *Kaun Banega Crorepati?* and wins 20 million rupees in prize money. Set in the slums of Mumbai but written and directed by a British screenwriter and a British film director, the film combines the use of Hindi—for early scenes about the young life of Jamal in the slums—with English—for the scenes of his later life and encounters with and escapes from Mumbai gangsters. Commercial releases in both the United States and Great Britain led to the winning of eight Academy Awards in 2009, including the awards for Best Picture, Best Director, and Best Adapted Screenplay. By the close of its release the film had grossed $377,417,293.

In India, reaction was more mixed. Most reviews were favorable and the box office intake was more than $6 million—slightly more than one-third of the $17 million taken in by *Dhoom 2,* a police action Hindi film that has been one of the decade's highest grossing films. However, the film also generated both controversy and criticism. In Patna, slum residents picketed the film with placards reading "I Am Not a Dog" (Time.com). In Mumbai, Shyamal Sengupta, a local film professor, criticized the film's stereotypical portraits: "It's a white man's imagined India. It's not quite snake charmers, but it's close. It's a poverty tour" (Magnier). One taxi driver interviewed in New Delhi, however, disagreed: "It's those who are making lots of money who are cribbing about the film showing the dark side of India," he said

(continues)

KAUN BANEGA CROREPATI? (continued)

"Those left behind are loving it because they can empathize with the film's hero" (Time.com).

Sources: Magnier, Mark. "Indians Don't Feel Good about *Slumdog Millionaire.*" *Los Angeles Times,* 24 January, 2009; Singh, Madhur. "*Slumdog Millionaire,* an Oscar Favorite, Is No Hit in India." Time.com (2009). Available online URL: www.time.com/time/arts/article/0,8599,1873926,00.html. Accessed January 26, 2009.

years, however, the Hindu festivals of northern India have become more standardized in their forms and practices, as regional celebrations are adapted to the forms and festivities described in the news media or shown on television. Older festival formats—the pilgrimage to a holy site, the procession of a deity in a chariot around a village's perimeter—

Durga Puja pandal, New Delhi. *The Bengali regional celebration of Durga Puja now takes place in many different parts of India wherever Bengali people have settled. This pandal (clay tableau) from a New Delhi celebration in 1978 shows the 10-armed goddess Durga with her lion as she slays a demon. The pandals are first worshipped in temples or community halls, then paraded around the city before being brought to a local river (here, the Yamuna River) and immersed.* (courtesy of Judith E. Walsh)

have been widely used in political organizing in recent years, particularly by the BJP and the VHP. And even decisions about public holidays now become the occasion for communal sniping in the highly politicized atmosphere that currently surrounds all religious observances.

Traditional Hindu Festivals

Traditionally Hindu festivals occurred either at harvest or planting times within the agricultural cycle. They marked the seasonal appearances of epidemic diseases (which they were held to ward off), celebrated events in the lives of gods and goddesses, or marked significant astronomical changes such as the phases of the Moon, eclipses, and solstices. The major Hindu festivals widely celebrated across northern India are the 10-day celebration of Dassehra ("10th"), the festival of Diwali ("lights"), and the spring festival of Holi. Dassehra occurs during the first 10 days of the Hindu month Asvin (October) and coincides with the harvest of the summer crop. The festival celebrates the victory of the god Rama over the evil demon Ravana, and its celebration is often marked—in larger villages and in urban centers—by performances of the *Ramlila,* a dramatic presentation of major episodes from the god Rama's life, held over several evenings.

Diwali, which is celebrated in November, is an end-of-harvest celebration and a festival for the worship of Lakshmi, the goddess of wealth. In some regions it is also a festival celebrating the return of Rama and Sita to their Ayodhya kingdom. Traditionally Diwali is celebrated by placing lit lamps and candles throughout the village or locale. Gambling with dice is also traditionally associated with Diwali.

Holi takes place in the spring, in Phalgun (March), the last month in the traditional Hindu calendar. Scholars identify Holi as a spring harvest festival and fertility rite. It is celebrated with bonfires and the roasting of grain. It is also the occasion for licentious behavior and cross-class, cross-caste abuse; members of lower castes and/or younger members of families splash red-colored water on caste superiors or family elders.

Many more local, regional, and communal festivals are still common in India but too numerous to detail at length. The two major Muslim festivals are the Id (feast day), which falls in the last month of the Muslim calendar year and at which animals are sacrificed and food shared within the community, and the second Id feast that follows the monthlong dawn to dusk fasting of Ramadan. In western India, since the 19th century, Maharashtrians have celebrated the birth of the

Sarasvati Puja, Calcutta. A priest worships the goddess of learning, Sarasvati, in an outdoor pandal as onlookers watch. (courtesy of Judith E. Walsh)

elephant-headed god Ganesh in August–September. In Tamil Nadu the harvest festival of Pongal occurs in mid-January.

Political *Yatras* and *Raths*

In the 1980s and 1990s Hindu nationalists frequently adapted traditional Hindu ritual and festival forms for use in their campaigns. *Yatras,* journeys or pilgrimages to a religious site, are a common form of Hindu religious worship. *Raths,* the chariot processions of a god's image around a village, town, or city, are also common. The chariots themselves (*raths*) also carry associations with the Hindu gods and heroes of the Hindu epics, particularly since the appearance on television of versions of the *Mahabharata* and *Ramayana.*

The VHP's first and most successful use of the yatra was the Ekatmata Yatra (pilgrimage for oneness) in 1983. This yatra was to demonstrate the unity of Hinduism, which it did symbolically by having three separate processions simultaneously crisscross India, visiting all of Hinduism's major pilgrimage sites before converging in the city of Nagpur at the end. One procession traveled from Nepal to Tamil Nadu; a second, from Bengal to Somnath in Gujarat; and a third, from Uttar Pradesh to Tamil Nadu. The *yatras* brought holy water, collected from all the religious sites and carried in jars along the way by members of the Sikh, Jain, and Untouchable communities. The separate processions met at Nagpur, the center of India (and not coincidentally the home city of the RSS in India), where the waters were all intermingled—the ultimate symbol of Hindu oneness. This first *yatra* brought together 312 separate processions, convened 4,323 meetings and rallies, and reached all but three of India's districts. RSS *swayamsevaks,* or volunteers, numbering 50,000 oversaw the logistics of the campaign and the processions' movements.

The processions also carried images of goddesses representing the Ganges and Mother India installed on raths and encouraged devotees to worship these images as they moved. The *yatra* was hugely successful and became the model for a number of later *yatras* and *raths* organized by both the VHP and BJP. The *yatra* was also a commercial success: In one procession alone 6,000 images of Mother India and 70,000 bottles of holy water were sold to devotees.

In 1990 L. K. Advani, leader of the BJP, used a different kind of procession, the *rath yatra* (chariot procession), to demonstrate the BJP's support for the Ramjanmabhoomi campaign. Advani traveled 10,000 kilometers (6,200 miles) through eight states in a Toyota decorated to look like an epic chariot, with the election symbol of the BJP and the Hindu symbol "Om" painted on its side. Saffron-clad associates dressed to look like the monkey god Hanuman accompanied the *rath,* as did women performing religious dances. Advani's speeches and Hindu militant songs were broadcast by loudspeakers atop the car, urging supporters to action. In Ahmedabad, Advani was met by a member of the Bajrang Dal who used his own blood to put a *tilak* (symbolic religious mark) on Advani's forehead.

Politicized Holidays

Modern religious holidays in India are often the occasion for public contention. State and local governments publish lists of the general holidays they recognize and the "restricted" holidays when their employees may choose not to work. (Government workers may generally choose two restricted holidays a year from the list offered them.) Restricted holidays will include most religious festivals—Dassehra, Diwali, and Holi for Hindus, Id for Muslims, Christmas for Christians—although Hindu holidays are also likely to be among the general holidays given to all workers. Restricted lists, however, can be used for political purposes and communal division. Just before national elections in 2004, for example, the BJP chief minister of Gujarat, Narendra Modi, removed a number of holidays for Christians, Muslims, Parsis, and Sikhs from the restricted list in what was probably intended as a bid for communal Hindu support.

"Pop" Diversification

Over the decades since independence, India became not only a more populous society but a more urbanized one. Indian popular culture developed along with and as a result of city life and a new consuming middle class. Initially the popularity of films and film songs gave Bollywood a monopoly over Indian audiences and guaranteed that its version of popular culture would dominate. Television, as first developed through the government-controlled Doordarshan, also seemed to offer another medium for the transmission of a centrally produced popular culture. But in the 1980s and 1990s, cheap cassette tapes and new satellite networks broke Bollywood's and Doordarshan's control over popular culture. Indian music now ranges from film songs to religious tapes, and from regional bawdy songs to virulent communalist propaganda. Television also now offers regional channels in the vernacular for the discussion and display of local issues and culture. Urban Indian culture still dominates India, and with 20 percent of villagers now owning TV sets, rural areas have grown increasingly conscious of the many forms of popular culture produced in the cities.

Village Indians, as it turned out in the elections of 2004, have also become more aware of other aspects of urban life. Not only have rural residents participated in the religious and political movements of the past 15 years, they have also made clear that they are aware, as perhaps never before, of the vast economic gulf that still separates urban and village ways of life.

10

INDIA IN THE TWENTY-FIRST CENTURY (1996–2010)

Anger. The major feeling is anger. You can call one chapter "anger."
The middle classes are 2 percent of the population and they are not being
represented. There is no representation. The interests of the
middle classes are not being represented by politicians.

■

Mumbai journalist in interview (Fernandez 2006, 186)

My own assessment is that Indian democracy is working quite well,
and is moving towards being more participative and giving power to
the lower caste. And it is through this movement that the lower caste
is asserting themselves. So I think it is within our reach through democracy
only to upset that hegemony of the upper caste.

■

Jawaharlal Nehru University Dalit student (Jaffrelot 2008, 48)

The rise of a Hindu majoritarian party in the 1980s and 1990s again highlighted the difficulties of democratic majority rule in a country with distinct minority populations and multiple religious communities. This had been an issue in debates over seat reservations and separate electorates before 1947. In the 1990s it reemerged as the VHP and BJP provoked riots over the Babri Masjid and as the BJP came to power in 1998 and 1999 at the head of coalition governments.

By 1999 observers had agreed that the BJP's main supporters were urban, upper-caste Hindus and those from the growing middle and/or upper classes. But, while Hindu nationalism was, in theory, an ideology that could appeal to the 80 percent of Indians who were Hindus, an election reversal in 2004 demonstrated that majoritarian politics might just as

BJP poster, New Delhi, 1996. An unofficial poster for the BJP urges (in Hindi) "Time for a Change—Your Decision" and "Come! Let's go with Bhajpa" (a colloquial name for the BJP). The lotus, the election symbol for the BJP, is the central image of the poster. (courtesy of Philip Oldenburg)

easily be defined along caste (or class) lines—and that in such divisions, the majority among voters could lie with rural voters, with the poor, and with the communities of OBCs and Untouchables. A second, and almost equally unexpected, national election in 2009 saw further victories for the Congress and a further erosion of BJP support. Analysts were left wondering if the Congress Party had managed to reassert its earlier dominance over Indian politics or if, alternatively, the golden bird of India's prosperous, globalized economy trumped the saffron identity of Hindutva.

Fragmented National Power

In the aftermath of the Babri Masjid demolition and violence, the BJP dropped its emphasis on Ayodhya and attempted to widen its constituency by focusing on an economic and social agenda. In 1996 the party won 161 seats in Parliament and tried for 13 days to form a government with Vajpayee as prime minister but failed to find coalition partners because of its aggressive Hindutva stand. Janata Dal politician H. D. Deve Gowda (1933–   ) became prime minister instead, heading a new coalition government, the United Front, made up of 13 leftist, regional, and low-caste parties and supported from outside the coalition by Congress (I) seats.

Gowda was the first regionally based prime minister in India's history. He came from a peasant proprietor background and had been chief minister of Karnataka. He spoke Kannada, the regional language of Karnataka, and was reputed to know little English or Hindi. Within 10 months of Gowda's becoming prime minister, Congress (I) had forced his resignation, replacing him with Inder Kumar Gujral (1919–   ), a relatively obscure Janata Dal member who had served in Congress governments during the 1960s and '70s before joining the Janata Dal in the 1980s. Gujral headed the fourth coalition government to be formed within the year. In November, however, when a government commission identified the DMK party from Tamil Nadu (one of Gujral's coalition partners) as secret funders of the Tamil group responsible for Rajiv Gandhi's assassination, Congress withdrew its support from the coalition, and Gujral's government fell.

The BJP Takes Power

National elections in 1998 gave the BJP the largest block of votes in Parliament—182 seats and 25.5 percent of the popular vote—and the BJP successfully formed a coalition government with 20 other parties, including the Tamil non-Brahman DMK and the tiny Bahujan Samaj Party (BSP). The BJP gained these coalition partners, however, only by abandoning substantial sections of its Hindutva agenda. The party's 1998 National Agenda for Governance dropped several long-standing goals: the building of the Ram temple in Ayodhya, a uniform civil code (a covert attack on the separate Muslim personal law), and ending the special constitutional status of the Muslim majority state of Jammu and Kashmir.

The BJP coalition remained in power with Vajpayee as prime minister for 13 months, until April 1999. Violent attacks against Indian Christians during 1998–99 raised fears that such violence would be tolerated by a Hindu nationalist government, but the BJP's fall in 1999 was caused by internal coalition politics. Squabbling led to the defection of both the DMK and the BSP. In the general elections of 1999, the BJP emerged with the same number of Lok Sabha seats (182) but with a much stronger coalition (294 seats out of the Lok Sabha's 543). Congress (I), now under the presidency of Sonia Gandhi (the Italian-born wife of Rajiv Gandhi), won only 114 seats. Vajpayee's return as prime minister marked the first time in 27 years an incumbent prime minister had been voted back into office.

Analysts from *Frontline,* a national English-language newsmagazine, declared at the time that the BJP (and its allies) had created "a new social block" in election politics (Yadav et al. 1999). This was not the creation of a "simple Hindu majoritarianism," for the BJP had gained its new allies only by abandoning much of its explicitly Hindutva agenda. Rather, it was the creation of a voting bloc in which caste hierarchy and class hierarchy reinforced each other in supporting the BJP coalition. Poll data collected by the Center for the Study of Developing Societies (CSDS) indicated that the BJP and its allies had secured 60 percent of the votes of upper-caste Hindus and 52 percent of the votes of

| | | | | | | All Votes |
| | Congress | BJP | | | Regional | in 1999 |
	(I)	BJP allies	Left	BSP	Parties	Election
Upper strata	34	69 49	28	13	39	45
Lower strata	66	31 51	72	87	61	55

Economic Class in the Elections of 1999
(as a percentage of each party's total votes)

Source: CSDS poll data as summarized in Yadav et al. 1999.

dominant (non-OBC) Hindu peasant castes. Looked at in class terms—through a simple division of the electorate into an "upper strata" and a "lower strata"—the BJP drew 69 percent of its votes from the 45 percent of Indian voters in the upper strata. Thus, the BJP might be said (with only some exaggeration) to represent "the rebellion of the elite" or, at least "the emergence of a new social group that is defined by an overlap of social and economic privileges" (Yadav et al. 1999).

Upward Caste Mobility

Frontline's 1999 analysis of the elections concluded with the question: ". . . if the privileged can form a bloc, why not the underprivileged?" In the 1980s and 1990s a new type of upward caste mobility had appeared in the North Indian Hindi belt region. This mobility had appeared first in South India during the late 19th and early 20th centuries: Non-Brahman castes changed their social status through ethnicization, that is, by moving outside narrow, endogamous *jati* definitions to establish broader ethnic identities. The caste associations of the 1880s–1930s were often the vehicles for such new identities in south India. Some associations even replaced Sanskrit *varna* classifications with the regional and ethnic identity of Dravidians. In the 1920s and '30s, the Tamil leader Periyar had used the idea of Dravidian identity to organize his Self-Respect Movement. Even before 1947 a strong non-Brahman movement in Tamil Nadu had forced its members into the region's English-language schools and had gained control of the regional Congress movement.

In contrast, in northern India Sanskritization had long been the preferred method for upward caste mobility. Even as late as 1947, the English-educated elite of North India came mostly from the upper castes, and these upper-caste members provided the leadership for most of the North's social and political movements. In the 1980s and '90s, however, North Indian social and political groups began to organize low castes and Untouchables outside the rituals, customs, and practices of Brahmanic Hinduism and into politicized ethnic identities analogous to those of the south.

Rising Power of Lower Castes

That upper-caste mobilizations against the Mandal Commission reforms had produced counter-organization among low-caste and Dalit (Untouchable) communities became clear in Lok Sabha and state elections in the 1990s. The two parties that benefited most

THE BANDIT QUEEN

The dramatic life of Phoolan Devi (1963–2001) made Indian news-paper headlines in the 1980s and 1990s, offering Indian readers an illustration of rural low-caste women's lives and of the growing vis-ibility of the Other Backward Classes (OBCs). Phoolan Devi was the second daughter of a lower-caste peasant in a small Uttar Pradesh vil-lage. By age 20 she had became the mistress of Vikram Mallah, leader of a local *dacoit* (bandit) gang. When Mallah was killed by a treacherous friend, Phoolan Devi was kidnapped, raped, and humiliated by high-caste *thakur* men from the village of Behmai. In revenge, on Valentine's Day 1981, she and her *dacoits* massacred 22 *thakur* men from Behmai, later said to be the same men who had raped her. She escaped capture for two years, becoming famous as one of India's most hunted *dacoits,* before surrendering under a plea agreement in 1983.

During her 11-year imprisonment Phoolan Devi was befriended by a journalist who published her story as *India's Bandit Queen,* a best-selling book and then a Bollywood film of the same name. After release from prison in 1994, Phoolan Devi married and converted to Buddhism; in 1996 she ran for Parliament as a Samajwadi Party can-didate in Uttar Pradesh, defeating an upper-caste candidate for the Lok Sabha seat, part of the rise to power of OBCs in that state. In 2001 Phoolan Devi was killed outside her New Delhi home by three masked gunmen. The man accused of her murder, Sher Singh Rana, claimed he had killed her to avenge the death of high-caste Uttar Pradesh men, but other reports suggested Phoolan Devi's husband had been involved in her murder.

from this politicization were the Samajwadi (Socialist) Party, an organization founded in 1992 that focused on OBCs in Bihar and Uttar Pradesh, and the Bahujan Samaj Party (Party of the Majority, or BSP), an Untouchable party that had worked on organizing coali-tions of low castes and Dalits since its founding in 1984. Two OBC leaders from the regional, low-caste Yadav community—Mulayam Singh Yadav (1939–) in Uttar Pradesh and Laloo Prasad Yadav in Bihar—used the Mandal reservations and the more politicized lower-caste climate for the benefit of their own OBC Yadav community in these states.

The BSP was founded by Kanshi Ram (1932–2006), a Punjabi from a low-caste family. During the late 1960s Kanshi Ram had cut himself

MAYAWATI

The elephant (BSP logo) is really the wise Ganesh, the trinity of gods (Brahma, Vishnu, Shiva) rolled into one. (BSP campaign slogan, 2007)

In 1995 a BSP coalition took control of the state government of Uttar Pradesh, and Mayawati (1956–), an Untouchable convert to Buddhism, became the state's chief minister. Mayawati was born into a Jatav (Untouchable) community in the Uttar Pradesh district of Bulandsahar and grew up in New Delhi where her father was a clerk in a government office. She graduated from college in New Delhi and has bachelor degrees in both law and education. She initially worked as a teacher in New Delhi until 1977 when she met Kanshi Ram and gave up plans to study for the Indian Administrative Service to join him in political work. "You won't even become a local municipal corporator," her father is said to have warned, "if you hang around losers like Kanshi Ram" (Bose 2008). In 2001, Kanshi Ram named Mayawati as his successor in the BSP organization.

Her first appointment as chief minister in Uttar Pradesh lasted less than five months, but she was returned to power in 1997 and again in 2002–03; all three times she was at the head of coalition governments. In the summer of 2007, however, the BSP won an absolute majority in the state, and Mayawati and the BSP came to power.

Throughout her terms in office Mayawati has attracted both controversy and criticism. It is said that she has accumulated a large personal fortune and has a vast collection of diamonds and silk

Mayawati, 2007. Bahujan Samaj Party (BSP) leader Mayawati standing before statues of herself, the Dalit leader Ambedkar (center), and the founder of the BSP party, Kanshi Ram in Lucknow, Uttar Pradesh. Mayawati was celebrating the 2007 election victory that would make her chief minister of Uttar Pradesh, India's largest state. (Ajay Kumar Singh/Associated Press)

(continues)

MAYAWATI (continued)

saris. Her 2007 filing with the government stated her cash and assets at 520 million rupees ($10.4 million). Claims of corruption (common in most Indian political parties) have resulted in lawsuits against her.

Some political analysts, however, believe that the BSP and Mayawati have built their strong following in Uttar Pradesh through a combination of policies that consolidate Dalit support and policies that benefit other impoverished communities. In her first term in office in 1995, Mayawati demonstrated the possible benefits of political power for low-caste and Untouchable communities in the state. She put BSP supporters into key administrative posts throughout the state, appointing Untouchable district magistrates in almost half of Uttar Pradesh's districts. A village redevelopment scheme was expanded to include Untouchable villages and to locate its roads, pumps, and houses within Untouchable neighborhoods. Grants were increased to allow Untouchable and Muslim children to attend primary school; 20 percent of police inspector posts were reserved for Untouchables. Muslims were also made eligible for reserved seats in the state administration. As of 2009, one in every five voters in Uttar Pradesh was a Dalit and almost 80 percent support the BSP. In the 2007 election, Mayawati further consolidated her party's hold by reaching out to other castes in the state, giving even Brahman candidates seats on her party's ticket.

An *Indian Express* reporter wrote in 2003 of the changes seen by Dalits in Uttar Pradesh:

> *Check with the Dalits of these villages. They will tell you this was God's forsaken country. They tilled the land of the upper castes, looked after their animals, washed their clothes, shaped their pots, made their shoes and cleaned their mess. In turn, they were declared untouchable and unclean—and forced to live in the dirtiest quarters of the village. . . . "There was a time when we were scared to speak out, even look up [one villager told the reporter]. Now we go and meet the tehsildar, the thanedar [government officials] and they listen to our complaints.". . . Everyone concedes that there can be no comparison between the old days and the present. (Sheth 2004)*

Source: Bose, Ajoy. "Excerpt from Behenji." *Tehelka Magazine* 5, no. 18 (2008). Available online. URL: http://www.tehelka.com/story_main39. asp?filename=Ne100508a_miracle.asp. Accessed January 27, 2010; Sheth, D. L. *Caste, Ethnicity and Exclusion in South Asia: The Role of Affirmative Action Policies in Building Inclusive Societies* (United Nations Development Programme, Human Development Report Office, 2004), pp. 50–51.

off from his family, vowed never to marry, and dedicated himself full time to the organization of low-caste people. Inspired by the writings of Ambedkar and Phule, Kanshi Ram believed that the future of low castes lay in political unity. Between 1989 and 1991 the BSP averaged almost 2 percent of the vote in national elections and had won several seats in the Lok Sabha. In the 1996 national elections, the party won 11 seats, and in 1998 it won five seats.

OBCs and Dalits in Government

By 1999 more-politicized OBC communities had made significant gains in both the Lok Sabha and state assemblies in Hindi-belt states. In general the Lok Sabha became much less upper caste in the decades between 1952 and 2002. Where in 1952, 66 percent of all Lok Sabha members were from the upper castes, in 2002 only 33 percent were. The OBCs' overall parliamentary presence also increased. Where in 1977 OBCs made up 10 percent of the Lok Sabha's members, in 2002 they made up 25 percent.

In the Hindi-belt states of Uttar Pradesh, Madhya Pradesh, and Bihar, the years from 1989 to 1999 saw a dramatic change in the representation of OBCs in state assemblies. In 1989 the percentage of OBCs in Parliament had been only 10.6 percent in Uttar Pradesh, 7.5 percent in Madhya Pradesh, and 18.5 percent in Bihar. Ten years later, however, OBCs were 25 percent of the members of Parliament from Uttar Pradesh, 23 percent from Madhya Pradesh, and 29 percent from Bihar. At the same time, the percentage of upper-caste members of Parliament from the three states had also fallen, from an average of 48 percent in 1989 to only 33 percent by 1999.

At the same time, the Bahujan Samaj Party (BSP) was contesting elections on a national basis by 1998 and by 1999 was averaging 4 percent of the national vote and had been certified as a national party. The BSP's greatest strength was in Uttar Pradesh, Madhya Pradesh, and the Punjab. In 1995, 1997, and from 2002 to 2003, the BSP ran the state government in Uttar Pradesh in coalition with other parties. But in 2007, the party won the state government outright and has remained in power ever since.

The BJP in Power

The BJP's new National Democratic Alliance (NDA), a coalition of 23 political parties, was strong enough to remain in power for five years. Chief among its goals was a pledge to continue the globalization reforms begun by the Congress Party in 1991. These reforms had brought prosperity to India's urban middle classes and were backed by the business classes, whose support the BJP was courting. Over the next five years the BJP introduced probusiness policies that further liberalized and privatized India's economy. The government cut taxes on capital gains and dividends. It began the privatization of state-controlled companies. It eased limits on the percentage of Indian companies that could be controlled by foreign investors. It removed import restrictions on more than 700 types of goods. New labor laws were proposed to make it easier for companies to fire employees and contract out work. But although a commitment to improve rural water supplies, housing, and education had been part of the BJP's initial agenda, the party offered reform proposals in these areas only in its 2004 (election-year) budget.

Nuclear Strategy

Although the BJP had had to give up parts of its agenda to form the governments of 1998 and 1999, the party was determined to make good on long-standing pledges to strengthen India militarily and as a world

---

CAMPAIGNS OF HATE

The years 1998 and 1999 saw 116 attacks against Christians in India, more than at any time since independence. The violence was worst in the tribal areas of Gujarat, Madhya Pradesh, and Orissa. In Orissa members of the Bajrang Dal were implicated in inciting a mob attack that killed an Australian missionary and his two young sons. In Gujarat attacks reached their peak during Christmas week 1998 into January 1999. A rally on December 25 in a tribal region of southeastern Gujarat was organized by a local Hindu extremist group. Anti-Christian slogans were shouted by 4,000 people, some of which were recorded on tape. "Hindus rise Christians run," the mob shouted. "Whoever gets in our way Will be ground to dust . . . Who will protect our faith? Bajrang Dal, Bajrang Dal." The rally was followed by forced conversions of Christian tribals to Hinduism and attacks on churches, missionary schools, and Christian and Muslim shops.

Source: Quotation from Human Rights Watch. Politics by Other Means: Attacks against Christians in India. October 1999. Available online. URL: http://www.hrw.org/reports/1999/indiachr/. Accessed February 10, 2010.

Rise (and Fall) of the Bharatiya Janata Party (BJP)								
	1984	1989	1991	1996	1998	1999	2004	2009
Seats in Lok Sabha	2	85	119	161	182	182	138	116
Percent of national vote	7.4	11.5	20.11	20.29	25.59	23.75	22.16	18.84

Source: Hasan, Zoya, ed. *Parties and Party Politics in India* (New Delhi: Oxford University Press, 2002), pp. 478–480, 509; Jaffrelot, Christophe, and Gilles Verniers. "India's 2009 Elections: The Resilience of Regionalism and Ethnicity." In *South Asia Multidisciplinary Academic Journal* 3 (2009). Available online. URL: http://samaj.revues.org/index2787. html. Accessed June 21, 2010.

power. In response to Pakistan's testing of a medium-range missile, the government authorized the explosion of five underground nuclear tests. Pakistan immediately exploded its own nuclear device, but in fall 1998 world pressure forced both countries to declare moratoriums on nuclear tests and to open talks on Kashmir. Again in April 1999 both nations tested ballistic missiles in a new round of saber-rattling. By 1999 the Indian government was spending $12 billion to fund equipment and salaries for 1 million people in the Indian army, navy, and air force and an additional 1 million staff in paramilitary units.

Kargil, the Fifty-Day War

By 1999 as many as 12 militant Muslim groups were fighting to free Kashmir from India's control, most supported economically and militarily by Pakistan. Among these groups were also Kashmiri separatists, groups that wanted to establish Kashmir as an independent state. In May 1999, shepherds in the Kargil district of India's Jammu and Kashmir spotted armed militants (Kashmiri and Pakistani) in Pathan dress infiltrating the mountaintops. Two weeks later the Indian air force and army swarmed into the region. Through all of June, Indian forces fought to clear the intruders from the occupied mountaintops. By July, the Indian army had driven the insurgents back across the Line of Control drawn up by the United Nations in 1972 for a new cease-fire in Kashmir. Approximately 500 Indian soldiers died in the Kargil War and, according to Indian reports, an estimated 2,000 of the enemy also died. Indian patriotic sentiment in favor of the Kargil soldiers was extremely high in the year following the war; soldiers' coffins were displayed in

303

public places throughout the country and in New Delhi a tribute to the war and the dead soldiers—The Fifty Day War—was enacted for 10 days in January 2000. In 2000, the BJP increased defense spending by 28 percent, an increase justified by the conflict of the preceding year.

Gujarat Earthquake, 2001

On the morning of Republic Day (January 26), the city of Bhuj in the Kutch region of the state of Gujarat was hit by an earthquake that would come to be reported as the second largest in India's recorded history. (The largest earthquake was reported to have occurred in 1737.) The quake, caused by the release of pressure from tectonic plate movements, was said to have measured 7.9 on the Richter scale. It leveled 95 percent of the town of Bhuj and killed more than 12,000 people in the region of Kutch alone and as many as 20,000 people overall. More than 1 million homes in the region were destroyed or damaged and more than 600,000 people were left homeless. Shocks from the quake were felt throughout northwestern India and the bordering regions of Pakistan; in the commercial capital of Ahmedabad, 50 multistory buildings were said to have collapsed. Traveling in the region in late October 2001, Narendra Modi (1950–   ), an RSS *pracharak* and protégé of BJP leader Advani, now chief minister of Gujarat as a result of a BJP state victory, urged a quick return to economic and trade normalization.

Terrorism and Military Mobilization

On December 22, 2000, a Pakistan-based militant group attacked New Delhi's 17th-century Red Fort, killing one soldier and two civilians. Almost one year later, on December 13, 2001, five armed terrorists in a car attacked New Delhi's Parliament complex; the five attackers and seven police and staff were killed. Both attacks were believed to have been planned by Lashkar-e-Taiba (LeT), a Pakistan-based terrorist group. In October 2002 Kashmiri militants killed 38 people in Kashmir's parliament.

Vajpayee's government increased the Indian army presence on Kashmir's border, and Pakistan did the same. By 2002 the two countries had 1 million soldiers mobilized on the border. By January 2003 each country had expelled the other's political envoy, and both were threatening retaliation if the other side began a nuclear conflict. If Pakistan used nuclear weapons against India, said the Indian defense minister George Fernandez at the time, Pakistan would be "erased from the world map" (Duff-Brown 2003). By 2003 deaths in the Kashmir insurgency were estimated to have reached 38,000–60,000.

Then in 2004, as the BJP called for new elections, Prime Minister Vajpayee called for the resumption of dialogue with Pakistan. On May 8, shortly before voting began, Vajpayee announced the restoration of both diplomatic and transportation ties between India and Pakistan and said a new round of peace talks would begin soon.

Gujarat Violence

The BJP distanced itself from the VHP in the election cycles that followed the demolition and violence of the Babri Masjid campaign. The VHP also found its activities curtailed immediately after 1992 by various government restrictions and bans on its activities. But by the late 1990s the VHP had again returned to its earlier themes, the building

Modi's Pride Yatra, Gujarat 2002. Black Cat Indian commandos (members of India's elite National Security Guard) protect Gujarat chief minister Narendra Modi's "chariot" north of Ahmedabad. Modi's Pride Yatra—a procession that traveled throughout Gujarat—was part of an election campaign calculated to appeal to Hindu nationalist sentiments in the aftermath of the state's worst Hindu-Muslim riots since partition. (AP/Wide World Photos)

305

MUSLIMS IN INDIA AFTER PARTITION

The 2001 census identified more than 138 million Muslims in India, accounting for 13.4 percent of the population. Indian Muslims live in all of India's states and union territories but constitute a majority in none. In northern and central interior India, rural Muslims work as small farmers or landless laborers; in towns and cities, as artisans or in middle- and lower-middle-class urban occupations. On the western and southwestern coasts, in contrast, numerous prosperous Muslim business communities and sects are found. Urdu is the first language of almost half of India's Muslims; the rest speak regional languages such as Assamese, Bengali, Gujarati, and Tamil, among others. Most Indian Muslims belong to the Sunni sect of Islam.

To date, a separate Muslim personal law code from before independence regulates Indian Muslims' lives. This code was first challenged in 1985 by an Indian Supreme Court ruling that awarded alimony to a divorced Muslim woman, Shah Bano Begum. Protests by orthodox Muslims at the time forced the government to reverse the court's ruling and to guarantee that sharia law (orthodox Islamic customary practices) would remain secular law for Indian Muslims. But since the Shah Bano case Hindu nationalists have repeatedly demanded a uni-

of the Ram temple at Ayodhya and the dismantling of Muslim religious structures in places such as Kashi (Benares) and Mathura.

In 2002, in the aftermath of Muslim terrorist attacks, the VHP put forward plans for the celebration of the 10-year anniversary of the Babri Masjid demolition. It set March 15 as the deadline for stone pillars to be brought to Ayodhya. Although the Supreme Court ordered construction stopped two days before the deadline, activists continued to travel between Ayodhya and the western Indian state of Gujarat (among other places). In February 2002 a clash between Hindu volunteers returning from Ayodhya and Muslim vendors at the Godhra rail station in Gujarat led to the train being burned; 58 Hindus died, many women and children.

The conflict began the worst Hindu-Muslim riots seen in India since partition. In Gujarat more than 1,000 people died, mostly Muslims, in violent clashes that occurred almost daily for the next several months. The violence included rapes, murder, and burned homes. In Gujarat's form civil law code, arguing that a separate Muslim code amounts to preferential treatment.

Communal violence is probably the single greatest concern of Indian Muslims today, particularly in northern India. Before 1947, communal riots were "reciprocal," equally harming Hindus and Muslims. Since 1947, however, riots have become more one-sided, with "the victims mainly Muslims, whether in the numbers of people killed, wounded or arrested." Starting in the late 1980s and continuing to the present, Hindu nationalist campaigns have precipitated communal violence on a scale not seen since partition. Rioting across northern India occurred in 1990–92, in Bombay in 1993, and in Gujarat in 2002. In the same period armed conflict between India and Pakistan over Kashmir, as well as Muslim terrorist attacks within India itself, only compounded communal tensions.

As India's largest and most visible religious minority, it seems likely that Indian Muslims will remain the target of Hindu nationalist rhetoric and agitation for the foreseeable future. The defeat of the BJP government in 2004 and 2009, however, and the rise of low-caste political movements in the late 20th and early 21st centuries may offer poor rural and urban Indian Muslims an alternative path to political influence—one that may be used without compromising their religious identities.

Source: quotation from Khalidi, Omar. *Indian Muslims since Independence* (New Delhi: Vikas, 1995), p. 17.

state capital, Ahmedabad, more than 100,000 Muslims fled their homes for refugee camps.

Reports suggested that police did little to stop the violence, much of which was not spontaneous but planned and carried out under the direction of local Hindu nationalist groups. The BJP had controlled the Gujarat state government since 1998. It had "saffronized" (appointed Sangh Parivar supporters to) district and regional boards and removed an earlier prohibition against civil servants joining the RSS. The state's chief minister at the time was the BJP leader Narendra Modi. Newspaper reports after the riots suggested the state had systematically kept its Muslim police officers out of the field and that 27 senior officers who had taken action against the rioting had been punished with transfers. Before the Gujarat riots political observers had predicted that the BJP's ineffective running of the state would cost them the government, but in the December 2002 state elections, after campaigning

SONIA GANDHI STEPS FORWARD

In the years since Rajiv Gandhi left us, I had chosen to remain a private person and live a life away from the political arena. My grief and loss have been deeply personal. But a time has come when I feel compelled to put aside my own inclinations and step forward. The tradition of duty before personal considerations has been the deepest conviction of the family to which I belong. (Quoted in Dettman 2001)

Although the Italian-born Sonia Gandhi was offered the leadership of the Congress Party almost immediately after the assassination of her husband in 1991, she spent the six years following his death in political seclusion, refusing to speak publicly about politics. Only at the end of 1997, as a badly disorganized Congress was preparing to contest the 1998 Lok Sabha elections, did Sonia Gandhi indicate her willingness to campaign. Although Congress lost to the BJP's coalition in those elections, it managed to hold onto 141 seats, an accomplishment many attributed to Sonia Gandhi (*Frontline* 1998). She became the president of the Congress Party in May of that year and went on to lead her party to victory in the 2004 elections. Facing a barrage of criticism for her foreign origins, she chose not to become prime minister after the elections, an office taken instead by Manmohan Singh. She continued as head of the Congress Party, however, and continued to speak out on behalf of the poor and against communalism.

Sources: Athreya, Venkatesh. "Sonia Effect Checks BJP Advance." *Frontline* 15, no. 4 (Feb. 21–Mar. 6 1998). Available online. URL: http://www.hinduonnet.com/fline/fl1504/15040060.htm. Accessed February 12, 2010; Dettman, Paul R. *India Changes Course: Golden Jubilee to Millennium* (New York: Praeger, 2001), p. 9.

aggressively on a Hindutva platform, Modi was returned to office with a large state majority.

Elections of 2004

Prime Minister Vajpayee called for early national elections in May 2004 hoping to benefit from the momentum of the 2003 state elections, which had produced victories for the BJP in three out of the four contested states, Madhya Pradesh, Rajasthan, and Chhattisgarh. Congress, still the BJP's major rival in the coalition politics of the last 20 years, had won only the state of Delhi. Campaigning for the 2004 elections the BJP focused on India's strong (now globalized) economy, on improved relations with Pakistan, and on its own competent government. The main theme of the BJP's campaign was "India Shining," a media blitz on which the BJP alliance spent $20 million and which emphasized the economic prosperity and strength India had achieved under BJP rule. One glossy poster showed a smiling yellow-sari-clad woman playing cricket: the caption read, "You've never had a better time to shine brighter" (Zora and Woreck 2004). Later commentators suggested that rural Indians, who had shared in little of the recent economic growth, might have been surprised to learn that India had

Congress victory celebration, New Delhi 2004. Jubilant Congress supporters parade images of three Gandhis—Sonia, Rajiv, and Indira—in a victory procession following the May national elections. But while Italian-born Sonia Gandhi was widely credited with bringing about the Congress victory, a virulent antiforeign campaign by BJP leaders prevented her from accepting the office of prime minister. Instead Manmohan Singh, an internationally known economist and second in authority within the Congress, became India's prime minister. (AP/Wide World Photos)

Urban v. Rural Turnout in National Elections		
Year of Election	Percent of Urban Voters	Percent of Rural Voters
1977	61.4	57.2
1980	58.3	53.9
1984	64.0	63.0
1989	61.3	60.8
1991	53.8	56.1
1996	54.6	57.8
1998	57.7	61.5
1999	53.7	60.7
2004	53.1	58.9

Source: Based on poll data from CSDS Data Unit. Christophe, and Peter van der Veer, eds. *Patterns of Middle Class Consumption in India and China* (New Delhi, Sage 2008), p. 37.

already achieved prosperity. During the campaign Sonia Gandhi, president of the Congress Party and widow of Rajiv Gandhi, criticized the BJP's waste of money on the campaign. Gandhi pointed out that the majority of India did not share the lifestyle lauded in the BJP ads, and she instead campaigned on a platform promising employment and economic betterment for India's poor.

Most political pundits predicted a BJP victory, but the party lost badly in the 2004 elections. The BJP had, postelection, 138 Lok Sabha seats (down from 182 in 1999) and only 22 percent of the national vote. Meanwhile, the Congress Party, whose demise many had thought imminent, won 145 Lok Sabha seats and 26 percent of the national vote. The BJP was voted out of power in Gujarat, the state where its communal policies had been victorious only two years before.

Approximately 390 million votes were cast in the 2004 election, 56 percent of India's 675 million registered voters. Later analyses of the Congress victory pointed out that in India the poor vote in greater proportions than the country's upper and middle classes. Vajpayee, who resigned as prime minister immediately, would later call the India Shining campaign a major mistake. Gandhi, whose campaigning was seen as a major factor in the Congress victory, refused to become prime minister. (BJP members of Parliament had campaigned vigorously against the idea of a person of "foreign origin" holding the prime minister's office.) Instead Manmohan Singh, the Sikh economist responsible for starting India's globalization in 1991, became India's first non-Hindu prime minister.

The "Exceptional" Pattern of Indian Voting

In most Western democracies, the rule holds true that the higher one's economic bracket, the more likely one is to vote. However, as Christophe Jaffrelot discusses in a recent article "Why Should We Vote?" (2008), in India the reverse is true. In the 2004 U.S. election, for instance, 63.5 percent of those earning $10,000 (or less) did not vote, while only 21.7 percent of those earning $150,000 missed voting. In India, however, in the 2004 Lok Sabha elections, the percentage of the "rich" who voted was 56.7, while the percentage of the "very poor" who voted was 59.3. The pattern is even more marked when comparing rural to urban voters: In every national election since 1991, Jaffrelot notes, rural voters turned out to vote in higher percentages than urban voters. And in urban states, such as Delhi, the difference can be even more pronounced: In the 2003 state elections in Delhi, 60 percent of the poor and very poor voted, while only 48.3 percent of the rich and very rich voted.

Some analysts have suggested that the rich and middle class in India have become "disenchanted" with democracy, believing along with BJP leader Vajpayee that "the present system of parliamentary democracy has failed to deliver the goods" (Rediff Special 1996). India's government, it is suggested, has been taken over by cult leaders and mass protests: "Strikes, shutdowns, marches, and fasts" now determine pub-

Rich v. Poor Turnout (Delhi State Elections, 2003)		
Social Class	Percent of Voters	Percent of Nonvoters
Very poor Poor	60.0	40.0
Lower middle class Middle class	53.6	46.4
Rich Very Rich	48.3	51.7

Source: Based on poll data from 2003 state elections in Delhi. Jaffrelot, Christophe, and Peter van der Veer, eds. *Patterns of Middle Class Consumption in India and China* (New Delhi: Sage, 2008), p. 37.

lic policy, and Indian democracy is no longer a "constitutional democracy" in which public decisions are made in a rational manner but a "populist democracy" (Guha 2007, 680–681).

Other analysts suggest that at the bottom of calls for a rejection of India's democracy is the growing recognition of the rich and middle classes, since the Mandal protests of the late 1980s, that Indian government is no longer in their hands. As one analyst suggests, India's social structure has changed, from "an elite-mass structure to one with a substantial middle class sandwiched between these two poles" (Sridharan 2004, 19). "There is a kind of cynicism about how is it going to make a difference if we go to vote or do not go to vote," said a Delhi state minister to Jaffrelot when asked why the middle classes in Delhi abstained from voting. ". . . Their attitude is 'I am not ready to try and make a difference,' because they feel they are not in numbers adequate enough to bring about a change" (2008, 46). This perception is echoed by Pavan Varma in *The Great Indian Middle Class* (2007): One reason, he writes, "for middle-class disenchantment with democratic politics is the perception that the electoral system no longer serves its interests, either exclusively as it would like, or even preponderantly as was the case in the past. Elections are about numbers, and the rural and urban poor are many more in number than the middle class" (55).

Interviewing Dalit students at Jawaharlal Nehru University in 2005, Jaffrelot found they agreed that the upper castes were now criticizing democracy because they were losing power in relation to the lower castes. "There are moves now to subvert democracy," one Dalit student told Christophe Jaffrelot. ". . . When democracy was in shambles in the beginning of the 1940s–1950s, Indian democracy was portrayed as the shining light of the world. And now when it is actually coming into its own, when people are participating, people are beginning to voice what they feel, then democracy becomes something on which we have surveys conducted about if it is good to vote or not" (2008, 49).

Congress Plans

Although analysts generally agree that it was the BJP that lost the 2004 elections rather than the Congress United Progressive Alliance (UPA) coalition that won it, nevertheless, the election offered Congress the opportunity to take power and the possibility of resurrecting its earlier popularity. Up to the 1980s, the success of Congress had lain in its ability to be a "catchall" party, to combine voters from contending social groups—from upper castes, Dalits, and Muslims, for instance—to create a coalition sometimes of voter extremes. Such coalitions gave the Congress the ability to poll between 36 percent and 51 percent of the vote from a wide range of social groups up into the 1990s (Jaffrelot and Verniers 2009, 3). But the 1990s witnessed the disintegration of the Congress's social coalition as the BJP and BSP at the national level and

THE COMMON MINIMUM PROGRAM, 2004

In May 2004, the Congress-led United Progress Alliance released its Common Minimum Program, a list of programs and commitments its alliance made for the future government of India. What follows is a statement of the six basic principles to which the government pledged itself.

To preserve, protect and promote social harmony and to enforce the law without fear or favour to deal with all obscurantist and fundamentalist elements who seek to disturb social amity and peace.

To ensure that the economy grows at least 7–8% per year in a sustained manner over a decade and more and in a manner that generates employment so that each family is assured of a safe and viable livelihood.

To enhance the welfare and well-being of farmers, farm labour and workers, particularly those in the unorganized sector, and assure a secure future for their families in every respect.

To fully empower women politically, educationally, economically and legally.

To provide for full equality of opportunity, particularly in education and employment for the Scheduled Castes, Scheduled Tirbes, OBCs and religious minorities.

To unleash the creative energies of our entrepreneurs, businessmen, scientists, engineers and all other professionals and productive forces of society. . . .

Source: Young India. "2004: India's Common Minimum Program." Available online. URL: http://www.yidream.org/2004/cmp.shtml. Accessed February 1, 2010.

the growing number of regional parties in the different states took votes that had previously gone to the Congress.

Now, in the aftermath of the 2004 elections, with Sonia Gandhi speaking for the poor and disadvantaged, Manmohan Singh speaking for economic reforms popular among the wealthy and middle class, and rural voters angry at the BJP over an economic prosperity in which they did not share, Congress saw the possibility of reestablishing its old dominance. In a Common Minimum Program announced by the Congress-led United Progressive Alliance (UPA) in 2004, the new government committed itself to policies designed to maintain the support of its coalition members. The Common Minimum Program offered a pledge to grow India's economy at 7 to 8 percent a year "in a manner that generates employment," a commitment to protect the welfare of farmers and farmer workers, a promise to introduce a new National Employment Guarantee Act that would guarantee 100 days of employment to the urban and rural poor and the lower middle classes, and a promise not to privatize public companies that were profitable and to consider privatization of companies only on a case-by-case basis (Young India 2004).

Economic Gains

Indian economic reforms had produced dramatic changes in the 1991 to 1996 period in part spurred on by the government's balance of payments crisis and measures designed to globalize India's economy and introduce competition to formerly protected Indian industries. But during the coalition governments from 1996 to 2001, market-oriented reforms had slowed as Indian industries, beginning to feel the effects of external liberalization and increased competition, became less supportive of reforms. By the time of the elections of 2004, the BJP government had begun a new phase of reforms, this time focusing on the privatization of state-owned companies, new labor laws intended to make it easier to fire employees, and foreign investments.

India's high fiscal deficits, public debt, and weak infrastructure (power, ports, transport) were among the most problematic aspects of its economy. The reforms of 1991–96 had succeeded in lowering the combined center and states fiscal deficit from 9.4 percent of GDP in 1990–91 to 6.4 percent in 1996–97. But by 2000–01 the consolidated deficit had risen again to 9.5 percent and by 2002–03 to 10 percent. As the fiscal deficit worsened, the ratio of India's public debt (the amount owed by the country to either internal or external investors) to its GDP also rose from 66 percent of GDP in 1996–97 to 85 percent in 2002–03 (Ahluwalia 2005, 60).

By 2004, however, the country was seeing renewed growth in agriculture and industry and in a booming service sector that now accounted
for about half of all GDP. Much of this service sector growth was due to
the Indian software industry, which had grown at an average of 8 percent throughout the 1990s. By 2004 this industry employed 600,0000
people and exported $13 billion of services (Guha 2007, 686). In addi-
tion the outsourcing of work to India had resulted in growth in Indian
centers performing work that ranged from the screening of U.S. medical tests to the running of Indian-based call centers for credit card and
airline companies. In 2002 there were more than 300 such call centers
in India employing 110,000 people (Guha 2007, 688). Before the 2004
elections, the GDP growth rate had jumped to 8.5 percent (from a low
of 3.8 percent in 2002–03). Although the BJP's claims of Indian "resur-
gence" were rejected by voters in the election of 2004, some analysts

India's GDP Growth Rates	
Period	Percent of GDP Growth
1950–72	3.5
1972–82	3.6
1982–92	5.0
1992–2002	6.0
2001–02	5.8
2002–03	3.8
2003–04	8.5
2004–05	7.5
2005–06	9.5
2006–07	9.7
2007–08	9.0
2008–09	6.7
2009–10	7.5

Source: Reserve Bank of India. "Table 233: Select Macroeconomic Aggregates—Growth
Rate and Investment Rate (at Constant Prices)." Handbook of Statistics on Indian
Economy 2008–09 (2009). Available online. URL: http://www.rbi.org.in/scripts/
AnnualPublications.aspx?head=Handbook%20of%20Statistics%20on%20Indian%20
Economy. Accessed February 1, 2010.
Note that figures for 2007–09 are estimates.
*2009–10 data is the RBI estimate as of January 2010.

Government Debt as a Percentage of GDP (2009)	
Country	Government Debt as a Percentage of Gross Domestic Product (GDP)
India	85
United States	85
China	20
Japan	219
Source: *New York Times*, 8 February 2010, B1 and B6.	

now think that the India economy was already poised for strong future growth at that time (Ahluwalia 2005, 57).

Between 2004 and 2009, the Indian economy grew at the average yearly rate of 8.5 percent, even with the global financial crisis and economic slowdown of 2007–09. India escaped the worst of the financial crisis because of its relatively cautious banking policies and low dependence on exports for growth. Instead domestic demand drove the Indian economy, especially in the areas of consumer durables and automobiles. Agriculture contributed approximately 20 percent of India's GDP while remaining the area of the economy that employed the most people (slightly more than half the Indian workforce). The service sector, on the other hand, led by computer software and outsourcing companies, continued to contribute more than half of India's GDP, even while employing only one-third of its workers. Inflation remained in the single digits, although it rose from 3.8 percent in 2004 to a predicted rate of more than 8 percent in 2009.

Although efforts were made to reduce the country's fiscal deficit through 2007, fuel and fertilizer subsidies caused it to rise substantially in 2008 and 2009. Public debt also continued high, at 85 percent of GDP in 2009. By 2009, however, the weakened global economy had caused the debt ratios of other world economies to rise even above the Indian level. As in the 1990s and early 2000s, an estimated 90 percent of India's public debt was owed to its own citizens (not to external investors), a relatively stronger position. For 2010, the Indian government announced plans to reduce its deficits by selling shares of government-owned companies and by reducing fertilizer and fuel subsidies, although it remained to be seen if internal political pressure would allow these policies to be carried out (*New York Times* 2010). For the long term, India's fiscal deficit, high level of public debt, weak infrastructure, need for employment opportunities, and need to strengthen both basic and higher educational opportunities remained problems for its economy.

Agrarian Woes

Since the late 19th century, peasant farmers in India had been producing crops for both world and all-Indian markets. This commercialization of agriculture had contributed to the growth of Indian famines at the turn of the century as peasant-produced food crops were replaced by crops aimed at nonlocal markets. Now, at the end of the 20th and start of the 21st century, the increased globalization of the Indian rural economy again produced distress and disruption among rural communities as farmer suicides and regional and local struggles over water and pollution plagued the Indian countryside.

Farmer Suicides

In 2004, shortly after taking office, Prime Minister Manmohan Singh took official notice of the high rate of farmer suicides by visiting rural Andhra Pradesh, a state which, by then, had seen 3,000 such suicides and in which 70 percent of the population depended on agriculture for their living (BBC News 2004). Newspaper reports of the suicides of farmers had begun to appear regularly in the late 1990s. The heads of farm families, often deeply in debt to local moneylenders, committed suicide by hanging, electrocution, or, most often, by drinking pesticide. By 2007, the total number of suicides for the past 11 years had reached 182,936, an average of 16,631 suicides per year, and much higher than the rate of suicide among nonfarming populations (Sainath 2009). Almost two-thirds of farmer suicides had taken place in just five Indian states: Maharashtra, Karnataka, Andhra Pradesh, Madhya Pradesh, and Chattisgarh.

Farmer suicides are attributed to crop failures, high expenses of cultivation, and high levels of farmer indebtedness, particularly in regions where farmers grow cash crops. Food crop farmers in states in the Gangetic plain and eastern India have seen fewer suicides; these regions are not as intensively farmed, their cultivation costs are lower, and government supports for food crops provide some needed stability. Cash crops, on the other hand, such as cotton, coffee, sugarcane, groundnut, pepper, and vanilla, require the heavy use of fertilizers, water, and specialized seeds. These crops are vulnerable to highly volatile global commodity prices and, at the same time, they have much higher per acre cultivation costs. For instance, as P. Sainath, a journalist who has written extensively on farmer suicides, shows, while a farmer in 1991 in a Maharashtrian district might

317

Farmer Suicides, 1997–2007		
Period	Total Number of Farmer Suicides in India	Average Per Year
1997–2001	78,737	15,747 per year
2002–06	87,567	17,513 per year
2007	16,632	16,632
Total 1997–2007	182,936	16,631 per year

Source: Sainath, P. "The Largest Wave of Suicides in History." *Counterpunch,* 12 February 2009, p. 2. Available online. URL: http://www.counterpunch.org/sainath02122009.html. Accessed January 14, 2010.

have bought local seeds for Rs. 7 to Rs. 9 per 1,000 grams, in 2004 farmers growing hybrid cotton from Monsanto seeds would have had to pay between Rs 1,650 to Rs. 1,800 for a bag of only 450 grams of seed (2009). In Kerala, as P. Sainath reports, farmers switching from growing paddy to growing vanilla in 2003–04 saw their per acre costs rise from Rs. 8,000 for paddy to almost Rs. 150,000 for vanilla.

In 2004, both the Congress coalition at the center and selected state governments began to provide compensation packages (estimated at about $3,000) to the families of farmers who took their own lives. In addition, some states, such as Kerala, have created commissions to review indebtedness on a case-by-case basis. As news reports point out, the numbers of farmer suicides has grown even as the number of Indian people working at farming has decreased: 8 million Indian workers left farming as a livelihood between the censuses of 1991 and 2001.

Water Fights

Even as high indebtedness and the difficulties of farming commercial cash crops drove individual farmers to suicide, rural villages had to contend collectively with water disputes, water shortages, and/or water pollution, caused either by regional interstate conflicts or by global multinationals. As water is increasingly in demand in India, whether for high-tech crops, bottled water and sodas, or urban city dwellers, some suggest that water, even more than oil, will be the resource most crucial for India's future economic development (Guha 2007, 660).

The regionalization of Indian politics and the concomitant strengthening of state governments vis-à-vis the national government (and national courts) have left the central government increasingly unable

This undated picture shows young men filling water cans from a supply truck of the Delhi Jal (Water) Board, Delhi Government. In water-short cities such as New Delhi, the city governments contract out to tankers to serve areas without piped connections or clean groundwater. The Delhi Jal Board was constituted through an act of the Delhi Legislative Assembly in 1998. According to its Web site, it currently sends out tankers on routes through 18 different locations in the city. (Paul Prescott/Shutterstock)

to compel states to accept its mediated decisions in cases of water disputes. States that hold the headwaters of important irrigation rivers have begun to seize those waters for their own uses. One example is the struggle between the states of Karnataka and Tamil Nadu over the Kaveri (formerly Cauvery) River waters. The Kaveri originates in Karnataka and then flows east into Tamil Nadu. While initially most irrigated farmlands using these waters were in Tamil Nadu, by the end of the 20th century, the number of acres in Karnataka under irrigation farming was fast approaching that of Tamil Nadu. The two states disputed each other's claims to these waters throughout the 1970s and 1980s without resolution. The Cauvery Water Disputes Tribunal, set up in 1991, has been unable over the past years to bring this dispute to a negotiated conclusion. By 2007 four states—Karnataka, Tamil Nadu, Kerala, and Puduchery—were involved in the dispute, and when the tribunal announced its final resolution in 2007, all four states found it unacceptable and planned to reopen negotiations.

A similar dispute occurred in northern India. The state of Punjab had been negotiating the sharing of the waters of the Ravi and Beas Rivers (whose headwaters were in Punjab) with other states in the region from the 1920s. But in 2004, the Punjab state legislature passed a Termination of Agreement Act, declaring it would appropriate as much of the Ravi and Beas Rivers as it wished before allowing these rivers to flow on to the states of Haryana and Rajasthan. This act is also still under review by the central government and by the courts.

Coca-Cola and Pollution

Finally, a third kind of water dispute arose in 2005 in the rural village of Plachimada in the southeastern state of Kerala where the international company Coca-Cola established a bottling plant in 2000. The growing competition for water in rural regions is part of the ongoing agrarian crisis in India, as water privatization threatens to deprive numerous rural communities of the resources for growing crops essential to their livelihood.

Multinational soda companies Coca-Cola and PepsiCo returned to India in 1993, as part of India's liberalization of license rules and regulations. The growth and increased prosperity of the middle class in India have caused both the soft drink and bottled water industries to grow rapidly. By 2005 the two multinational companies owned 90 factories in India: 52 for Coca-Cola and 38 for PepsiCo. Soft drink sales alone had increased by 2007 to $2 billion a year, and almost 80 percent of this market was controlled by Coca-Cola and PepsiCo. The bottled water

Thums Up, New Delhi, ca. 1978. One indigenous product whose market share was not damaged by the liberalization of India's economy was Thums Up, a Coca-Cola look-alike with a red upward-pointing thumb on its bottle, the flagship drink of the Parle soft drink company. In the late 1970s, when Coca-Cola, along with other foreign companies, abandoned operations in India, Parle stepped in, offering Thums Up to a thirsty Indian market. But when PepsiCo and Coca-Cola reentered India's newly liberalized economy in the 1990s, Parle sold their company to the international Coca-Cola. Ever since, and in spite of Coca-Cola's subsequent efforts to kill off the Thums Up product line—a direct competitor with its own Coke product—Thums Up has continued to maintain a strong market share, some suggest as much as half of cola sales in India. (courtesy of Judith E. Walsh)

industry has also grown rapidly over the past 20 years, and about 40 percent of this industry was also controlled by the same two companies. Bottled water in India is primarily just treated and purified groundwater, which can be extracted at little cost by any entity that has access to it. Even after purification and treatment, the major cost for this water is in its packaging and marketing. In the same way, although the companies describe their soda factories as "bottling plants," according to one report they are just "pumping stations" that extract as much as "1.5 m litres of water a day from the ground" for the production of soft drinks and/or bottled water (Shiva 2005).

By 2000 Coca-Cola had acquired the land and licensing rights to build a 40-acre bottling plant in the small, primarily low-caste, Muslim, and Scheduled Tribe community of Plachimada. Over the next two years, the company's extraction of groundwater from its lands caused the region's water table to fall, producing contamination in local water. By 2003 the toxic nature of sludge dumped by the plant was attracting BBC radio newscasts and the attention of the local CPI-(M) politicians. Publicity from the protest spread to New Delhi, where a local analysis of Coca-Cola and PepsiCo soft drinks in 2003 was reported to contain high levels of pesticides. The Indian Parliament promptly banned these products in its own cafeterias and clubs but not in the entire country. In Plachimada, attention shifted from the issue of groundwater depletion to that of pollution and to whether Coca-Cola would be permanently enjoined from operating a plant in that village.

National Rural Employment Guarantee Scheme

The National Rural Employment Guarantee Scheme (NREGS—subsequently renamed the Mahatma Gandhi National Rural Employment Guarantee Act) was proposed by the Congress coalition immediately after the 2004 elections as part of its Common Minimum Program, but it was enacted only in 2005 and put into operation in 2006. The NREGS was to provide a legal guarantee of 100 days of employment every year to rural adults willing to do public works unskilled labor at the statutory minimum wage of Rs. 100 per day. The purpose of the act was to boost rural economies and enhance overall economic growth.

The scheme shares the costs of this employment with state governments, with the center paying the costs of the work allowances and the state governments mandated to provide an unemployment allowance to workers for whom they cannot authorize work. The village *panchayats* register households for the purpose of this work and assigns work. Men and women must be treated equally under the act, and all adults in a village can apply for employment.

For 2006 the NREGS covered only 200 districts, but by 2008 it was mandated for all 593 districts in India. The initial budget for 2006–07 was Rs. 11,000 crores, sharply increased to Rs. 39,100 crores (approximately $8 billion) for 2009–10. The huge size of the program and the difficulties in implementation have raised criticisms and the inevitable charges of corruption. The World Bank criticized the program as misguided in its 2009 development report since, the report claimed, the program interfered with the migration of rural workers to cities and thus did not allow those communities "to fully capture the benefits of labour mobility" (Business Standard 2009). The Society for Participatory Research in Asia (PRIA) conducted a study of the implementation of the NREGS by local *panchayats* in 13 states and noted that the average employment was only 42 days, not 100 as specified by the act. However, the study noted, a large number of households in the 13 states were getting employment under the scheme (The *Hindu* 2009). This observation was echoed by respondents to the Center for the Study of Developing Societys (CSDS) exit polls after the 2009 elections. Some 31 percent of the rural poor and 29 percent of the rural "very poor" told pollsters that they had benefited from the program, a higher level of support, CSDS pollsters noted, than for any previous or existing poverty program (Jaffrelot and Verniers 2009, 16).

More Reserved Seats for OBCs

In 2005, the Congress-led UPA coalition proposed extending reservations for OBCs to 27 percent of the seats at elite technical and management institutions throughout the country, including institutions such as the All India Institute of Medical Studies (AIMS), the Indian Institutes of Technology (IITs), and the Indian Institutes of Management (IIMs) as well as other central higher education institutions. Reservations for Dalits had increased their numbers at these institutions, but the previous Mandal quotas for OBCs had not applied to these institutions. When Congress attempted to extend these reservations to private institutions, it was blocked from doing so by court order. In response, both houses of Parliament unanimously passed the 93rd Constitutional Amendment, an amendment that allows the central and state governments to enact seat reservations in private institutions.

The planned implementation of seat reservations for OBCs in elite institutions and central universities sparked a series of anti-reservation protests (and some pro-reservation protests) throughout May by students and supporters at affected schools in centers such as Mumbai, Delhi, and Chennai. Protesters against the reservation policies charged that the plan was a "vote bank" effort on the part of the Congress. The BJP did not denounce the reservations, but both it and the Left parties called for the exclusion of the "creamy layer" from the reservations. (The "creamy layer" is an expression used to refer to the wealthier families and/or households within groups that are eligible for reservations.) The matter was referred to the Supreme Court. It upheld the law two years later, directing the government, however, to exclude the creamy layer of OBCs from its implementation.

Mumbai Terrorism

Since the 1990s there have been numerous terror attacks within India and in the Indian-controlled section of Kashmir, including the 2000 attack on the Red Fort in New Delhi and the 2001 and 2002 attacks on the Indian Parliament and the parliament in Kashmir. In Mumbai alone, there were at least seven separate bombing attacks (some involving multiple bombs) between 1993 and 2006. But the November 2008 terrorist attack on Mumbai was unique among all these incidents for its sustained ferocity and warlike intensity. For more than two days, from the evening of November 26 through the morning of November 29, 10 terrorists, armed with AK-47s, bombs, and grenades, attacked sites in south Mumbai, including the railway station, the Cama hospital, a local café, the Nariman House (home to a Jewish outreach center), the Oberoi Trident Hotel, and the historic Taj Mahal Hotel. Reports of the numbers of dead and injured vary, but more than 170 were killed and more than 300 wounded in these attacks.

Only one of the attackers survived. Ajmal Kasab, a 21-year-old Pakistani, was captured early in the attacks, and it was from him that most subsequent information came. The attackers were said to have been trained by Lashkar-e-Taiba (LeT) at guerrilla warfare training camps in Pakistan. Having hijacked an Indian fishing boat and killed its crew and captain, they arrived at Mumbai's docks near the Gateway of India on the evening of November 26. They then broke into five teams of two men each and fanned out through southern Mumbai toward locations identified earlier. Although most attacks had ended by late evening November 26, the occupation and seizing of hostages at Nariman House and the two luxury hotels lasted longer, with the attack on the Oberoi Hotel ending around midday on November 28,

Equipment of Terrorists in Mumbai Attacks

During the investigation of these offences it has come to light that for the purpose of attacking the targetted [sic] sites in Mumbai, a total of 10 terrorists were selected and grouped in 5 Buddy pairs of two terrorists each. Each of these 10 highly trained and motivated terrorists was equipped and provided with the following firearms, live ammunition, explosives and other material as follows:

Serial No.	Material	Quantity
1	AK 47	1
2	pistol	1
3	hand grenades	8 to 10 each
4	AK 47 magazine	8 (each magazine hosting 30 rounds)
5	pistol magazine	2 (each magazine hosting 7 rounds)
6	Khanjir	1
7	dry fruit (badam, manuka, etc.)	2 kg
8	cash (Indian rupees)	ranging from Rs. 4000 to Rs. 6000+/- each
9	Nokia mobile handset	1 each
10	headphone	1 each
11	water bottle	1 each
12	G.P.S.	1 (each group)
13	RDX-laden IED (with timer)	1 (Approximately each 8 kgs)
14	9-volt battery	3
15	haver sack	1
16	bag (for carrying RDX-laden IED)	1
17	satellite phone	1 (for all)
18	rubberized dinghy with outboard engine	1

Source: *Final Report Mumbai Terror Attack Cases*, 26 November 2008, p. 8.

the Nariman House siege ending by the evening of November 28, and the Taj Mahal occupation ending only by the morning of November 29. The terrorists were in touch with "handlers" by satellite phone throughout the operation and were thought to have taken cocaine and LSD to keep themselves alert during the 50-hour siege.

A characteristic of the Mumbai attacks was the randomness and brutality of the killing. Hostages were taken not for negotiation purposes but only to prolong the attack: "The hostages are of use only as long as you do not come under fire," one supervisor was recorded saying. "If you are still threatened, then don't saddle yourself with the burden of the hostages. Immediately kill them" (Sengupta 2009). Along their various routes the teams commandeered taxis and private cars and planted a number of time-delayed bombs that later killed numerous people and added to the confusion and chaos of the attack.

The coordination and violence of the attacks made news worldwide. In India criticism was directed at the government's incompetence and lack of preparation—it took more than 10 hours for India's elite National Security Guard commandos to reach the occupied hotels—and for its failure to heed earlier warnings of potential attacks. The home minister, Shivraj Patil, resigned, and the Indian government accused Pakistan of supporting terrorist organizations. The Indian Parliament subsequently created the National Investigation Agency, a central counterterrorism group with functions similar to the U.S. Federal Bureau of Investigation. The Unlawful Activities (Prevention) Act was strengthened to facilitate the containment and investigation of terrorism. The surviving terrorist was put on trial in spring of 2009, and by December the prosecution had concluded the presentation of its case. In Pakistan seven members of LeT were arrested and put on trial, none, however, from the highest levels of the organization.

Elections of 2009

The national elections of 2009 were almost as much a surprise to Indian politicians and analysts as the elections of 2004. The Congress-led UPA coalition was returned to power in an election in which 58 percent of eligible voters (or 714 million Indians) voted. The Congress Party won 206 seats in the Lok Sabha, more seats than it had won since 1991. In addition, Congress seemed to have neutralized the "anti-incumbency" vote. The elections returned Prime Minister Manmohan Singh to power after a full five-year term in office—the first time this had happened since 1962. Congress attrib-

Congress and the BJP: Seats Won, Percent of Seats Won, and Percent of Vote Won, 2004 and 2009

	Congress			BJP		
	2004	2009	won/lost	2004	2009	won/lost
National seats	145	206	+ 61	138	116	-22
Percentage of seats won	26.7%	37.94%	+11.20%	25.4%	21.36%	-4 %
Percentage of votes won	26.53%	28.52%	+1.99 %	22.16%	18.84%	-3.32%

Sources: Arora, Balveer, and Stephanie Tawa Lama-Rewal. "Introduction: Contextualizing and Interpreting the 15th Lok Sabha Elections." *SAMAJ: South Asia Multidisciplinary Academic Journal* 3, "Contests in Context: Indian Elections 2009" (2009): pp. 4–5; Jaffrelot, Christophe, and Gilles Verniers. "India's 2009 Elections: The Resilience of Regionalism and Ethnicity." *South Asia Multidisciplinary Academic Journal* 3 (2009). Available online. URL: http://samaj.revues.org/index2787.html. Accessed June 21, 2010.

uted its success to its renewed ability to construct an inclusive voter alliance. "My government sees the overwhelming mandate it has received as a vindication of the policy architecture of inclusion that it put in place," said president Pratibha Patil (1934–   ), the country's first woman president, in a speech to the newly elected Parliament. "It is a mandate for inclusive growth, equitable development and a secular and plural India" (Patil 2009).

In 2004 it had been generally true that the poorer an Indian voter was, the more likely he or she was to vote for Congress. But in 2009, among rural voters (an estimated 71.8 percent of the electorate), the rich and middle classes voted for Congress candidates in almost the same proportions as the poor. Even among urban voters, wealthier voters chose Congress more often than the BJP. The success of Congress in the election was attributed (in equal measure) to: (1) the economic policies of Manmohan Singh and the general strength of the Indian economy; (2) the Congress's labor employment policies for rural workers (NREGS) and reservation policies for OBCs; and (3) the prestige and negotiating skills of Sonia Gandhi, president of the Congress Party, who had kept it and the UPA coalition together (Jaffrelot and Verniers 2009).

The major loser of the 2009 election was the BJP. Overall the party won only 116 seats and not quite 19 percent of the electoral vote, putting it back to its levels in the election of 1991. The party lost seats in 21 out of 28 states, including states like Delhi and Rajasthan where

New Gandhis, Election 2009. Congress supporters celebrate their election victory out-side the home of Sonia Gandhi in New Delhi. The posters waved on this account were of Sonia Gandhi and her son, Rahul Gandhi, who represents the Amethi constituency in Uttar Pradesh. (AP/Wide World Photos)

it had previously been strong. In part, this weak showing was due to the dissolution of the BJP's NDA coalition: The BJP had had 23 coalition partners in 2004 but only seven in 2009. Parties dropped out in order to contest the elections on their own or because the BJP seemed more likely to lose after 2004 or, in some cases, because they were uncomfortable with the BJP's Hindutva discourse and feared Sangh Parivar practices might alienate Muslims or Christian voters (Jaffrelot and Verniers 2009, 9). In a number of states, the loss of coalition partners put the BJP into three-way contests, to the great benefit of the Congress.

At the same time, the BJP's "new social bloc"—that is the preference for the BJP on the part of both high-class and high-caste voters noted after the 1999 election—also failed in 2009. Although the BJP lost in 2004, it had still been the preferred choice of rich and middle-class voters: "the richer the Indian voter, the more he/she voted for the BJP" (Jaffrelot and Verniers 2009, 12). But in 2009, as noted above, all economic classes of Indian voters, from the very rich to the very poor, preferred Congress to the BJP. Only among the higher castes did the BJP's

328

earlier appeal hold true. Exit polling showed that, throughout India, almost 38 percent of the upper castes voted for the BJP; this was the only social group in which the BJP was preferred to Congress.

Mayawati's Bahujan Samaj Party (BSP) also failed to meet analyst expectations in 2009, particularly in comparison with its 2007 success in winning control of the Uttar Pradesh state government. Nevertheless, the BSP won more seats (21) than it had in 2004 (19) and fielded 500 candidates overall. India's "first past the post" voting system meant that the BSP won only one seat outside of Uttar Pradesh even though it won almost 5 percent of the votes in the Punjab, Madhya Pradesh, and Maharashtra and 15 percent of the vote in Haryana. The BSP did not succeed—as it had in the Uttar Pradesh state elections—in dramatically broadening its voter base. Exit polls showed that more than half its votes came from its core Dalit constituency. Still, as India's only national Dalit party, the BSP emerged from the 2009 elections with a full 6 percent of the electoral vote, making it the third largest national party in India.

Recognized National Parties in 2009 Election			
	Seats Won	Percent of Seats	Percent of All India	State/States
Congress	206	37.94	28.52	All India
BJP	116	21.36	18.84	All India
Bahujan Samaj Party (BSP)	21	4.99	6.17	Uttar Pradesh
Communist Parts of India (Marxist)	16	2.95	5.34	W. Bengal, Kerala, Tripura
Nationalist Congress Party	9	1.66	2.04	Maharashtra, Meghalaya
Communist Party of India	4	0.74	1.43	W. Bengal, Kerala
Rashtriya Janata Dal	4	0.74	1.27	Bihar

Sources: Arora, Balveer, and Stephanie Tawa Lama-Rewal. "Introduction: Contextualizing and Interpreting the 15th Lok Sabha Elections." *SAMAJ: South Asia Multidisciplinary Academic Journal* 3, "Contests in Context: Indian Elections 2009" (2009): 4–5; Jaffrelot, Christophe, and Gilles Verniers. "India's 2009 Elections: The Resilience of Regionalism and Ethnicity." *South Asia Multidisciplinary Academic Journal* 3 (2009). Available online. URL: http://samaj.revues.org/index2787.html. Accessed June 21, 2010.

Regionalization, Fragmentation, or Federalization?

"Is it the end of caste and communal politics?" asked the *Hindu* in a 2009 post-election analysis. "Or is it the beginning of yet another 'rainbow coalition' for the Congress?" (2009). Did the Congress victory in 2009 mean a return to its dominance as a "catchall" party and to nationally defined elections? Many analysts would later argue that, in spite of the Congress's victory, the answer to these questions was "no."

The trend towards the regionalization—some say the fragmentation—of India's political processes could be seen in the 2009 elections as it had been seen earlier in 2004. While the Indian election commission recognized seven "national" parties in the 2009 elections, there were fully 30 state or regional parties that contested and won seats in the election. Even among the seven national parties only two—Congress and the BJP—won seats throughout all of India.

And even with Congress's impressive increase in the number of seats it won, the party polled only 2 percentage points higher in its share of the national vote than it had in 2004. This was roughly the same percentage share of votes it had polled in elections since 1996. The Indian system of counting votes (first-past-the-post) helped give Congress seats even in states where regional parties polled strongly against it. Notably, even taken together, the two true "all-India" parties—Congress and the BJP—polled only 47 percent of election votes. Regional parties won almost 53 percent of the total votes cast, continuing a trend seen in 2004.

National v. Regional Parties, 1991–2009 (as percent of election votes)						
Parties	1991	1996	1998	1999	2004	2009
Congress	36.26	28.80	25.82	28.30	26.53	28.52
BJP	20.11	20.29	25.59	23.75	22.16	18.84
Total (Cong + BJP)	56.37	49.09	51.41	52.05	48.59	47.36
Regional parties	43.63	50.91	48.59	47.95	51.41	52.54

Sources: Arora, Balveer, and Stephanie Tawa Lama-Rewal. "Introduction: Contextualizing and Interpreting the 15th Lok Sabha Elections." *SAMAJ: South Asia Multidisciplinary Academic Journal* 3, "Contests in Context: Indian Elections 2009" (2009): 4–5; Jaffrelot, Christophe, and Gilles Verniers. "India's 2009 Elections: The Resilience of Regionalism and Ethnicity." *South Asia Multidisciplinary Academic Journal* 3 (2009). Available online. URL: http://samaj.revues.org/index2787.html. Accessed June 21, 2010.

The 2009 election, then, does not indicate a return to nationally defined elections; instead it demonstrates the continuation of the "constant trend towards regionalization in Indian national and state elections" (Jaffrelot and Verniers 2009, 7). It is at the regional or state level that ethnic voting (that is, voting by caste or by religious community) becomes visible. Most caste communities do not spread past their linguistic areas but are usually defined by or within a single state. At the state level, castes or subcastes still often vote in blocs. In Rajasthan, for example, in 2009, 74 percent of Brahmans voted for the BJP; in Andhra Pradesh, 65 percent of the Reddys (one of three dominant caste groups) voted for Congress; and in Gujarat, 67 percent of Muslims voted for Congress (Jaffrelot and Verniers 2009, 11). Although in 2009 Congress did succeed in attracting votes from different communities—its old "catchall" strategy—nevertheless, elections at the regional level are now the determining ones. "The Indian general elections continue to be the aggregate of 28 regional elections, each displaying its social political and economic specificities" (Jaffrelot and Verniers 2009, 14). This "federalization" of the political system, as one analysis prefers to call it, means that state assembly elections are increasingly the main site for election contests, while national elections and national coalitions are becoming increasingly "derivative"—that is, dependent on and determined by the state or regional level (Aurora 2009).

Poverty

After the 2009 elections, Prime Minister Manmohan Singh—perhaps with the dual aim of demonstrating the effectiveness of his economic policies even while taking steps to please an important rural constituency—appointed a special committee, headed by the economist Suresh Tendulkar, to review and revise the formula used to estimate poverty in India. As the government moved toward targeting services in its public distribution system to households defined as "below the poverty line," the line itself, and its calculation, had become increasingly controversial. "The Great Indian Poverty Debate" (as the book of the same name edited by the economists Angus Deaton and Valerie Kozel called it) was also a debate about the efficacy and fairness of India's economic liberalization policies—another context in which the measure of poverty had become controversial.

From the late 1970s, the Planning Commission had compiled estimates of Indian poverty using statistics on household and individual income included in National Sample Surveys and calculating the "poverty line" with an income-based formula that estimated the

Planning Commission Estimates of Poverty, 1973–2005			
	Poverty Ratio		
Year	Percent of Rural	Percent of Urban	Percent Total
1973–74	56.4	49.0	54.9
1977–78	53.1	45.2	51.3
1983	45.6	40.8	44.5
1987–88	39.1	38.2	38.9
1993–94	37.3	32.4	36.0
2004–05	28.3	25.7	27.5

Source: Planning Commission of India. "Percentage and Number of Poor in India (73–74 to 04–05)." (2010). Available online. URL: http://planningcommission.nic.in/data/b_misdch.html. Accessed June 1, 2010.

income level needed for an individual to purchase the necessary food calories each day. People living in rural areas, it was estimated, needed incomes sufficient to consume 2,400 calories per day; those in urban areas needed 2,100 calories. Using this methodology, the Planning Commission estimated that 54.9 percent of Indians had lived below the poverty line in 1973–74, in 2004–05, 27.5 percent did so.

There were many criticisms of the Planning Commission's methods of calculation. Critics said that the income level it established (for rural Indians Rs. 11.90 per day in 2004–05) were levels indicating not just poverty but destitution. Other critics found the income estimates drawn from the periodic National Sample Surveys to be too high; they did not match estimates of nutrition and poverty coming from other surveys. In 2008, for example, when the World Bank updated its statistics on worldwide poverty, its new calculations gave a much higher estimation of Indian poverty. Using an international income level of $1.25 per day to define poverty, the World Bank estimated that in 1981, 60 percent of Indians had lived at or below the poverty level, while in 2005, 42 percent did so.

When the Tendulkar Committee submitted its final report to the Planning Commission in December 2009, it suggested a revised formula for estimating poverty. The new formula no longer used a caloric norm and based all poverty calculations on 2004–05 urban poverty estimates. Under the committee's new methodology, the poverty line was raised for rural Indians from an income level of Rs. 12 to Rs. 15 per day. This revision, small as it was, added an estimated 100 million people to the category of Indian poor. Under this new method, the overall estimation of Indian poverty became 37.5 percent, 10 percentage points higher than under the earlier formulation.

At the same time, the committee reestimated Indian poverty levels for 1993–94; they were now estimated overall at 45.3 percent. At a speech in Bhubaneswar, Prime Minister Manmohan Singh emphasized the point that poverty had not increased since the beginning of economic liberalization: "In fact, it has continued to decline after the economic reforms at least at the same rate as it did before. It is true," the Prime Minister added, "that the rate of decline has not been faster and I personally feel it should be. But that it has declined, there is no doubt" (Das 2009).

Conclusion

India is approximately the size of Europe and contains numerous well-defined ethnic and linguistic regions that have not always meshed easily with the goals and requirements of democratic majoritarian government. Since independence, political pundits have frequently predicted the dissolution of the Indian state and its fragmentation into numerous regional divisions. In the years immediately following 1947, political and public pressure forced the central government to create numerous linguistic states. Then in the 1980s, separatist movements raised the possibility that entire regions would secede from the

Tendulkar Committee: Revised Poverty Rates, 1993–1994 and 2004–2005		
Poverty Ratio		
Year	Percent of Rural	Percent of Urban	Percent Total
1993–94 (reestimated)	50.1	31.8	45.3
2004–05	41.8	25.7	37.2

Source: Planning Commission of India. "Percentage and Number of Poor in India (73–74 to 04–05)." (2010). Available online. URL: http://planningcommission.nic.in/data/b_misdch.html. Accessed June 1, 2010.

center. Now in the first decade of the 21st century, the Indian political system—instead of breaking apart—is coming to reflect the country's diversity in the increasing regionalization of political parties and ethnic (caste and religious communities) voting patterns.

Nevertheless, the Indian political system, the world's largest democracy, still remains today, as it has since independence in 1947, a problematic vehicle for meeting the needs of India's multiple castes, religions, minorities, and urban and rural voters. The Hindu nationalist BJP party and its Hindutva identity looked for a while as if it might unite a significant number of the 80 percent majority of Hindus behind its political agenda. But, whatever the theoretical potential of Hindu political unity (in the eyes of Hindu nationalists), the past history and economic and social realities of the Indian caste system have stood in the way of that unity. The Hindutva movement, for all its continuing appeal to upper-caste Hindus, has, at least for the moment, stalled at something below 20 percent of the Indian vote.

The Congress victory in both 2004 and 2009 underscored once again the effectiveness of election campaigns that promise to improve the lot of India's poor. Politicians have won Indian elections on this basis in the past and have then failed to act on their pledges. But the self-conscious emergence of low-caste and Untouchable political parties in the late 20th and early 21st centuries—combined with what was widely seen as a decisive rural vote against the BJP in 2004—have added new dimensions to the Indian political and social scene. Currently, democratic majority rule has great appeal to those Dalit, OBC, or rural voters who can see themselves as part of a potential Indian voting majority— among whom are the more than 37 percent of the population living below the Indian poverty line. And the poor in India, as all observers are now well aware, vote more than the rich.

To the great surprise of political pundits and politicians alike, the Congress Party has now managed through two elections to simultaneously court the rich and middle class who want economic reforms and the rural and urban poor who want better lives. It is not clear if Congress leaders will be able, in the future, to continue to combine economic growth with economic betterment. But if they can, then perhaps the "golden bird" of India's economic prosperity will continue to fly upward, redeeming the pledges of equality, inclusion, and social justice made by those earlier leaders who began the journey of Indian democracy more than 60 long years ago.

APPENDIX 1
BASIC FACTS ABOUT INDIA

Official Name
Republic of India

Government
Since the late 1970s, India's constitution has defined its government as a "sovereign, socialist, secular, democratic republic." Suffrage is universal, with all Indians over the age of 18 eligible to vote in governmental elections.

The government is a federated mixed parliamentary-presidential system. The central government has two houses: the Lok Sabha (People's Assembly), the lower house, based on proportional representation with no more than 550 members directly elected to five-year terms; and the Rajya Sabha (Council of State), a 250-member upper house elected by provincial legislative assemblies for six-year terms. Within the Lok Sabha, a prime minister and cabinet (the Council of Ministers) head the government and must retain the support of a majority of Lok Sabha members to remain in power. The central government's administrative powers are exercised in the name of a president and vice president elected by a special electoral college for five-year terms; the president's duties, however, are largely ceremonial. India also has an independent judiciary headed by the Supreme Court made up of a chief justice and (as of 2008) no more than 30 other judges, all appointed by the president.

India's 28 state governments are run by chief ministers responsible to state legislatures, some of which are bicameral. In addition, India's president appoints a governor for each state who may take over the state's government in times of emergency. The central government has greater authority over the republic's seven union territories. The

335

relative powers of central and state governments are specifically defined in the Constitution of 1950. Since 1985 a special act has given village *panchayats* (councils) considerable authority over local social, health, educational, and developmental issues.

Political Divisions

Capital
New Delhi

States
There are 28 states: Andhra Pradesh, Arunachal Pradesh, Assam, Bihar, Chhattisgarh, Goa, Gujarat, Haryana, Himachal Pradesh, Jammu and Kashmir, Jharkhand, Karnataka, Kerala, Madhya Pradesh, Maharashtra, Manipur, Meghalaya, Mizoram, Nagaland, Orissa, Punjab, Rajasthan, Sikkim, Tamil Nadu, Tripura, Uttarakhand (formerly Uttaranchal), Uttar Pradesh, and West Bengal.

Union Territories
The seven union territories are Andaman and Nicobar Islands, Chandigarh, Dadra and Nagar Haveli, Daman and Diu, Delhi, Lakshadweep, and Puducherry (formerly Pondicherry).

Geography

Area
India covers an area of 1,269,219.34 square miles (3,287,263 sq. km). It is the largest country on the South Asian subcontinent and is slightly more than one-third the size of the United States. It is the seventh-largest country in the world.

Boundaries
India's triangular-shaped landmass is bounded by water on two sides: the Arabian Sea on the west and the Bay of Bengal on the east. (These seas merge into the Indian Ocean to the south.) Immediately to the east of India's southernmost tip lies the country of Sri Lanka. In the northwest India shares a long border with Pakistan; in the north and northeast it shares borders with China, Nepal, Bhutan, Bangladesh, and Myanmar (Burma).

Topography
India is made up of four topographical regions: 1) the mountain rim to the far north, including the Himalayan and the Karakoram ranges

and the Hindu Kush; 2) the rich Indo-Gangetic alluvial plain across the north, cut by the Indus River to the west and the Ganges River system to the east and including desert regions in the west; 3) the Deccan Plateau and the highlands of peninsular India; and 4) the narrow strips of the coastal fringe regions that run along India's southwestern and southeastern coastline.

Climate

India's climate varies from tropical monsoon in the south to temperate in the north and is determined by its basic topography. The relative flatness of Indian lands south of the high northern mountain ranges draws in air currents from the surrounding seas to the south, while the extreme height of the northern mountains keeps airstreams from moving further north into the main Asian continent. The pattern of seasons throughout most of India includes a cool, dry winter from October to March; a hot season with temperatures well above 100° Fahrenheit (38° Celsius) between March/April and June/July; and a rainy season that lasts into September, caused by the southwestern monsoon.

Highest Elevation

India's highest elevation is at Mount Kanchenjunga, the world's third-highest mountain, measuring 28,208.7 feet (8,598 m) and lying along its border with Nepal.

Demographics

Population

India is the second most populous country in the world after China. Its population in the last Indian census (2001) was 1,027,015,247. As of 2010 (July) the population is now estimated at 1,173,108,018. Although India occupies approximately 2 percent of the world's land area, it supports more than 17 percent of the world's population.

Urban v. Rural Populations

According to the 2001 census, 72.2 percent of India's population lives in more than 638,588 villages; 27.8 percent lives in India's 5,161 cities and towns. In 2009 the urban population was estimated to have grown to 29 percent; the rural to have fallen to 71 percent.

Major Cities

According to the 2001 census, India has 27 cities with populations above 1 million. The three largest cities were (in 2001) Mumbai

(Bombay), with 11,914,398 residents (within the official city limits); Delhi, with 9,817,439 residents; and Kolkata (Calcutta) with 4,580,544 residents. After these three, the next 10 largest cities are Bangalore, Chennai (Madras), Ahmedabad, Hyderabad, Pune, Kanpur, Surat, Jaipur, Nagpur, and Indore.

Literacy Rates
According to the 2001 census, 64.8 percent of the Indian population is literate: 75.3 percent of the male population is literate, and 53.7 percent of the female population.

Languages
The 16 spoken languages officially recognized in India are Assamese, Bengali, English, Gujarati, Hindi, Kannada, Kashmiri, Malayalam, Marathi, Oriya, Punjabi, Sanskrit, Sindhi, Tamil, Telugu, and Urdu.

Religions
According to the 2001 Indian census, major religions in India are practiced among the population as follows: 80.5 percent Hindus, 13.4 percent Muslims, 2.3 percent Christians, 1.9 percent Sikhs, 0.8 percent Buddhists, 0.4 percent Jains. (Census figures for 2001 included population figures for the states of Jammu and Kashmir and Assam, two heavily Muslim regions, for the first time since 1971.)

Economy

Gross Domestic Product
For 2009 India's gross domestic product (GDP) was estimated at $3.578 trillion (when measured by purchasing power). The Indian economy had an average growth rate of more than 7 percent between 1999 and 2010. As of 2010 the agricultural sector was estimated as producing 17. percent of India's GDP the industrial sector; 29 percent; and the service sector, 54.9 percent.

Currency
The Indian currency is the rupee.

Agricultural Products
Major agricultural products are rice, wheat, oilseed, cotton, jute, tea, sugarcane, lentils, potatoes, onions, dairy products, sheep, goats, poultry, fish

Natural Resources

Major mineral resources include coal (the fourth-largest reserves in the world), iron ore, manganese, mica, bauxite, titanium ore, chromite, natural gas, diamonds, petroleum, and limestone. India imports petroleum, but it has oil resources in Assam, Gujarat, and offshore oil fields.

Industrial Products

Indian industrial products include textiles, chemicals, food processing, steel, transportation equipment, cement, mining, petroleum, machinery, software, and pharmaceuticals. In addition, India has developed a large computer software industry. The large India film industry is located in Mumbai, Kolkata, and Chennai. Since the globalization of India's economy in the 1990s, international call centers have also been located in India.

Trade

India's major exports include petroleum products, textile goods, gems and jewelry, engineering goods, chemicals, and leather manufactures. In the early years of Indian independence and up to the breakup of the Soviet Union, the USSR was India's largest trading partner as well as its biggest supplier of defense weaponry. Since the liberalization of India's economy in the 1990s, India's trading partners have changed. In 2008 India's three top exporting partners were the United States (12.3 percent), the United Arab Emirates (9.4 percent), and China (9.3 percent). India imported the most products from the following: China (11.1 percent), Saudi Arabia (7.5 percent), the United States (6.6 percent), the United Arab Emirates (5.1 percent), Iran (4.2 percent), Singapore (4.2 percent), and Germany (4.2 percent).

APPENDIX 2

CHRONOLOGY

Prehistory

50 million years ago	Tectonic plate movements bring island landmass into collision with Eurasian continent; collision forms Himalaya Mountains, Tibetan Plateau, and the South Asian subcontinent
ca. 30,000–10,000 B.C.E.	Stone Age communities in northern Pakistan and in states of Andhra Pradesh, Madhya Pradesh, Gujarat, Rajasthan, Uttar Pradesh, and Bihar
ca. 8,000–ca. 2000 B.C.E.	Neolithic stone age sites found in western and northern Pakistan and in northern and southern India. Earliest site is at Mehrgarh in Baluchistan, Pakistan; southern Indian sites date from third millennium B.C.E. and continue into the second millennium B.C.E.
ca. 6,500 B.C.E.	Agriculture and domestication of animals begins at Mehrgarh in Baluchistan, Pakistan
2600–1900 B.C.E.	Harappan civilization: mature, urban phase develops in the Indus River Valley region
late third millennium B.C.E.– second millennium B.C.E.	Indo-Aryan tribes migrate into Indian subcontinent
By ca. 1500 B.C.E.	Rig Veda composed, primarily in the greater Punjab region of subcontinent

The Hindu World Order

ca. 1200–400 B.C.E.	Indo-Aryan tribes and culture spread into Ganges River Valley, and urban culture develops
By ca. 500 B.C.E.	Composition of three other Vedas and major Upanishads (following recent changes in dating death of the Buddha)
ca. 500 B.C.E.	Composition of core stories of *Mahabharata* and *Ramayana*
fifth century B.C.E.	Sixteen *mahajanapadas* (great clan's territories) form in Gangetic region
ca. late sixth– fifth century B.C.E.	Life and death of Mahavira Vardhamana, historical founder of Jainism
ca. fifth century B.C.E.	Life and death of Siddhartha Gautama, founder of Buddhism
ca. mid-fourth century B.C.E.	Mahapadma Nanda establishes political control of Magadha region and other Gangetic states
327 B.C.E.	Alexander of Macedonia crosses Indus River and invades India
ca. 321 B.C.E.	Mauryan dynasty founded by Chandragupta Maurya
ca. 268–233 B.C.E.	Ashoka rules Mauryan Empire
ca. mid-third century B.C.E.	Third Buddhist Council convenes under auspices of Ashoka, according to Buddhist traditions
ca. second– first century B.C.E.	Indo-Bactrian-Greek kingdoms are established in north India; King Menander rules ca. 155–130 B.C.E.
ca. late second century B.C.E.–late fourth century C.E.	Scythian (Shaka) tribes move into northern India. Western Shakas rule in Rajasthan, Sind through fourth century C.E.
185 B.C.E.	Shunga dynasty overthrows Mauryan dynasty
ca. fifth century B.C.E.– fourth century C.E.	Composition and compilation of epics, *Mahabharata* and *Ramayana;* composition of the Bhagavad Gita (ca. first century C.E.)
ca. 200 B.C.E.–ca. 200 C.E.	Composition of the Laws of Manu
100 B.C.E.–800 C.E.	Trade routes established between Roman Empire (and its successors) and Indian coasts

first–third centuries C.E.	Kushan tribes defeat Scythians (Shakas) in northern India; Kushan ruler Kanishka governs ca. 78 or 144 C.E.
	Satavahana dynasty rules Deccan region; Chola, Chera, and Pandya dynasties compete for regional power in southern India
first–fifth centuries	Spread of Hinduism, Buddhism, and Jainism along with Sanskrit-based culture into southern and western India
52 C.E.	St. Thomas is martyred on Malabar Coast according to legend
320–ca. mid-sixth century	Gupta dynasty establishes empire across north India
ca. 500	Composition of the major Puranas
ca. mid-fifth century– mid-sixth century	Hunas (tribes) repeatedly attack northern and western India
570–632	Muhammad, founder of the Islamic religion, in Saudi Arabia
606–647	Harsha establishes empire across north India

Turks, Afghans, and Mughals

sixth–ninth centuries	Southern Indian dynasties of Chalukyas (Karnataka), Pallavas (Kanchipuram), Pandyas (Madurai), and Cholas (Tanjore) compete for power
seventh–10th centuries	Bhakti religious sects appear in south India; 63 Shaivite saints (the Nayanars) and 12 Vaishnavites (the Alvars) are associated with these bhakti sects
by 10th century	Bhakti has spread to north India
seventh–12th centuries	Persecution of Jain and Buddhist communities in southern India
ca. eighth–ninth centuries	Shankara founds Vedanta school of philosophy
mid-seventh century– ninth century	Arab traders settle on Malabar Coast and in Konkan region
711	Arabs invade Sind
mid-ninth century–1279	Chola dynasty expands and rules in southern India and Sri Lanka

998–1030	Mahmud of Ghazni rules Afghan empire and raids northwest of subcontinent between 1000 and 1027
1137	Death of Ramanuja, South Indian Brahman founder of a school of Vedanta emphasizing the importance of bhakti
1151–1206	Ghurid dynasty rules Afghan region and northern India
12th–18th centuries	Bhakti sects spread throughout India; among the saints associated with these sects in North India are Kabir (ca. 1440), Chaitanya (ca. 1485), Surdas and Mirabai (both b. ca. 15th century), Tulsidas (b. 16th century), and Tukaram (b. 1608)
1206–1526	Dynasties of the Delhi Sultanate rule northern India; major dynasties are the Slave dynasty (founded 1206), Khalji dynasty (1290), Tughluq dynasty (1320), Sayyid dynasty (1414), and Lodi dynasty (1451)
1258	Mongol armies destroy caliphate at Baghdad
1297–1307	Mongol armies make four successive invasions of India
1335–42	Famine kills residents in Delhi and surrounding regions
1346–1565	Vijayanagar kingdom rules the southern peninsula of India
1347–1518	Bahmani Sultanate rules the Deccan
1398–99	Timur (Tamerlane) invades India and sacks Delhi
1469–1539	Guru Nanak, founder of the Sikh religion
1510	Portuguese establish a settlement at Goa
1526–30	Babur founds the Mughal Empire (1526–1857) by defeating the Lodi sultan in battle at Panipat
1530–56	Humayun rules the Mughal Empire
1542	Jesuit St. Francis Xavier travels to Goa
1556–1605	Akbar rules the Mughal Empire
1600	Founding of the East India Company in England
1605–27	Jahangir rules the Mughal Empire
1612–90	English establish warehouses ("factories") at Surat, Bombay (Mumbai), Madras (Chennai), and Calcutta (Kolkata)

1627–58	Shah Jahan rules the Mughal Empire
1630–80	Shivaji Bhonsle, founder of Maratha power in Maharashtra
mid-17th century	Dutch establish control over the spice trade from bases in Southeast Asia and Sri Lanka
1658–1707	Aurangzeb rules the Mughal Empire
1660s	French establish settlements at Surat and Pondicherry (Puducherry) and in Bengal

The British Raj

1746–63	Three Carnatic Wars are fought between the French and English in India
ca. 1750s–1818	Maratha Confederacy rules from Pune
1757	East India Company armies defeat the nawab of Bengal at the Battle of Plassey
1764	English armies defeat a coalition led by the Mughal emperor at the Battle of Baksar (Buxar); from 1765 the East India Company is granted the *diwani* (right to collect land revenues) in province of Bengal
1767–99	In the four Anglo-Mysore Wars, East India Company fights and ultimately defeats the Mysore rulers Haidar Ali Khan and his son Tipu Sultan
1769–70	Famine in Bengal kills an estimated one-quarter of the region's population
1773	British Regulating Act reorganizes East India Company operations; Warren Hastings is first governor-general appointed under this act
1784	Sir William Jones founds the Asiatic Society of Bengal; William Pitt's India Act is passed in England to bring East India Company more directly under parliamentary controls; Governor-General Cornwallis passes wide-ranging reforms of company operations, collectively called the Cornwallis Code
1793	Cornwallis's permanent settlement of Bengal gives landownership to local zamindars in perpetuity

1802–18	East India Company armies defeat Maratha Confederacy and annex Maratha lands
1813	Charter of East India Company is renewed by Parliament; new charter provisions allow private traders and missionaries to travel to and work in company territories
1816	*Bengali Gazette*, first newspaper published in an Indian language, is founded in Calcutta
1817	English-language Hindu College is founded in Calcutta
1820s	Sir Thomas Munro develops *ryotwari* land settlements in Madras Presidency, making revenue settlements with individual cultivators (*ryots*) for fixed periods of time
1828	Rammohan Roy founds the religious association the Brahmo Sabha (later Brahmo Samaj) in Calcutta
1829	Governor-General William Bentinck makes sati illegal in company territories
1833	Parliament's Charter Act ends East India Company's commercial functions
1835	Thomas Babington Macaulay writes his "Minute on Education" arguing that English, not Indian languages, should be the medium for Indian education
1836–1921	Muslim Moplah communities along the Malabar Coast carry out periodic rebellions against Hindu landlords and British government
1845–49	British armies defeat Sikh forces in two Anglo-Sikh wars and annex the Punjab
1849–56	Governor-General Dalhousie's government annexes princely states in Bengal, Rajasthan, the Punjab, and Oudh
1853	India's first passenger railroad opens in Bombay; major rail lines are laid up through the 1920s
1854	Wood Dispatch authorizes creation of university centers at Bombay, Madras, and Calcutta for English-language college education in India; appointments to the Indian Civil Service (ICS)

	are made on the basis of competitive examinations held in England
1857–58	Rebellion (known to the British as the Indian Mutiny) begins with sepoy (soldier) mutiny near Delhi and develops into a widespread but not united uprising against British rule; put down by the British with great difficulty
1858	British government in England passes laws abolishing East India Company and placing the Indian empire under direct Crown rule; by the end of the 19th century two-thirds of India is ruled directly by the British; princely (or native) states (totaling almost 500–600 princes) make up almost one-third of Indian territories and are ruled indirectly
1861	Indian Councils Act allows appointment of between three and six Indian members to the governor-general's council
1866–78	Famines spread across north and south India
1868	Deoband Dar-ul-Ulum, a modernized Muslim madrassa for the education of *ulamas,* is founded at Deoband
1869	Suez Canal opens, shortening trip from Great Britain to India to just more than three weeks
1870–85	English-educated Indians form regional political associations in cities such as Pune (1870), Calcutta (1875), Madras (1878), and Bombay (1885)
1871	Start of the decennial (10-year) Indian census
1873	Jyotirao Phule founds the Satyashodhak Samaj (Truth-Seeking Society) to unify lower-caste and Untouchable communities
	In Pabna district, eastern Bengal, prosperous peasants organize protest meetings, rent strikes, and legal challenges to fight zamindar rent increases
1875	Sir Sayyid Ahmad Khan founds the Muhammadan Anglo-Oriental College at Aligarh to provide elite Muslim students with English-language education

	Peasants protest falling cotton prices in the Deccan cotton riots
1875–77	Dayananda Saraswati founds the Arya Samaj, a reform Hindu society, in western and northern India
1876	Queen Victoria is proclaimed empress of India
1878	Vernacular Press Act requires Indian-language presses (but not those published in English) to post bonds for their conduct with the government; English-educated Indians in major Indian cities organize to protest the act
1878–80	British fight a war against the Afghan regime to their northwest to gain protection against possible Russian encroachments into Afghanistan and India
1880s–90s	Cow protection riots between Hindu and Muslim communities over issues of the slaughter of cattle for meat erupt across northern Indian
1882	Theosophist Society establishes its Indian headquarters at Madras
1883–84	British Indian government proposes Ilbert Bill, an act that would allow Indian judges to try cases involving Europeans; public protests by the Anglo-Indian community force the altering of the bill

Toward Freedom

1885	First meeting of the Indian National Congress is held in Bombay, attended by 73 delegates from every British Indian province
1887	M. G. Ranade founds the Indian National Social Conference, a meeting of social reformers
1891	Government's Age of Consent bill raises the age of statutory rape of girls from 10 to 12 and provokes mass meetings and protests from Hindu communities in Bengal and Maharashtra
1892	Indian Councils Act provides for indirect elections of candidates to the central and regional Legislative Councils in Bengal, Bombay, and Madras

	Maximum age for taking the Indian Civil Service exams is raised to 23
1893–95	Bal Gangadhar Tilak inaugurates two political Hindu festivals in Maharashtra: one celebrating the birthday of the Hindu god Ganesh, the other celebrating the Marathi hero Shivaji
1896–97	Famine causes 5 million deaths across India
1897	Swami Vivekananda founds the Ramakrishna Mission in Calcutta
	Damodar and Balkrishna Chapedar assassinate Pune's unpopular plague commissioner, Walter Rand; Tilak is imprisoned for sedition
1899–1900	A second all-India famine causes another 5 million deaths
	Birsa Munda leads Munda tribe members in Bihar in a two-month rebellion against the British government
1905	Governor-General Curzon's government partitions the province of Bengal; the partition is protested through the *swadeshi* movement, a widespread boycott of British goods, honors, and institutions
1906	All-Indian Muslim League is founded
1907	Indian National Congress splits between its older "moderate" members and its younger "extremists" during its meeting at Surat
1909	Morley-Minto reforms (officially known as the Indian Councils Act) enacted in London to give Indians more members in legislative councils at the center and in the provinces and to begin election to the councils from a variety of constituencies
1911	A Delhi durbar is held to celebrate the coronation of the British king, George V
	Partition of Bengal is rescinded
	Transfer of the capital from Calcutta to Delhi is announced
1914	British Indian government declares India at war against Germany
1915	Hindu Mahasabha is founded

1916	Lucknow Pact is jointly proposed by a reunited Congress and the Muslim League; the pact is a plan for constitutional reforms to give elected Indian representatives additional power at the provincial and the central levels; the principle of separate electorates for Muslims is accepted and detailed in the pact
1916–24	A worldwide pan-Islamic Khilafat movement forms to preserve the Ottoman sultan's role as caliph and Islamic holy places in the Middle East; it ends in 1924 when Kemal Atatürk, ruler of Turkey, abolishes the Ottoman caliphate
1919	The Montagu-Chelmsford reforms propose a new system called "dyarchy," under which the British Indian government would turn over responsibility for some areas of government to elected Indians
	Rowlatt Acts make temporary sedition laws permanent; Mohandas K. Gandhi calls for a nationwide *hartal* (strike) that turns violent
	British general Reginald Dyer orders troops to fire on a peaceful crowd in Jallianwalla Bagh in Amritsar
1920	M. N. Roy founds the Communist Party of India

Gandhi and the Nationalist Movement

ca. 1920s	Periyar (E. V. Ramaswami Naicker) founds the Self-Respect Movement for Dravidians in Madras
1921–22	Gandhi and Indian Khilafat movement organize a national noncooperation campaign against the British; 20,000 Indians are jailed for civil disobedience; Gandhi abruptly ends the campaign when violence erupts
1923	Indian Civil Service examinations are held simultaneously in England and India for the first time
1925	The RSS (Rashtriya Swayamsevak Sangh), a paramilitary Hindu nationalist organization, is founded at Nagpur

1927	The British-appointed Simon Commission tours India to recommend future political reforms and is boycotted because it has no Indian members
	Indian radio begins under a government monopoly
1928	At a Congress-sponsored All-Parties Conference, Mahasabha members block Mohammed Ali Jinnah's compromise proposal for minority representation; Jinnah joins the All-India Muslim Conference, which demands separate electorates for Muslims in any future government
1930	Gandhi and the Congress begin a new campaign, the Salt March, against the British; an estimated 90,000 Indians are jailed for civil disobedience; during this campaign British government convenes the first Round Table Conference, inviting all Indian constituencies to debate future governmental reforms; Congress boycotts the first conference
1931	Gandhi and the British viceroy, Baron Irwin, reach the Gandhi-Irwin pact, which ends civil disobedience, releases protesters from jail, and commits Gandhi to attend the Round Table Conference in London.
	First Indian film with sound is produced in Bombay
1931–32	The second Round Table Conference, with Gandhi attending, deadlocks over the question of minority representation in a future central government
1932	The Indian government awards separate electorates to a number of Indian groups, among them Untouchables; Gandhi begins a fast-to-the-death in protest; Poona Pact, between Gandhi and Untouchable leader B. R. Ambedkar, replaces separate electorates with reserved seats for Untouchables
1933	Cambridge University Muslim student coins a name for the future separate Islamic Indian state: "Pakistan"

| 1935 | Government of India Act creates a federated government in India in which the provinces are run by elected Indian officials and the center by the British Indian government; many provisions of this act carry over into the government of independent India |

1937   Congress wins provincial elections and forms governments in eight Indian provinces; Muslim League fails to form a single government; as governors, Congress politicians make few concessions to Muslim politicians

1939   British government declares India at war with Germany in World War II

1940   Muslim League's Lahore Resolution demands an independent Muslim state

1942   Cripps Mission offers Congress only a guarantee of dominion status at the end of the war; Congress rejects the plan, demanding an immediate share in the central governing of India

Congress launches the Quit India civil disobedience campaign; all Congress leaders are immediately jailed, but widespread protest occurs nonetheless

1942–45   Subhas Bose joins the Axis powers and leads his Indian National Army against British troops in Burma; Bose dies in a plane crash in 1945

1942–46   Famine in Bengal kills between 1 to 3 million people

1945–46   In central and provincial elections Jinnah and the Muslim League campaign for an independent Muslim state in India; the League wins most Muslim seats; Congress wins 91 percent of all non-Muslim seats

1946   British cabinet mission to India fails to find a formula for granting independence because Jinnah and Congress cannot agree on the structure of any future central Indian government

Jinnah calls for "Direct Action Day" to demonstrate Muslims' commitment to Pakistan;

	violent communal rioting breaks out, killing 4,000 in Calcutta and spreading across northern India
1947	Lord Mountbatten is appointed the last British viceroy to India and brokers a final plan to partition British India into two separate countries, India and Pakistan
	India and Pakistan become independent dominions at midnight on August 14
	Partition boundaries, announced August 17, produce communal violence in which 10 million people become refugees
1947–49	Most Indian princes agree to transfer their states to either India or Pakistan; India seizes control of the princely states of Hyderabad and Junagadh
	India and Pakistan go to war over the state of Kashmir; United Nations cease-fire and a temporary division of the disputed state ends the war; India agrees to hold a plebiscite to determine Kashmir's future
1948	Gandhi is assassinated in New Delhi by Naturam Godse, a right-wing militant Hindu
1949	Hindu Marriage Validating Act removes legal barriers to intercaste marriage

Constructing the Nation

1950	New Indian constitution becomes law, establishing India as a democratic republic
1951–52	Congress Party wins the first elections held under the new constitution and forms India's first government; Jawaharlal Nehru becomes India's first prime minister; Nehru remains prime minister at the head of Congress governments until his death in 1964
1951–56	First Five-Year Plan successfully reestablishes the stability of India's economy
1955–56	Hindu Marriage Act, Hindu Succession Act, and Adoption and Maintenance Act reform

marriage customs and equalize women's access to paternal property

Untouchability (Offences) Act provides penalties for discrimination against Untouchables; government establishes quotas (reserved seats) in the Lok Sabha, provincial legislatures, educational institutions, and government departments for members of Scheduled Castes (Untouchable castes) and Scheduled Tribes

1956   Indian government creates 14 language-based states

Untouchable leader B. R. Ambedkar converts to Buddhism, as do many of his followers

1956–61; 1961–66   Second and Third Five-Year Plans focus economic efforts on industrializing the Indian economy

1959   Panchayati Raj Plan organizes agricultural and village development work in Indian states

Indian television begins as a government monopoly

1962   Sino-Indian War: India and China go to war over disputed boundaries in the northeast, resulting in an Indian military defeat and the loss of the Karakoram Pass to China

1964   Nehru dies after a long illness; Lal Bahadur Shastri is elected prime minister

1965–85   New strains of wheat and rice introduced into the Punjab and other Indian regions produce a "Green Revolution," dramatically increasing crop production, particularly in the Punjab

1966   India's refusal to hold a plebiscite in Kashmir leads to a brief war with Pakistan in which Indian forces dominate; truce mediated by the Soviet Union returns Kashmir to its 1949 status; Shastri dies suddenly immediately following the negotiations

In midst of escalating food shortages and rising prices, Congress Party bosses choose Indira Gandhi as prime minister

1967   Congress wins reelection by its smallest margin to date as India's food crisis worsens;

	anti-Brahman DMK party takes power in Madras; Sikh party Akali Dal wins control of the newly created province of the Punjab
1969	Gandhi nationalizes 14 of India's private banks
1970–71	Gandhi abolishes the privy purses awarded to former Indian princes
1971	Gandhi, expelled from Congress, wins election through her own Congress (R) Party on a platform of abolishing poverty
	War between East and West Pakistan leads India into a brief war with West Pakistan; Pakistan surrenders, and East Pakistan becomes the independent country of Bangladesh
1972–74	Monsoon failures create food shortages, rising prices, and near famine conditions; international loans restrict India's economic plans
1974	India detonates an underground nuclear device
1975	Coalition of opposition parties protesting government corruption and rising prices becomes a national movement, the Janata Morcha (People's Front), against Gandhi's government
	High Court of Uttar Pradesh finds Gandhi guilty of corrupt election practices and bars her from holding office
1975–77	Gandhi has the president of India declare national emergency, jails her political opponents, suspends civil rights, and takes control of the government
	Sanjay Gandhi leads efforts to raze urban slums and effect birth control through sterilization
1977	Indira Gandhi calls for new elections, ending the Emergency and freeing her political opponents; Janata coalition wins the election, and Morarji Desai becomes prime minister
1978–80	Janata government's Mandal Commission Report identifies more than 3,000 castes and communities ("Other Backward Classes") that deserve preferential treatment in government jobs and education

1980	Janata coalition loses election to Indira Gandhi and her Congress (I) Party; Sanjay Gandhi dies in a plane crash; Rajiv Gandhi wins election to Parliament
1981	In Tamil Nadu mass conversions of Untouchables to Islam in ceremonies sponsored by the Muslim League raise Hindu nationalist fears of a threat to the Hindu majority in India
1982	Doordarshan, the government television station, adds programming and expands its audience through satellites
1983	The VHP (Vishwa Hindu Parishad) organizes the Ekatmata Yatra (procession for oneness) to demonstrate Hindu unity
	Phoolan Devi, India's "Bandit Queen," surrenders and is imprisoned
1983–84	VHP begins a national Ramjanmabhoomi campaign, an effort to restore the god Rama's birthplace in Ayodhya by destroying a 16th-century Muslim mosque, Babri Masjid, said to have been built over that site
	RSS founds a new youth wing, the Bajrang Dal, to work on the Ramjanmabhoomi campaign and is involved in forming a new political party, the BJP (Bharatiya Janata Party), out of the old Hindu nationalist Jana Sangh party
1984	Indian army in "Operation Bluestar" invades the sacred Sikh temple at Amritsar to destroy the Sikh militant leader Bhindranwale and his followers
	Indira Gandhi is assassinated by Sikh members of her bodyguard; Rajiv Gandhi becomes prime minister and calls for new elections, which Congress wins overwhelmingly
	Gas tank at a Union Carbide factory in Bhopal, Madhya Pradesh, explodes, killing 7,000 to 10,000 people within the first three days and injuring at least 10,000 more
	Kanshi Ram founds the Bahujan Samaj Party to organize low castes and Dalits (Untouchables) as a political party

1985	After a legal judgment in the *Shah Bano* case antagonizes conservative Muslims, Gandhi's government passes a bill making sharia practices the law for Indian Muslims
1986	As the number of dowry deaths increases, government makes such deaths a special category of crime to facilitate prosecution
1987	V. P. Singh exposes the Bofors scandal in the Gandhi government and is expelled from the Congress Party; Singh founds an opposition party, the Janata Dal
1987–90	Indian army unsuccessfully fights the Tamil Tiger guerrilla movement in Sri Lanka
1989	Singh's Janata Dal and National Front defeat Congress; the front forms a coalition government with support from the BJP; Singh becomes prime minister.
1990	Singh government's decision to implement the Mandal Report recommendations produces upper-caste protests and student suicides; VHP announces that construction of its Rama temple in Ayodhya will begin in October; BJP leader L. K. Advani begins a party procession from Gujarat in support of the campaign; Prime Minister V. P. Singh orders Advani's arrest in Bihar, and the BJP withdraws from Singh's government
1991	Rajiv Gandhi is assassinated in Tamil Nadu by a member of the Sri Lankan Tamil Tigers; Congress wins enough votes in the elections to form a coalition government with Narasimha Rao as prime minister
	Rao's finance minister, Manmohan Singh, implements an economic program to open India's economy to global markets
	Cauvery Water Disputes Tribunal is set up to negotiate water rights on the Kaveri (Cauvery) River between Karnataka and Tamil Nadu
1992	VHP volunteers break into the Babri Masjid grounds in Ayodhya and destroy the mosque; communal rioting breaks out across northern

India; Prime Minister Rao arrests major Hindu nationalists and temporarily bans the RSS, VHP, and Bajrang Dal from further activity

Samajwadi Party is founded to organize Other Backward Classes (OBCs) in Bihar and Uttar Pradesh

India in the Twenty-first Century

1996	Elections give the BJP a plurality, but the party is unable to form a coalition government; coalition of small parties forms government, first with Deve Gowda and then with Inder Kumar Gujral as prime minister
	Phoolan Devi wins election to Uttar Pradesh seat as Samajwadi Party candidate
1996, 1997, 2002–03	Bahujan Samaj Party forms brief coalition governments in Uttar Pradesh
1998	BJP succeeds in forming a coalition government by abandoning key elements of its Hindutva (Hindu nationalist) agenda
1998–99	More than 100 violent attacks are made against Christians in the tribal areas of several states and in Orissa
	Tensions worsen between India and Pakistan as both countries explode nuclear devices
1999	BJP emerges from a new national election at the head of a stronger coalition government
	50-day Kargil War won by India after heavy fighting at Kargil, on the Indian side of Kashmir border, between Pakistani and Kashmiri insurgents and Indian military forces
2000	Dowry deaths are now estimated to number 5,000 per year according to UNICEF
	Pakistan-based militants attack the Red Fort in New Delhi, killing three people
2001	An earthquake in Gujarat kills 20,000 people
2001–02	Armed terrorists attack the Indian Parliament complex killing eight people; in 2002 terrorists kill 38 people in the Kashmir parliament

2002	As VHP celebrates 10-year anniversary of Ayodhya movement, Muslims kill 58 Hindu nationalist volunteers on a train in Godhra, Gujarat; communal riots rage in Gujarat over several months
2002–03	India and Pakistan withdraw political envoys and mass soldiers on borders in Kashmir
2003	Amid claims that a Coca-Cola bottling plant had polluted water in a Kerala village, an analysis of Coca-Cola and PepsiCo soft drinks reports that they contain high levels of pesticides
2004	BJP announces restoration of diplomatic and transportation ties with Pakistan and says a new round of peace talks will soon start
	BJP loses national election after running on a campaign of "India Shining"; Congress Party forms government with economist Manmohan Singh as prime minister
	India, Brazil, Japan, and Germany ask for permanent seats on the UN Security Council
	A tsunami caused by an undersea earthquake off the coast of Sumatra destroys coastal communities in South and Southeast Asia, killing thousands in southern India and the Andaman and Nicobar Islands
	Punjab state legislature passes act terminating its water agreements with states of Haryana and Rajasthan
2005	Bus service resumes, between the Indian and Pakistani regions of Kashmir; Kashmiri terrorist bombs in New Delhi kill 60 people; in Bangalore, Kashmiri terrorists open fire on a technology conference
	Congress enacts the National Rural Employment Guarantee Scheme (NREGS), a legal guarantee of 100 days employment every year to rural adults willing to do public works
2006	India and the United States sign a nuclear co-operation agreement allowing India to buy nuclear fuel in exchange for external inspection of its civilian nuclear plants

Kashmiri terrorists explode bombs in eight locations on a Mumbai commuter rail line, killing 182 people; bombings result in a four-month suspension of India and Pakistan peace talks

2007   Terrorist bombs kill 68 passengers on an India-to-Pakistan train, part of resumed rail service between the two countries

The Bahujan Samaj Party (BSP) wins a landslide victory in Uttar Pradesh, returning Mayawati as chief minister; 25 die in Rajasthan as the OBC Gujjar caste demands the lowering of its caste status to gain access to more reserved government jobs

Pratibha Devisingh Patil (1934–   ) is elected president of India on July 19, the first woman to hold this position

Indian crime statistics number dowry deaths at 8,093

Farmer suicides, predominantly in five states, average 16,631 per year from 1997 to 2007

Cauvery Water Disputes Tribunal announces its decisions; four states involved refuse to accept and plan appeals

2008   Supreme Court allows government to proceed with plan to expand 27 percent reservation of seats for OBCs in elite technical and medical institutions but requires wealthier OBCs (the "creamy layer") to be excluded from the reservations

India and the United States conclude a civilian nuclear trade deal that would allow the United States to sell nuclear fuel, technology, and reactors to India for peaceful use

Terrorist attacks on tourist and other sites in southern section of Mumbai between November 26 and 29 kill more than 170 people

2009   Congress wins 206 seats in unpredicted election victory and easily forms a coalition government; BJP seats in Lok Sabha return to their level in 1991; regional political parties poll more than 50 percent of the electoral vote for the second time since 2004

Tendulkar Committee revises formula by which poverty is estimated in India: percentage of Indian people living at or below the poverty level now estimated at 37.5 percent

2010   Twenty-six years after the 1984 Union Carbide factory gas leak, a court in Bhopal, Madhya Pradesh, finds eight Indians guilty of "death by negligence" and sentences the seven who remain alive to two years each in prison; those sentenced include the chairman of Union Carbide in India, the Indian managing director, the vice president, the works manager, the production manager, the plant superintendent, and the plant production assistant

A majority Allahabad High Court ruling divides the disputed holy site of Ayodhya into thirds; the court awards Hindus control over the section where the Babri mosque had been torn down in 1992 and divides the remaining two-thirds equally between Muslims and a Hindu minority sect, Nirmohi Akhara, which had been an early litigant in the case

XIX Commonwealth Games take place in New Delhi

APPENDIX 3

BIBLIOGRAPHY

Ahluwalia, Isher Judge. "Indian Economy: New Pathways to Growth and Development." In *India Briefing: Takeoff at Last?* edited by Alyssa Ayres and Philip Oldenburg, 45–81. New York: Asia Society and M. E. Sharpe, 2005.

Ahmed, I., and H. Reifeld, eds. *Middle Class Values in India and Western Europe.* New Delhi: Social Science Press, 2001.

Aiyer, Ananthkrishnan. "The Allure of the Transnational: Notes on Some Aspects of the Political Economy of Water in India." *Cultural Anthropology* 22, no. 4 (2007): 640–658.

Alam, Muzaffar, and Sanjay Subrahmanyam. *The Mughal State, 1526–1750.* Delhi and New York: Oxford University Press, 1998.

Alberuni, Muhammad ibn Ahmad, and Ainslie T. Embree. *Alberuni's India.* Abridged ed. New York: Norton, 1971.

Ali, Daud. *Courtly Culture and Political Life in Early Medieval India.* Cambridge Studies in Indian History and Society, vol. 10. Cambridge: Cambridge University Press, 2004.

Allchin, Bridget, and Raymond Allchin. *The Birth of Indian Civilization.* New York: Penguin, 1968.

———. *The Rise of Civilization in India and Pakistan.* Cambridge: Cambridge University Press, 1982.

Allchin, F. R. *The Archaeology of Early Historic South Asia: The Emergence of Cities and States.* Cambridge: Cambridge University Press, 1995.

Allen, Charles, and Michael Mason. *Plain Tales from the Raj: Images of British India in the Twentieth Century.* London: Macdonald Futura, 1976.

Ambasta, Pramathesh. "Programming NREGS to Succeed." *Hindu,* 31 October, 2009. Available online. URL: http://beta.thehindu.com/opinion/lead/article41154.ece. Accessed February 12, 2010.

Amnesty International. "Clouds of Injustice: Bhopal Disaster 20 Years On." (2004). Available online. URL: www.amnesty.org/en/library/info/ASA20/015/2004. Accessed February 10, 2010.

Arnold, David. *Science, Technology, and Medicine in Colonial India*. In *The New Cambridge History of India*, vol. 5, pt. 3. New York: Cambridge University Press, 2000.

Arora, Balveer, and Stephanie Tawa Lama-Rewal. "Introduction: Contextualizing and Interpreting the 15th Lok Sabha Elections." *SAMAJ: South Asia Multidisciplinary Academic Journal* 3 (2009). Contests in Context: Indian Elections 2009. Available online. URL: http://samaj.revues.org/index1092.html. Accessed June 1, 2010.

Asher, Catherine Ella Blanshard. *Architecture of Mughal India*. In *The New Cambridge History of India*, vol. 1, pt. 4. Cambridge: Cambridge University Press, 1992.

Ashoka. "Ashokan Rock and Pillar Edicts." *Project South Asia*. Available online. URL: http://projectsouthasia.sdstate.edu/Docs/index.htm. Accessed February 13, 2010.

Athreya, Venkatesh. "Sonia Effect Checks BJP Advance." *Frontline* 15, no. 4 (February 21–March 6, 1998). Available online. URL: http://www.hinduonnet.com/fline/fl1504/15040060.htm. Accessed February 12, 2010.

Ayres, Alyssa, and Philip Oldenburg, eds. *India Briefing: Takeoff at Last?* New York: Asia Society and M. E. Sharpe, 2005.

Bailey, Gregory. "The Puranas: A Study in the Development of Hinduism." In *The Study of Hinduism*, edited by Arvind Sharma, 139–169. Columbia: University of South Carolina Press, 2003.

Bama. *Sangati: Events*. Translated by Lakshmi Holmstrom. New Delhi: Oxford University Press, 2005.

Bana. *Harsacarita*. Translated by E. B. Cowell and F. W. Thomas. Delhi: Motilal Banarsidass, 1961.

Bartlett, John. *Familiar Quotations: A Collection of Passages, Phrases, and Proverbs Traced to Their Sources in Ancient and Modern Literature*. 16th ed. Edited by Justin Kaplan. Boston: Little, Brown, 1992.

Basham, A. L. *The Wonder That Was India*. London: Sidgwick & Jackson, 1958.

Bayly, C. A. *Indian Society and the Making of the British Empire*. Cambridge: Cambridge University Press, 1988.

———. *Rulers, Townsmen and Bazaars: North Indian Society in the Age of British Expansion, 1770–1870*. Delhi and Oxford: Oxford University Press, 1992.

Bayly, C. A., Brian Allen, and National Portrait Gallery. *The Raj: India and the British, 1600–1947*. London: National Portrait Gallery Publications, 1990.

Bayly, Susan. *Caste, Society and Politics in India from the Eighteenth Century to the Modern Age. The New Cambridge History of India,* vol. 4. Cambridge: Cambridge University Press, 1999.

BBC News. "India Pm Pledge over Suicide Farmers." BBC News online, July 1, 2004.

Bechert, Heinz, and Siglinde Dietz, eds. *When Did the Buddha Live?: Controversy on the Dating of the Historical Buddha—Selected Papers Based on a Symposium Held under the Auspices of the Academy of Sciences (Bibliotheca Indo-Buddhica).* New Delhi: Sri Satguru Publications, 1996.

Begum, Gul-Badan. *Humayun-Nama (the History of Humayun) with Persian Text.* Translated by Annette S. Beveridge. Lahore: Sang-e-meel Publications, 2002.

Belnos, S. C., and A. Colin. *Twenty Four Plates Illustrative of Hindoo and European Manners in Bengal.* Calcutta: Riddhi-India, 1979.

Bhagavad Gita: A New Translation. Translated by George Thompson. New York: North Point Press, 2008.

Bhagavan, Manu Belur, Anne Feldhaus, and Eleanor Zelliot. *"Speaking Truth to Power": Religion, Caste, and the Subaltern Question in India.* New Delhi: Oxford University Press, 2008.

Bhattacharjee, K. S. *The Bengal Renaissance: Social and Political Thoughts.* New Delhi: Classical Publishing, 1986.

"Bhopal." Union Carbide Corporation. Available online. URL: http://www.bhopal.com/facts.htm. Accessed June 1, 2010.

Birodkar, Sudheer. "Hindu History: The Intervention of Alien Rule from 1194 C.E. up to 1947 C.E." 2004. Available online. URL: http:/www.hindutva.org/landalienrule.html. Accessed March 31, 2005.

Blakely, Rhys. "Activists Mark Bhopal Anniversary with Renewed Call for Justice." Timesonline, December 3, 2009.

"Bombay University Calendar and Examination Papers." Bombay: Bombay University, 1861 and 1900–1901.

Borthwick, Meredith. *Changing Role of Women in Bengal, 1849–1905.* Princeton, N.J.: Princeton University Press, 1984.

Bose, Ajoy. "Excerpt from *Behenji.*" *Tehelka Magazine* 5, no. 18 (2008). Available online. URL: http://www.tehelka.com/story_main39.asp?filename=Ne100508a_miracle.asp. Accessed January 27, 2010.

Bose, Subhas Chandra. *An Indian Pilgrim: An Unfinished Autobiography and Collected Letters, 1897–1921.* Calcutta: Asia Publishing House, 1965.

Brahmankar, D. "By Invitation: Great Indian Consumers." Available online. URL: http://web.lexis-nexis.com. Accessed September 27, 2004.

Brass, Paul R. *The Politics of India since Independence.* 2d ed. Cambridge: Cambridge University Press, 1994.

Brecher, Michael. *Nehru: A Political Biography.* Abridged ed. Boston: Oxford University Press, 1961.

Brockington, John. "The Sanskrit Epics." In *The Blackwell Companion to Hinduism* (2005). Available online. URL: http://www.blackwell reference.com/subscriber/tocnode?id=g9780631215356_chunk_ g978063 12153568. Accessed October 4, 2009.

Brown, Judith M. *Gandhi and Civil Disobedience: The Mahatma in Indian Politics, 1928–34.* Cambridge: Cambridge University Press, 1977.

―――. *Nehru: A Political Life.* New Haven, Conn., and London: Yale University Press, 2003.

Brown, W. Norman. "Mythologies of India." In *Mythologies of the Ancient World,* edited by S. N. Kramer, 277–331. New York: Anchor, 1961.

Bryant, Edwin. *The Quest for the Origins of Vedic Culture: The Indo-Aryan Migration Debate.* Oxford: Oxford University Press, 2001.

Bryant, Edwin F., and Laurie L. Patton, eds. *The Indo-Aryan Controversy: Evidence and Inference in Indian History.* New York: Routledge, 2005.

Buck, William, and Valmiki. *Ramayana: King Rama's Way.* Berkeley: University of California Press, 1976.

Bulliet, Lucy. "The Indigenous Aryan Debate for Beginners." New York: 2002.

Burton, Antoinette. *Dwelling in the Archive: Women Writing House, Home and History.* New York: Oxford University Press, 2003.

Butalia, Urvashi. *The Other Side of Silence: Voices from the Partition of India.* Durham, N.C.: Duke University Press, 2000.

"Calcutta University Calendar and Examination Papers." Calcutta: Calcutta University, 1861.

Carstairs, G. Morris. *The Twice-Born.* Bloomington: Indiana University Press, 1967.

Census of India, 2001. Office of the Registrar General. January 7, 2004. Available online. URL: http://www.censusindia.net. Accessed January 11, 2010.

―――. "Provisional Population Totals: Census of India 2001." Office of the Registrar General, India. Available online. URL: http://census india.gov.in/Data_Products/Library/Provisional_Population_Total_link/ webed.html. Accessed January 21, 2010.

Chadwick, John, and Gerard Clausson. "Indus Script Deciphered." *Antiquity* 43 (1969): 200–207.

Chakrabarty, Dipesh. "The Difference—Deferral of (a) Colonial Modernity: Public Debates on Domesticity in British Bengal." *History Workshop* 36 (Autumn 1993): 1–35.

————. *Rethinking Working-Class History: Bengal, 1890 to 1940.* Princeton, N.J.: Princeton University Press, 2000.

Chakravarti, Uma. "Whatever Happened to the Vedic *Dasi?* Orientalism, Nationalism and a Script for the Past." In *Recasting Women,* edited by Kumkum Sangari and Sudesh Vaid, 27–87. New Brunswick, N.J.: Rutgers University Press, 1990.

Chakravarti, Ranabir. *Trade in Early India.* Oxford in India Readings. Themes in Indian History. New Delhi: Oxford University Press, 2001.

Chanana, Karuna. "Social Change or Social Reform: The Education of Women in Pre-Independence India." In *Socialisation, Education and Women,* edited by Karuna Chanana, 96–129. New Delhi: Orient Longman, 1988.

"Chapter 3: Size, Growth Rate and Distribution of Population." In *Provisional Population Totals: Census of India 2001.* New Delhi: Office of the Registrar General, India, 2001.

Chatterjee, Partha. *The Nation and Its Fragments: Colonial and Postcolonial Histories.* Delhi and New York: Oxford University Press, 1995.

Chatterji, Bankim Chandra. *Anandamath.* Translated by Basanta Koomar Roy. New Delhi: Orient Paperbacks, 1992.

————. *Bankim Racanabali* [Collected works of Bankim]. 13th ed. Calcutta: Sahitya Sangsad, 1989.

Chaudhuri, Nirad C. *The Autobiography of an Unknown Indian.* Berkeley: University of California Press, 1968.

Chopra, Aditya. *Dilwale Dulhania Le Jayenge* [The lover will carry away the bride]. India: 190 minutes, 1995. Motion picture.

Chowdhury-Sengupta, Indira. "The Return of the Sati: A Note on Heroism and Domesticity in Colonial Bengal." *Resources for Feminist Research* 22, nos. 3–4 (1993): 41–44.

CIA. "India: The World Factbook." Available online. URL: www.odci.gov/cia/publications/factbook/geos/in.html. Accessed February 12, 2010.

Codell, Julie F., ed. *Imperial Co-Histories: National Identities and the British and Colonial Press.* Madison, N.J.: Fairleigh Dickinson University Press, 2003.

Cohen, Stephen Philip. *India: Emerging Power.* Washington, D.C.: Brookings Institute Press, 2002.

Cohn, Bernard. *An Anthropologist among the Historians and Other Essays.* Delhi: Oxford University Press, 1987.

————. "The British in Benares." *Comparative Studies in Society and History* 4 (1962): 169–199.

————. *Colonialism and Its Forms of Knowledge: The British in India.* Princeton, N.J.: Princeton University Press, 1996.

————. *India: The Social Anthropology of a Civilization.* New York: Prentice-Hall, 1971.

————. "The Initial British Impact on India." *Journal of Asian Studies* 19 (1960): 418–431.

————. "Political Systems in Eighteenth Century India." *Journal of the American Oriental Society* 82 (1962): 360–380.

Conze, Edward. *Buddhism: Its Essence and Development.* New York: Harper Torchbook, 1959.

Copland, Ian. *The Princes of India in the Endgame of Empire, 1917–1947.* Cambridge Studies in Indian History and Society 2. Cambridge: Cambridge University Press, 1997.

Cort, John. *Open Boundaries: Jain Communities and Culture in Indian History.* Albany: State University of New York Press, 1998.

Countrywatch. "India Review 2003." Available online. URL: http://www.countrywatch.com. Accessed May 1, 2003.

Cousins, Lance S. "The Dating of the Historical Buddha: A Review Article." *Journal of the Royal Asiatic Society of Great Britain and Ireland* 3, no. 6 (1996). Available online. URL: http://indology.info/papers/cousins/. Accessed September 20, 2009.

Curzon, George Nathaniel. *British Government in India: The Story of the Viceroys and Government Houses.* Vol. 1. London: Cassell and Company, Ltd, 1925.

Danino, Michel. "The Riddle of India's Ancient Past." 1999. Available online. URL: http://micheldanino.voiceofdharma.com/riddle.html. Accessed February 28, 2005.

Das, Gurcharan. *India Unbound.* New York: Anchor Books, 2002.

Das, Prafulla. "Poverty Is Surely Declining, but Not Fast Enough: Manmohan Singh." *Hindu,* 28 December 2009.

Datta, Pranati. "Urbanisation in India." Paper for European Population Conference, hosted by Office of Population Research at Princeton University, 2006.

Davis, Richard H. "The Story of the Disappearing Jains: Retelling the Saiva-Jain Encounter in Medieval South India." In *Open Boundaries: Jain Communities and Cultures in Indian History,* edited by John E. Cort, 213–224. Albany: State University of New York Press, 1998.

Deaton, Angus, and Valerie Kozel, eds. *The Great Indian Poverty Debate.* New Delhi: MacMillan India, 2005.

De Bary, Wm. Theodore, ed. *Sources of Indian Tradition.* New York: Columbia University Press, 1958.

Desai, Jigna. *Beyond Bollywood: The Cultural Politics of South Asian Diasporic Film.* New York: Routledge, 2004.

Dettman, Paul R. *India Changes Course: Golden Jubilee to Millennium.* New York: Praeger, 2001.

Devahuti, D. *Harsha: A Political Study.* 3d ed. Delhi: Oxford University Press, 1998.

Dirks, Nicholas B. "Castes of Mind." *Representations* 37 (Winter 1992): 56–78.

———. *Castes of Mind: Colonialism and the Making of Modern India.* Princeton, N.J.: Princeton University Press, 2001.

———. *The Hollow Crown: Ethnohistory of an Indian Kingdom.* 2d ed. Ann Arbor: University of Michigan Press, 1993.

Doniger, Wendy, and Brian K. Smith, trans. *The Laws of Manu.* London: Penguin, 1991.

Donner, Henrike. *Domestic Goddesses: Maternity, Globalization and Middle-Class Identity in Contemporary India.* Urban Anthropology Series. Aldershot, UK, and Burlington, Vt.: Ashgate, 2008.

Duff-Brown, Beth. "India Issues Tough Threat If Pakistan Uses Nuclear Weapons." Associated Press. January 27, 2003. Available online. URL: http://www.sfgate.com/cgi-bin/article.cgi?f=/news/archive/2003/01/27/international1842EST0813.DTL. Accessed May 23, 2005.

Dunn, Ross E. *The Adventures of Ibn Battuta, a Muslim Traveler of the Fourteenth Century.* London: Croom Helm, 1986.

Duraphe, Ashok T. *Final Report/Charge Sheet.* Mumbai: Commissioner of Police, 2009.

Eaton, Richard M. *Essays on Islam and Indian History.* New Delhi: Oxford University Press, 2000.

———. *A Social History of the Deccan, 1300–1761: Eight Indian Lives.* New Cambridge History of India I, p. 8. Cambridge: Cambridge University Press, 2005.

———. *The Rise of Islam and the Bengal Frontier, 1204–1760.* New Delhi: Oxford University Press, 1993.

———. "Temple Desecration and Indo-Muslim States." *Journal of Islamic Studies* 11, no. 3 (2000): 283–319.

Eder, Milton. "The Bhagavadgita and Classical Hinduism: A Sketch." In *The Study of Hinduism,* edited by Arvind Sharma, 169–199. Columbia: University of South Carolina Press, 2003.

Edney, Matthew H. *Mapping an Empire: The Geographical Construction of British India, 1765–1843.* Chicago: University of Chicago Press, 1997.

Embree, Ainslie T., ed. *1857 in India: Mutiny or War of Independence?* Boston: D. C. Heath, 1963.

Embree, Ainslie T., and William Theodore De Bary, eds. *The Hindu Tradition.* New York: Random House, 1972.

Embree, Ainslie Thomas. *India's Search for National Identity*. New York: Alfred A. Knopf, 1972.

———. *Utopias in Conflict: Religion and Nationalism in Modern India*. Berkeley: University of California Press, 1990.

Embree, Ainslie Thomas, and Mark Juergensmeyer. *Imagining India: Essays on Indian History*. Delhi and New York: Oxford University Press, 1989.

Embree, Ainslie Thomas, et al., eds. *Sources of Indian Tradition*. Vol. 1: *From the Beginning to 1800*. 2d ed. New York: Columbia University Press, 1988.

Farmer, Steve, Richard Sproat, and Michael Witzel. "The Collapse of the Indus-Script Thesis: The Myth of a Literate Harappan Civilization." *Electronic Journal of Vedic Studies* 11, no. 2 (2004).

Federal Research Division, Library of Congress. Country Studies: *India*. 1998. Available online. URL: http://countrystudies.us/india/. Accessed September 27, 2004.

Fernandes, Leela. *India's New Middle Class: Democratic Politics in an Era of Economic Reform*. Minneapolis: University of Minnesota Press, 2006.

Fischer, Louis. *The Life of Mahatma Gandhi*. New York: Harper Paperback, 1983.

Frank, Katherine. *Indira: The Life of Indira Nehru Gandhi*. Boston: Houghton Mifflin, 2002.

Fraser, Andrew H. L. *Among Indian Rajahs and Ryots: A Civil Servant's Recollections and Impressions of Thirty-Seven Years of Work and Sport in the Central Provinces and Bengal*. 3d ed. London: Seeley, Service and Co., 1912.

Freed, Stanley A., and Ruth S. Freed. *Hindu Festivals in a North Indian Village*. New York: American Museum of Natural History, 1998.

Gandhi, Mohandas K. *An Autobiography: The Story of My Experiments with Truth*. Translated by Mahadev Desai. Boston: Beacon Press, 1957.

———. "Gandhi's Letter to H. S. L. Polak." 1909. The Official Mahatma Gandhi eArchive & Reference Library. Available online. URL: http://www.mahatma.org.in/books/showbook.jsp?id=204&link=bg&book=bg0005&lang=en&cat=books&image.x=11&image.y=9. Accessed January 10, 2005.

———. *Indian Home Rule [or Hind Swaraj]* 1910. The Official Mahatma Gandhi eArchive & Reference Library. Available online. URL: http://www.mahatma.org.in/books/showbook.jsp?id=76&link=bg&book=bg0005&lang=en&cat=books. Accessed February 16, 2005.

Gangoly, O. C., ed. *The Humorous Art of Gogonendranath Tagore*. Calcutta: Birla Academy of Art and Culture, 1981.

Geetha, V. "Periyar, Women and an Ethic of Citizenship." In *Economic and Political Weekly* 33, no. 17 (April 25–May 1, 1998): WS9–WS15.

Geetha, V., and S. V. Rajadurai. "Dalits and Non-Brahmin Consciousness in Colonial Tamil Nadu." *Economic and Political Weekly* 28, no. 39 (September 25, 1993): 2,091–2,098.

Gentleman, Amelia. "Indian Prime Minister Denounces Abortion of Females." *New York Times,* 29 April 29 2008.

George, Rosemary Marangoly, ed. *Burning Down the House: Recycling Domesticity.* Boulder, Colo.: Westview Press, 1998.

Gimbutas, Marija. "Review of Archaeology and Language: The Puzzle of Indo-European Origins." *American Historical Review* 95, no. 1 (1990): 125–127.

Gordon, Richard. "The Hindu Mahasabha and the Indian National Congress, 1915 to 1926." *Modern Asian Studies* 9, no. 2 (1975): 145–203.

———. "Non-Cooperation and Council Entry, 1919 to 1920." *Modern Asian Studies* 7, no. 3 (1973): 443–473.

Gordon, Stewart. *The Marathas, 1600–1818.* New York: Cambridge University Press, 2007.

Grewal, J. S. *The Sikhs of the Punjab.* Rev. ed. Cambridge: Cambridge University Press, 1998.

Guha, Ramachandra. *India after Gandhi: The History of the World's Largest Democracy.* New York: HarperCollins, 2007.

Guilmoto, Christophe Z. "Characteristics of Sex-Ratio Imbalance in India, and Future Scenarios." In *4th Asia Pacific Conference on Reproductive and Sexual Health and Rights.* Hyderabad, India: United Nations Population Fund, 2007.

Gupta, Purnacandra. *Bangali Bau* [The Bengali wife]. Calcutta: A. K. Banerji, 1885.

Harper, Edward. "Two Systems of Economic Exchange in Village India." *American Anthropologist* 61 (1958): 760–778.

Hasan, Zoya, ed. *Parties and Party Politics in India.* New Delhi: Oxford University Press, 2002.

Hawley, John Stratton, and Mark Juergensmeyer. *Songs of the Saints of India.* Rev. ed. New York: Oxford University Press, 2004.

Hay, Stephen, ed. *Sources of Indian Tradition.* Vol. 2: *Modern India and Pakistan.* 2d ed. New York: Columbia University Press, 1988.

Heeter, Chad. "Seeds of Suicide: India's Desperate Farmers." *Frontline.* Available online. URL: http://www.pbs.org/frontlineworld/rough/2005/07/seeds_of_suicide.html. Accessed February 1, 2010.

Hitchcock, Amanda. "Rising Number of Dowry Deaths in India." World Socialist Web Site. July 4, 2001. Available online. URL: http://www.

wsws.org/articles/2001/jul2001/ind-j04.shtml. Accessed October 9, 2004.

Howe, Irving, ed. *The Portable Kipling*. New York: Penguin Books, 1982.

Human Rights Watch. *Politics by Other Means: Attacks against Christians in India*. October 1999. Available online. URL: http://www.hrw.org/reports/1999/indiachr/. Accessed September 26, 2004.

IANS. "Slum Dwellers in Patna Burn Effigies of 'Slumdog Millionaire' Director." *Indo-Asian News Service (IANS)*, February 22, 2009.

"India's BJP Eyes Up Poorer Voters." BBC News. June 23, 2004. Available online. URL: http://news.bbc.co.uk/1/hi/world/south_asia/3831719.stm. Accessed February 28, 2005.

INSA. "Agriculture." In *Pursuit and Promotion of Science—The Indian Experience*. Indian National Science Academy (INSA). Available online. URL: http://www.iisc.ernet.in/INSA/ch21.pdf. Accessed April 5, 2005.

Irschick, Eugene F. *Dialogue and History: Constructing South India, 1795–1895*. Berkeley: University of California Press, 1994.

Institute of Science in Society. *Farmer Suicides and Bt Cotton Nightmare Unfolding in India*. London: The Institute of Science in Society, 2010. Available online. URL: http://www.i-sis.org.uk/farmersSuicidesBtCotton India.php. Accessed June 1, 2010.

Jackson, Peter. *The Mongols and the West, 1221–1410*. In *The Medieval World*. Harlow, UK, and New York: Pearson Longman, 2005.

Jackson, Peter A. *The Delhi Sultanate: A Political and Military History*. Cambridge Studies in Islamic Civilization. Cambridge: Cambridge University Press, 1999.

Jaffrelot, Christophe. *Dr. Ambedkar and Untouchability: Fighting the Indian Caste System*. New York: Columbia University Press, 2005.

———. *The Hindu Nationalist Movement in India*. New York: Columbia University Press, 1996.

———. *India's Silent Revolution: The Rise of the Lower Castes in North India*. New York: Columbia University Press, 2003.

———. "The Strategy Pays Off." *Tehelka* 26 May 2007. Available online. URL: http:www.tehekla./story_main30.asp?filename=Ne260507The_strategy_CS.asp. Accessed January 27, 2010.

Jaffrelot, Christophe, and Peter van der Veer, eds. *Patterns of Middle Class Consumption in India and China*. New Delhi: Sage, 2008.

Jaffrelot, Christophe, and Gilles Verniers. "India's 2009 Elections: The Resilience of Regionalism and Ethnicity." *SAMAJ: South Asia Multidisciplinary Academic Journal* 3 (2009). Contests in Context: Indian Elections 2009. Available online. URL: http://samaj.revues.org/index2787.html. Accessed January 11, 2009.

Jalal, Ayesha. *The Sole Spokesman: Jinnah, the Muslim League and the Demand for Pakistan.* Cambridge: Cambridge University Press, 1985.

Jamison, Stephanie W. *Sacrificed Wife/Sacrificer's Wife: Women, Ritual, and Hospitality in Ancient India.* New York: Oxford University Press, 1996.

Jamison, Stephanie W., and Michael Witzel. "Vedic Hinduism." In *The Study of Hinduism,* edited by Arvind Sharma, 65–113. Columbia: University of South Carolina Press, 2003.

Jayakar, Pupul. *Indira Gandhi: An Intimate Biography.* New York: Pantheon Books, 1993.

Jones, Kenneth W. *Socio-Religious Reform Movements in British India. The New Cambridge History of India,* vol. 1, pt. 3. New York: Cambridge University Press, 1989.

Kalahana. *Rajatarangini.* Translated by R. Shamastry. Westminster, UK: A. Constable & Co., 1956.

Kalidasa. "Shakuntala and the Ring of Recollection." In *Theater of Memory,* edited by Barbara Stoler Miller. New York: Columbia University Press, 1984.

Kangle, R. P., ed. *The Kautiliya Arthasastra. Part II: An English Translation with Critical and Explanatory Notes.* Delhi: Motilal Banarsidas, 1972.

Katzenstin, Mary Fainsod, Uday Singh Mehta, and Usha Thakkar. "The Rebirth of the Shiv Sena: The Symbiosis of Discursive and Organizational Power." In *Parties and Party Politics in India,* edited by Zoya Hasan, 257–286. New Delhi: Oxford University Press, 2002.

Kelkar, Vijay L. "India: On the Growth Turnpike." *2004 Narayanan Oration* 24. Canberra: Australia National University, 2004.

Kennedy, Kenneth A. R. "Review of *Ancient Cities of the Indus Valley Civilization.*" *American Anthropologist* 102, no. 2 (June 2000): 365–366.

Kenoyer, Jonathan Mark. *Ancient Cities of the Indus Valley Civilization.* Karachi: Oxford University Press, 1998.

Kenoyer, Jonathan Mark, and R. H. Meadow. "Fifty-Five Years of Archaeological Research in Pakistan: The Prehistoric Periods." In *Pakistan on the Brink: Politics, Economics, Society,* edited by Craig Baxter, 191–219. Lanham, Md.: Lexington Books, 2004.

Khalidi, Omar. *Indian Muslims since Independence.* New Delhi: Vikas, 1995.

Khan, Omar, and Jim McCall. "Harappa." Available online. URL: www.harappa.com. Accessed February 13, 2010.

Kincaid, Dennis. *British Social Life in India, 1608–1937.* Newton Abbot, UK: Readers Union, 1974.

Kling, Blair B. *Partner in Empire: Dwarkanath Tagore and the Age of Enterprise in Eastern India.* Berkeley: University of California Press, 1976.

Kochanek, Stanley A. "Mrs. Gandhi's Pyramid: The New Congress." In *Parties and Party Politics in India,* edited by Zoya Hasan, 76–106. New Delhi: Oxford University Press, 2002.

Kondo, Hideo. "An Invitation to the Indus Civilization." Available online. URL: http://pubweb.cc.u-tokai.ac.jp/indus/english/index.html. Accessed February 13, 2010.

Kopf, David. *The Brahmo Samaj.* Princeton, N.J.: Princeton University Press, 1979.

Kosambi, D. D. *Ancient India: A History of Its Culture and Civilization.* New Delhi: Pantheon, 1965.

Kumar, Vivek. "BSP and Dalit Aspirations." *Economic and Political Weekly* 39, no. 18 (May 1–7, 2004): 1,778–1,781.

Lal, Ruby. *Domesticity and Power in the Early Mughal World.* New York: Cambridge University Press, 2005.

Law Code of Manu: A New Translation by Patrick Olivelle. Oxford: Oxford University Press, 2004.

Lawler, Andrew. "The Indus Script—Write or Wrong." *Science* 306, no. 17 (December 2004). Available online. URL: www.sciencemag.org. Accessed September 10, 2009.

Laws of Manu. Translated by Georg Buhler. Vol. 25: Sacred Books of the East. Oxford: Clarendon Press, 1886.

Lippman, Thomas W. *Understanding Islam: An Introduction to the Muslim World.* New York: Meridian, 1995.

Lochan, Meeta, and Rajiv Lochan. *Farmers' Suicide: Facts & Possibly Policy Interventions.* Mumbai: Yashwantrao Chavan Academy of Development Administration, 2006. Available online. URL: www.yashada.org/organisation/FarmersSuicideExcerpts.pdf. Accessed January 15, 2009.

Ludden, David E. *Peasant History in South India.* Princeton, N.J.: Princeton University Press, 1985.

Lutgendorf, Philip. "Medieval Devotional Traditions: An Annotated Survey of Recent Scholarship." In *The Study of Hinduism,* edited by Arvind Sharma, 200–260. Columbia: University of South Carolina Press, 2003.

———. "Sholay." Philip's Fil-Ums: Notes on Indian Popular Cinema. 2002. Available from http://www.uiowa.edu/~incinema/. Accessed October 5, 2004.

Macaulay, Thomas Babington. "Macaulay's Minute on Education, February 2, 1835." Project South Asia. Available online. URL: http://www.mssu.edu/projectsouthasia/history/primarydocs/education/Macaulay001.htm. Accessed March 30, 2004.

MacInnes, Paul. "How 'Slumdog Millionaire' Is Changing Film-Making in India." *The Guardian,* 4 June 2009.

Macnicol, Nicol, ed. *Hindu Scriptures.* New York: E. P. Dutton, 1963.

Magnier, Mark. "Indians Don't Feel Good About 'Slumdog Millionaire.'" *Los Angeles Times,* 24 January 2009.

Malhotra, Anshu. *Gender, Caste, and Religious Identities: Restructuring Class in Colonial Punjab.* Delhi: Oxford University Press, 2002.

Malhotra, Inder. *Indira Gandhi: A Personal and Political Biography.* Boston: Northeastern University Press, 1989.

Mankekar, Purnima. *Screening Culture, Viewing Politics: An Ethnography of Television, Womanhood, and Nation in Postcolonial India.* Durham, N.C.: Duke University Press, 1999.

Manor, James. "Parties and the Party System." In *Parties and Party Politics in India,* edited by Zoya Hasan, 431–474. New Delhi: Oxford University Press, 2002.

Manuel, Peter. *Cassette Culture: Popular Music and Technology in North India.* Chicago: University of Chicago Press, 1993.

Marriot, McKim, ed. *Village India: Studies in the Little Community.* Chicago: University of Chicago Press, 1955.

Masson, Charles. *Narrative of Various Journeys in Balochistan, Afghanistan, and the Panjab.* 4 vols. Karachi: Oxford University Press, 1974.

McCrindle, John W. *Ancient India as Described by Megasthenes and Arrian.* New Delhi: Munshiram Manoharlal, 2000.

McCully, Bruce. *English Education and the Origins of Indian Nationalism.* New York: Columbia University Press, 1940.

McKenzie, David, and Isha Ray. "Urban Water Supply in India: Status, Reform Options and Possible Lessons." *Water Policy* 11, no. 4 (2009). Available online. URL: http://www.iwaponline.com/wp/01104/wp011040 42.htm. Accessed June 1, 2010.

McKinsey Global Institute. *The 'Bird of Gold': The Rise of India's Consumer Market:* McKinsey Global Institute, 2007. Available online. URL: MGI_india_birdofgold2008.pdf(SECURED). Accessed February 10, 2010.

Menon, Parvathi. "'Dowry Deaths' in Bangalore." *Frontline* 16, no. 17 (August 14–27, 1999). Available online. URL: http://www.flonnet.com/fl1617/16170640.htm. Accessed July 26, 2010.

Metcalf, Barbara Daly, and Thomas R. Metcalf. *A Concise History of Modern India.* 2d ed. Cambridge Concise Histories. New York: Cambridge University Press, 2006.

Miller, Heidi J. "India, an Archaeological History: Palaeolithic Beginnings to Early Historic Foundations (Review)." *Asian Perspectives* 42, no. 2 (Fall 2003): 380–383.

Mishra, Vijay. *Bollywood Cinema: Temples of Desire.* New York: Routledge, 2002.

Mitter, Partha. *Art and Nationalism in Colonial India 1850–1920: Occidental Orientations.* Cambridge and New York: Cambridge University Press, 1994.

Mohanty, B. B. "'We Are Like the Living Dead': Farmer Suicides in Maharashtra, Western India." *The Journal of Peasant Studies* 32, no. 2 (April 2005): 243–276.

Mohanty, B. B., and Sangeeta Shroff. "Farmers' Suicides in Maharashtra." *Economic and Political Weekly* 39, no. 52 (December 25–31, 2004): 5,599–5,606.

Mozumder, Sudip, and Merrell Tuck. "New Data Show 1.4 Billion Live on Less Than \$1.25 a Day, but Progress against Poverty Remains Strong." Available online. URL: http://go.worldbank.org/DQKD6WV4TO. Accessed February 1, 2010.

Muir, Ramsay. *The Making of British India, 1756–1858, Described in a Series of Dispatches, Treaties, Statutes, and Other Documents.* Lahore: Oxford University Press, 1969.

Nanda, B. R. *The Nehrus: Motilal and Jawaharlal.* Chicago: University of Chicago Press, 1962.

NCAER (National Council of Applied Economic Research). *The Great Indian Market: Results from NCAER's Market Information Survey of Households.* New Delhi: 2005.

Noorani, A. G., ed. *The Muslims of India: A Documentary Record.* New Delhi: Oxford University Press, 2003.

O'Flaherty, Wendy, ed. *Hindu Myths.* London: Penguin, 1975.

———. *Textual Sources for the Study of Hinduism.* Chicago: University of Chicago Press, 1988.

O'Hanlon, Rosalind. *Caste, Conflict, and Ideology: Mahatma Jotirao Phule and Low Caste Protest in Nineteenth-Century Western India.* Cambridge: Cambridge University Press, 1985.

Olivelle, Patrick, trans. *Upanisads.* New York: Oxford University Press, 1996.

Pandey, Gyanendra. *Remembering Partition: Violence, Nationalism and History in India.* Cambridge: Cambridge University Press, 2001.

Parpola, Asko. "Is the Indus Script Indeed Not a Writing System?" In *Airavati: Felicitation Volume in Honour of Iravatham Mahadevan,* edited by Varalaaru.com, 111–131. Chennai: varalaaru.com, 2008.

————. "Study of the Indus Script." *International Conference of Eastern Studies* (2005 and after). Available online. URL: http://www.harappa.com/script/indusscript.pdf. Accessed June 1, 2010.

Patil, Pratibha DeviSingh. President of India. *Speech to Parliament,* 2009.

Patwardhan, R. P., ed. *Dadabhai Naoroji Correspondence.* Vol. 2, Part 1: *Correspondence with D. E. Wacha 4-11-1884 to 23-3-1895.* Bombay: Allied Publishers, 1977.

Peterson, Indira Viswanathan. "Sramanas against the Tamil Way: Jains as Others in Tamil Saiva Literature." In *Open Boundaries: Jain Communities and Cultures in Indian History,* edited by John E. Cort, 163–187. Albany: State University of New York Press, 1998.

Planning Commission of India. "Percentage and Number of Poor in India (73–74 to 04–05)." (2010). Available online. URL: http://planning commission.nic.in/data/misdch.html. Accessed February 10, 2010.

Possehl, Gregory L. *The Indus Civilization: A Contemporary Perspective.* Walnut Creek, Calif.: AltaMira, 2002.

Prentiss, Karen Pechilis. *The Embodiment of Bhakti.* New York: Oxford University Press, 1999.

Presentation on Religion Data: Census of India 2001. Office of the Registrar General. September 6, 2004. Available online. URL: http:// www.census india.net/religiondata/presentation_on_religion.pdf. Accessed April 6, 2005.

Press Trust of India. "World Bank Sees NREGS as a Barrier to Economic Development." *Business Standard,* 16 March 2009. Available online. URL: http://www.business-standard.com/india/storypage.php?autono =351922. Accessed January 31, 2010.

Provisional Population Totals: Census of India 2001. Office of the Registrar General, India. April 18, 2001. Available online. URL: http://www.census india.net/results/webed.html. Accessed January 11, 2005.

"Punjab University College Calendar and Examination Papers." Punjab: Punjab University, 1874–75.

Rajan, V. G. Julie. "Will India's Ban on Prenatal Sex Determination Slow Abortion of Girls?" 2003. Hindu Women's Universe. Available online. URL: http://www.hinduwomen.org/issues/infanticide.htm. Accessed October 9, 2004.

Rajaram, N. S. "Aryan Invasion." 1995. Available online. URL: http://www.hindunet.org/alt_hindu_home/1995_July_2/msg00086.html. Accessed October 27, 2003.

Ramakumar, R. "The Unsettled Debate on Indian Poverty." *Hindu,* 2 January 2010. Available online. URL: http://www.thehindu.com/2010/01/02/stories/2010010252981000.htm. Accessed February 5, 2010.

Ramusack, Barbara N., ed. *The Indian Princes and Their States*. Cambridge: Cambridge University Press, 2004.

Ranade, Ramabai. *Ranade, His Wife's Reminiscences*. Translated by Kusumavati Deshpande. Delhi: Ministry of Information and Broadcasting, 1963.

Rao, P. N., Nisha Yadav, et al. "Entropic Evidence for Linguistic Structure in the Indus Script." *Science* 324 (May 2009). Available online. URL: http://www.sciencemag.org. Accessed September 6, 2009.

Ratnagar, Shereen. "The Bronze Age: Unique Instance of a Pre-Industrial World System?" *Current Anthropology* 42, no. 3 (2001): 351–379.

———. *Trading Encounters: From the Euphrates to the Indus in the Bronze Age*. New Delhi: Oxford University Press, 2004.

Rawat, Basant. "Minority Hole in Gujarat Police Force." Available online. URL: http://www.telegraphindia.com/archives/archive.html. Accessed September 26, 2004.

Raychaudhuri, Tapan, and Irfan Habib. *The Cambridge Economic History of India*. Cambridge and New York: Cambridge University Press, 1981.

Reichel, Clemens. "Clay Sealings and Tablets from Tell Asmar: An Ancient Mesopotamian Palace Reinvestigated." Oriental Institute—The University of Chicago. 1998. Available online. URL: http://oi.uchicago.edu/OI/PROJ/DIY/NN_FAL98/NN_Fal98.html. Accessed October 27, 2003.

Reserve Bank of India. "Table 233: Select Macroeconomic Aggregates—Growth Rate and Investment Rate (at Constant Prices)." In *Handbook of Statistics on Indian Economy 2008–09 (2009)*. Available online. URL: http://www.rbi.org.in/scripts/AnnualPublications.aspx?head=Handbook%20of%20Statistics%20on%20Indian%20Economy. Accessed February 1, 2010.

Rgveda Samhita with the Commentary of Sayanacharya. Vol. 2. Poona: Vaidika Samshodhana Mandala, 1936.

Richards, John F. *Kingship and Authority in South Asia*. Delhi and New York: Oxford University Press, 1998.

———. *The Mughal Empire*. Cambridge: Cambridge University Press, 1993.

Rig Veda. Translated by Wendy Doniger O'Flaherty. London: Penguin Books, 1981.

Roberts, Earl. *Forty-One Years in India: From Subaltern to Commander-in-Chief*. 34th ed. London: Macmillan, 1905.

Rushdie, Salman. "Religion, as Ever, Is the Poison in India's Blood." *Guardian Unlimited*. 9 March 2002. Available online. URL: http://

books.guardian.co.uk/departments/politicsphilosophyandsociety/ story/0,6000,664342,00.html. Accessed January 4, 2005.

Said, Edward W. *Orientalism.* New York: Pantheon Books, 1978.

Sainath, P. "The Largest Wave of Suicides in History." *Counterpunch,* 12 February 2009. Available online. URL: http://www.counterpunch.org/ sainath02122009.html. Accessed January 14, 2010.

Sangari, Kumkum, and Uma Chakravarti, eds. *From Myths to Markets: Essays on Gender.* New Delhi: Manohar, 2001.

Sanghavi, Prachi, Kavi Bhalla, and Veena Das. "Fire-Related Deaths in India in 2001: A Retrospective Analysis of Data." *Lancet* 373, no. 967 (2009). Available online. URL: http://www.thelancet.com/journals/ lancet/article/PIIS0140-6736%2809%2960235-X/fulltext#article_ upsell. Accessed January 26, 2010.

Sarkar, Sumit. *Beyond Nationalist Frames: Postmodernism, Hindu Fundamentalism, History.* Bloomington: Indiana University Press, 2002.

———. *Modern India, 1885–1947.* Madras: Macmillan India, 1983.

———. *Writing Social History.* Delhi and New York: Oxford University Press, 1997.

Savarkar, V. D. *Hindutva.* New Delhi: Hindi Sahitya Sadan, 2005.

Schmidt, Karl J. *An Atlas and Survey of South Asian History.* London: M. E. Sharpe, 1995.

Schwartzberg, Joseph E., et al., eds. *A Historical Atlas of South Asia.* Chicago: University of Chicago, 1978.

Sen, Amartya. "Many Faces of Gender Inequality." *Frontline* 18, no. 22 (October 27–November 9, 2001). Available online. URL: http://www. flonnet.com/fl1822/18220040.htm. Accessed June 1, 2005.

Sengupta, Somini. "Dossier Gives Details of Mumbai Attacks." *New York Times,* 7 January 2009.

Sharma, Arvind, ed. *The Study of Hinduism.* Columbia: University of South Carolina Press, 2003.

Sheth, D. L. *Caste, Ethnicity and Exclusion in South Asia: The Role of Affirmative Action Policies in Building Inclusive Societies.* United Nations Development Programme, Human Development Report Office. 2004. Available online. URL: http://hdr.undp.org/docs/publications/back ground_papers/2004/HDR2004_DL_Sheth.pdf. Accessed September 29, 2004.

———. "Secularisation of Caste and Making of New Middle Class." *Economic and Political Weekly* 34 (August 21–28, 1999). Available online. URL: http://jan.ucc.nau.edu/~sj6/epwshethmclass1.htm#hdg2. Accessed February 1, 2010.

Sheth, Shirish, Prabhat Jha, et al. "Low Male-to-Female Sex Ratio of Children Born in India: National Survey of 1–1 Million Households." *Lancet* 367, no. 9,506 (2006): 185–186, 211–218.

Shiva, Vandana. "India: Soft Drinks, Hard Cases." *Le Monde diplomatique* (English edition), 14 March 2005. Accessed January 16, 2010.

Shukla, Sonal. "Cultivating Minds: 19th Century Gujarati Women's Journals." *Economic and Political Weekly,* 26 October 1991, pp. 63–66.

Singh, Madhur. "'Slumdog Millionaire,' an Oscar Favorite, Is No Hit in India." Time.com (2009). Available online. URL: www.time.com/time/arts/article/0,8599,1873926,00.html. Accessed January 26, 2009.

Sinha, Mrinalini. "Britishness, Clubbability, and the Colonial Public Sphere: The Genealogy of an Imperial Institution in Colonial India." *Journal of British Studies* 40, no. 4 (2001): 489–521.

Sippy, Ramesh. *Sholay* [Flames]. India: 199 minutes, 1975. Motion picture.

Smith, Vincent A. *The Oxford History of India.* 3d ed. Oxford: Clarendon Press, 1958.

Spear, Percival. *The Nabobs: A Study of the Social Life of the English in Eighteenth Century India.* London: Oxford University Press, 1963.

Sridharan, E. "The Growth and Sectoral Composition of India's Middle Class: Its Impact on the Politics of Economic Liberalization." *India Review* 3, no. 4 (October, 2004): 405–428.

Stark, Herbert. *India under Company and Crown.* 4th ed. Calcutta: Macmillan, 1921.

"Statistical Reports of Lok Sabha Elections." *Election Results—Full Statistical Reports* (1952 to 2009). Available online. URL: http://eci.nic.in/eci_main/StatisticalReports/ElectionStatistics.asp. Accessed January 12, 2009.

Steel, F. A., and G. Gardiner. *The Complete Indian Housekeeper and Cook; Giving the Duties of Mistress and Servants, the General Management of the House and Practical Recipes for Cooking in All Its Branches.* 4th ed. London: W. Heinemann, 1902.

Stein, Burton. *A History of India.* Oxford: Blackwell, 1998.

———. *Peasant State and Society in Medieval South India.* Delhi and New York: Oxford University Press, 1985.

Subbarao, D. *Third Quarter Review of Monetary Policy 2009–10.* Press statement by Dr. D. Subbarao, Governor, 2010.

Sundar, Nandini. "Caste as Census Category: Implications for Sociology." *Current Sociology* 48 (2000): 111–126. Available online. URL: http://csi.sagepub.com/cgi/reprint/48/3/111.pdf. Accessed September 29, 2004.

Tandon, Prakash. *Punjabi Century.* Berkeley: University of California Press, 1968.

Tata Institute of Social Sciences. *Causes of Farmer Suicide in Maharashtra: An Enquiry: Final Report Submitted to the Mumbai High Court.* Mumbai, 2005. Available online. URL: www.tiss.edu/Causes%20 of%20Farmer%20Suicides%20in%20Maharashtra.pdf. Accessed January 24, 2010.

Tendulkar, Suresh. *Report of the Expert Group to Review the Methodology for Estimation of Poverty.* New Delhi: Government of India Planning Commission, 2009.

Tewari, Jyotsna. "Sabarmati to Dandi: Speech at Dabhan." Raj Publications, 1995. Available online. URL: http://www.mkgandhi.org/Civil%20 Disobedience/civil_dis.htm. Accessed August 2, 2004.

Thackston, Wheeler M., ed. *The Baburnama: Memoirs of Babur, Prince and Emperor.* New York: Modern Library, 2002.

Thakur, Himendra. "Are Our Sisters and Daughters for Sale?" IndiaTogether. org. June 1999. Available online. URL: http://www.indiatogether.org/ wehost/nodowri/stats.htm. Accessed October 9, 2004.

Thapar, Romila. *Asoka and the Decline of the Mauryas.* London: Oxford University Press, 1961.

———. *Early India: From the Origins to A.D. 1300.* Berkeley: University of California Press, 2002.

———. "Somanatha and Mahmud." *Frontline* 16, no. 8 (April 10–23, 1999). Available online. URL: http://www.flonnet.com/fl1608/16081210. htm. Accessed July 26, 2005.

Tharoor, Sashi. *Nehru: The Invention of India.* New York: Arcade Publishing, 2003.

Thieme, Paul. "The 'Aryan' Gods of the Mitanni Treaties." *Journal of the American Oriental Society* 80, no. 4 (October–December 1960): 301–317.

Thompson, Edward. *Suttee.* London: George Allen & Unwin, 1928.

Thompson, E. W. *A History of India for High Schools and Colleges.* Madras: Christian Literature Society, 1908.

Tomlinson, B. R. *The Economy of Modern India, 1860–1970.* Cambridge and New York: Cambridge University Press, 1993.

Topinard, Paul. *Éléments d'anthropologie générale.* Paris: A. Delahaya et É. Lecrosnier, 1885.

Trautmann, Thomas R. *Aryans and British India.* New Delhi: Vistaar, 1997.

———. *The Aryan Debate.* Oxford in India Readings. Debates in Indian History and Society. New Delhi: Oxford University Press, 2005.

Trivedi, Lisa N. "Visually Mapping the 'Nation': Swadeshi Politics in Nationalist India, 1920–1930." *Journal of Asian Studies* 62, no. 1 (February 2003): 11–41.

UNICEF Innocenti Research Centre. *Domestic Violence against Women and Girls.* June 1997. Available online. URL: www.unicef-icdc.org/publications/pdf/digest6e.pdf. Accessed October 9, 2004.

United States Geological Survey. "The Himalayas: Two Continents Collide." Available online. URL: http:pubs.usgs.gov/gip/dynamic/himalaya.html. Accessed August 24, 2009.

————. "Understanding Plate Motions." Available online. URL: http://pubs.usgs.gov/publications/text/understanding.html. Accessed October 10, 2003.

Vajpayee, Atal Bihari. "We Need to Rejuvenate Our Democratic Process." *The Rediff Special* 1996. Available online. URL: http://www.rediff.com/news/1998/aug/05atal.htm. Accessed February 2, 2010.

Van Buitenen, J. A. B., and James L. Fitzgerald, eds. *The Mahabharata.* Chicago: University of Chicago Press, 1973–1978.

Van Der Veer, Peter. *Imperial Encounters: Religion and Modernity in India and Britain.* Princeton, N.J.: Princeton University Press, 2001.

Van Wessel, Margit. "Talking about Consumption: How an Indian Middle Class Dissociates from Middle-Class Life." *Cultural Dynamics* 16, no. 1 (2004): 93–116. Available online. URL: http://cdy.sagepub.com/cgi/content/refs/16/1/93. Accessed September 27, 2004.

Varma, Pawan. *The Great Indian Middle Class.* Revised ed. New Delhi: Viking, 2007.

Walsh, Judith E. *Domesticity in Colonial India: What Women Learned When Men Gave Them Advice.* Lanham, Md.: Rowman & Littlefield, 2004.

————. *Growing Up in British India: Indian Autobiographers on Childhood and Education under the Raj.* New York: Holmes & Meier, 1983.

Walters, Jonathan S. "Buddhist History: The Sri Lankan Pali Vamsas and Their Community." In *Querying the Medieval: Texts and the History of Practices in South Asia,* edited by Ronald Inden, Jonathan Walters, and Daud Ali, 99–164. New York: Oxford University Press, 2000.

"Why the Congress Did as Well as It Did." *The Hindu Online* (May 25, 2009). Available online. URL: www.hinduonnet.com/nic/howindiavoted2009/page5.pdf. Accessed May 26, 2009.

Witzel, Michael. "Autochthonous Aryans? The Evidence from Old Indian and Iranian Texts." *Electronic Journal of Vedic Studies* 7, no. 3 (2001): 1–115.

————. "Rama's Realm: Indocentric Rewritings of Early South Asian Archaeology and History." In *Archaeological Fantasies: How Pseudoarchaeology Misrepresents the Past and Misleads the Public,* edited by Garrett G. Fagan, 203–232. New York: Routledge, 2006.

Witzel, Michael, and Steve Farmer. "Horseplay in Harappa: The Indus Valley Decipherment Hoax." *Frontline* (October 13, 2000). Available online. URL: http://www.flonnet.com/fl1720/17200040.htm. Accessed April 26, 2004.

Wolpert, Stanley. *A New History of India.* 2d ed. New York: Oxford University Press, 1982.

———. *A New History of India.* 3d ed. New York: Oxford University Press, 1989.

———. *A New History of India.* 8th ed. New York: Oxford University Press, 2008.

———. *Tilak and Gokhale: Revolution and Reform in the Making of Modern India.* Berkeley and Los Angeles: University of California Press, 1962.

Wright, Theodore. "Muslims in South Asia." In *Encyclopedia of the World's Minorities,* edited by Carl Skutsch, 873–877. New York: Routledge, 2005.

Yada, Yogendra, Sanjay Kumar, and Oliver Heath. "The BJP's New Social Bloc." *Frontline* 16, no. 23 (November 6–19, 1999). Available online. URL: http://www.hinduonnet.com/fline/fl1623/16230310.htm. Accessed February 12, 2010.

Young India. "2004: India's Common Minimum Program." Available online. URL: http://www.yidream.org/2004/cmp.shtml. Accessed February 1, 2010.

Zora, Parwini, and Daniel Woreck. "The BJP's 'India Shining' Campaign: Myth and Reality." *World Socialist Web Site.* May 7, 2004. Available online. URL: http://www.wsws.org/articles/testdir/may2004/ind-m07.shtml. Accessed September 26, 2004.

APPENDIX 4
SUGGESTED READING

Surveys and Anthologies

Bose, Sugata, and Ayesha Jalal. *Modern South Asia*. 2d ed. London and New York: Routledge, 2003.

Brown, Judith M. *Modern India: The Origins of an Asian Democracy*. 2d ed. Oxford and New York: Oxford University Press, 1994.

CIA. "India: The World Factbook." Available online. URL: www.odci. gov/cia/publications/factbook/geos/in.html. Accessed February 12, 2010.

Countrywatch. "India Review 2003." Available online. URL: http:// www.countrywatch.com. Accessed May 1, 2003.

Daniélou, Alain. *A Brief History of India*. Rochester, Vt.: Inner Traditions, 2003.

Embree, Ainslie T., et al., eds. *Sources of Indian Tradition*. Vol. 1: *From the Beginning to 1800*. 2d ed. New York: Columbia University Press, 1988.

Gautier, François. *A New History of India*. New Delhi: Har-Anand Publications, 2008.

Guha, Ramachandra. *India after Gandhi: The History of the World's Largest Democracy*. New York: HarperCollins, 2007.

Guha, Ranajit, ed. *A Subaltern Studies Reader, 1986–1995*. Minneapolis: University of Minnesota Press, 1997.

Hay, Stephen, ed. *Sources of Indian Tradition*. Vol. 2: *Modern India and Pakistan*. 2d ed. New York: Columbia University Press, 1988.

Keay, John. *India, a History*. New York: Grove Press, 2001.

Kulke, Hermann, and Dietmar Rothermund. *A History of India*. 4th ed. New York: Routledge, 2004.

Ludden, David. *India and South Asia*. Oxford: Oneworld Publications, 2002.

McLeod, John. *The History of India*. Westport, Conn.: Greenwood Press, 2002.

Metcalf, Barbara Daly, and Thomas R. Metcalf. *A Concise History of Modern India*. 2d ed. Cambridge Concise Histories. New York: Cambridge University Press, 2006.

Mines, Diane P., and Sarah Lamb. *Everyday Life in South Asia*. Bloomington: Indiana University Press, 2002.

Robb, Peter. *A History of India*. Palgrave Essential Histories. Houndmills, UK: Palgrave, 2002.

Sarkar, Sumit. *Modern India 1885–1947*. Madras: Macmillan India, 1983.

Schmidt, Karl J. *An Atlas and Survey of South Asian History*. London: M. E. Sharpe, 1995.

———. "Project South Asia." South Dakota State University Web-based digital library. 2003. Available online. URL: http://projectsouthasia. sdstate.edu/. Accessed February 13, 2010.

Schwartzberg, Joseph E. *A Historical Atlas of South Asia*. 2d printing with additional material. Oxford: Oxford University Press, 1992. Available online. URL: http://dsal.uchicago.edu/reference/schwartzberg.html. Accessed June 1, 2010.

Smith, Vincent A. *The Oxford History of India*. 3d ed. Edited by Percival Spear. Oxford: Clarendon Press, 1958.

Stein, Burton. *A History of India*. Oxford: Blackwell, 1998.

Thapar, Romila. *A History of India*. Vol. 1. London: Penguin, 1990.

Tharu, Susie, and K. Lalita, eds. *Women Writing in India: 600 B.C. to the Early 20th Century*. 2 vols. New York: Feminist Press, 1991.

Wolpert, Stanley A. *A New History of India*. 8th ed. New York: Oxford University Press, 2008.

Land, Climate, and Prehistory

Allchin, F. R. *The Archaeology of Early Historic South Asia: The Emergence of Cities and States*. Cambridge: Cambridge University Press, 1995.

Bryant, Edwin. *The Quest for the Origins of Vedic Culture: The Indo-Aryan Migration Debate*. Oxford: Oxford University Press, 2001.

Bryant, Edwin, and Laurie L. Patton, eds. *The Indo-Aryan Controversy: Evidence and Inference in Indian History*. New York: Routledge, 2005.

Farmer, Steve, Richard Sproat, and Michael Witzel. "The Collapse of the Indus-Script Thesis: The Myth of a Literate Harappan Civilization." *Electronic Journal of Vedic Studies* 11, no. 2 (2004).

Frawley, David. "The Myth of the Aryan Invasion of India." 2003. Available online. URL: http://www.hindunet.org/hindu_history/ancient/aryan/aryan_frawley.html. Accessed March 1, 2005.

Guha, Sudeshna. "Negotiating Evidence: History, Archaeology and the Indus Civilisation." *Modern Asian Studies* 39, no. 2 (2005): 399–426.

Jamison, Stephanie W., and Michael Witzel. "Vedic Hinduism." In *The Study of Hinduism*, edited by Arvind Sharma. Columbia: University of South Carolina Press, 2003, 65–113.

Kenoyer, Jonathan Mark. *Ancient Cities of the Indus Valley Civilization.* Karachi: Oxford University Press, 1998.

Khan, Omar, and Jim McCall. "Harappa." Available online. URL: www. harappa.com. Accessed February 13, 2010.

Kochhar, Rajesh. *The Vedic People: Their History and Geography.* New Delhi: Orient Longman, 2000.

Kondo, Hideo, "An Invitation to the Indus Civilization." Available online. URL: http://pubweb.cc.u-tokai.ac.jp/indus/english/index. html. Accessed February 13, 2010.

Lal, B. B. "The Homeland of the Indo-European Languages and Culture: Some Thoughts." (2002). Available online. URL: http://www.geocities. com/ifihhome/articles/bbl001.html. Accessed January 2002.

Lawler, Andrew. "The Indus Script—Write or Wrong." *Science* 306, no. 17 (December 2004). Available online. URL: www.sciencemag.org. Accessed September 10, 2009.

Parpola, Asko. "Study of the Indus Script." *International Conference of Eastern Studies* (2005 and after). Available online. URL: http://www. harappa.com/script/indusscript.pdf. Accessed June 1, 2010.

Possehl, Gregory L. *The Indus Civilization: A Contemporary Perspective.* Walnut Creek, Calif.: AltaMira, 2002.

Ratnagar, Shereen. *Trading Encounters: From the Euphrates to the Indus in the Bronze Age.* New Delhi: Oxford University Press, 2004.

Schmidt, Karl J. *An Atlas and Survey of South Asian History.* London: M. E. Sharpe, 1995.

Schwartzberg, Joseph E. *A Historical Atlas of South Asia.* 2d printing with additional material. New York and Oxford: Oxford University Press, 1992. Available online. URL: http://dsal.uchicago.edu/reference/ schwartzberg. Accessed June 1, 2010.

Thapar, Romila. *Early India: From the Origins to A.D. 1300.* Berkeley: University of California Press, 2002.

Trautmann, Thomas R. *The Aryan Debate.* Oxford in India Readings. Debates in Indian History and Society. New Delhi: Oxford University Press, 2005.

United States Geological Survey. "The Himalayas: Two Continents Collide." Available online. URL: http://pubs.usgs.gov/publications/ text/himalaya.html. Accessed August 24, 2009.

Witzel, Michael. "Autochthonous Aryans? The Evidence from Old Indian and Iranian Texts." *Electronic Journal of Vedic Studies* 7, no. 3 (2001): 1–115.

———. "Rama's Realm: Indocentric Rewritings of Early South Asian Archaeology and History." In *Archaeological Fantasies: How Pseudoarchaeology Misrepresents the Past and Misleads the Public,* edited by Garrett G. Fagan, 203–232. New York: Routledge, 2006.

Witzel, Michael, and Steve Farmer. "Horseplay in Harappa: The Indus Valley Decipherment Hoax." *Frontline* 17, no. 20 (September 30–October 13, 2000). Available online. URL: http://www.flonnet.com/fl1720/17200040.htm. Accessed October 13, 2009.

Caste, Kings, and the Hindu World Order

Ashoka. "Ashokan Rock and Pillar Edicts." *Project South Asia.* Available online. URL: http://projectsouthasia.sdstate.edu/Docs/index.htm. Accessed February 13, 2010.

Auboyer, Jeannine. *Daily Life in Ancient India: From 200 B.C. to 700 A.D.* London: Phoenix, 2002.

Basham, A. L. *The Wonder That Was India.* London: Sidgwick & Jackson, 1963.

The Bhagavad Gita: Krishna's Counsel in Time of War. Translated by Barbara Stoler Miller. New York: Bantam Books, 1991.

The Bhagavad Gita: A New Translation. Translated by George Thompson. New York: North Point Press, 2008.

Cort, John. *Open Boundaries: Jain Communities and Culture in Indian History.* SUNY Series in Hindu Studies. Albany: State University of New York Press, 1998.

Cousins, Lance S. "The Dating of the Historical Buddha: A Review Article." *Journal of the Royal Asiatic Society of Great Britain and Ireland* 3, no. 6 (1996). Available online. URL: http://indology.info/papers/cousins/. Accessed September 20, 2009.

De Bary, Wm. Theodore. *Buddhist Tradition: In India, China and Japan.* New York: Vintage Books, 1990.

Dundas, Paul. *The Jains.* London: Routledge, 2002.

Embree, Ainslie T. *The Hindu Tradition.* New York: Random House, 1972.

Jamison, Stephanie W., and Michael Witzel. "Vedic Hinduism." In *The Study of Hinduism,* edited by Arvind Sharma, 65–113. Columbia: University of South Carolina Press, 2003.

Kalidasa. "Shakuntala and the Ring of Recollection." In *Theater of Memory*, edited by Barbara Stoler Miller. New York: Columbia University Press, 1984.

Law Code of Manu: A New Translation by Patrick Olivelle. Oxford: Oxford University Press, 2004.

Laws of Manu. Translated by Wendy Doniger and Brian K. Smith. London: Penguin, 1991.

O'Flaherty, Wendy, ed. *Hindu Myths*. London: Penguin, 1975.

O'Flaherty, Wendy Doniger, ed. *Textual Sources for the Study of Hinduism*. Chicago: University of Chicago Press, 1988.

Olson, Carl. *The Different Paths of Buddhism*. New Brunswick, N.J.: Rutgers University Press, 2005.

Ramanujan, A. K. *Folktales from India: A Selection of Oral Tales from Twenty-two Languages*. New York: Pantheon Books, 1991.

Richman, Paula, ed. *Many Ramayanas: The Diversity of a Narrative Tradition in South Asia*. Berkeley: University of California Press, 1991.

Rig Veda. Translated by Wendy Doniger O'Flaherty. London: Penguin Books, 1981.

Thapar, Romila. *Early India: From the Origins to A.D. 1300*. Berkeley: University of California Press, 2002.

Upanishads. Translated by Patrick Olivelle. New York: Oxford University Press, 1996.

Van Buitenen, J. A. B., and James L. Fitzgerald, eds. 1973–1978. *The Mahabharata*. 4 vols. Chicago: University of Chicago Press.

Zimmer, Heinrich Robert, and Joseph Campbell. *Myths and Symbols in Indian Art and Civilization*. Princeton, N.J.: Princeton University Press, 1972.

Turks, Afghans, and Mughals

Alam, Muzaffar, and Sanjay Subrahmanyam. *The Mughal State, 1526–1750*. Delhi and New York: Oxford University Press, 1998.

Alberuni, Muhammad Ibn Ahmad. *Alberuni's India*. Abridged ed. Edited by Ainslie T. Embree. New York: Norton, 1971.

Asher, Catherine Ella Blanshard. *Architecture of Mughal India. The New Cambridge History of India*, vol. 1, pt. 4. Cambridge and New York: Cambridge University Press, 1992.

Bayly, Susan. *Caste, Society and Politics in India from the Eighteenth Century to the Modern Age*. Cambridge: Cambridge University Press, 1999.

Dalrymple, William. *White Mughals: Love and Betrayal in Eighteenth-Century India*. London: HarperCollins, 2002.

Das Gupta, Ashin, and Uma Dasgupta. *The World of the Indian Ocean Merchant, 1500–1800: Collected Essays of Ashin Das Gupta*. New Delhi and New York: Oxford University Press, 2001.

Dunn, Ross E. *The Adventures of Ibn Battuta, a Muslim Traveler of the Fourteenth Century*. London: Croom Helm, 1986.

Eaton, Richard M. *Essays on Islam and Indian History*. New Delhi: Oxford University Press, 2000.

————. *The Rise of Islam and the Bengal Frontier, 1204–1760*. New Delhi: Oxford University Press, 1993.

————. "Temple Desecration and Indo-Muslim States." *Journal of Islamic Studies* 11, no. 3 (2000): 283–319.

Gordon, Stewart. *The Marathas 1600–1818*. New York: Cambridge University Press, 2007.

Grewal, J. S. *The Sikhs of the Punjab*. Rev. ed. Cambridge and New York: Cambridge University Press, 1998.

Hardy, Peter. *Historians of Medieval India*. New Delhi: Munshiram Manoharlal, 1997.

Hawley, John Stratton, and Mark Juergensmeyer. *Songs of the Saints of India*. Rev. ed. New York: Oxford University Press, 2004.

Jackson, Peter A. *The Delhi Sultanate: A Political and Military History*. Cambridge and New York: Cambridge University Press, 1999.

Lal, Ruby. *Domesticity and Power in the Early Mughal World*. New York: Cambridge University Press, 2005.

Lippman, Thomas W. *Understanding Islam: An Introduction to the Muslim World*. New York: Meridian, 1995.

Peterson, Indira Viswanathan. "Sramanas against the Tamil Way: Jains as Others in Tamil Saiva Literature." In *Open Boundaries: Jain Communities and Cultures in Indian History*, edited by John E. Cort, 163–187. Albany: State University of New York Press, 1998.

Pinch, William R. *Warrior Ascetics and Indian Empires*. Cambridge Studies in Indian History and Society. New York: Cambridge University Press, 2006.

Richards, John F. *The Mughal Empire*. Cambridge: Cambridge University Press, 1993.

Spear, Percival. *The Nabobs: A Study of the Social Life of the English in Eighteenth Century India*. London: Oxford University Press, 1963.

Subrahmanyam, Sanjay, ed. *Money and the Market in India, 1100–1700*. Delhi and New York: Oxford University Press, 1994.

Thackston, Wheeler M., ed. *The Baburnama: Memoirs of Babur, Prince and Emperor.* New York: Modern Library, 2002.

Thapar, Romila. "Somanatha and Mahmud." *Frontline* 16, no. 8 (1999). Available online. URL: http://www.flonnet.com/fl1608/16081210.htm. Accessed January 23, 2004.

The Jewel in the Crown

Allen, Charles, and Michael Mason. *Plain Tales from the Raj: Images of British India in the Twentieth Century.* London: Macdonald Futura, 1976.

Bayly, C. A. *Indian Society and the Making of the British Empire.* Cambridge: Cambridge University Press, 1988.

———. *Rulers, Townsmen and Bazaars: North Indian Society in the Age of British Expansion, 1770–1870.* Delhi and Oxford: Oxford University Press, 1992.

Bayly, Susan. *Caste, Society and Politics in India from the Eighteenth Century to the Modern Age.* Vol. 4. The New Cambridge History of India, edited by Gordon Johnson. Cambridge: Cambridge University Press, 1999.

Burton, Antoinette. *Burdens of History: British Feminists, Indian Women, and Imperial Culture, 1865–1915.* Chapel Hill: University of North Carolina Press, 1994.

Cohn, Bernard. *Colonialism and Its Forms of Knowledge: The British in India.* Princeton, N.J.: Princeton University Press, 1996.

Dalrymple, William. *The Last Mughal: The Fall of a Dynasty: Delhi, 1857.* New York: Vintage Books, 2008.

———. *White Mughals: Love and Betrayal in Eighteenth-Century India.* Hammersmith and London: HarperCollins, 2002.

Dirks, Nicholas B. "Castes of Mind." *Representations* 37 (Winter 1992): 56–78.

———. *Castes of Mind: Colonialism and the Making of Modern India.* N.J.: Princeton: Princeton University Press, 2001.

Edney, Matthew H. *Mapping an Empire: The Geographical Construction of British India, 1765–1843.* Chicago: University of Chicago Press, 1997.

Embree, Ainslie T., ed. *1857 in India: Mutiny or War of Independence?* Boston: D. C. Heath, 1963.

Howe, Irving, ed. *The Portable Kipling.* New York: Penguin Books, 1982.

Kincaid, Dennis. *British Social Life in India, 1608–1937.* Newton Abbot, UK: Readers Union, 1974.

Kopf, David. *British Orientalism and the Bengal Renaissance; The Dynamics of Indian Modernization, 1773–1835*. Berkeley: University of California Press, 1969.

Macaulay, Thomas Babington, "Macaulay's Minute on Education, February 2, 1835." Project South Asia. Available online. URL: http://projectsouthasia.sdstate.edu/Docs/history/primarydocs/education/Macaulay001.htm. Accessed February 13, 2010.

Metcalf, Thomas R. *Ideologies of the Raj*. Cambridge and New York: Cambridge University Press, 1994.

Mukherjee, Rudrangshu. *Awadh in Revolt, 1857–1858: A Study of Popular Resistance*. 2d ed. London: Anthem, 2002.

———. "Satan Let Loose upon Earth: The Kanpur Massacres in India in the Revolt of 1857." *Past & Present*, no. 128 (August 1990): 92–116.

Said, Edward W. *Orientalism*. New York: Pantheon Books, 1978.

Spear, Percival. *The Nabobs: A Study of the Social Life of the English in Eighteenth Century India*. London: Oxford University Press, 1963.

Stokes, Eric. *The English Utilitarians and India*. Delhi and New York: Oxford University Press, 1989.

Tomlinson, B. R. *The Economy of Modern India, 1860–1970*. Cambridge and New York: Cambridge University Press, 1993.

Trautmann, Thomas R. *Aryans and British India*. New Delhi: Vistaar, 1997.

Worswick, Clark, and Ainslie Thomas Embree. *The Last Empire: Photography in British India, 1855–1911*. New York and London: Aperture, Robert Hale, 2001.

Becoming Modern—the Colonial Way

Bayly, Susan. *Caste, Society and Politics in India from the Eighteenth Century to the Modern Age. The New Cambridge History of India*, vol. 4. Cambridge: Cambridge University Press, 1999.

Borthwick, Meredith. *Changing Role of Women in Bengal 1849–1905*. Princeton, N.J.: Princeton, University Press, 1984.

Burton, Antoinette. *Burdens of History: British Feminists, Indian Women, and Imperial Culture, 1865–1915*. Chapel Hill: University of North Carolina Press, 1994.

Chakrabarty, Dipesh. *Provincializing Europe: Postcolonial Thought and Historical Difference*. Princeton, N.J.: Princeton University Press, 2000.

Chanana, Karuna. "Social Change or Social Reform: The Education of Women in Pre-Independence India." In *Socialisation, Education and Women,* edited by Karuna Chanana, 96–129. New Delhi: Orient Longman, 1988.

Chatterjee, Partha. *Nationalist Thought and the Colonial World.* Minneapolis: University of Minnesota Press, 1986.

Forbes, Geraldine. *Women in Modern India.* Cambridge: Cambridge University Press, 1996.

Hatcher, Brian. *Idioms of Improvement: Vidyasagar and Cultural Encounters in Bengal.* Delhi: Oxford University Press, 1996.

————. "Remembering Rammohan: An Essay on the (Re-)Emergence of Modern Hinduism." *History of Religions* 46, no. 1 (2006): 50–80.

Irschick, Eugene F. *Dialogue and History: Constructing South India, 1795–1895.* Berkeley: University of California Press, 1994.

Jain, Jyotindra. *Kalighat Painting: Images from a Changing World.* Ahmedabad, India: Mapin, 1999.

Jones, Kenneth W. *Socio-Religious Reform Movements in British India. The New Cambridge History of India,* vol. 1, pt. 3. New York: Cambridge University Press, 1989.

Joshi, Sanjay. *Fractured Modernity: Making of a Middle Class in Colonial North India.* Delhi: Oxford University Press, 2001.

Karve, D. D. *The New Brahmans: Five Maharashtrian Families.* Berkeley: University of California Press, 1963.

Kling, Blair B. *Partner in Empire: Dwarkanath Tagore and the Age of Enterprise in Eastern India.* Berkeley: University of California Press, 1976.

Kopf, David. *The Brahmo Samaj.* Princeton, N.J.: Princeton University Press, 1979.

Lelyveld, David. *Aligarh's First Generation: Muslim Solidarity in British India.* Reprint, Delhi: Oxford University Press, 1996.

Malhotra, Anshu. *Gender, Caste, and Religious Identities: Restructuring Class in Colonial Punjab.* Delhi: Oxford University Press, 2002.

McCully, Bruce. *English Education and the Origins of Indian Nationalism.* New York: Columbia University Press, 1940.

Minault, Gail. *Secluded Scholars: Women's Education and Muslim Social Reform in Colonial India.* New Delhi: Oxford University Press, 1998.

Mitter, Partha. *Art and Nationalism in Colonial India 1850–1920: Occidental Orientations.* Cambridge: Cambridge University Press, 1994.

O'Hanlon, Rosalind. *Caste, Conflict, and Ideology: Mahatma Jotirao Phule and Low Caste Protest in Nineteenth-Century Western India.* Cambridge and New York: Cambridge University Press, 1985.

Sangari, Kumkum, and Sudesh Vaid, eds. *Recasting Women*. New Brunswick, N.J.: Rutgers University Press, 1990.

Sarkar, Sumit. "Colonial Times: Clocks and Kali-Yuga." In *Beyond Nationalist Frames: Postmodernism, Hindu Fundamentalism, History*. Bloomington: Indiana University Press, 2002.

Sarkar, Tanika. *Hindu Wife, Hindu Nation*. Bloomington: Indiana University Press, 2001.

Sinha, Mrinalini. *Colonial Masculinity: The "Manly Englishman" and the "Effeminate Bengali" in the Late Nineteenth Century*. New Delhi: Kali for Women, 1997.

Walsh, Judith E. *Domesticity in Colonial India: What Women Learned When Men Gave Them Advice*. Lanham, Md.: Rowman & Littlefield, 2004.

———. *Growing Up in British India: Indian Autobiographers on Childhood and Education under the Raj*. New York: Holmes & Meier, 1983.

———. *How to Be the Goddess of Your Home: An Anthology of Bengali Domestic Manuals*. Translated by Judith E. Walsh. New Delhi: Yoda Press, 2005.

Toward Freedom

Bose, Subhas Chandra. *An Indian Pilgrim: An Unfinished Autobiography and Collected Letters, 1897–1921*. Calcutta: Asia Publishing House, 1965.

Burton, Antoinette. *Dwelling in the Archive: Women Writing House, Home and History in Late Colonial India*. New York: Oxford University Press, 2003.

Chatterjee, Partha. *Nationalist Thought and the Colonial World*. Minneapolis: University of Minnesota Press, 1986.

Embree, Ainslie Thomas. *India's Search for National Identity*. New York: Alfred A. Knopf, 1972.

Forbes, Geraldine. *Women in Modern India*. Cambridge: Cambridge University Press, 1996.

Freitag, Sandria B. *Collective Action and Community: Public Arenas and the Emergence of Communalism in North India*. Berkeley: University of California Press, 1989.

Guha, Sumit. *Growth, Stagnation or Decline? Agricultural Productivity in British India*. Delhi and New York: Oxford University Press, 1992.

Irschick, Eugene F. *Dialogue and History: Constructing South India, 1795–1895*. Berkeley: University of California Press, 1994.

Jones, Kenneth W. *Socio-Religious Reform Movements in British India*. New Cambridge History of India. New York: Cambridge University Press, 1989.

Minault, Gail. *Secluded Scholars: Women's Education and Muslim Social Reform in Colonial India*. New Delhi: Oxford University Press, 1998.

Mitter, Partha. *Art and Nationalism in Colonial India 1850–1920: Occidental Orientations*. Cambridge and New York: Cambridge University Press, 1994.

Nanda, B. R. *The Nehrus: Motilal and Jawaharlal*. Chicago: University of Chicago Press, 1962.

Prakash, Gyan, ed. *The World of the Rural Labourer in Colonial India*. Delhi and New York: Oxford University Press, 1992.

Ramusack, Barbara N., ed. *The Indian Princes and Their States*. Cambridge: Cambridge University Press, 2004.

Sarkar, Sumit. *The Swadeshi Movement in Bengal, 1903–1908*. Reprint, New Delhi: Peoples Pub. House, 1994.

Wolpert, Stanley. *Tilak and Gokhale: Revolution and Reform in the Making of Modern India*. Berkeley and Los Angeles: University of California Press, 1962.

Gandhi and the Nationalist Movement

Brown, Judith M. *Gandhi and Civil Disobedience: The Mahatma in Indian Politics, 1928–34*. Cambridge: Cambridge University Press, 1977.

———. *Nehru: A Political Life*. New Haven and London: Yale University Press, 2003.

Chatterjee, Partha. *Nationalist Thought and the Colonial World*. Minneapolis: University of Minnesota Press, 1986.

Chaudhuri, Nirad C. *The Autobiography of an Unknown Indian*. Berkeley: University of California Press, 1968.

Copland, Ian. *The Princes of India in the Endgame of Empire, 1917–1947*. Cambridge and New York: Cambridge University Press, 1997.

Dalton, Dennis. *Mahatma Gandhi: Nonviolent Power in Action*. New York: Columbia University Press, 2000.

Erikson, Erik H. *Gandhi's Truth: On the Origins of Militant Nonviolence*. New York: Norton, 1993.

Fischer, Louis, ed. *The Essential Gandhi: An Anthology of His Writings on His Life, Work, and Ideas*. New York: Vintage, 2002.

———. *The Life of Mahatma Gandhi*. New York: Harper Paperback, 1983.

Gandhi, Mohandas K. *An Autobiography: The Story of My Experiments with Truth*. Translated by Mahadev Desai. Boston: Beacon Press, 1957.
————. *The Penguin Gandhi Reader*. Edited by Rudrangshu Mukherjee. New Delhi and New York: Penguin Books, 1993.
Gordon, Leonard A. *Brothers against the Raj: A Biography of Indian Nationalists Sarat and Subhas Chandra Bose*. New York: Columbia University Press, 1990.
Mayo, Katherine. *Mother India*. Edited by Mrinalini Sinha. Reprint, Ann Arbor: University of Michigan Press, 2000.
Nandy, Ashis. *The Intimate Enemy: Loss and Recovery of Self under Colonialism*. New Delhi: Oxford University Press, 1983.
Nehru, Jawaharlal. *The Discovery of India*. New York: John Day, 1946.
Savarkar, V. D. *Hindutva*. New Delhi: Hindi Sahitya Sadan, 2005.

Constructing the Nation

Brass, Paul R. *The Politics of India since Independence*. Cambridge: Cambridge University Press, 1994.
Brown, Judith M. *Nehru: A Political Life*. New Haven, Conn., and London: Yale University Press, 2003.
Butalia, Urvashi. *The Other Side of Silence: Voices from the Partition of India*. Durham, N.C.: Duke University Press, 2000.
Embree, Ainslie T. *Utopias in Conflict: Religion and Nationalism in Modern India*. Berkeley: University of California Press, 1990.
Frank, Katherine. *Indira: The Life of Indira Nehru Gandhi*. Boston: Houghton Mifflin, 2002.
Frankel, Francine R. *India's Political Economy, 1947–1977: The Gradual Revolution*. Princeton, N.J.: Princeton University Press, 1978.
Hasan, Zoya, ed. *Parties and Party Politics in India*. New Delhi: Oxford University Press, 2002.
Jaffrelot, Christophe. *Dr. Ambedkar and Untouchability: Fighting the Indian Caste System*. New York: Columbia University Press, 2005.
————. *The Hindu Nationalist Movement in India*. New York: Columbia University Press, 1996.
Jalal, Ayesha. *The Sole Spokesman: Jinnah, the Muslim League and the Demand for Pakistan*. Cambridge: Cambridge University Press, 1985.
Mahar, J. Michael, ed. *The Untouchables in Contemporary India*. Tucson: University of Arizona Press, 1972.
Malhotra, Inder. *Indira Gandhi: A Personal and Political Biography*. Boston: Northeastern University Press, 1989.

Manor, James. "Parties and the Party System." In *Parties and Party Politics in India,* edited by Zoya Hasan, 431–474. New Delhi: Oxford University Press, 2002.

Menon, Ritu, and Kamla Bhasin. *Borders and Boundaries: Women in India's Partition.* New Brunswick, N.J.: Rutgers University Press, 1998.

Moon, Vasant, and Gail Omvedt. *Growing Up Untouchable in India: A Dalit Autobiography.* Asian Voices. Lanham, Md.: Rowman & Littlefield, 2001.

Noorani, A. G., ed. *The Muslims of India: A Documentary Record.* New Delhi: Oxford University Press, 2003.

Omvedt, Gail. *Buddhism in India: Challenging Brahmanism and Caste.* New Delhi and Thousand Oaks, Calif.: Sage, 2003.

Pandey, Gyanendra. *Remembering Partition: Violence, Nationalism and History in India.* Cambridge: Cambridge University Press, 2001.

Sarkar, Tanika, and Urvashi Butalia, eds. *Women and the Hindu Right.* New Delhi: Kali for Women, 1995.

"Statistical Reports of Lok Sabha Elections." *Election Results—Full Statistical Reports* (1952 to 2009). Available online. URL: http://eci.nic.in/eci_main/StatisticalReports/ElectionStatistics.asp. Accessed January 12, 2009.

Tharoor, Sashi. *Nehru: The Invention of India.* New York: Arcade Publishing, 2003.

Tomlinson, B. R. *The Economy of Modern India, 1860–1970.* Cambridge: Cambridge University Press, 1993.

Varshney, Ashutosh. *Ethnic Conflict and Civic Life: Hindus and Muslims in India.* New Haven, Conn.: Yale University Press, 2002.

Zelliot, Eleanor. *From Untouchable to Dalit: Essays on the Ambedkar Movement.* 2d rev. ed. New Delhi: Manohar, 1996.

Bollywood and Beyond

Census of India. "Provisional Population Totals: Census of India 2001." Office of the Registrar General. Available online. URL: http://censusindia.gov.in/Data_Products/Library/Provisional_Population_Total_link/webed.html. Accessed January 21, 2010.

Chopra, Aditya. *Dilwale Dulhania Le Jayenge* [The lover will carry away the bride]. India: 190 minutes, 1995. Motion picture.

Davis, Richard H. *Lives of Indian Images.* Princeton, N.J.: Princeton University Press, 1997.

Desai, Jigna. *Beyond Bollywood: The Cultural Politics of South Asian Diasporic Film.* New York: Routledge, 2004.

Fernandes, Leela. *India's New Middle Class: Democratic Politics in an Era of Economic Reform*. Minneapolis: University of Minnesota Press, 2006.

Freed, Stanley A., and Ruth S. Freed. *Hindu Festivals in a North Indian Village*. New York: American Museum of Natural History, 1998.

Guilmoto, Christophe Z. "Characteristics of Sex-Ratio Imbalance in India, and Future Scenarios." In *4th Asia Pacific Conference on Reproductive and Sexual Health and Rights*. Hyderabad, India: United Nations Population Fund, 2007.

Kishwar, Madhu. *Off the Beaten Track: Rethinking Gender Justice for Indian Women*. New Delhi: Oxford University Press, 1999.

Laxman, R. K. *Brushing up the Years: A Cartoonist's History of India, 1947–2004*. New Delhi: Penguin Viking, 2005.

Lutgendorf, Philip. *The Life of a Text: Performing the Ramcaritmanas of Tulsidas*. Berkeley: University of California Press, 1991.

———. Philip's Fil-Ums: Notes on Indian Popular Cinema. Available online. URL: http://www.uiowa.edu/~~incinema/. Accessed October 5, 2004.

Mankekar, Purnima. *Screening Culture, Viewing Politics: An Ethnography of Television, Womanhood, and Nation in Postcolonial India*. Durham, N.C.: Duke University Press, 1999.

Manuel, Peter. *Cassette Culture: Popular Music and Technology in North India*. Chicago: University of Chicago Press, 1993.

Mazumdar, Sudip. "Man Bites 'Slumdog.'" *Newsweek*, 21 February 2009.

Mishra, Vijay. *Bollywood Cinema: Temples of Desire*. New York: Routledge, 2002.

Oldenburg, Veena Talwar. *Dowry Murder: The Imperial Origins of a Cultural Crime*. New York: Oxford University Press, 2002.

Sheth, D. L. "Secularisation of Caste and Making of New Middle Class." *Economic and Political Weekly* 34 (August 21–28, 1999). Available online. URL: http://jan.ucc.nau.edu/~sj6/epwshethmclass1.htm#hdg2. Accessed August 21–28, 1999.

Singh, Madhur. "Slumdog Millionaire, an Oscar Favorite, Is No Hit in India." Time.com (2009). Available online. URL: www.time.com/time/arts/article/0,8599,1873926,00.html. Accessed January 26, 2009.

Sippy, Ramesh. *Sholay* [Flames]. India: 199 minutes, 1975. Motion picture.

Sridharan, E. "The Growth and Sectoral Composition of India's Middle Class: Its Impact on the Politics of Economic Liberalization." *India Review* 3, no. 4 (October 2004): 405–428.

Tarlo, Emma. *Clothing Matters: Dress and Identity in India.* Chicago: University of Chicago Press, 1996.

Varma, Pawan. *The Great Indian Middle Class.* Rev. ed. New Delhi: Viking, 2007.

India in the Twenty-first Century

Ahmed, I., and H. Reifeld, eds. *Middle Class Values in India and Western Europe.* New Delhi: Social Science Press, 2001.

Ambasta, Pramathesh. "Programming NREGS to Succeed." *Hindu* 31 October 2009. Available online. URL: http://beta.thehindu.com/opinion/lead/article41154.ece. Accessed February 12, 2010.

Arora, Balveer, and Stephanie Tawa Lama-Rewal. "Introduction: Contextualizing and Interpreting the 15th Lok Sabha Elections." *SAMAJ: South Asia Multidisciplinary Academic Journal* (2009). Available online. URL: http://samaj.revues.org/index1092.html. Accessed June 1, 2010.

Athreya, Venkatesh. "Sonia Effect Checks Bjp Advance." *Frontline* 15, no. 04 (February 21–March 6, 1998). Available online. URL: http://www.hinduonnet.com/fline/fl1504/15040060.htm. Accessed February 12, 2010.

Ayres, Alyssa, and Philip Oldenburg, eds. *India Briefing: Takeoff at Last?* New York: Asia Society and M. E. Sharpe, 2005.

Bose, Ajoy. "Excerpt from *Behenji* [Mayawati]." *Tehelka Magazine* 5, no. 18 (2008). Available online. URL: http://www.tehelka.com/story_main39.asp?filename=Ne100508a_miracle.asp. Accessed January 27, 2010.

CIA. "India: The World Factbook." Available online. URL: www.odci.gov/cia/publications/factbook/geos/in.html. Accessed February 12, 2010.

Cohen, Stephen Philip. *India: Emerging Power.* Washington, D.C.: Brookings Institute Press, 2002.

Countrywatch. "India Review 2003." Available online. URL: http://www.countrywatch.com. Accessed May 1, 2003.

Duraphe, Ashok T. *Final Report/Charge Sheet.* Mumbai: Commissioner of Police, 2009.

Fernandes, Leela. *India's New Middle Class: Democratic Politics in an Era of Economic Reform.* Minneapolis: University of Minnesota Press, 2006.

Guha, Ramachandra. *India after Gandhi: The History of the World's Largest Democracy.* New York: HarperCollins, 2007.

Hasan, Zoya, ed. *Parties and Party Politics in India.* New Delhi: Oxford University Press, 2002.

Heeter, Chad. "Seeds of Suicide: India's Desperate Farmers." Frontline. 2005. Available online. URL: http://www.pbs.org/frontlineworld/rough/2005/07/seeds_of_suicide.html. Accessed February 1, 2010.

Human Rights Watch. "Politics by Other Means: Attacks against Christians in India." 1999. Available online. URL: http://www.hrw.org/reports/1999/indiachr/. Accessed September 26, 2004.

Ilaiah, Kancha. *Why I Am Not a Hindu: A Sudra Critique of Hindutva Philosophy, Culture and Political Economy.* Calcutta: Samya, 1996.

Jaffrelot, Christophe. *India's Silent Revolution: The Rise of the Lower Castes in North India.* New York: Columbia University Press, 2003.

Jaffrelot, Christophe, and Peter van der Veer, eds. *Patterns of Middle Class Consumption in India and China.* New Delhi: Sage, 2008.

Jaffrelot, Christophe, and Gilles Verniers. "India's 2009 Elections: The Resilience of Regionalism and Ethnicity." *SAMAJ: South Asia Multidisciplinary Academic Journal* 3 (2009).

McKinsey Global Institute. *The 'Bird of Gold': The Rise of India's Consumer Market.* McKinsey Global Institute 2007. Available online. URL: MGI_india_birdofgold2008.pdf(SECURED). Accessed February 10, 2010.

Metcalf, Barbara D., ed. *Islam in South Asia: In Practice.* Princeton, N.J.: Princeton University Press, 2009.

Mohanty, B. B. "'We Are Like the Living Dead': Farmer Suicides in Maharashtra, Western India." *Journal of Peasant Studies* 32, no. 2 (April 2005): 243–276.

Planning Commission of India. "Percentage and Number of Poor in India (73–74 to 04–05)." 2010. Available online. URL: http://planningcommission.nic.in/data/misdch.html. Accessed June 1, 2010.

Ramakumar, R. "The Unsettled Debate on Indian Poverty." *Hindu* 2 January 2010. Available online. URL: http://www.thehindu.com/2010/01/02/stories/2010010252981000.htm. Accessed February 5, 2010.

Reserve Bank of India. "Table 233: Select Macroeconomic Aggregates—Growth Rate and Investment Rate (at Constant Prices)." *Handbook of Statistics on Indian Economy 2008–09* (2009). Available online. URL: http://www.rbi.org.in/scripts/AnnualPublications.aspx?head=Handbook%20of%20Statistics%20on%20Indian%20Economy. Accessed February 1, 2010.

Sainath, P. "The Largest Wave of Suicides in History." *Counterpunch* 12 February 2009. Available online. URL: http://www.counterpunch.org/sainath02122009.html. Accessed January 14, 2010.

Sen, Mala. *India's Bandit Queen: The True Story of Phoolan Devi.* London: Hartville, 1991.

Shiva, Vandana. "India: Soft Drinks, Hard Cases." *Le Monde diplomatique* (English edition), 14 March 2005.

Tendulkar, Suresh. *Report of the Expert Group to Review the Methodology for Estimation of Poverty.* New Delhi: Government of India Planning Commission, 2009.

Varma, Pawan. *The Great Indian Middle Class.* Rev. ed. New Delhi: Viking, 2007.

Yada, Yogendra, Sanjay Kumar, and Oliver Heath. "The BJP' New Social Bloc." *Frontline* 16, no. 23 (November 6–19, 1999). Available online. URL: http://www.hinduonnet.com/fline/fl1623/16230310.htm. Accessed February 12, 2010.

INDEX

Note: **Boldface** page numbers indicate primary discussion of a topic. Page numbers in *italic* refer to illustrations. Italicized letters *c* and *m* following page numbers refer to the chronology and maps, respectively.

A BRIEF HISTORY OF INDIA

Sikhism 76, 88, 90, 91, 94, 151, 174
Sikh kingdom 113, **117**, 122–123
Sikhs 182, 209
  after independence 227–228
  effects of "divide and rule"
    on 216
  festivals and holidays 291–292
  I. Gandhi's assassination 249
  government and politics 113,
    209, 211, 214, 219, 236,
    243–244, 291, 311
  partition and 221, 227–228
  population 285
  in the Punjab 251
  riots and 218
Simla 134, 182–183, 184–185
Simon, John 202–203
Sind(h) 17, 54, 70, 80, 83, 91, 101,
  117, 214, 219
Singh, Ajit 254
Singh, Beant 249
Singh, Chaudhuri Charan 175,
  242, 254
Singh, Hari 220
Singh, Kalyan 261
Singh, Manmohan 308, *309,* 326–
  327, *358c*
  on aborting of female fetuses
    285
  economic policies of 258–259,
    314, 327
  farmer suicides 317
  as first non-Hindu prime min-
    ister 311
  poverty programs 331–333
Singh, Ranjit 113, 117
Singh, Satwant 249
Singh, Vishwanath Pratap (V. P.)
  253–257
Sino-Indian War of 1962 232
Sirajuddaula 103–104
Sita 289
"Sky-clad" sect (Jainism) 38
Slave (Mamluk) dynasty 78, 79, 80
slavery, women and 43
Slumdog Millionaire (film) xii,
  287–288
slums 237, 241, 266, 270, 287–288
smrti 24
smuggling 241
Soan River Valley 5–6
Social Conference movement 162,
  176
social reform **146–152**, 162,
  168–170, 178. *See also specific*
  association or reform
socialism 195, 204, 216, 223–224,
  228, 298
Socialist Independence for India
  League 204
Society for Participatory Research in
  Asia (PRIA) 323
Society for the Encouragement of
  Widow Remarriage 149
soft drink industry 320–322
Soma 30
Somnath, temple at 70, **72**
soul. *See* atman
South Africa, Gandhi in 187–189

south India 50–52, **71–74**, 81. *See*
  also specific location
  bhakti in 74, 75–76, 78
  birth groups and 63
  Christian communities in 54
  housing 268
  language and writing 36, 45
  temples built 57
  trade 51–52
  upward caste mobility in 297
Soviet Union. *See* USSR (Union of
  Soviet Socialist Republics)
spinning and weaving 115–116, 129,
  196–198, 200, 209
spinning wheel 196, 200
SRB. *See* "sex–ratio at birth" (SRB)
Sri Lanka 47, 50, 54, 74, 88,
  252–253, 257
Sridharan, E. 275
sruti 24
St. Mary's Church (Madras) *133*
states 109–110, 117–119, 225,
  227, 238–241, 323–324. *See also*
  princely states; *specific state*
Steel, Flora Annie 131–132, 134
steel industry 129–130, 180
Stein, Burton 42
sterilization 241
stone age communities **5–6**
Story of My Experiments with Truth,
  The (Gandhi) 199
Strachey, John 166, 169
Stribodh 154
strikes
  banning of 241
  against landlords 193
  peasant 198
  railway 240
  Rowlatt Acts 190
  textile industry 208
  Tilak's imprisonment 183–184
student protests 179, 183, 216,
  255, 256
stupas 55–56, 57
Subhadra 57
Sudas 76–77
Suez Canal 126, 128, 132
Sufism 68, 88, 92
suicide 255, 256, **317–318**
sultans/sultanates 78–82. *See also*
  specific sultan/sultanate
Sunni Muslims 68, 92
Supreme Court 225, 251, 252, 259,
  306, 324
surveys. *See also* census
  archaeological 7, 72
  geographical 127
  household 273–275
  land revenues and 87, 155
  poverty 331–332
Surya 25, 30, 57, 59
swadeshi 179–180, 183, 184
swaraj 165, 183, 184, 194, 204. *See*
  also self-rule
Swarup, Vikas 287
Swat Valley 3, 6, 17, 23
Swatantra Party 235, 240
swayamsevaks 245, 260, 292

symbols. *See* Indus script; signs and
  symbols
Syndicate, the 233, 234, 235, 236
Syrian Christians 54

T

Tagore, Debendranath 147, 148,
  151
Tagore, Dwarkanath 140, 141
Tagore, Gaganendranath 153
Tagore, Rabindranath 153, 191
Taj Mahal 92, *93*
Tamil 97
  bhakti in 75–76, 78
  farms and farming 74
  legends and myths 71
  non-Brahman movement 205,
    297
  songs 74, 75, 78
Tamil language 36, 45, 51, 52, 54,
  227, 306
Tamil Nadu
  festivals and holidays 290
  R. Gandhi's assassination in 257
  government and politics 251–
    253, 257, 258, 295
  language and writing 227
  non-Brahman movement 205,
    296, 297
  population 266
  religion and beliefs 244,
    251–252
  riots 261
  water disputes in 320
Tamil Tigers 252–253, 257
Tantia Tope 122
Tara Bai 95
Tariff Board 200
Tata, J. N. 129–130
Tata Iron and Steel Company
  (TISCO) 129–130, 180
taxation. *See also* land revenues
  East India Company and 105,
    106–107, 109, 113–114
  non-Muslims and 81, 85, 86,
    87, 94
  Salt March **206–209**, *207*
Taxila 29, 48
technology 14, 26, 28, 29, 119, *129,*
  250. *See also* industrialization;
  transportation
telegraphs 119
Telegu language 227
television 250, 288. *See also specific*
  show
  government and politics 276,
    282–283, 286, 290, 292
  middle-class and 271–272, 274
  popular culture and 264, 275,
    276–277, 292
  urban life and 266
temples 58–59, 64, 77–78, *148. See*
  also Ramjanmabhoomi (Rama's
  birthplace/Babri Masjid mosque)
  campaign; *specific temple*
  destruction of 57, 69, 72, 80
  looting of 70
  rebuilding of 87

412